The Childhood of Jesus

The Childhood of Jesus

Decoding the Apocryphal Infancy Gospel of Thomas

REIDAR AASGAARD

CASCADE *Books* · Eugene, Oregon

THE CHILDHOOD OF JESUS
Decoding the Apocryphal Infancy Gospel of Thomas

Cascade Books
A Division of Wipf and Stock Publishers
199 W. 8th Ave., Suite 3
Eugene, OR 97401

www.wipfandstock.com

ISBN 13: 978-1-60608-126-6

Scripture quotations are from the New Revised Standard Version Bible, copyright
© 1989 by the Division of Christian Education of the National Council of the
Churches of Christ in the USA and used by permission.

BWHEBB, BWHEBL, BWTRANSH [Hebrew]; BWGRKL, BWGRKN, and BWGRKI
[Greek] Postscript® Type 1 and TrueTypeT fonts Copyright © 1994–2009 BibleWorks,
LLC. All rights reserved. These Biblical Greek and Hebrew fonts are used with
permission and are from BibleWorks, software for Biblical exegesis and research.

Cataloging-in-Publication data:

Aasgaard, Reidar.

   The childhood of Jesus : decoding the apocryphal Infancy Gospel of Thomas /
Reidar Aasgaard.

   xii + 286 p.; 23 cm. Includes bibliographical references and indexes.

   ISBN 13: 978-1-60608-126-6

   1. Gospel of Thomas (Infancy Gospel)—Criticism, interpretation, etc.
2. Apocryphal Infancy Gospels. 3. Apocryphal books (New Testament)—Criticism,
interpretation, etc. I. Title.

BS2860 T42 A27 2009

Manufactured in the U.S.A

Respectfully dedicated to

Espen A.
Pippi L.
Lisa and Bart S.

Contents

Preface / *ix*
Abbreviations / *x*

1. The History of Research / 1
2. Oral/Written Tradition / 14
3. Narrative and Literary Features / 35
4. Daily Life and Social Relations / 53
5. Cultural Concepts and Values / 73
6. Jesus as a Child / 86
7. Jesus from Boy to Man / 103
8. Intertextuality—Reflections of the Bible / 113
9. Strange Sayings / 137
10. Main Theological Issues / 149
11. A Popular Tale from Early Rural Christianity / 166
12. Christianity's First Children's Story / 192
13. Conclusions / 214

Appendixes

1. Greek Text / 219
2. English Translation / 233
3. The Structure of Ga/Gb/Gd / 243
4. Designations of Individual Episodes / 245
5. Survey of Greek Variants and the Versions / 248
6. Survey of IGT Evidence by Century / 252
7. Survey of Early Christian Infancy Stories / 254

Bibliography / *259*
Index of Biblical Writings / *277*
Index of Infancy Gospel of Thomas / *280*
Index of Ancient Authors and Writings / *282*

Preface

This book is a central outcome of a three-year period of research on children in antiquity and early Christianity (2003–2006). The project was funded by the Norwegian Research Council and located at the Faculty of Theology, University of Oslo.

Chapters and parts of the book have been presented on several occasions, at the annual meetings of the Society of Biblical Literature/American Academy of Religion (2005–2007), the Oxford Patristics Conference (2007), and the AELAC meeting (Association pour l'étude de la littérature apocryphe chrétienne, 2008). I have also had the opportunity to discuss the material with individuals and groups of colleagues at the Faculty of Theology, in the Oslo-based cross-institutional Patristic study group, and with colleagues abroad. An anonymous peer reader gave me very skilled and valuable advice in a final stage of the work.

I am grateful for the many invitations and opportunities to present my work on IGT and for the numerous insightful comments and constructive suggestions from friendly co-scholars. I appreciate highly the enthusiastic support that many have given of my ideas about this gospel—and also the sober objections of some. These contributions—no names mentioned and none forgotten—have very much served to improve the book. Thus, what weaknesses remain are entirely my responsibility.

Easter, Anno Domini 2009
Reidar Aasgaard

ABBREVIATIONS

Ancient

Acts Thom.	Acts of Thomas
Ant.	Josephus *Antiquities of the Judeans*
Ap. Jas.	Apocryphon of James
Arab. Gos. Inf.	Arabic Gospel of the Infancy
Arm. Gos. Inf.	Armenian Gospel of the Infancy
Assum. Vir.	Assumption of the Virgin
Civ.	Augustine *De civitate Dei* (*City of God*)
1 Clem.	1 Clement
Conf.	Augustine *Confessiones*
Deipn.	Athenaeus *Deipnosophists*
Dial.	Justin *Dialogue with Trypho*
Ep.	Pliny the Younger *Epistles*
Ep. Apos.	Epistle of the Apostles
Gos. Bart.	Gospel of Bartholomew
Gos. Nic.	Gospel of Nicodemus
Gos. Thom.	Gospel of Thomas
Gos. Truth	Gospel of Truth
Haer.	Irenaeus *Against Heresies*
Herm. Vis.	Shepherd of Hermas *Visions*
Hist. Jos. Carp.	History of Joseph the Carpenter
Hom. Jo.	John Chrysostom *Homilies on John*
Ign. Pol.	Ignatius *To Polycarp*
IGT	*Infancy Gospel of Thomas*
Inan. glor.	John Chrysostom *De inani gloria* (*Address on Vainglory and the Right Way for Parents to Bring Up Their Children*)
Inst.	Quintilian *Institutio Oratoria* (*The Orator's Education*)
Itin.	Antoninus Placentinus *Itinerarium*
J.W.	Josephus *The Judean War*
LXX	Septuagint
Metam.	Ovid *Metamorphoses*
NT	New Testament
Or.	Dio Chrysostom *Orationes*

OT	Old Testament
Pan.	Epiphanius *Panarion*
Pap. Eg.	*Papyrus Egerton*
Prot. Jas.	*Protevangelium of James/Infancy Gospel of James*
Ps.-Mt.	*Gospel of Pseudo-Matthew*

Modern

ACW	Ancient Christian Writers
AKA	Abhandlungen (Akademie der Wissenschaften und der Literatur)
BTB	*Biblical Theology Bulletin*
BZRGG	Beihefte zur Zeitschrift für Religions- und Geistegeschichte
CCSA	Corpus Christianorum: Series Apocryphorum
CP	*Classical Philology*
CSCO	Corpus Scriptorum Christianorum Orientalium
FC	Fathers of the Church
HTR	*Harvard Theological Review*
HTS	Harvard Theological Studies
JBL	*Journal of Biblical Literature*
JECS	*Journal of Early Christian Studies*
JRS	*Journal of Roman Studies*
JSJ	*Journal for the Study of Judaism in the Persian, Hellenistic, and Roman Periods*
JSNT	*Journal for the Study of the New Testament*
JSNTSup	Journal for the Study of the New Testament Supplement Series
JTS	*Journal of Theological Studies*
LAA	Late Antique Archaeology
LCL	Loeb Classical Library
LNTS	Library of New Testament Studies
Neot	*Neotestamentica*
NHMS	Nag Hammadi and Manichaean Studies
NovT	Novum Testamentum
NTTS	New Testament Tools and Studies
OrChr	*Oriens Christianus*
PG	Patrologia Graeca
PTS	Patristische Texte und Studien
SacPag	Sacra Pagina
SBLMS	Society of Biblical Literature Monograph Series
SBLRBS	Society of Biblical Literature Resources for Biblical Studies

SBLSymS	Society of Biblical Literature Symposium Series
SemeiaSt	Semeia Studies
SHC	Studies in Hellenistic Civilization
SHR	Studies in the History of Religions (Supplements to Numen)
SNTU	Studien zum Neuen Testament und seiner Umwelt
TLG	Thesaurus Linguae Graecae
TJT	*Toronto Journal of Theology*
TRW	Transformation of the Roman World
TSK	*Theologische Studien und Kritiken*
TU	Texte und Untersuchungen
TUGAL	Texte und Untersuchungen zur Geschichte der altchristlichen Literatur
VCSup	Vigiliae Christianae Supplements
VerbEccl	*Verbum et Ecclesia*
WUNT	Wissenschaftliche Untersuchungen zum Neuen Testament
YCS	Yale Classical Studies

1

The History of Research

The apocryphal *Infancy Gospel of Thomas* presents a fascinating story: a description of the childhood of Jesus. The gospel, which covers about six to seven book pages, consists of a number of miracle accounts and some discourses: it begins with the five-year-old Jesus playing by a brook and ends with the well-known episode from the Gospel of Luke about Jesus at twelve discussing Scripture with the learned men in the temple. From these early years, we hear of Jesus' play with other children. He is said to perform nature wonders by making clay sparrows come alive and by carrying water in a cloak. We are told that he heals a young man after a deadly axe cut and his brother James from a poisonous snakebite. We hear of his father Joseph taking the boy to school three times and of conflicts with teachers as he outshines them all in knowledge. Indeed, Jesus' wisdom is so great that it must come from God himself.

But we also come to know of stranger features. When Jesus is instructed in the art of reading, he not only knows the alphabet, but also the hidden meaning of each letter—he interprets the A in inscrutable ways. When he is criticized, he becomes infuriated. On occasion, he ridicules others. And still more shocking: when a child destroys the pools Jesus has made and when another bumps into him, Jesus' curse causes both to die. An imprudent teacher meets the same fate when attempting to correct his precocious student.

The *Infancy Gospel of Thomas* (IGT) is also special in that it is the only account of Jesus' childhood to have come down from early Christianity. To be sure, the gospels of Matthew and Luke, the apocryphal *Infancy Gospel of James* (*Protevangelium of James* [*Prot. Jas.*]), and a few ancient gospel fragments also have something to say about his early life.[1] But they almost exclusively focus on his birth and the events taking place immediately after. Thus, IGT is the only writing to tell about Jesus'

---

1. See appendix 7.

childhood, a period of his life for which we have elsewhere no reliable historical data. Regrettably, IGT too has no such data to offer us—its value is of another kind.

The tradition history and reception history of the gospel are as fascinating as troublesome to follow. IGT can, at least in core, be traced back to the middle of the second century CE within a Greek-speaking context.[2] It proved popular and was early translated into other languages, first into Latin and Syriac, and a little later into Ethiopic, Armenian, Georgian, Arabic, Irish, and Slavonic. It occurs in varying forms—in Greek there are at least four different variants: Ga, Gb, Gd, and Gs.[3] The gospel is also found in combination with other legendary material, such as *Prot. Jas.* Judging from the geographical spread and the age of its preserved manuscripts (fifth–sixteenth centuries), IGT appears to have been in frequent use way up in the medieval period, when it was made an integral part of other gospels, such as the *Gospel of Pseudo-Matthew* (*Ps.-Mt.*). Only around the time of the Reformation it seems gradually to have fallen into disuse.

It is no wonder that this infancy gospel has attracted interest, but also caused bewilderment and even disgust among present day readers. With its mixture of ingratiating and unsavory elements, particularly in its depiction of Jesus, with its frequent attribution to heretical groups, and with its unruly transmission process, IGT has become an object that scholarship has had great problems addressing. Often, it has been placed at some margin in early Christianity. Sometimes its Jesus has been accounted for by appealing to similar material in other religions. Frequently, the gospel has been viewed as banal and theologically uninteresting. For brief periods, it has been eagerly studied, but then fallen into near oblivion. And whereas much work has been done during the last decades to situate other apocryphal material within the framework of nascent Christianity, this has not been true of IGT. In modern analyses of the early Christians and their communities, history, faith, and theology, the gospel plays virtually no role.[4] Seldom has it been

2. See Chartrand-Burke, "Infancy Gospel," 247–54, 265–69 for discussions about the language and time of composition. I agree with his conclusions (which concur with many other scholars).

3. See ibid., 100.

4. IGT is either not mentioned or only very briefly commented on, see Hurtado, *Lord Jesus*, 449–51; Ehrman, *Lost Christianities*, 203–5; Young, *Cambridge History*,

taken into the family and to heart; instead, it has become a neglected outsider—an exposed orphan within the study of early Christianity.

The *Infancy Gospel of Thomas* does not deserve such a fate. The aim of this book is to contribute to a renewal of the debate on this gospel. I shall do so by analyses of its material, by offering interpretations on central issues, and eventually by presenting a fresh understanding of the story as a whole. Hopefully, this can advance the interest in IGT in general, but also create a deeper appreciation of the story itself and of its place in early Christianity.

Research Prior to 1950

A brief survey of IGT's research history is necessary so as to give a picture of current main issues and views and to prepare the ground for the analyses to follow.[5] Modern research on IGT commenced in the late seventeenth century and into the eighteenth century, with scholars devoted to the search for ancient manuscripts containing apocryphal gospel materials, and among them IGT. The gospel was edited by J. Fabricius as early as 1703, but the first ripe fruit of this quest was Johann C. Thilo's text-critical work *Codex Apocryphus Novi Testamenti* (1832), which became the basis for several translations into modern languages. His edition, however, was surpassed by Constantin von Tischendorf's *De evangeliorum apocryphorum origine et usu* (1851). It presented the text in four variants—the so-called Greek A and Greek B, and two Latin versions (Lv and Lt, see pp. 181–82). This work has in its second edition (1876) remained the standard text-critical edition so far.

Following Thilo's edition some discussion of IGT's origin arose. Usually, IGT was thought to be the *Gospel of Thomas* (*Gos. Thom.*) mentioned by early patristic sources (see p. 174, n. 30), and both in them and in modern times often considered to be of gnostic origin. Some scholars also argued for docetic or Manichean origins.[6] It was generally held that IGT was originally much longer than what was extant, and that it had been cleaned of its heretical contents by orthodox

---

29–30; Burrus, *Ancient Christianity* (IGT scarcely mentioned); Moreschini and Norelli, *Greek and Latin Literature*, 151–52.

5. The research history in Chartrand-Burke, "Infancy Gospel," 19–99, has been of great value here.

6. For a presentation and more references, see ibid., 22–30.

redactors, a so-called "expurgation theory." Progress in research was small, however, and during the fifty years after Tischendorf's edition little significant work took place. Very often, IGT was denigrated as being banal and offensive in contents.[7] At the beginning of the twentieth century, scholars influenced by the history-of-religion school pointed to Indian and Egyptian parallels.[8] Similar views have been repeated and developed until recently.[9]

Some discussion also took place about the social setting of IGT. Michel Nicolas (1866) suggested that IGT was to be situated among common people.[10] This was followed by Jean Variot (1878), who noted similarities between IGT and miracle accounts in hagiographical literature.[11] Such an origin among commoners was later supported by Arnold Meyer (1904), who saw in IGT a collection of folktales, and also credited it for its realistic and agreeable portrayal of everyday life.[12] Their insights, however, were by and large neglected until taken up again in recent years.[13]

In the late nineteenth and early twentieth centuries, research profited from discoveries of several new manuscripts, especially versions in Syriac, Georgian, Slavonic, and Ethiopic. Much energy was put into studying the complex relationships among the growing number of witnesses.[14] Edgar Hennecke's edition of NT apocrypha in German (1904) created new interest in the material.[15] Here, Arnold Meyer questioned the expurgation theory, and held that IGT was originally a brief collection of folktales similar to Indian childhood stories about Buddha and Krishna, but that it was adopted by Gnostics and expanded with

---

7. See for example Cowper, *Apocryphal Gospels*, x–xi.

8. For example Resch, *Aussercanonische Parallelltexte*; Conrady, *Quelle der kanonischen Kindheitsgeschichte*.

9. Particularly by Thundy, *Buddha and Christ*.

10. Nicolas, *Études*, 295–99.

11. Variot, *Les Évangiles Apocryphes*, 214–15, 232–34.

12. Meyer, "Erzählung Des Thomas," 65–66; Stählin, *Altchristliche Griechische Literatur*, 1196; also Enslin, "Along Highways and Byways," 92.

13. By Chartrand-Burke in particular (see p. 10). But such ideas are also hinted at by Gero, "Infancy Gospel," 47, 77; Elliott, *The Apocryphal Jesus*, 1–3.

14. For a presentation, see Chartrand-Burke, "Infancy Gospel," 41–43, 47–56. Cf. also the discussion in Peeters, "Introduction," i–lix.

15. Hennecke, *Handbuch*; Hennecke, *Neutestamentliche Apokryphen*.

speculative material, which later was excluded through orthodox revision.[16] His views were supported by Walter Bauer (1909), Felix Haase (1913), and James Moffatt (1915–1918).[17] Moffatt held that there was little in IGT to support docetic or gnostic origin.[18] Against the common view that IGT was composed in Greek, Paul Peeters (1914) argued that it originated in a Syriac speaking setting.[19]

New manuscript findings from the 1920s on enabled further progress in the study of forms and variants of IGT.[20] Important was Armand Delatte's publication (1927) of a manuscript, A, which later became a main witness to variant Gd.[21] The translation of the Georgian version (1956) and the publication of the Irish version (1958; 1964) were also of great benefit.[22] Views of IGT as inferior and of gnostic origin, however, continued to dominate. Occasionally, the idea of Jewish-Christian origins was launched, but with little acclaim.[23]

Research from the 1950 to 1990

An important turn in IGT research took place in 1956 with the publication of the *Gospel of Thomas*.[24] From this it became clear that IGT had often within modern scholarship been confused with this sayings gospel. A positive effect of this was that scholars began to question the expurgation theory and the idea of gnostic origin, and instead to search

16. Meyer, "Erzählung Des Thomas," 63–66.

17. Bauer, *Leben Jesu*, 87–100; Haase, *Literarkritische Untersuchungen*, 38–48; Moffatt, "Gospels," 485–88.

18. Moffatt, "Gospels."

19. Peeters, "Introduction."

20. Especially as concerns variant Gd, see Chartrand-Burke, "Infancy Gospel," 58–60.

21. Delatte, "Évangile De L'enfance." Delatte used the term Greek C, but Voicu, "Verso," 26 and others have established Gd as its scholarly designation.

22. Garitte, "Fragment Géorgien," 511–20; Carney, "Two Old Irish Poems," 1–43; Carney, *Poems of Blathmac*. See also Herren and Brown, *Christ in Celtic Christianity*, 162–65.

23. Such views were advanced by Wilde and Schonfield, see Chartrand-Burke, "Infancy Gospel," 61–62.

24. It first became accessible to scholars with the publication of Labib, *Coptic Gnostic Papyri*. For a brief survey of its finding and publication, see Robinson, "Nag Hammadi."

for other settings for the gospel. More negatively, interest in IGT waned as focus turned toward the newly discovered *Gos. Thom.* Consequently, research stagnated, with scholars often repeating old views about IGT, particularly as to its banal character and its heretical leanings. In various ways, the gnostic hypothesis has been repeated, sometimes uncritically, by scholars such as Philipp Vielhauer (1975), Alfred Schindler (1988), Walter Rebell (1992), Gerhard Schneider (1995), and—in greatest detail—by W. Baars and J. Helderman (1993; 1994).[25]

Some progress in research was made in more limited areas. Aurelio de Santos Otero (1967) did significant work on IGT's Slavonic version (tenth century).[26] He produced a (much criticized) retro-version into Greek, claiming that this hypothetical Vorlage reflected more superior evidence to the original IGT than did the oldest Greek manuscripts. He also held that this Vorlage had more gnostic features than other variants of IGT. His arguments have been decisively refuted, though. In spite of its shortcomings, Santos Otero's work served to weaken the confidence in the Greek manuscripts as main evidence to the earliest text of IGT.[27] Thomas Rosén (1997) has continued the work on the Slavonic versions, as editor of a very important critical edition of this branch of the IGT tradition.[28]

Valuable work was done on IGT's Latin (fifth century) and Ethiopic (no later than the seventh century) versions, showing that they were rooted in old Greek Vorlagen.[29] New findings of Greek manuscripts were also made, among them the sole witness to variant Gs, the Codex Sabaiticus 259 (H),[30] and also of an Arabic version.[31] Some scholars also

25. Vielhauer, *Geschichte*, 676–77; Schindler, *Apokryphen*, 439; Rebell, *Neutestamentliche Apokryphen*, 134–35; Schneider, *Evangelia Infantiae*, 37–38; Baars and Helderman, "Neue Materialien (I)," 203–4; ibid., "Neue Materialien (Fortsetz.)," 30–31.

26. Santos Otero, *Das kirchenslavische Evangelium.*

27. For a critique of Santos Otero, see Chartrand-Burke, "Infancy Gospel," 70–73; Esbroeck, "Review," 261–63.

28. Rosén, *Slavonic Translation.*

29. Particularly by Arras and Rompay, "Manuscrits Éthiopiens," 133–46; Philippart, "Fragments Palimpsestes," 391–411; Rompay, "Ethiopische Versie," 119–32.

30. Probably first in Esbroeck, "Review," 262.

31. Cf. Chartrand-Burke, "Infancy Gospel," 88–89.

attempted to argue for the primacy of origin of the Greek variant Gb, but unconvincingly.[32]

Whereas scholarship during this period emphasized transmission history and textual criticism, some scholars also discussed issues of form and content. Johannes B. Bauer (1964) suggested that the story originated from the need of non-intellectual early Christians to account for the "hidden years" of Jesus.[33] This was supported by Oscar Cullmann in his influential introduction to IGT in Wilhelm Schneemelcher's *New Testament Apocrypha* (1991); here, Cullmann also concedes that IGT has some qualities of good storytelling.[34] Scholars such as Craig A. Evans (1992) renewed the search for Jewish parallels to IGT and pointed to similarities with accounts about famous rabbis.[35] And Albert Fuchs and Franz Weissengruber (1978) published a concordance of the variants Ga and Gb, crediting their authors with talents for storytelling.[36]

The most important contribution in this period, however, was that by Stephen Gero (1971), who made a thorough form-critical analysis of IGT's individual episodes. Gero rejected gnostic origin and favored Greek, not Syriac, as IGT's original language. Importantly, he also argued in favor of an oral setting for the material and suggested that some of the episodes in IGT may once have been independent units.[37]

Discussion of IGT's provenance within this period usually favored Syrian and Palestinian, occasionally Asia Minor, origin.[38] A few scholars also argued that IGT incorporated traces of Christian or Jewish-Christian tensions with a Jewish milieu. For example, Stephen Wilson (1995) has held that the Jewish spectators' concession in IGT of Jesus' divinity reflects ongoing Jewish-Christian disputes.[39]

32. Cf. Lowe, "*Ioudaioi*," 76–78; Mirecki, "Infancy Gospel," 191–201. Cf. also the detailed discussion in Chartrand-Burke, "Infancy Gospel," 78–80.

33. Bauer, "Entstehung Apokrypher Evangelien," 269–70.

34. Cullmann, "Infancy Gospels," 416–17, 442.

35. Evans, *Noncanonical Writings*, 234–36; also McNeil, "Jesus and the Alphabet," 126–28.

36. Fuchs and Weissengruber, *Konkordanz*, 226, 247.

37. Gero, "Infancy Gospel," 56–64. I return to his contributions on pp. 29, 38, and 39. I agree with Chartrand-Burke, "Infancy Gospel," 73 in that Gero (56 n. 1) is far too cautious in dating the writing down of IGT as late as the fifth century.

38. See the discussions in ibid., 81–84, 269–76.

39. Wilson, *Related Strangers*, 84–85.

Central Contributions Since 1990

Especially significant contributions since 1990 have been made by
Sever J. Voicu, Ronald F. Hock, Tony Chartrand-Burke, and—to an extent—Andries G. van Aarde.[40]

Voicu (1991; 1997; 1998) has greatly improved on earlier work
on IGT's transmission.[41] He pointed out the primacy of IGT's shorter
variant(s), which he sees reflected in the early versions (particularly the
Ethiopic and the Syriac), thus further undermining the expurgation
theory.[42] By means of a careful synoptic comparison he has also shown
that Codex Sabaiticus 259 (H) forms a distinctive variant, Gs, which
represents an early stage in the Greek transmission, closer to the early
versions than other Greek witnesses. He has, however, not fully integrated the Gs material in his synopsis and probably also overestimated
the value of the Ethiopic version as witness to IGT's earliest text.[43]

Hock (1995) has contributed to IGT research through an accessible
text edition, giving a parallel Greek-English presentation of the material.
The hybrid character of his main text—a combination of Tischendorf A
and B, and Gd and others—is problematic, however.[44] More important
than the text itself is Hock's introduction and commentaries, which
in spite of their brevity represent considerable advances in the understanding of IGT's setting and contents. Hock develops the form-critical
analysis of Gero, thus supporting the idea of IGT's narrative sophistication.[45] He also points out similarities in genre and content between IGT
and other ancient literature, for example the Alexander Romance and
emperor biographies, in which descriptions of the childhood of their
heroes aim at foreshadowing their future greatness as adults. Thus, IGT
reflects common patterns within ancient biography, also seen in other
early Christian literature including the gospels of Matthew and Luke.[46]

40. Elliott, *Synopsis* is also of some value as a tool for comparing variants, although
it very much relies on the text edition of Tischendorf.

41. Voicu, "Histoire," 191–204; ibid., "Notes," 119–32; ibid., "Verso."

42. Ibid., "Notes," 130–32.

43. Cf. the criticism in Chartrand-Burke, "Infancy Gospel," 92–93. Some of Voicu's
views are followed up by Schneider in his Greek-German edition of the infancy gospels, see Schneider, *Evangelia Infantiae*, 41–47.

44. Hock, *Infancy Gospels*.

45. Ibid., 92–95.

46. Ibid., 96–97.

According to Hock, features that had been thought to represent heretical leanings in IGT should instead be seen as mirroring general cultural conventions in late antiquity and early Christianity.[47]

In his thesis "The Infancy Gospel of Thomas: The Text, its Origins, and its Transmission" (2001), Chartrand-Burke has developed the views of Voicu and Hock, but also made other important contributions to the study of IGT.[48] In his work, Chartrand-Burke presents an extensive chronological history of research.[49] He describes the Greek manuscripts and the versions, presents the Greek variants (Gs, Ga, Gb, Gd) in a synopsis with a detailed apparatus, gives an English translation of Gs with notes rendering translations of differing texts, and discusses in detail IGT's development, variants, origins, transmission, and stemma. This makes his work the most complete presentation of IGT's text and transmission.[50] In Chartrand-Burke's opinion, Gs (H) is—together with the earliest versions (the Syriac and Latin)—the closest witness to the original text of IGT.[51]

Chartrand-Burke focuses in particular on IGT's Christology and its depiction of Jesus as a child. He dismisses the idea of Jesus as a gnostic saviour figure and with it also the expurgation theory. Instead, he finds some resemblance to IGT's Jesus in stories of ancient heroes and miracle workers; the closest parallels, however, are with ancient Israelite holy men such as the prophets Elijah and Elisha.[52] In his view, the problematic features such as Jesus' cursing can be explained on this basis, since such activity is also attributed to them.[53]

Chartrand-Burke considers the life of children in antiquity and early Christianity as a background for IGT's depiction of Jesus. In his

---

47. Ibid., 98–99.

48. The thesis, which is of great value for further IGT research, is under revision and to be published; it is accessible online: http://www.collectionscanada.ca/obj/s4/f2/dsk3/ftp05/NQ63782.pdf.

49. Chartrand-Burke, "Infancy Gospel," 10–99. The only other research history of any length is Gero, "Apocryphal Gospels," 3969–96, esp. 3981–84. On the church Slavonic, see Rosén, *Slavonic Translation*, 17–38.

50. It will make Tischendorf's edition finally obsolete and should be the requisite starting point for future study.

51. Chartrand-Burke, "Infancy Gospel," 259–62; also ibid., "Greek Manuscript Tradition," 150–51.

52. Ibid., "Infancy Gospel," 305–11.

53. Ibid., 309–10.

view, children's living conditions were very demanding, with little or no understanding of the special character of childhood. Children were valued for what they were to become: they were unfinished adults.[54] Accordingly, IGT's Jesus is an adult in disguise, and the gospel aims at showing, "following convention, that Jesus' character, and with it his abilities, was already apparent at birth."[55] IGT does not present Jesus as a real child in any way, but as an idealized child, as adults saw children.[56]

Occasionally, Chartrand-Burke also touches on IGT's social setting, taking up again the ideas of Nicholas, Variot, and Meyer (p. 4). He places IGT within an early Christian "middle class" stratum, a mixed and broad group above the level of slaves, but below the very few belonging to the social elite.[57]

Finally, van Aarde has launched an alternative to the idea of gnostic origin in his thesis "Die Kindheidsevangelie van Tomas as 'n heroïese mite van die God-kind Jesus in die konteks van die Ebionitiese vroeë Christendom" (2005).[58] In his opinion, IGT reflects, or is at least influenced by, Ebionite Christianity.[59] He also sees in IGT a presentation of Jesus in the form of a god-child myth.[60] In his view of Jesus as an adult

---

54. Ibid., 321–61.

55. Ibid., 316.

56. Ibid., 366–403.

57. Ibid., 363–64.

58. Van Aarde, "Kindheidsevangelie" (in Afrikaans). He has also presented his view in some articles, see Van Aarde, "Infancy Gospel"; "Griekse Manusckrip"; "Kindheidsevangelie van Tomas"; "Ebionite Tendencies."

59. Van Aarde builds his analysis on the manuscript S (Codex Sinaiticus Gr. 453), which belongs to variant Gb, see below (p. 16). He concedes that other manuscripts can be colored by gnostic thinking, but holds that this is not the case with Gr. 453, see ibid., "Infancy Gospel," 832–35. He bases his view very much on IGT's prolog and argues that it should be read as if Thomas is writing to his "brothers" (i.e. Jewish Christians) in the diaspora, not to Christians among the Gentiles. Van Aarde's emphasis on the prolog and his reading of it is puzzling and little convincing (see "Kindheidsevangelie," 68–74, also 93–115). In my opinion, he has exaggerated the Jewish coloring of IGT; on this, see my chapter 8.

60. Van Aarde, "Infancy Gospel," 838–42; and "Kindheidsevangelie van Tomas," 477–84. His interpretation, in which he holds that IGT should be read as a myth, in a "tautegorical" and not allegorical, symbolic, or metaphorical way, is not convincing (Van Aarde, "Kindheidsevangelie van Tomas," esp. chaps. 5–6.) and very similar to earlier (allegorical) attempts at reading theological or ecclesial conflicts out of IGT's story; on this, see chap. 10 below.

in disguise, van Aarde is—despite some nuances—in agreement with Hock and Chartrand-Burke.[61]

Main Challenges for IGT Research

Much IGT research has until recently been seriously misguided, primarily due to its association with Gnosticism. In addition, scholarship has been long preoccupied with, and hampered by, problems related to IGT's transmission. As a consequence, study of its actual contents has been nearly neglected. In fact, research on IGT must in several respects start anew.[62] With the recent works of Voicu, Hock, and Chartrand-Burke, however, important advances have been made both as concerns IGT's transmission and socio-cultural and theological setting, which will facilitate future study of IGT.

In this book I address a variety of issues regarding IGT. Some have already been discussed within research, whereas others are in need of being raised. On some points my views concur with earlier insights, particularly those of Hock and Chartrand-Burke. On others I bring in radically new perspectives, and also present ideas which should evoke controversy.

It is also my contention that some of the issues that have been seen as obstacles to the study of IGT, can in fact help deepen our understanding of it. Instead of causing scholarly bewilderment and even despair, they can be turned to advantage: by taking fresh points of departure as concerns perspectives and methods new avenues to the story and setting of IGT can be opened up.

The main challenges in IGT research can be related to four areas in particular. The four—which are closely interconnected—are:

1. *Transmission history*. Although the understanding of the relations among the different manuscripts, variants, and versions of IGT has improved, especially with the contributions of Voicu and Chartrand-Burke, the great variation among them has not been sufficiently accounted for. Why the great differences in form, style, and even contents of the texts? And why is it so difficult to produce a clear stemma for the preserved manuscripts?

---

61. Van Aarde, "Infancy Gospel," 843–46.
62. I here agree with the verdict of Chartrand-Burke, "Infancy Gospel," 100.

2. *Story.* Due to IGT's complex transmission history and the charges of heresy and lack of narrative sophistication, limited energy has been spent on the story itself. How is the story constructed? What is it about? Except for the form-critical analyses of Gero and Hock, and a brief narrative analysis by Chartrand-Burke, IGT has in fact not been made subject to thorough analysis, neither as concerns structure nor individual elements.[63] The need for such an undertaking is overripe.

3. *Theological and ideological profile.* Except for Chartrand-Burke's and van Aarde's discussions of IGT's Christology, neither the various aspects of IGT's theology nor its theology as a whole have been systematically treated. Most such analyses have been fragmentary, often merely indicating possible gnostic or history-of-religion parallels to expressions and concepts in the story. Also, very little has been done to advance our understanding of IGT's broader ideological horizon, such as the social and cultural values reflected or its perceptions of childhood and of gender.[64]

4. *Social setting and audience.* Except for those who have considered IGT heretical, very few scholars have addressed and discussed its social setting and audience. Some have loosely assumed the addressees to have been among common people. Far more needs to be said about issues such as these, however. Can such scrutiny for example tell us something new about IGT's place within early Christianity? And can it also be that a new appreciation of IGT may somehow enrich our understanding of early Christianity itself?

Approaches in This Book

These are the basic questions addressed in the chapters below. The procedure will be as follows: first, the transmission of IGT will be treated as a starting point for the study of the material (chap. 2). An analysis of its story follows (chap. 3). Third, IGT's narrative world will be presented, with a view to social and cultural aspects (chaps. 4–5). Then I shall dis-

63. For this seminal narrative analysis, see ibid., 262–64. There are also many valuable observations in the notes in Hock, *Infancy Gospels.*

64. With the exception of the discussion of ideas about children and childhood in Chartrand-Burke, "Infancy Gospel," chaps. 6–8.

cuss issues related to IGT's Jesus, viz., the depiction of him as a child and a boy, highlighting questions about childhood and gender (chaps. 6–7). The subsequent chapters analyze IGT's theology, based on exegetical readings of the story, so as to draw up its theological and ideological profile (chaps. 8–10). Then the issue of audience is addressed, with the aim of investigating the social and cultural context within which IGT can have belonged (chaps. 11–12). Finally, I reflect on some implications following from my study and its findings (chap. 13). Since many of the passages in IGT will be dealt with from different perspectives, some repetition and overlap will occur throughout the chapters.

The appendixes provide material in support of reading and for further study. The text and translation of IGT in appendixes 1 and 2 can be used for reference as one works through each chapter. Appendix 3 lists titles and short titles of individual episodes; these will be employed throughout the book. Verse numbering follows Chartrand-Burke's text of IGT.

One caveat is needed from the outset: since IGT is so difficult to situate in time and place, we will have to relate to its ideological, cultural, and social context in rather general terms. Thus, I shall sometimes be sweeping in my descriptions of ancient perceptions on gender, childhood, values, and the like. My use of the designation "late antiquity" will also be fairly open: unless otherwise stated, it will cover the period from IGT's time of origin, mid-second century CE and up to the fifth–sixth centuries.

2

ORAL/WRITTEN TRADITION

The transmission history of IGT has shown itself very difficult to untangle. Since the manuscripts, both Greek and non-Greek, differ widely, much research has been devoted to reconstructing some kind of *original* text. The view has been that without such a text little substantial can be said about IGT's contents. Thus, it has been a pressing aim within research to establish a firm text-critical basis to enable further progress in the study of IGT.[1]

IGT has undergone many changes during transmission. It is, at least in core, rooted in the second century, but it has proven difficult to trace the developments of the material and to produce a precise stemma of the manuscripts preserved. An additional problem is that the Greek manuscripts are late (eleventh–sixteenth centuries), and that older forms of IGT are primarily preserved in the versions, particularly the Latin and the Syriac.

Certain main forms of the IGT material are nonetheless visible. The manuscripts reflect four such forms:[2]

1. A short form, containing 15 units (Gs 2–15, 17, see p. 37; appendix 5). This is found in most of the versions.

2. An intermediate form, with two units added (Gs 1 and 16). This is found in one Greek manuscript (H).

3. A long form with two additional units placed before the final episode, 19 units in all. This form is found in most Greek manuscripts.

4. A combined form, viz., together with other infancy stories (see pp. 182–85)

---

1. Cf. Chartrand-Burke, "Infancy Gospel," 98.
2. Ibid., 246, 255–64.

Very likely, the short form is the oldest, with various kinds of material being added, but occasionally also taken away, and in a long and unruly process.[3]

In this chapter, focus will be on the Greek material. One aim will be to give an impression of the character of this material. It will become clear that it is marked by considerable diversity. Thus, another aim will be to account for this variation and to clarify its implications for our overall understanding of IGT. The versions will be presented at a later point (pp. 180–85).

The Greek Variants

The Greek manuscripts—fourteen are known to survive—can be sorted into four main variants, in chronological order: Gs, Ga, Gd, and Gb.[4] Within scholarship, they have usually been denoted recensions—for reasons that will become clear later (pp. 32–33), I shall call them *variants*.

Variant Gs is represented by one manuscript only: H (Codex Sabaiticus 259; eleventh century). It is in spite of its relatively late date the earliest manuscript in Greek, but is dependent on an old archetype (probably ca. fifth century). The variant reflects the short and oldest known form of IGT, but has rather late in transmission had chapters 1 and 10 added, thus belonging to the intermediate form.[5]

The Ga variant, the long form, can most likely be dated to the ninth century, when chapters 17–18 were included. It is represented by eight more or less complete manuscripts. The main witness to the variant is W (fourteenth–fifteenth centuries). Other, mutually independent manuscripts are V (fourteenth–sixteenth centuries), P (1422/23), and O (before 1455). The four remaining manuscripts share a common Vorlage and are denoted family α: B (fifteenth century), L (fifteenth century), M (fifteenth century), and D (sixteenth century).

Variant Gd, dating back to the eleventh century, is characterized by its addition of long prologs about Jesus and his family in Egypt, its at-

---

3. Ibid., 261–64. Chartrand-Burke has convincingly rejected the theory that IGT was at an early point a larger work that was later cleansed of its heretical content.

4. Ibid., 101–16, 279–85.

5. Ibid., 260–64, 279–81. I agree with him that Gs/H is the oldest form of IGT preserved in Greek, not least because of its similarities with the early versional manuscripts (see pp. 181–85).

tribution to James (instead of Thomas), and its very different language and syntax.[6] It is found in three manuscripts: T (thirteenth century, the second earliest Greek manuscript, cf. H), R (fifteenth century), and A (fifteenth century). A is customarily regarded the main witness to Gd.

The Gb variant is shorter than Ga in the sayings and dialog episodes, and has by many scholars been viewed as an abridgement of it. In addition, the narratives are substantially reformulated. The variant is thought to have originated before the fifteenth century. It is found in two manuscripts: S (fourteenth–fifteenth centuries) and C (fifteenth–sixteenth centuries), the former being considered its best representative.[7]

In view of the rather late dates given for the variants, it is very important to note that this primarily refers to the overall structure of IGT. It says little about its individual episodes, which in both form and contents are likely to be considerably older, cf. for example Gs with its fifth-century precursor.

Comparison of Greek Variants

In the following, I shall not enter into a broad discussion of the transmission history of IGT. Rather, focus will be on aspects that can give a framework for my presentation in the chapters to come. In order to show the relationship between the variants, I shall set up a synopsis of three representative passages, viz., Curse on a Careless Boy, 1 Teacher (Alpha Lesson), and Healing of James' Snakebite. The three will be compared with special attention to verbal agreements and differences. To make the material surveyable, only variants Gs, Ga, and Gd will be employed.[8]

In the synopsis shading indicates verbal agreement between all three variants (minor differences in spelling are disregarded), underlining agreement only between Gs and Ga, *italics* only between Gs and Gd,

6. Ibid., 113–14. Chartrand-Burke considers Gd a radical, but gradual rewriting of Ga and of little use for reconstructing the original text.

7. See ibid., 112, 283. Chartrand-Burke supports this notion of abridgement and in his stemma (p. 287) presents Gb as derived from Ga.

8. My translation follows the main texts of Chartrand-Burke's Greek synopsis, which employs H as witness for Gs, W (with some substitutions) for Ga, and A (occasionally T) for Gd. Cf. ibid., 134–35. The way I use Ga and Gd is problematic, however, since they—differently from Gs—are eclectic-compound, and thus hypothetical, texts; still, the material suffices to demonstrate my points.

and **bold** only between Ga and Gd. The common elements between all variants are thus easily observed by a glance at the shaded text. If one for example wishes to survey the common elements between Gs and Ga both shaded and underlined text must be read. To facilitate quick comparison, the texts are given in translation, and in a fairly literal form.

Sample 1: Curse on a Careless Boy (4:1–2)

We start with a typical miracle account with alternating actions and sayings:

Gs	Ga	Gd
When he left there *with* his father *Joseph*, someone running bumped into his shoulder.	**Then** again **Jesus** went through **the village**, and a running **child** bumped hard into his shoulder.	**Then**, when **Jesus** a few days later was walking *with Joseph* in **the village** one **child** who ran pushed Jesus in the shoulder.
And Jesus *says* to him: "Cursed be your ruling power!" And *immediately* he died.	And being irritated, Jesus said to him: "**You shall not go your way!**" And straight away **he fell and** died.	And becoming angry, Jesus *says* to him: "**You shall not go your way!**" And *immediately* **he fell and** died.
When the people saw that he died, they at once *cried* out and said: "From where was *this* child begotten, since his word becomes deed?"	When they saw what happened some said: "From where was that child begotten, since every word turns real and into deed?"	When the Jews saw the miracle, they made an outcry, saying: "From where is this child?"
But when the parents of the dead child noticed what had happened, they blamed his father Joseph, saying:	And when the parents of the deceased arrived, they blamed Joseph, his father, saying:	And they said to Joseph:
"Because you have this child, you can't live with us in this village. *If you want* to be here, teach him to bless and not to curse.	"Since you have such a child, you can't be with us or live in this village, or else teach him to bless and not to curse.	"You can't live with us having **such a** child. Take him and stay away from now on. *If you want* to live with us, teach him to bless and not to curse.
For our child has been taken away from us."	For he puts **our children** to death."	For he has made **our children** into cripples."

In this passage, some features are worth particular notice. Most of the common elements consist of single yet important words: shoulder, Jesus, died, from where, child, Joseph. Some verbal agreements are minor and coincidental: and, to him, saw, for. There are two striking similarities, the verbatim rendering of the advice given: "teach him to bless and not to curse, and the reproach of Joseph: "you can't be/live with us (having such a child)."[9]

Second, Gs/Ga have additional elements in common, particularly these words: running, bumped into, parents, blamed, his father, in this village. More striking, however, is the similarity in the spectator response to Jesus' action: the almost identical question "From where was this/that child begotten" with the common vocabulary in the justification: since . . . word . . . deed. Here, Gd differs significantly in its very brief response, and in not mentioning the child's parents.

Furthermore, Gs/Gd have some elements in common as against Ga. Both at the beginning state that Jesus was with Joseph, and at the end indicate Joseph's wish: "If you wish (to be/live here/with us)." In addition, they have some minor, probably accidental, verbal agreements: says, immediately, cried/cry.

Finally, there are also some agreements in Ga/Gd against Gs. The most important is the identical formulation of Jesus' reaction: "You shall not go your way," and the information that "he (the child) fell."[10] Less significant is the occurrence of words such as: Jesus, the village, child, our children.

Several inferences can be made from these observations. First, it goes without saying that we here have the same episode, with a number of narrative elements constituting a common framework: the village, Jesus, the careless child, Jesus' curse, the boy's death, the general response ("from where"), Joseph, the reproach of him, and the advice given about Jesus, i.e. "to bless and not to curse." The last two elements are those having the closest verbal affinity, particularly the latter, which has a proverbial form and may reflect a biblical phrase (Rom 12:14; see p. 122). Apart from these instances, verbatim agreements are limited: some central, but not very conspicuous terms are common (shoulder, child etc.); other words are so ordinary that they might be expected to

9. Word order and phrasing differ somewhat in the latter case.

10. They correspond verbatim with Gb as concerns Jesus' saying; and Gb also notes that the child fell.

occur (and, saw etc.). More often, agreements are based on similarity in content rather than in wording: Jesus left/went/was walking; the child was running/ran; he bumped/bumped hard/pushed; he died immediately/straight away; he was dead/deceased. Sometimes Gs/Ga agree against Gd, and at other times Gd/Ga against Gs, but with no specific pattern one or the other way.

A number of differences should also be noted. For example, Gs mentions only after a while that the careless person was a child; and its Jesus saying is totally different from the others (see p. 138). Ga develops upon the spectators' response: Jesus' "every word turns real and into deed"; it does not, however, mention Joseph's wish to remain in the village; and it also states that Jesus became irritated. Gd too describes Jesus' agitation, but characterizes him as "angry"; the spectators' response is considerably briefer than in both the others, whereas its reproach of Joseph is far more verbose; strikingly, the child's parents does not appear in the episode. In Gd the event is said to take place "a few days later"; thus, the episode seems more detached from the preceding episode than in Gs/Ga.

All variants differ in their accusation against Jesus: in Gs he is said to take the child away from his parents, in Ga generally to put people's children to death, in Gd to make them cripples—the seriousness of the accusation appears more important than its precise nature. In addition, there are several stylistic differences, for example in word order, parataxis/hypotaxis, use of particles and style (cf. pp. 47–49).

Thus, the analysis indicates that we here have a narrative with several basic common elements, a few of which—particularly the reproach of Joseph—are verbally very close. Other elements, however, are rather differently phrased: each variant has its characteristics, sometimes in common with one of the others, but just as often peculiar to itself. The impression left is that we here have variants of an episode with a basic storyline and with one or two core sayings, but that the episode apart from this is rather freely rephrased or retold.

Sample 2: First Teacher (Alpha Lesson) (6:10)

In the second sample we turn to a speech that is part of the dialog between Jesus and his first teacher. Here, Jesus explains the hidden meaning of the alpha:

Gs	Ga	Gd
With many listening *he* said to the teacher:	With many listening the child said to **Zacchaeus:**	With many listening *he* said to **Zacchaeus:**
"Listen, master, *and be mindful of* the order of the *first* letter,	"Listen, master, to the order of the alpha letter,	"Listen, master, *and be mindful of* the order of the *first* letter,
and pay close attention	and pay close attention	
how it has	how it has	how it has
sharp lines and	lines and	two lines and
a middle stroke,	middle-strokes,	middle strokes,
which you see	which you see	
sharpening,	being common,	*sharpening,*
intersecting,	intersecting,	continuing,
joining,	joining,	joining,
creeping out,		
drawing back,		
elevated,	elevated,	elevated,
dancing,	dancing,	dancing,
missile-bearing,	shimmer-shining,	
three-marked,	three-marked,	three-edged,
double-edged,		*double-edged,*
		not antagonistic,
same-formed,		
same-placed,		
same-kinded,	same-kinded,	same-kinded,
raised,	subtracted,	parallel,
balanced,	balanced,	balance-cornered,
equally-measured,	equally-measured	equally-measured
equally-proportioned		
—such lines does *the alpha* have."	—such lines has the A."	—such lines has *the alpha.*"

As for contents, this is a difficult passage indeed. Here, however, focus will be on comparing variants, and the meaning of the speech will be discussed later (pp. 143–46).

There are several elements common to all three variants, particularly in the first half of the passage; here, they agree nearly verbatim in some phrases: "With many listening," "the order of the first/alpha letter, how it has (sharp/two) lines and (a) middle(-)stroke(s)." Many terms are common and follow a similar sequence: "lines . . . stroke(s) . . . joining . . . elevated . . . dancing . . . same-kinded." The three variants have common elements at the end of the speech too, although they are more limited: "balance(d) . . . equally-measured . . . lines has/does the alpha (the A) have."[11]

The variants also have some characteristics. As in sample 1 there is a crisscrossing of elements, but with no evident special loyalties: first, Ga/Gd go against Gs in naming the teacher (however, all three mention his name earlier in the episode). They also concur in the closing formulation, which is verbatim nearly identical: ". . . equally-measured—such lines has the A/alpha." Furthermore, Gs/Ga differ from Gd in having similar additions in the first half: "pay close attention to", "which you see", "intersecting." However, Gs/Gd also concur against Ga in having the words "and be mindful of" and "first" in the same phrase, and in the terms "sharpening" and "double-edged."

There is one striking feature in this crisscrossing, however: Gs appears to be picking up elements from both Ga and Gd, thus producing a longer text. This adding up is particularly visible at the beginning (from Gd: and be mindful of, first; from Ga: pay close attention, which you see, intersecting).

All three variants also have words peculiar to them. Ga has: two (lines), being common, shimmer-shining, subtracted. Gd has: not antagonistic, parallel. And Gs has: teacher, sharp (lines), creeping out, drawing back, missile-bearing, same-formed, same-placed, raised, equally-proportioned—the many additions of Gs make the text stand even more out as against the others.[12]

Clearly, the variants are more similar in this passage than in the previous: it seems to have a more stable shape as concerns vocabulary and phrases as well as in sequence of elements.[13] This may suggest some kind of mutual dependency, particularly of Gs on the others. However, the differences seem too big so as to suggest direct or close literary dependency, cf. the variation in vocabulary, spelling, and addition/

---

11. Some Greek terms are also more similar in spelling and pronunciation than is visible in translation: ὀξυνομένους/ὀξυσμένους (Gs/Gd) – ξυνοὺς (sharpening – being common), διαβαίνοντας – διαμένοντας (intersecting – continuing), and ἐπαρτικούς – ὑπάρπουχους – παρόχους (raised – subtracted – parallel).

12. The words "missile-bearing" and "same-placed" are difficult to read and make sense of in Gs.

13. However, differences among manuscripts within each variant are considerable (particularly within Ga) and require closer scrutiny.

omission. Instead, the affinities—particularly in the descriptions of the alpha—remind of some kind of jingles or enumerations like those of the New Testament vice and virtue lists.[14] What this might imply will be developed upon below (pp. 143–46).

Sample 3: Healing of James' Snakebite (15:1–2)

Our final example is a miracle episode consisting only of narrative and no sayings, viz., Healing of James' Snakebite:

Gs	Ga	Gd
James went out into the forest to tie up *sticks* to use for baking bread. And Jesus went with him. And while they were gathering the sticks a miscreant snake bit James on his hand. As he was wracked with pain and dying, the child Jesus ran to James, and blew on the bite. Then straight away the bite was healed, [and] the snake was destroyed, and James stood up.	Joseph sent his son James to tie up wood and carry to his house. And the child Jesus followed him. And while James was gathering the sticks a snake bit James' hand. And as he was wracked with pain and dying, Jesus came and blew on the bite. Then straight away it (he?) was healed, [and] the animal burst apart.	And Joseph sent James to gather *sticks* for the oven. And Jesus followed James. And while gathering the sticks a snake bit James. And falling to the ground he was about to end his life from the pain caused by the poison. But Jesus healed James, and the animal died.

Here, similarities are much more sparse than in the previous sample. Verbatim agreements among all are few and primarily consist of words central to the narrative: James, Jesus, gathering . . . sticks, snake, bit, healed. Agreements between two are more common, however. This is evident with Gs/Ga, which concur in several words and expressions: to tie up, hand, as he was wracked with pain and dying, blew on the bite, straight away. Ga/Gd agree against Gs in three instances: by introducing Joseph as sending James, by stating that Jesus followed James, and—less conspicuously—by describing the snake as "the animal."

14. Cf. Charles, "Vice and Virtue Lists," 1252–57.

Beyond elements common to all, however, the literary agreements between Gs and Gd are minimal. Thus, Gs/Ga and Ga/Gd affinities are clearly much stronger than in the case of Gs/Gd.

The differences among the three are considerable, with several features characteristic of each of them: in Gs James goes into a forest, the sticks are meant for baking bread, the snake is "miscreant," James runs to Jesus for help, and the snake is "destroyed," with James standing up. In Ga James is characterized as the son of Joseph, the "wood" is to be carried to the house, Jesus comes to help James, and the snake "burst apart." And Gd states that the sticks are meant for the oven (for heating?), that James falls to the ground, that his pain is due to poison, and that the snake died. Except for James' reaction to the bite, Gd is much briefer than the others. Interestingly, however, its description of James' reaction differs much from the others in wording, but is at the same time very similar in content.

What we have here, then, are three variants of a narrative, which in their main elements and contents are very similar, but which differ much in wording and detail. Most of the verbatim agreements, especially between Gd and the others, seem due to a common storyline rather than to some literary link.[15]

An Oral/Written Approach to IGT

What can be inferred from the analyses of these texts? It is evident that they have much in common as concerns general presentation and main elements, but that they differ considerably in wording and detail. Verbatim agreement occurs in a number of cases, but with shifting constellations. No clear patterns can be gleaned, except that Gs and Ga agree slightly more often in wording than does Gd with them, and that Ga and Gd agree more often in storyline than does Gs with them. Only in the description of the alpha (6:10) are verbal similarities so marked that we may speak of a more fixed tradition (see pp. 143–46). But beyond this instance, little can be inferred as to specific dependencies or

15. The literary affinity between Gs and Ga seems at first glance stronger, especially in their middle part. However, the impression does not hold good, since Ga's main manuscript (W) has a lacuna here and is supplemented with readings from V, α, and the Slavonic version. W lacks nearly all of "And while . . . Jesus came," 16:1b–2a. This makes this part of the text hybrid and less reliable for comparison.

affinities, and the passages emerge as fairly free renditions of a common reservoir of IGT material.[16]

How can this state of affairs be accounted for? The few scholars who have discussed this question have viewed the matter with focus almost exclusively on tracing an original or archetypal *text*. The picture given of IGT's transmission has very much been that of a written process, with scribes more or less judiciously copying the text of older exemplars. Accordingly, scholars have often accounted for the differences among the manuscripts through explanations taken from New Testament textual criticism: the problem is seen as the result of limitations in scribal skills, or of a gradual process during which several levels of copies have been lost. And faced with this great diversity, scholars have either resigned as to the possibility of reconstructing an archetype or found themselves compelled to present preliminary or synoptic texts.[17]

In my opinion such approaches are not able to render account of the matter. Lack of restraint is unlikely to explain the great textual variation, even though some may be due to scribal freedom. And there is equally little to support the idea of missing links in the written transmission. Instead, it seems more adequate to approach the material from a different angle, namely from the perspective of oral tradition: the variants of IGT should be studied as written manifestations of material that has to a large extent been orally transmitted. As I argue below, the almost exclusively literary paradigm in IGT research needs to be replaced by a combined *oral/written* paradigm, possibly even with main emphasis on the oral side.[18]

IGT was transmitted in a culture that was fundamentally oral. Only a small percentage of the late antique population was able to read and/or write, probably 5–15%, and with much local and social diversity.[19]

16. If Gb had been included in the comparisons, the discrepancies are likely to have appeared even greater, cf. the description of it on p. 16.

17. For examples of resignation, see Koester; of preliminary reconstruction, see Tischendorf and Hock; and of synoptic approach, see Fuchs and Weissengruber, Moffat, Voicu, and Chartrand-Burke.

18. A similar broadening of focus is also argued forcefully in the case of the canonical gospels, by Dunn, "Jesus in Oral Memory," 123–24, and at length in Mournet, *Oral Tradition*. For a similar view on apocryphal acts, see Thomas, *Acts of Peter*; on folklore and fairytales, Anderson, *Fairytale*, 15.

19. For a thorough discussion, see Harris, *Ancient Literacy*, particularly chap. 8 and the conclusion.

Oral-rhetorical performance was often held in higher esteem than the written word.[20] Knowledge, occupational skills, history, religious and cultural traditions—the great reservoir of human experience—nearly all of this was handed on from person to person and from generation to generation by way of oral transmission.

In recent years, there has been a growing recognition of the pervasively oral character of communication in antiquity, with a number of studies dealing with classical (e.g., fairytales), Jewish (e.g., midrashim) as well as early Christian material (e.g., canonical gospels and apocryphal acts).[21] With its thematic focus, simple form, and brevity, IGT would be a kind of material suitable for oral transmission.

Oral Features in Written Texts

Research on orality in antiquity has been accompanied by much reflection on methodological issues.[22] One basic idea has been that within such transmission traditions are not written, but *performed*, i.e. presented as a totality of words, gestures and look.[23] Since much of what was written was also meant to be performed orally, however, the differences between oral and written should not be overestimated. Nevertheless, several elements appear indicative of oral transmission; these are elements that for example function as means for embellishment, memorization or narrative intervention. Although they do not individually prove oral character, the occurrence of many such features together clearly heightens the probability.[24] A common denominator of many of them is that they serve to balance stability (esp. through fixity in storyline and main characters) and flexibility (fluidity, esp. through adaptation of minor elements to new contexts).[25] Another common denominator is

20. See Shiner, *Proclaiming the Gospel*, 14–16; also Vitz, *Performing Medieval Narrative*.

21. In addition to the works mentioned above, other important contributions are Byrskog, *Story as History*; Hearon, *Mary Magdalene Tradition*; Mackay, *Signs of Orality*; Rhoads, "Performance Criticism" (parts I–II).

22. See Byrskog, *Story as History*, esp. 107–44.

23. See Shiner, *Proclaiming the Gospel*; and Mournet, *Oral Tradition*, esp. chap. 4.

24. Mournet, *Oral Tradition*, 155–58.

25. See Thomas, *Acts of Peter*, chaps. 3–4; ibid., "Stories without Texts."

that of redundancy, i.e. of repetition of stylistic, narrative, and rhetorical elements.[26] The most important indicators of orality are:[27]

1. In the Story as a Whole and Its Structure
- multiform stories (e.g., variants), indicating reshaping within oral transmission
- episodic character, thus, e.g., allowing for performance of individual episodes
- independent occurrence of individual episodes
- transmission of similar material in blocks, as thematic concentration or aid for memorization, often in blocks of three; this is, e.g., a common feature in fairytales
- anonymity, indicating the public domain character of the material

2. The Occurrence of Certain Narrative Features
- conventionality in form (recognizable type of story or episode)
- fixed and single storyline (so as to form an independent, unified episode)
- balancing of stability and flexibility in narrative ("program with open source code")
- stability in main actions and events
- flexibility in motivations for actions and causations of events
- relative stability in central sayings, flexibility in general
- stability of main characters (identity and personality)
- flexibility of secondary characters
- stability in naming of characters
- stability in chronological information
- use of only two main characters (or groups of characters) in a scene
- tolerance of inconsistency within an episode or between episodes
- interpretative comments (explicit or implicit), illustrations, and asides

26. See particularly ibid., 274–79.

27. There are some overlaps between the four categories. The organization of elements is developed on the basis of listings in Kelber, *Oral and Written Gospel*, 27–33; Thomas, *Acts of Peter*, esp. chap. 3; Hearon, *Mary Magdalene Tradition*, 45–47; Mournet, *Oral Tradition*, esp. chap. 5.

3. The Occurrence of Certain Rhetorical Features
   - repetition of narrative elements, phrases, and keywords, often in threes, the so-called *trikolon*, or *trikolon crescens* (with increase in length or drama)
   - verbal echoing
   - ring composition or symmetry (e.g., chiasm)
   - repetition of elements at the start and end of a unit of material (inclusio)
   - flashback/anticipation (analepsis/prolepsis)
   - formulaic or proverb-like expressions
   - refrains
   - parallelisms
   - antitheses
   - rhyme and assonance
   - alliterations
   - rhythmic patterns

4. In the Character of the Language
   - simple syntax
   - paratactic sentence structure
   - frequent use of conjunctive elements (καί, δέ etc.)
   - colloquial style

Oral Features in IGT

From the analyses above we can observe several instances of such oral features. The diversity of the parallel passages points in such a direction, as does the episodic character of each of them. Generally, the passages are characterized by stability in core, through the use either of a specific wording (6:10) or of basic narrative elements (4; 15). Thus, there is in these samples enough narrative coherence for them to be preserved as units during the process of transmission, and also no doubt that they deal with the same basic material. At the same time there is considerable flexibility in detail. Narrative elements can be added/omitted, for example in characterization (4, Jesus' reaction; 15, the snake is miscreant), in reasons given (4, Jesus' every word becomes deed; anger because of Jesus' misdeeds) and explanations (15, wood fetching in order to bake bread/for the oven). Even such important—but not essential—narrative elements as the parents of the careless boy can be left out (4).

Parts of passages can also be variously phrased. In the description of the snakebite, Gd differs much in wording from Gs/Ga. Ga and Gd differ on Jesus' motivations in Careless Boy: in Ga he is irritated, in Gd angry. There are also deviations in narrative sequence (the point at which information is introduced: 4, child; 6:10, the name Zacchaeus). Such variation can reflect adaptation to the differing preferences of storytellers and/or their audiences.

Common rhetorical devices are also employed, such as threefold repetition (*trikolon*, Gs 6:10, same/same/same), counting (Gs/Gd 6:10, three-/two-), and similar opening/ending (inclusio, 6:10, the alpha has lines). The high frequency (cf. redundancy) of stylistic elements such as the conjunctive "and" in the sample passages also signals their oral character. The relative verbal stability in the alpha passage (6:10) can very much be due to it having a formulaic character (see pp. 145–46). A number of the other listed oral features also occur in the sample passages, but cannot be developed on here.[28]

Some differences among the variants may even come from the act of hearing. In 6:10 (end) Gs/Gd have "alpha" written out in full, whereas Ga has "A." Although this can be due to scribal change, it can just as likely reflect oral performance being written down, with the "alpha" being heard or memorized, not copied. Similarly, words which sound rather similar have been differently rendered in writing (6:10, cf. above), and have been retained in spite of being incomprehensible. Both differences can of course have arisen from a reader dictating to scribes, but they are just as likely explained as stories being written down from oral performance or from memory.[29]

---

28. Some will, however, be referred to later. Some oral features do not occur in IGT: there are for example (almost) no interpretative comments, illustrations or asides. But oral material does not at all have to exhibit such features.

29. It can be illuminating to compare the character and degree of textual variation in IGT with that of the canonical gospels. On a superficial look the deviance among each IGT manuscript and variant appears to be considerably greater than with the NT gospels. This may speak in favor of less textual fixity and a greater degree of orality in IGT (although recent NT research emphasizes the gospels' oral character more strongly than has been done the last decades, cf. particularly Mournet, *Oral Tradition*, 278–93).

In sum, the analyses strongly indicate the oral coloring of IGT. Although further scrutiny is needed, the samples suffice to make the claim plausible.[30]

The notion about IGT's oral character is of course not completely new: it has, as noted (p. 7), already been proposed by Gero as concerns the main structure of IGT. On the basis of nearly all witnesses Gero attempted to describe different stages of oral tradition and to correlate them with IGT's main literary forms.[31] His view is that IGT consisted of an orally based cycle of episodes, with the less well-attested episodes being added at late stages, and with episodes introduced or omitted over the centuries depending on how they were dogmatically or morally valued.[32] Gero has, particularly through his form-critical analyses of the material, made a strong case for IGT as orally transmitted. My discussion of narrative and rhetorical features in the sample texts has substantiated and developed this view. However, Gero's idea about dogmatic or moral reasons lying behind addition/omission of episodes appears to overstate the ideological element in IGT's transmission and redaction—here he unwittingly allies with those who consider IGT heretical or unethical—although he dismisses gnostic affinities. The fact that the framework of IGT remains basically the same throughout

---

30. The many individual episodes which sometimes appear independently of IGT, but also sometimes were integrated into it (see appendixes 4–5), clearly point to the oral basis of the material. So does the fact that similar accounts can turn up in widely diverse areas and versions (see pp. 180–85). It is worth noting that some distinctive narrative elements recur in different versions without any demonstrable translational links between them. For example, Ir differs from its Latin precursors in that it has Zeno (9:3) die again after being revived; this detail is elsewhere only found in Gs and *Arm. Gos. Inf.* The Syriac version has Zeno die on a Sabbath; this is also found in the early Latin tradition (Lv, Lm, and Ir), but not in the Greek. In addition, Syr and Lv, Lm, Ir share two other special narrative elements: that Jesus learns the Hebrew alphabet (aleph instead of alpha), and that the bed in the workshop measured six cubits (cf. Voicu, "Verso," 36; Chartrand-Burke, "Infancy Gospel," 127). Scholars usually account for such similarities by assuming some common written ancestor. Occasionally, this may be the case. However, such crisscrossing of elements can often more readily be seen as reflecting the material's oral character: with its combination of stability and fluidity, oral transmission is well fit to explain that episodes could be conflated, narrative elements be transferred to other episodes and—within a world that was very much bi-lingual—even exchanged between different language versions.

31. Gero, "Infancy Gospel," 47, 56–59. He also constructed a stemma for the transmission of the material (p. 56).

32. Ibid., 47–57, 75–76.

the manuscripts, Greek and non-Greek, and in spite of differing forms (cf. above) weakens such a view. And the episodes which are added or omitted appear no more dogmatically or morally problematic than those always included.[33] More likely, these changes are part of the vicissitudes to which such accounts are exposed within oral transmission.[34]

Ron Cameron follows Gero's lead and sees in the IGT material a process of both oral and written transmission, in which episodes "circulated from the oral to the written tradition and back again with relative fluidity."[35] Also J. Keith Elliott subscribes to this: he assumes that there was a mixture of written and oral transmission, with the story's "encapsulating in writing at various points in history of a developing cycle of oral tradition."[36] Although neither Cameron nor Elliott present arguments in favor of their view, they are in my opinion essentially correct.

According to the oral/written approach that I have argued in favor of above, the transmission of IGT can be seen as follows: the story originated in the mid-second century CE, and was composed in an oral and/or written shape by an otherwise unknown author. Its core is now impossible to determine definitively, but very likely included substantial parts of or most of the short written form. It was transmitted throughout the centuries, with episodes being added or omitted, and with its shape and contents adapted to shifting contexts. At different points of time, the storytellers or persons within their audiences wrote the stories down. The process of transmission was a double and interrelated one: oral and written, with mutual exchange, but with the oral tradition as dominant. The transmission is likely to have had much in common with that of ancient fairytales. Very early, IGT was translated—orally and/or written[37]—into other languages. It was also gradually combined with or integrated into similar material, thus taking on a more extensive

33. The characteristics of oral transmission are visible in the addition and omission of narrative details in the manuscripts for no other than pedagogical reasons, cf. for example in Ga the omissions of the Greek manuscript V (Chartrand-Burke, "Infancy Gospel," 106–7) and the abridgements in Gb in comparison to Ga (ibid., 112).

34. For a similar example, cf. John 7:53—8:11 (Pericope of the Adulteress); see Metzger, *Textual Commentary*, 187–89.

35. Cameron, *Other Gospels*, 123.

36. Elliott, *Apocryphal New Testament*, 69. Cf. also ibid., *The Apocryphal Jesus*, 3.

37. Very likely, there would have been made several, and unrelated, translations to other languages, cf. Chartrand-Burke, "Infancy Gospel," 52–54.

and more strongly literary-written shape, such as found in the *Gospel of Pseudo-Matthew* (see p. 182). In the chapters following, this view of IGT will be further developed.

Implications of an Oral/Written Approach to IGT

The view presented above has important implications for IGT scholarship. First, the search for an original or archetypal text that has been so prevalent, should be strongly toned down. Previous research has through its repeated failures to establish such a text indirectly shown the futility of the endeavor. And the turning away from an overly literary approach to an oral/written approach precludes the possibility of attaining to such a text, say something close to it. If an oral/written approach is accepted, even only in part, the quest for an original text in fact becomes methodologically and practically impossible, since there will be no way to control the transformations taking place with the material on its journey from archetype to the variety of written manifestations in the manuscripts.

This does not discount the idea that IGT once had a main originator. In fact, it is likely that it had, and that this person was not only a compiler, but someone who put a distinctive narrative mark on the story, and in a way still discernible (cf. chap. 3).[38] But the oral/written approach means that we can no longer get very close to such an author, or even decide whether IGT first had a written or an oral form.

The inaccessibility of an archetype should not, however, prevent us from searching for the old layers of IGT material. Rather, such a quest must go on, but with sobriety and as part of a study of the transmission process in all its chronological and geographical breadth.[39]

Second, abandoning the quest for an original does not mean that we are prevented from or hampered in the study of IGT's contents. Even though this has been the opinion of several, the view is misguided. Instead of considering divergence a problem, it should be regarded a

38. This is partly against ibid., 364–66, who is more indefinite as to the individuality of the author although he often speaks of the originator as a "writer." Cf. also the valuable general reflections on authorship in Thomas, *Acts of Peter*, 78–82.

39. Important work on this has been done by Gero, "Infancy Gospel"; Voicu, "Notes"; ibid., "Verso"; Chartrand-Burke, "Infancy Gospel," chaps. 3 and 5.

value: it is a resource for the study of IGT in all its richness, for example as concerns textual individuality, diversity in settings, and adaptation to context. The differing texts should not primarily be regarded as tools to gain access to an original IGT, but serve as windows into the individual "worlds" reflected in its multiform written manifestations.[40] Thus, each manuscript, variant, and version can be studied in their own right and on their own terms, as telling their part of the history of IGT. In the future, such a "diplomatic" approach to IGT may turn out to be the most fruitful. This has only to a very limited extent been practised within previous research, but will be a guiding principle below.[41]

An oral/written approach has important implications for our understanding of the relationships among the written sources, and particularly the concepts of variant/recension and of stemma. As noted (p. 14), IGT emerges in the written tradition in certain main forms, and in Greek in four distinct variants which have commonly been denoted "recensions." Usually, scholars use "recension" in the sense of "revision," signalling a process of conscious editing with the aim to simplify, shorten or amplify, censor or purge a text.[42] Such instances of revision may of course have occurred in the case of IGT. From an oral perspective, however, the variation should rather be seen as a less controlled, more gradual, sometimes arbitrary, process resulting from frequent retelling of the material. Thus, the Greek variants may even reflect separate written manifestations of oral transmission of IGT. The analyses of the (although) few sample texts above did not uncover any conscious reworking of the story out of dogmatic or moral concerns, but rather narrative rephrasing of a common reservoir of material within new contexts. Thus, to speak of "variants"—which is more open in meaning, and includes the oral element—rather than of "recen-

40. A similar change in attitude has already for some time taken place within NT textual criticism, see Epp, "Issues in New Testament Textual Criticism," 52–61, 70–76; Hurtado, "Beyond the Interlude," 26–48.

41. The main example of such an approach is Baars and Helderman, "Neue Materialien" (parts I–II); they are, however, misguided in many respects, see Chartrand-Burke, "Infancy Gospel," 88. Another example is that of van Aarde, "Die Kindheidsevangelie van Tomas." So far, study of the contents of IGT has been based on an eclectic-hybrid text, viz., that of Tischendorf.

42. Cf. for example the discussions in Chartrand-Burke, "Infancy Gospel," 245–64.

sions" appears more adequate in the case of IGT, and I shall do so in the following.[43]

The oral/written approach also makes attempts at constructing a stemma for the transmission of IGT more difficult. It does not make the production of a stemma superfluous or unwarranted, however. On the contrary, a stemma is needed in order to trace relationships and developments. But a stemma has to take fully account of the character of such transmission, and the interchange between the oral and the written.[44]

The oral perspective does of course not exclude a more literary oriented approach. Rather, both are fully legitimate and can be balanced against one another. In some cases, the literary links between manuscripts are obvious, such as in the Greek family α (cf. above). In other cases, manuscripts within the same variant (Greek or versional) may differ so much that we must reckon with several missing oral/written links between them. Occasionally, manuscripts can also be seen as shooting scripts for oral performances, or—conversely—as written manifestations of such performances. However, this has to be studied thoroughly on the basis of individual manuscripts and their relationships.[45]

Finally, an oral/written approach is of consequence for the study of IGT's socio-cultural and theological contexts. By analyzing the material in its diversity we may be able to perceive more clearly the milieus in which the story was transmitted and how they might have been similar or differed. Just as each canonical gospel is seen to reflect the life of some specific early Christian groups, each variant of IGT can be viewed as glimpses into different settings within late antique Christianity.[46]

43. There may be some pattern(s) in the relations between them, but this has to be developed on a broader basis than can be done here. To speak of variants is also on a level with the practice within modern research on folk- and fairytales.

44. The stemma in Chartrand-Burke, "Infancy Gospel," 285–87 is very valuable, but can probably be developed further, so as to reflect degrees of dependence, oral/written relations etc. See also the stemma in Voicu, "Verso," 95.

45. For reflections on the relationship between transmission and performance, see Shiner, *Proclaiming the Gospel*.

46. An interesting illustration of this is that whereas Zeno in the Greek variants and most Latin versions fell down from a roof, the boy in the Irish version (Ir 41; text and translation in Herbert and McNamara, "Versified Narrative," 478–79) fell over a cliff. In Ireland they did not have houses with flat roofs, but they have plenty of cliffs!

Implications for This Book

The following chapters will take account of such an oral/written ap-proach. I shall do so by concentrating primarily on one of the Greek variants, namely *Gs* (manuscript *H*). There are a number of reasons for selecting this one in particular: it appears to reflect a fairly early stage in the process of transmission, namely late antiquity, the period of special interest here. It is the Greek manuscript which is closest to the oldest versions (the Latin and the Syriac), and thus likely to mirror a primitive form of IGT. And since the manuscript *H* is the single representative in its variant, we do not have to handle the many problems related to tex-tual transmission and variation. When I speak in the following of IGT, it is usually the text of Gs that is implied. However, since my interest not lies only in this text, but in attaining a broader grasp of the material, I shall occasionally consult other variants, and in particular the other Greek ones. Several such references can be found in the notes.[47]

---

47. For an overview, see the entries in index on pp. 280–81 (also appendix 5).

3

Narrative and Literary Features

The *Infancy Gospel of Thomas* has generally been considered a product of inferior literary quality. According to scholars, it is lacking in narrative nerve and plot, and is—with an oft repeated phrase—said to consist "of a series of loosely connected episodes."[1] It is also said to fall short in literary standards, since it contains merely "savorless and inartistic tales."[2] Only rarely have more sympathetic evaluations been offered.[3] Usually, the only structuring principle in IGT is considered to be the age indications of Jesus.[4] And even this turns out not to be fully reliable, since the indications of age on several occasions differ in the manuscripts.[5]

On a superficial look, then, claims of incoherence and literary inferiority seem to hold true. But the claims can be countered. Although it is true that IGT is held in a simple language, there are qualities to be found, as will be shown. The narrative skills also seem to vary among the manuscripts.[6] And even though IGT does not reach up to the literary

1. It "besteht aus Sammelgut" which is "literarisch nur notdürftig zusammengehalten," Vielhauer, *Geschichte*, 674; Schneider, *Evangelia Infantiae*, 37. Rebell, *Neutestamentliche Apokryphen*, 132 ponders "ob man, wenn man nach dem 'Urtext' sucht, nicht hinter einer Schimäre ist; vielleicht war die Kindheitserzählung des Thomas ursprünglich gar kein kohärent konzipiertes Werk, sondern eine offene Sammlung von autarken Einzelstücken"; also Hock, *Infancy Gospels*, 169–74; Voicu, "Verso," 50–51.

2. Enslin, "Along Highways and Byways," 84. For other characterizations, such as "barbarous," "trivial," and "platt," see the references in Chartrand-Burke, "Infancy Gospel," 80 (nn. 259–62).

3. One of the most positive is the concession in Cullmann, "Infancy Gospels," 442 that the author "was endowed with a gift of vivid story-telling, especially when he depicts scenes from everyday childhood."

4. Cf. Miller, *Complete Gospels*, 369, who notes that apart from some temporal markers (Jesus' age) "there are no other overt indications of structure."

5. For example, in Gabd/Lm 10:1 Jesus is said to be six years old (not seven), and in Ga already in 11:2 (and not in 12:1) said to be eight years old.

6. A partial explanation of this has been offered above, in its basis in oral tradition (cf. chapter 2). But its "simple" character also has to do with its social background; I return to this in later chapters.

standards expected from classical writings, it contains obvious traces of rhetorical abilities.[7] Besides, IGT is not necessarily the kind of writing that should be measured according to the standards of ancient rhetoric. In this respect, IGT has much in common with several NT writings, for example Mark and Revelation, and with early Christian writings such as the *Shepherd of Hermas* (ca. 140 CE).

More important, however, is that such charges against IGT, particularly of incoherence, are usually based on modern presuppositions about literary quality. As has been shown in the case of *Life of Aesop* and the Gospel of Mark, modern criticism has not taken sufficiently into account the ways in which antique writings establish plots within episodic narratives.[8] Many such writings consist of collections of more or less self-contained episodes and often develop their plots on the basis of repetition of motifs and events, differently from modern novels which for example employ psychological development and dynamics of social interaction.

Similarly, modern criticism has not taken seriously the oral character of many ancient sources (cf. chap. 2). In orally based or marked material, the audience's appreciation very much depends on the effect of a story's individual episodes, since they are often performed individually or in clusters, but also—when the story is told as a whole—on the cumulative effect of its episodes.[9] In such material, coherence and plot are created for example by the retelling of similar episodes, by grouping of similar material, by repetition of conflicts between main characters, by weaving together episodes in order to create narrative tension or to give keys for interpretation, but also by elaborating different motifs to secure variation (cf. pp. 26–27).[10]

In this chapter, various narrative aspects of IGT will be analyzed, showing that IGT has far more narrative sophistication than has been usually allowed for: there are clear indications of narrative coherence, of a deliberate plot, and of artistic skills.[11] I shall, however, not go into

7. See particularly the form-critical analyses of Gero, "Infancy Gospel," 56–64 and Hock, *Infancy Gospels*, 92–95 as indications of this.

8. This is convincingly argued by Shiner, "Creating Plot."

9. Ibid., 155–57.

10. This is very usefully presented and exemplified in ibid., 169–74.

11. Such analysis is highly needed, since it has not been done systematically and at length. Chartrand-Burke, "Infancy Gospel," 262–64 (also 398–402) makes use of a narrative approach, however; his analyses are valuable, but relatively brief. Gero, "Infancy

great detail, but sketch IGT's main structure and develop on elements that in special ways contribute to its plot. Other aspects of its narrative world, such as the main characters, socio-cultural and ideological-theological settings, will be dealt with in other chapters. Focus will be on main structure, tradition-historical and form-critical aspects, narrative outline and plot, certain narrative motifs, narrative elaboration and style, and genre.

Main Structure

Gs has a simple and clearly set out structure. It can be outlined thus:[12]

Gs	Full title			Short title
1	Heading/Prolog			Prolog
2–3	Three Miracles			
	2:1	Cleaning of Pools		Pools
	2:2–5	Vivification of Sparrows		Sparrows
	3:1–3	Curse on Annas' Son		Annas' Son
4–5	A Miracle and the Responses to It			
	4:1–2	Curse on a Careless Boy		Careless Boy
	5:1–3	Joseph Rebukes Jesus		Joseph's Rebuke
6–8	Teacher Discourse			
	6:1—8:2	First teacher		1 Teacher
		6:1–7	Dialog	1 Teacher (Dial.)
		6:8–10	Alpha Lesson	1 Teacher (Alpha)
		7:1–4	Lament	1 Teacher (Lam.)
		8:1–2	Exclamation	1 Teacher (Exclam.)
9	A Miracle and the Responses to It			
	9:1	Raising of Zeno		Zeno
	9:2–4	Parents' Dialog with Jesus		Zeno
10–12	Three miracles			
	10:1–2	Carrying Water in a Cloak		Water in Cloak
	11:1–2	Miraculously Great Harvest		Harvest
	12:1–2	Miraculous Repair of a Bed		Bed
13–14	Teacher discourses			
	13:1–3	Second Teacher		2 Teacher
	14:1–4	Third Teacher		3 Teacher
15–16	Two miracles			
	15:1–2	Healing of James' Snakebite		Snakebite
	16:1–3	Healing of an Injured Foot		Injured Foot
17	Final discourse (epilog)			
	17:1–5	Jesus in the Temple		Jesus in Temple

Gospel," 46–80, and Hock, *Infancy Gospels*, 85–90, 92–97, occasionally touch on narrative aspects, but only in connection with individual episodes or cycles of episodes.

12. I here follow the numbering of Chartrand-Burke, "Infancy Gospel."

Gs has the same structure as most of the versions, the exception however being that 1 and 16 are missing in the versions (cf. p. 14). Gabd differs from Gs in that they have Gs 16 placed after Gs 9, and have two additional episodes after Gs 15 and before the final episode (Jesus in Temple); see appendixes 1–4.

Tradition-historical and Form-critical Aspects

From a tradition-historical perspective the structure of Gs give support to the idea of an oral/written transmission to IGT. The limited variation in type of material (mainly miracles and discourses) and the regular alternation between them give IGT a unified and lucid character, well fit for such transmission. Much of the material is organized in blocks, particularly of three. This is characteristic of the miracle episodes in 2–3 and 10–12.

There are also three teacher episodes: 6–8, 13, and 14. Although some scholars argue that they are a triplication of one single narrative,[13] it is far more likely that they—following a traditional oral pattern—have been three from the outset; the triad is witnessed in all manuscripts. It should also be noted that the reaction and action of the first and second teachers on Jesus' disobedience is identical: "the teacher became irritated and hit him" (6:8; 13:2)—here, IGT uses the narrative technique of verbatim repetition. In addition, if there originally was only one episode, the narrative would loose a central point, viz., the success of the third, wise teacher following the failures of the others.[14]

Two miracle episodes, 4–5, and 9, share a common basic structure: they appear as individual miracles with expanded responses. The last two miracles in Gs, 15–16, emerge as a group of brief, less firmly organized miracles.

It is not unlikely that parts of this material were transmitted orally in smaller or larger units independently of writing.[15] The occurrence of other episodes related to IGT, but less integrated into the tradition, im-

13. Gero, "Infancy Gospel," 63–64. Even if this should be the case, the development into a pattern of three must have taken place very early, cf. the cluster of three-organization of miracle stories and the tripartite structure of many of Jesus' sayings.

14. On the use of similar episodes for the creation of plot, see Shiner, "Creating Plot," 169, 173–74.

15. Chartrand-Burke, "Infancy Gospel," 74.

plies this. Examples of such episodes are Riding the Sunbeam, Children Made Swine, and Jesus and the Dyer (see appendix 4).

Form-critically IGT consists of three main types: prolog, miracles, and discourses.[16] The *prolog* has elements in common with prologs known from many ancient writings and serve to give IGT a literary taint. *Miracles* form a distinctive feature in IGT: they comprise the majority of episodes.[17] As in the NT, there are two main categories: nature and health miracles. Five are nature miracles: 2:1 (Pools); 2:2–5 (Sparrows); 10 (Water in Cloak); 11 (Harvest); 12 (Bed). Health miracles consist of two subtypes, cursing and healing miracles. There are three instances of cursing: 3 (Annas' Son); 4 (Careless Boy); 13 (2 Teacher). A fourth miracle can also be added, from Joseph's Rebuke (5:2, Blinding of Accusers). There are three healing episodes: 9 (Zeno); 15 (Snakebite); 16 (Injured Foot). To this can be added two healings that form part of other episodes: 8:2 (Healing of the Cursed); 14:4 (vivification in 2 Teacher).

The other main form-critical category, *discourse*, also has a broad place in IGT. Most striking are 1–3 Teacher (6–8; 13; 14), with the first episode as clearly the most elaborate. In addition, there are brief discourses functioning as responses to miracles: Joseph's Rebuke (5) and Jesus' dialog with Zeno's parents (9). Finally, Jesus in the Temple can be counted among the discourses (17:1–5); it has, however, also been classified as a personal legend.[18] The discourses mainly consist of dialogs (5:1–2; 6:1–3, 5–7, 8–9; 9:2–4; 13:1–3; 14:1–4), pointed sayings (8:1), and brief speeches (5:3; 6:4, 10; 7:1–4). The last of these speeches, the teacher's lament in 7:1–4, can also be classified as a speech-in-character, an ἠθοποιΐα.[19]

Although the episodes can be sorted into two main types, it is evident that many of them are not of a pure kind: they also contain elements from other types, for example with narrative elements within discourses (5:2; 6:7 etc.).

16. There has been done quite an amount of form-critical analysis of IGT, particularly by Gero, "Infancy Gospel." He has a slightly differing categorization: 1. short miracle stories with no Jesus saying (and no synoptic parallels), 2. healings with Jesus sayings attached (and synoptic parallels), and 3. curses (with Mark 11:20–26 as a NT parallel). In addition, he classifies some episodes (2 and 6–8) as apophthegms.

17. Among the canonical gospels, IGT the most clearly resembles Mark in this respect.

18. See Vielhauer, *Geschichte*, 674.

19. This is the well-argued view of Hock, *Infancy Gospels*, 94–95.

Narrative Outline and Plot

In the following, IGT will be outlined in order to show how its material is weaved together to form a coherent narrative.

First is the heading/prolog (1), which attributes IGT to "the Israelite" Thomas. The apostle Thomas is probably intended, or Thomas as Jesus' legendary twin brother. The prolog has the function of creating a solemn opening to the gospel and of giving it an air of authenticity and authority by linking it up with a well-known figure. It introduces the gospel Jesus' "great childhood deeds" and places the story in the geographical context of Nazareth. Apart from this, the prolog is only loosely integrated into the gospel and clearly secondary; it is for instance lacking in many of the oldest versions, such as the Georgian and some Syriac and Latin.[20]

Throughout IGT there are no explicit references to the narrator. Implicitly, however, he emerges as omniscient (he knows what Jesus and others feel and think) and omnipresent (as having direct access to all the events). He does not himself take part in the story, but tells it from outside of the events taking place. Nevertheless, what he tells is presented as reliable and as reflecting Jesus' own point of view.

After the introduction, the main body of IGT follows, with its alternation of miracles and discourses. Although miracles are clearly most frequent in number, the discourses in extent add up to more than 60% of the total story. The first triplet of miracles (2–3: Pools, Sparrows, Annas' Son) is performed by Jesus at the age of five. On a Sabbath, Jesus is playing at the ford of a stream making pools. In a miraculous way, he purifies the polluted water in the pools. Then he forms twelve sparrows out of clay, which he—to the marvel of a Pharisee—makes come alive. The son of Annas the High Priest observes the events, destroys the pools with a twig, and accuses Jesus of breaking the Sabbath. The result is, as noted, that Jesus curses him so that he withers away, i.e. dies.

The three miracles are closely knit together, in a chiastic a–b–a structure: the son of Annas acts in relation to Jesus' first miracle, that of

20. Cf. Chartrand-Burke, "Infancy Gospel," 279–81. There is for example nowhere else in Gs made a connection to Thomas, nor are there other links in vocabulary ("Gentile", "brothers", names of places etc.). Consequently, the prolog will only occasionally be included in the discussions below. In the heading of Gb, Thomas is presented as the "holy apostle," in Ga as a philosopher, whereas Gd does not have the prolog and does not mention Thomas at all.

the pools, and without explicit reference to the sparrow miracle. The insertion of the sparrow episode enhances the total effect of the account, both by heightening the impression of Jesus' miraculous power and by juxtaposing two different responses, that of the marveling Pharisee and of the averse son of Annas. Climax and conclusion to the events finally occur in the third miracle: the death of Annas' son. A similar pattern can be found in Mark 5:21–43 par., in the intertwined episodes of the raising of Jairus' daughter and the haemorrhaging woman.[21]

After this an episode follows (4–5: Careless Boy, Joseph's Rebuke) which has central features in common with that of Annas' son. When—as Gs relates it—Jesus is on his way from the ford, another boy runs by and bumps into him, to the effect that he too is cursed for his misdeed and dies. Whereas this episode too involves a boy who dies, it differs from the preceding by developing upon the reaction of the people witnessing the event. As concerns main motif, then, the episode is linked up with the preceding, but takes the issue of audience response much further. There is a threefold response: first, the response of the people, then of the boy's parents, and finally of Joseph. The last is by far the longest response; thus, we here seem to have a rhetorical *trikolon crescens*.

Now the first teacher episode follows (6–8: 1 Teacher), with Zacchaeus being introduced. He stands listening to Jesus' words and is inspired to impart even more wisdom to the boy. In the end, the result is near-fatal—not for Jesus, but for the teacher imagining that he were able to teach the pupil something he did not already know. Zacchaeus ends up by professing his uttermost despair and shame: he must "die, or have to flee from this village" (7:3); and he also proclaims that the boy must be something great, "whether a god, an angel, or whatever else" (7:4).

Following this confession, there now occurs a climax and turning point. Jesus first makes an assurance that now the "unfruitful [will] bear fruit, the blind see, and the foolish in heart become wise" (8:1). Interestingly, this listing appears to correspond, even in sequence, to his earlier instances of cursing: Annas' son who withered away (3:3, became unfruitful), the accusers who were blinded (5:5, probably the parents of the careless boy), and Zacchaeus, the stupid teacher (7:3–4)—all these are restored: they bear fruit, see, become wise. Read this way, the saying

21. See Shiner, "Creating Plot," 172–73.

gives a flashback which serves to bind this first half of IGT together. Jesus then breaks out in a praise quite similar to that of Matt 11:25–27 par, saying: "I have come from above in order to rescue those below and call them to what is above, just as the one who sent me to you ordered me," and as a result the cursed are saved and Jesus wins the respect of all: "no-one dared to make him angry after that" (8:2). Thus, the untimely deaths have been made good again, and they have had their (probably intended) effect, as warnings toward unbelieving spectators. No attention is paid, however, to the fact that the deaths of the children obviously are already a thing of the past, and that these incidents did not have any great consequences for Jesus—he could even be taken to school as if nothing problematic had occurred. Such illogical elements are typical of oral narratives (cf. p. 26).

With this climax, tensions created earlier in the plot are solved and balance re-established. Jesus' first day at school is also over, without any hints of further visits. The matter seems to be held in suspension, however: the unsuccessful event can indicate that new attempts will be necessary.

The next episode (9: Zeno) is more loosely tied to the preceding: it happens "many days later." The tension level is now considerably lowered. Again a miracle takes place, and again a dead boy is involved, in a way similar to Careless Boy (4). This time, however, it is not Jesus who causes his death: the boy himself falls down from a roof while at play. Nevertheless, the boy's parents accuse him: "You pushed our child down." No flashback to Jesus' previous "murders" is given, but clearly lies implicit in the narrative as the occasion for their accusation. Jesus, however, repudiates their claim by waking the boy, now called Zeno, from the dead and having him confirm his innocence. After this Jesus commands Zeno to "sleep," so that he dies again. Nonetheless his parents praise God and worship Jesus (9:3).

Now the next phase in Jesus' childhood is introduced: he has become seven years old, and performs a string of three miracles (10–12: Water in Cloak, Harvest, Bed). The two first miracles are briefly related, whereas the third is more elaborated and functions as a climax within the unit. The miracles are thematically closely related: they all deal with domestic activities (water fetching, sowing/harvesting, handiwork), places (house/hometown, field, workshop), and figures (mother and father).[22] They are also linked together by the similar reactions of Mary (10:2) and Joseph (12:2): both kiss Jesus and ask/thank God for his blessing of the child.[23] Thus, although these miracles are not as integrated as the first group of three (2–3), they are nevertheless strongly interconnected.[24]

By the time of the last miracle Jesus has become eight years old, and Joseph seeing his wisdom thinks it high time to take him to school again, three years after the first attempt, so that he shall not "be unacquainted with letters" (13:1). The return to this issue serves to create narrative cohesion in IGT as a whole and contributes markedly to the push in its plot. Provided that 1–3 Teacher tradition-historically were originally a single unit (cf. above), the way it has been worked into IGT shows considerable storytelling skills: in its present shape, the introduction to the second and third episodes—with its brief, analeptic reference to the first teacher (13:1: Joseph handed him over to "another master")—establishes a link to the first episode and also an expectation as to what will now happen. At the same time the introduction gives the narrative a fresh start: no indication is given of Joseph having realized from Jesus' first visit to school that he already had learned the letters and would have no need of education. Although IGT's audience knows better, the characters, Joseph in particular, do not appear to have learned anything from the previous incident.

Second teacher (13:2 Teacher) is very briefly narrated and clearly functions as a passageway leading to the climax of 3 Teacher. But it also serves to heighten the tension in this part of IGT, in two ways. First, by its fatal result: the second teacher is not only shamed like the first teacher, he is even—after having hit Jesus—cursed to death (13:2). And second, by its dramatic break with what was stated at the end of 1 Teacher, that "no-one dared to make him angry from after that" (8:2). What the author has "promised," in fact turns out not to hold good:

---

22. The workshop itself is not mentioned in Gs, but seems to be implied.

23. Chartrand-Burke, "Infancy Gospel," 237, 239, 399 holds that 10:2 and 12:2 are not original, but added later, since they are absent in the Syriac and some other versional manuscripts. Although this is a problematic claim, I refrain—since my focus is on Gs—from a discussion of this here.

24. On such clusters, see Shiner, "Creating Plot," 169–70. For a discussion of the episodes, see also chap. 7 below.

Jesus is nevertheless made angry, and is now confined to the house in order to avoid the death of others who might instigate him.

After a few days of confinement—a modest punishment for such a deed!—the third teacher offers to take Jesus to school. He is a wise man who immediately acknowledges Jesus' superiority and instead of doing the teaching lets Jesus teach him and the strongly impressed crowd. As a result of his truthful witness, the second teacher too is "saved," which implies that he is brought back to life (14:4). With this episode, a new climax is reached, and tensions created are solved again: the third teacher has displayed his competence; the second teacher has been restored to life; and—most importantly—a main point in 1–3 Teacher is displayed, viz., Jesus' superior "grace and wisdom."[25]

Following this, two rather loosely grouped miracles are told (15–16: Snakebite, Injured Foot).[26] We are now close to the end of IGT, and in Gs this appears to be the place for including remaining material. Nonetheless, there is a certain narrative coherence and development even here: both episodes deal with work activities (wood fetching and wood splitting) and with young men, viz., Jesus' brother James and "a young man." There is also a rise in drama from the first to the second episode: whereas James is at the verge of dying when rescued, the young man is already dead after having cut his foot. And whereas no audience reaction is reported in the first episode, this is central in the second. The reaction is special, since it anticipates the canonical gospels' story about the adult Jesus: the crowd exclaims: ". . . he will go on saving *all the days of his life*" (16:3, my emphasis).

Thus, the final miracle also leads up to the last episode (17: Jesus in Temple). This is IGT's most explicit narrative link to the canonical tradition, and serves to lend a certain authority to IGT as a whole: it does not compete with the canonical gospels, but shows them due respect by integrating one of their pericopes as its ending. The episode is not only an appendix, however, but functions in the words and concepts that it highlights as a natural rounding off (see p. 118): here, the childhood of Jesus is lead to its end, with him on the threshold of the adult world.

25. Cf. also Chartrand-Burke, "Infancy Gospel," 263.
26. Ga has here four miracles.

Finally, IGT as a whole is brought to a close by a brief concluding doxology, which in Gs is corrupt at the end: "To him [God] be the glory . . ."[27]

The analysis, then, shows that IGT has an ordered structure and a coherent storyline, with narrative climaxes and some instances of interconnecting flashbacks and anticipations. There is also a fairly regular alternation of main types of episodes (miracles and discourses) and subtypes (different kinds of miracles), which gives variation to the story, but at the same time secures unity. The somewhat differing length of the individual episodes also contributes to variation. In addition, some episodes are intertwined (Pools, Sparrows, and Annas' Son) in ways that provide keys for interpretation: it serves to emphasize Jesus' miraculous power and the differing reactions to him. But episodes are also split and postponed so as to maintain narrative tension (1–3 Teacher).

The main characters also serve to strengthen narrative cohesion: they are limited in number and appear repeatedly throughout the story. Apart from Jesus, this is particularly the case with Joseph and the teachers, but also the anonymous crowds (2:4; 4:1; 6:5, 7–8, 10; 10:1; 14:2; 16; 17:2). At the same time, the cast is broad enough to keep up interest in the story.

Thus, IGT in structure, storyline, and plot turns out to have considerably more narrative quality than has been assumed.

Narrative Motifs: Audience Response and Curse/Blessing

Two other factors also give indications of IGT's narrative sophistication. The first is its depiction of audience response. The spectator reactions provide the story with elements that bind it together, but also contribute to development. The most important thoroughgoing feature is how spectators relate to Jesus: they react with marvel. In the first group of miracles, the Pharisee marvels at Jesus' vivification of the sparrows (2:5, ἐθαύμασεν). In 1 Teacher, Zacchaeus marvels at Jesus' words to Joseph (6:1, ἐθαύμασεν), as do the Jews standing by (6:6, θαυμάζετε). Later, Zeno's parents marvel at Jesus' power (9:3, ἐθαύμασαν). The spectators at Jesus' third visit to school are stunned (14:2, ἐκπλήττεσθαι). The crowd marvels at his healing of the injured foot (16:3, ἐθαύμασαν).

27. Gs has ᾧ ἡ δό[ξα] . . .

Finally, those present in the temple are amazed (17:2, ἐξίσταντο). Sometimes, the spectators are also so overwhelmed as to be left speechless (6:6, 9; 17:2). Clearly, IGT wishes to underscore the wonder-inspiring effect of Jesus' activity.

A development can also be observed as concerns types of audience response. In the first half of the IGT, response is primarily negative: people react by accusing Jesus (2:3; 3:1; 5:1), by criticizing his parents (4:2; 5:1), by disbelief in his words (6:6), and by being afraid of him (7:2; 8:2). After the narrative climax at the end of 1 Teacher (8:2), when those who had earlier been cursed are restored to life, a change takes place. Except for the relapse of the second teacher (13:2–3, but cf. also 10:2), reactions are now positive: Zeno's parents praise God and worship Jesus (9:3). Mary kisses him seeing the signs he makes (10:2). A little later, Joseph both embraces and kisses him (12:2). The third teacher is "glad" to hear him and encourages him (14:2). And the scribes in the temple confirm his "wisdom" and "glory of virtue" (17:4).

There also occurs a change in the contents of the responses. Early in the story people ask: "From where was this child born, since his word becomes deed?" (4:1). The question is at this point left unanswered. Later on, the first teacher develops on the idea by asking: "What kind of womb bore him? What kind of mother raised him?" (7:2). Now, a mother is hinted at, but the answer is still open. At the end of IGT, in an addition to the Lukan temple account, the question is answered: when Mary has confirmed that she is Jesus' mother, the scribes and the Pharisees declare that "Blessed are you, for the Lord God has blessed the fruit of your womb" (17:4). Thus, from an unspecific question at the start, the narrative gradually clarifies the issue, until an answer is given: Mary is the mother of Jesus (cf. also p. 110).

A similar development can be seen in the description of Jesus. In 1 Teacher, the crowd states that Jesus must be something special, since "no-one, neither a teacher of the law nor a Pharisee, has spoken like this child" (6:5). A little later, the first teacher speculates whether Jesus is some kind of "god" or "angel" (7:4). With the last of Jesus' miracles, however, the crowd professes openly that "he has indeed saved many souls from death. And he will go on saving all the days of his life" (16:3).

Thus, the types and contents of audience response evince a drama which appears consciously worked out. Its elements contribute both to stableness and development: the awe-inspiring character of Jesus' words and deeds is emphasized, and reactions change from primarily negative to predominantly positive as the audiences—both individuals and groups—gradually realize the greatness of Jesus.[28]

The second factor contributing to narrative sophistication is the motif of curse and blessing. The motif is first hinted at in Jesus' curse on Annas' son (3). It is made explicit when the parents of the careless boy state that Joseph must teach Jesus "to bless and not to curse" (4:2). Cursing is again made a central issue in the narrative climax of 8:1–2: as an effect of Jesus' outbreak of praise, "all those who had fallen under his curse were saved." After this narrative climax blessing comes into focus: Jesus is—implicitly—blessed by God (10:2); Joseph states that God has blessed him with the boy (12:2); and Mary has been blessed by giving birth to him (17:4).

Thus, the ideas of curse and blessing run through IGT, with a significant turn at 8:1–2. This turn, however, is not a result of Jesus being taught to bless and not to curse (4:2). Instead, it follows from the various characters' realization of who Jesus is, as coming from God (4:1; 9:3). At the end the two narrative threads of audience response and of curse/blessing are tied together in the words to Mary in the temple: "Blessed are you, for the Lord God has blessed the fruit of your womb" (17:4).

Narrative Elaboration and Style

It may be true that Gs—and IGT in general—is not very developed artistically, at least according to modern literary standards. For example, events are presented in simple chronological order. There are few comments on the part of the narrator; the only ones are the secondary attribution to Thomas (1:1), the mention of "God's law" (14:2), and the brief final doxology (17:5). The language is also sometimes clumsy.[29] On the other hand, several elements show sophistication in narrative elabora-

28. Generally, Ga works out the reactions of characters in more detail than Gs (3:2; 6:2). Gd too often embroiders upon events and character responses (e.g., 9:2–3; 15:2).

29. For example, there are unnecessary repetitions (3:1, "he dried up the pools he had collected"; 7:3, "has been overcome by . . . was overcome by"), seemingly unmotivated sayings (11:1, "But Joseph took it from Jesus' seeds"), less intelligible sayings (4:1, "Cursed be your ruling power" etc.), and illogical use of information (2:3–5, Jesus' accuser in the sparrow miracle is first introduced as "a Jew", and at the end spoken of as "the Pharisee"). Occasionally, such unevenness can reflect corruptions in the process of transmission.

tion, in ways characteristic of episodic stories like this.[30] Some occurred in the sample passages above (chap. 2). Others show up elsewhere, for example rhetorical means such as repeated negation (6:5, οὐδέποτε . . . οὐδένος . . . οὐδὲ . . . οὐδὲ) and *trikolon crescens* (6:8, τὴν φωνὴν . . . τὴν δόξαν . . . τὴν δύναμιν τῆς συνέσεως, cf. also 8:1).

The storytelling of IGT is usually economical, with only the most vital information given. In a number of instances, however, the episodes are worked out in detail. The details provided very much conform to features characteristic of oral transmission, for example the use of names, both familiar (Joseph, Mary, James) and less familiar (Annas, Zacchaeus, Zeno), of vivid description of actions (2:4, Jesus clapping his hands; 5:1, the pulling of Jesus' ear etc.), and of dialog (5:1–3; 9:2–4). Even the well-known Jesus in Temple has extra details added (17:3; see pp. 115–18).[31]

The narrative elaboration of 1 Teacher merits special attention. Here, Zacchaeus' lament is developed in considerable detail (7:1–4), with him bemoaning his fate: he has become "miserable" since he has been overcome by Jesus, a child; he has been ignorant, even though he is expected to be a teacher; and he has made himself a fool to the spectators and the villagers. Jesus' way of dealing with the teacher also has much in common with other ancient stories that ridicule similar figures, for example, philosophers in Lucian's *Philosophies for Sale* (ca. 160 CE), opponents in Philostratus' *Life of Apollonius* (ca. 215 CE), and authorities in *Life of Aesop*.[32] Indeed, there is a distinct slapstick quality to the episode: the scene is construed in a way aiming at comic effect (see pp. 145–46 and 207).

As for style, Gs appears to have a distinctively oral character, for example with a generally simple syntax. Its use of grammatical forms reflects a popular, *koiné*, style, and it has a fairly varied and advanced—and even inscrutable—vocabulary. In spite of differences in content and wording (cf. pp. 16–23), Gs shares these characteristics with Ga (and

30. See Shiner, "Creating Plot," 171–72.

31. The formulations of Gb often differ from the other variants, with phrases being repeated and the same point being reiterated in a different wording (oral characteristic). Gb also focuses on action, whereas dialogs and Jesus sayings are usually brief.

32. Shiner, "Creating Plot," 162–66, on comic elements, see esp. p. 162. On Aesop, see particularly Hägg, "A Professor and His Slave," 177–203.

Gb). In general, its style can be described as unpretentious, fresh, and appealing—and thus well fit for finding a broad audience.[33]

Genre

The question of genre also has consequences for our understanding of IGT. Research has, however, had difficulties with deciding upon its genre since the story has elements in common with different kinds of material from the period. Obviously, it shares some narrative features with the *Hellenistic novels*. The similarities are not marked, however, and clearly not many enough to tie it closely up with this genre.[34] IGT appears to have more in common with *ancient biographies* on holy men and political leaders, such as Philo's *On the Life of Moses* (20 BCE—40 CE) and Suetonius' emperor biographies (ca. 70–130 CE), in which descriptions of the heroes' childhood are seen as anticipations of their future greatness.[35] However, this category of writings is very diverse and their fit with IGT rather limited.[36] There is for instance no other writing which deals only with a hero's childhood; this stage of life constitutes nearly always just a small part of the total story.

IGT has also some features in common with *fable literature* such as *Life of Aesop*. But its individual episodes appear less pointed and more dependent on the plot of the whole story than are the fables, which more easily function as separate units.[37] The many animals that make up the cast of the fables are also lacking in IGT.

---

33. This is the view of Fuchs and Weissengruber, *Konkordanz*, 207–47, esp. 225–26, 245–47 as concerns the style of Ga and Gb. The same verdict can be meted out to Gs, according to Greek expert Bjørn Helge Sandvei at the Norwegian Lutheran School of Theology, Oslo (as discussed with him in August 2005).

34. Cf. the discussion in Chartrand-Burke, "Infancy Gospel," 299–315. For discussions of the ancient novel, see Tatum, *Search for the Ancient Novel*; Hägg, *Parthenope*.

35. So Hock, *Infancy Gospels*, 96–97, and Chartrand-Burke, "Infancy Gospel," 313, stress the similarities of IGT's Jesus with stories about Jewish holy men (see pp. 8–9).

36. In discussions of these writings, scholars tend to overstate the common elements. In my opinion, they often seem more to share a common motif rather than to belong to a common genre. Cf. also Hägg, "Evangelierna som biografier" 44–56.

37. See Gibbs, *Aesop's Fables*, ix–xii; Shiner, "Creating Plot," 166–67. However, Pervo, "Nihilist Fabula," 84–97 argues in favor of (some) coherence in Aesop.

IGT can also be compared with other types of classical material. A very broad group is that of *fairytale, myth, legend, and sacred history*.[38] In oral cultures such as that of antiquity, this kind of—largely popular— material is very rich. It is also of a kind easily transformed from one subtype to another, for example from fairytale to myth, from myth to legend, and so on. Occasionally, fairytales were even turned into plots for novels.[39] Thus, it is notoriously difficult and not very rewarding to distinguish clearly among them.[40] In spite of the great variation within the group, IGT nonetheless appears to share some general thematic and stylistic features with it (with myth being the least relevant, however).[41] Such features are a main figure with unusual skills; the figure's conflicts with others; fairly self-contained episodes integrated into a narrative whole; relative anonymity as concerns place and time, which make it adaptable to new contexts and audiences, yet enough individuality in narrative detail so as to preserve an air of authenticity; and narrative fluidity reflecting oral transmission. Nonetheless, the fit between IGT and specific other such stories is not very close. For example, it differs from many types of fairytales in that its narrative world is presented as a real world and in that it pretends to be historically rooted. In sum, IGT appears to come closest to the legend type, possibly the belief legend, but with elements from some of the other categories.[42]

IGT has also elements in common with other *Jewish and early Christian literature*. This is the case with Jewish novels such as Tobit (third–second century BCE), *Joseph and Aseneth* (first century BCE— second century CE, possibly Christian), and Esther (ca. third century BCE), with apocryphal acts such as *Acts of Paul and Thecla* (mid-second century CE), *Acts of Peter* (late second century CE), and with hagiographical writings such as *Life of Antony* (356–362 CE). Here too,

---

38. I here employ the categories of Honko, "Folkloristic Theories," 4–25, esp. 21; cf. also Anderson, *Fairytale*, 16. For discussions about genre within folkloristic studies, see Honko, "Folkloristic Theories"; also Ben-Amos, "Folktale," 255–67. For detailed classifications of such tales, see Uther, *Types of International Folktales*.

39. Anderson, *Fairytale*, 22, 145–57; Shiner, "Creating Plot," 162–63.

40. So Anderson, *Fairytale*, 16.

41. Cf. ibid., 20–23. IGT appears to borrow features from a variety of story types, such as "tales of magic", "religious tales", and even "anecdotes and jokes", see the classifications in Uther, *Types of International Folktales*.

42. See the model in Honko, "Folkloristic Theories," 21.

however, similarities are not very close. This is even more the case with sayings gospels such as Q and *Gospel of Thomas.*

Neither is IGT's similarity with its twin, the *Infancy Gospel of James*, very striking, in spite of the shared issue of childhood. The two are more likely to reflect parallel, yet independent developments. In fact, *Prot. Jas.* seems both in form and content to have more in common with Hellenistic novels and apocryphal acts than with IGT. The frequent joint presentation of the two stories, due to their focus on the early years of Jesus and his family, has probably linked them more closely together than they should be.

The early Christian material to come the closest to IGT as concerns genre is in fact the *canonical gospels.* It is evident that IGT is drawing on Luke, and probably also on other gospels (see chap. 8). The influence can be seen in IGT's overall structure: (1) it is introduced by a prolog, in a way known from the NT gospels (Luke) and letters. Like the other gospels, (2) it has a biographical account; (3) the account consists of alternating narratives (miracles), discourses and Jesus sayings; and (4) these elements are linked together on the basis of chronology. Finally, (5) IGT ends with the episode of Jesus in the Temple, thus creating a link to the canonical gospels. The inclusion shows that a concern behind IGT was somehow to supplement the NT gospels with material from Jesus' childhood, and in a way thought congenial to their Jesus stories.

Whether IGT should be called a gospel, is of course a matter of definition.[43] For example, IGT is both in form and in content much closer to the NT gospels than to *Gospel of Thomas.* But like it, it also differs from them, particularly in its lack of explicit mention of Jesus' death or resurrection. Nonetheless, the similarities with the canonical material are so many that the customary modern description of IGT as a gospel is to an extent justifiable.

At the same time, however, such a classification must be done with proviso, since it can also conceal IGT's special character. In fact, this is signalled by what appears to be its oldest (self-)designation, namely not as a gospel, but as παιδικὰ μεγαλεῖα, a story about Jesus' "great childhood deeds."[44]

---

43. For a discussion of gospel as genre, see Burridge, *What Are the Gospels?*

44. Whether this should be regarded as some kind of literary or narrative genre is not clear; the matter needs closer scrutiny.

In sum, IGT emerges as a mixture of belief legend and gospel, together with some elements from ancient biography. Probably this is the closest one can get to a genre classification. Eventually, this makes IGT very much into a kind of its own: there is in fact no other material handed down from antiquity which can be seen as clear parallels.[45] This may give important signals as to IGT's literary-historical setting: it is a story that draws on and unifies a twofold tradition, viz., a popular oral/written heritage and a biblical-ecclesial heritage. Its uniqueness may even give us hints about its social setting and audience. But these are matters which we shall return to later.

Conclusion

The analysis has shown that IGT employs a broad variety of narrative tools. This is reflected on several levels, from its overall organization and down to its individual details. Contrary to what has been held, it has been demonstrated that IGT has considerable narrative quality. This is evident when it is compared to relevant types of works, for example *Life of Aesop*, the Gospel of Mark, and Revelation. But it also holds true when seen in relation to the standards of modern narrative theory. To an extent, IGT even possesses some of the qualities typical of classical rhetoric.

These narrative qualities are not coincidental, but a result of conscious composition and presentation: there is in IGT's story a clearly visible plot. This plot includes several central thoroughgoing elements, such as Jesus' display of his miraculous power and wisdom, and the motif of curse/blessing. But it also comprises a dynamic development, in which the growing recognition of Jesus' divinity is a basic motif. This development is conveyed in the story by means of varying levels of tension, solutions of tension, dramatic turns, and changing audience responses, and finally ends up with an event leading the way into the canonical gospels. In the following, several of these elements will be dealt with in more detail.

45. The lack of close precursors to IGT is also noted by Hock, *Infancy Gospels*, 97–98 and Chartrand-Burke, "Infancy Gospel," 397.

4

❧◈❧

DAILY LIFE AND SOCIAL RELATIONS

Analyses of the "world" of IGT have so far been few and brief. Some scholars have tried to locate IGT geographically, usually tracing its origin to somewhere in the eastern Mediterranean (p. 7). A few others have studied IGT with a view to social setting and suggested some kind of everyday life context for it (pp. 4 and 10). One scholar has noted its vivid portrayal of rural life.[1] Chartrand-Burke has the broadest discussion of social setting, but does not—in spite of many valuable observations—deal systematically with the matter.[2] Thus, there is a great need for further analysis.

In the following two chapters, I shall undertake a study of IGT's "world." I have two particular aims in mind. The first is the question as to what kind of world emerges from the story itself. What does its "narrative world" look like, both in its details and its totality? How is it construed as concerns space, time, entities, persons, social relations, and values? Such an analysis has not been made before, and a collection and classification of information will thus be valuable in itself.

Second, such a study of IGT's narrative world is required if we are to come to grips with the distinctive character and setting of this story. Without a thorough analysis of the text itself it will be impossible to deal responsibly with such issues. Some of these issues, such as historical setting and audience, will be touched on here, but further unfolded later (chaps. 11–12). Other issues, such as gender and theology, will be addressed, due to their importance, in separate chapters (chaps. 6–10).

The idea of a "narrative world" is of course a construct. What we have in IGT (Gs) is a world created by its author, an imaginary entity. As such, it can be governed by its own laws, and may have little or no

---

1. Cf. the analysis of Bagatti, "Nota sul vangelo," 486–87.

2. See Chartrand-Burke, "Infancy Gospel," chaps. 7–8, esp. pp. 398–404.

connection with a real world. On the other hand, it can also have a close affinity to some specific reality and its laws. On the surface, IGT is a story about Jesus' childhood days in Palestine. But apart from a few details such as some names and social practices, there is little to link it with that time and area. By and large, the depiction of the biblical world appears to be a thin veneer (see chap. 8). This does not mean, however, that the story is unrelated to reality. Instead, it is appropriate to see IGT as primarily reflecting another world, viz., the setting(s) in which it originated and was retold: the material should be viewed as a window into the world of its author and audience, or at least into a world recognizable to them. The differences between the text samples above have already given indications of adaptations to different contexts (pp. 16–23).[3]

I am of course acutely aware of the methodological challenges involved in making inferences from such a narrative world to a "real world." Developments in method during the last several decades, not least within hermeneutics (hermeneutics of suspicion) and literary criticism (deconstruction) have highlighted the dangers of mixing fiction and facts, along with the manifold problems inherent in mirror reading.[4] Nonetheless, the narrative world of a text is not context-free, it always has some relationship—close or distant, positive or negative— to the setting in which the text was produced. For instance, redaction criticism and various social-scientific approaches to the NT gospels base their analyses on the assumption that there is some correspondence between the world depicted in the text and the setting to which it belonged. We do, for example, presume that the gospel of Matthew is "transparent" in a way that lets us peek behind its scenes and get an impression of the social and religious milieu in which it originated.[5] In the following I shall deal with IGT in a similar manner. I shall first through

3. Several other examples can be found in the notes (see index on pp. 280–81 and appendix 5).

4. For a critical discussion of the problems related to this, see Bauckham, "For Whom Were Gospels Written." I agree with some of his critical remarks, but for a number of reasons think that he is overly skeptical as to the possibility of reading an audience "behind the text." In addition, I am not aiming at detecting a specific religious community or the like behind it, but to describe the narrative world of IGT and a more general socio-cultural milieu mirrored in it. This is on a level with the view of Barton, "Gospel Audiences," 173–94, esp. 193–94, with its focus on the world within the text.

5. On this, see for example Luz, Theology of the Gospel of Matthew.

detailed analysis try to describe the world of the text, and then relate it to what could have been an historical setting for the story. The picture painted will be tentative, and of course I do not think that it is possible to prove its validity. Rather, my aim is to sketch a *plausible* scenario of IGT's social and cultural context.[6]

IGT's narrative world can be analyzed in a variety of ways.[7] Here, I shall pay attention to the gospel's depiction of topography, objects, characters, human behavior, social activities, and social institutions and arrangements. The next chapter (chap. 5) will deal with additional aspects: the cultural concepts and values reflected in IGT. Although information is sometimes scanty, it can nonetheless—when studied closely and pieced carefully together—present a meaningful totality.

Topography

What picture does IGT give of its topography, of space, as organized by humans or given by nature? We encounter a variety of elements. Central in IGT's story is the village (κώμη, 1:1; 4:2; 7:3); the Greek word normally indicates a small town, which would be the domicile of a large number of people in late antiquity (cf. p. 70).[8]

Houses are mentioned several times (9:1; 13:3; 14:3–4), for example the home of Jesus and his family. The word οἶκος in itself tells us little about the houses involved.[9] It seems that some of them, however, have more than one floor: children are playing on the roof of an upstairs room (9:1, ὑπερῷον). Nothing is said to indicate that there was something unusual or particularly risky about such a place for play. Thus, the house—and possibly other houses—must have been built in materials

---

6. I agree here with Thomas, *Acts of Peter*, 82, that in basically oral communities the "past is not remembered as such, but is continually retold to reflect present history and social relations."

7. For my analysis I eclectically employ concepts from Neyrey, *Paul, in Other Words*; Malina, *New Testament World*; Peter Richardson, *Building Jewish*; Guijarro, "Domestic Space."

8. Brunt, "Labour," 701–3, 707.

9. For classifications, see Brödner, *Wohnen in der Antike*, 42–71, with numerous examples of houses in Italy and in the provinces on 125–246; George, "Repopulating the Roman House"; Guijarro, "Family in First-Century Galilee." For an important volume that is sensitive as to variation in time, place, and social level, see Ault and Nevett, *Ancient Greek Houses*.

solid enough for a group of children to be playing on top of it. However, the building referred to does not appear to be the *domus* of the rich, which usually was located in cities or larger villages, or the sometimes lavish, sometimes more modest, *villa* buildings at their countryside estates (*latifundia*).[10] Neither does it reflect the *insulae*, the big apartment buildings commonly found in bigger towns and cities. Rather, the houses described are more like the *tabernae*, the two to four storey houses built of brick or stone, with wooden, usually flat roofs, often with a staircase on the outside giving easy access also for children to the roof. This type of housing accommodated a considerable portion of the population, especially outside the big cities. There was much variation, however, frequently with no clear distinction between *tabernae* and (groups of) *villae*.[11] On the ground floor, the *tabernae* would often have workshops, shops, or taverns. On the first floor there would be a room (ὑπερῷον) for the family in charge of the business below, primarily a place for sleep. Very occasionally, there would be more rooms, or one or two more storeys with lodgings for tenants and others. For a fall to cause the death of a child (9:1), a two or more storey house seems the more probable.[12]

IGT also presupposes that Jesus' father Joseph had a place spacious enough to make plows, yokes, and beds. Although it is not stated explicitly what kind of locale this is, some kind of building seems implied: it may have been a workshop, which was usually situated on the ground floor of a *taberna*.

The village also has a schoolroom, a παιδευτήριον (6:8) or a διδασκαλεῖον (14:2), which presupposes that the village is of some size.[13] The place appears to be an established place for teaching, but no

10. See the articles on late antiquity villas by Carla Sfameni (Italy) and Lynda Mulvin (Danube-Balkan) in Bowden, *Recent Research*, and by Sarah Scott (Italy and Britain) and Alexandra Chavarría Arnau (Spain) in Christie, *Landscapes of Change*; also Bowes, "Rural Home."

11. Percival, "The Villa in Italy," 530–31.

12. In Ga/Gb Zeno is explicitly said to fall down from a two-storey house (9:1, διστέγου), from which Jesus afterwards jumps down unhurt (9:3). Gd is somewhat ambiguous: here Zeno is said to fall down from an ἀνώγαιον, which can refer to an unspecified elevated place, but also to an upper floor of a house (see Luke 22:12; also Liddell and Scott, *Greek-English Lexicon*, ad loc.

13. See for example Rawson, *Children*, 195–96.

information is given about its character.[14] But it is centrally located in the village, with quick and public access (6:7, 10; 14:3).[15] Even though we hear of three different teachers, the schoolroom seems to be the same.

Except for the temple in Jerusalem, no other edifices are spoken of, for example public buildings such as markets, town halls, baths, and stadiums, or religious buildings such as temples and synagogues. This lack may be due to the particular character of IGT. But it can also reflect a setting in which such edifices, many of which presupposed urban communities, were not common.[16]

Although it is not stated explicitly, it appears that the village has streets and areas in which crowds could gather (4:1; 10:1; 16:2). It also has a central location for fetching water (10:1). Whether this is a river, a brook, a well, a water fountain, or a cistern, the most common types of water supply for villages and cities, is not clear.[17] The last alternative, a cistern, may be the most probable.[18]

There seems to be no big threats to the village and its inhabitants from the outside: no defending walls, observation towers, or arms are mentioned. People move freely about; even children leave the village by themselves. The impression is given of a peaceful situation vis-à-vis the outside world.

The village appears to be located in a rural area. There is a stream near the village (2:1–2); the term ῥύαξ is usually employed of a small river, a "rushing stream" or a "mountain torrent."[19] The river is so close that even small children can go there. There has also recently been a rain (βροχή), which probably has made the water of the stream flood (ταράσσον). Thus, there appears to be no lack of water in the area. On the other hand, water does not emerge as a threatening element: the child Jesus is able to lead the water into pools and control it, as is the

14. For evidence of schools and types of accommodation, see Cribiore, *Writing*, 13–26; also ibid., *Gymnastics*, 18–20. The material she presents from Egypt is fairly representative of Mediterranean antiquity in general, see ibid., 1–2.

15. See Rawson, *Children*, 165.

16. For changes taking place in late antiquity as concerns rural abandonment of temples and building boom of churches, see Chavarría and Lewit, "Archaeological Research," 38–43; Caseau, "Fate of Rural Temples."

17. For water supplies, see Brödner, *Wohnen in Der Antike*, 99–106; Richardson, *Building Jewish*, 61–62.

18. In Gb/Gd 11:1 Jesus is said to fetch water at a "well" (πηγή).

19. Liddell and Scott, *Greek-English Lexicon*, ad loc.

son of Annas (3:1). Neither lakes nor seas are hinted at. This may be due to the location of Nazareth, but more likely as noted above, mirrors the topographical setting of IGT itself.[20]

There is farm land attached to the village on which Joseph and Jesus work (13:1–2). There is also a forest in its close vicinity where children can go to fetch wood (15:1–2, νάπη). The presence of these biotopes together (stream, farm land, forest) near the village indicates that the village is of moderate size. No other topographical elements, such as mountains, valleys, and roads, are hinted at.

IGT has little to say about flora and fauna. However, there are bushes (15:1, φρύγανον) and willow trees (3:1, ἰτέα). Willows were common in the Mediterranean, with a variety of species and used for many purposes, including woodworking.[21]

No domestic animals are mentioned. Use of draught animals is implied, however (12,1: yokes).[22] The sparrows (2:2, στρουθία) formed by Jesus may have been thought of as domestic animals, since such birds were popular pets in late antiquity.[23] The only wild animal is a snake (16). The reptile is clearly perceived as being very dangerous. This is in agreement with general Christian and Jewish views. Greco-Roman attitudes were far less skeptical: snakes were sometimes held as pets and could also be regarded holy.[24] In sum, however, the botany and zoology of IGT yield limited information as to its setting.

Thus, the topographical information is not very extensive. Nonetheless, a certain impression is given: there emerges a small-town setting, with mostly flat-roofed houses of a traditional two, maybe three to four, storey type. The fact that the village has a locale for first level education indicates a settlement of some size and some degree of specialization. But the setting is clearly not a big city. Geographically, the world described does not appear to lie on the seaside nor in dry inland

20. Gb does not mention a brook; Jesus is only playing "on the ground," and the pools come from a shower (2:1).

21. Bonnington, "Trees, Shrubs and Plants," 234–35.

22. On the use of animals within agriculture and on the value of archaeological finds for assessing economical circumstances, see Applebaum, "Animal Husbandry."

23. The most famous being that of Lesbia in Catullus' (84–54 BCE) *Poems* 2 and 3. See also Brödner, *Wohnen in Der Antike*, 93–98; Rawson, *Children*, 129–30; Horn, "Children's Play," 105–6.

24. Toynbee, *Animals in Roman Life*, 223–24, 233–36.

or high mountains, but in an area with small rivers, cultivated land, and woodland.

Objects

IGT describes a limited number of objects. Some household artefacts and articles of food are indicated. Jesus goes to fetch water in a pitcher (10:1, κάλπη). This was a common household item: it was a narrow-necked, almost ball-shaped vessel that was carried on the back or on the head.[25] As it was made of earthenware (clay, cf. also 2:2), it was not very solid. Since attention is paid in the cloak miracle to the loss of water rather than of the pitcher, it is clear that the artefact is viewed as invaluable.

Not much is said about food. In the miracle above, we hear of water, which of course had a central place in diet and cooking. There is no scarcity of it, however (cf. p. 57). Bread is central to the diet. It is made from meal (11, σπόρος, σῖτος), probably wheat or barley, and seems to be baked in ovens, since sticks (15:1) are burned in the process. Grain cultivation, one of the basic agricultural industries in the late antiquity Mediterranean, appears to have a central place. The two other main industries, olive and grape production, however, are not hinted at.[26]

As for clothing, only Jesus' dress is described (10:2). This πάλιον (also spelled πάλλιον) is a common term for a Greek cloak. It was worn over the tunic and suitable for different types of climate. It could vary in form and color depending on cultural context and fashion. The word could also designate a Roman toga, and sometimes a philosopher's cloak; nothing indicates the latter here, however.[27] Children were usually dressed in a way similar to adults; thus, Jesus appears to be dressed in a common, non-extraordinary way.[28]

No toys are referred to—with the possible exceptions of the clay sparrows (2:2) and a natural item used as a plaything, the willow twig

---

25. White, *Farm Equipment*, 152, 197–200.

26. On bread and baking, see Wilkins, *Food in Antiquity*, chaps. 2–3 and 5.

27. In Latin it is called *pallium*. See Croom, *Roman Clothing*, 49–51, 64, also 125–45 (provincial clothing).

28. Ibid., 120–22.

of Annas' son (3:1). This may indicate scarcity of such items within the setting of IGT.[29]

The mention of a bed (12:1) shows that at least the more affluent had beds for sleep. Such a κράβαττον could also serve as sofa at meals. It was usually made of wood, but the more expensive could have iron or bronze frames. Since the type mentioned had wooden planks, it probably was among the less expensive.[30]

In his workshop, Joseph makes plows and yokes (12:1), which implies that much of his production served agricultural purposes. Plows, ἄροτρα, were used in grain cultivation.[31] The ζυγοί probably refer to yokes for draught animals, used in agriculture or transport.[32] But Joseph also repairs objects for domestic use (a bed). The impression given is that wood is readily available as material, cf. also the reference to woodland (above) and to a wood-chopping youngster (16). Nothing is said, however, of fishing, an important industry in the Mediterranean, also at the coast of Palestine and in the Sea of Galilee.[33]

In the school, there is a book (14:2, βιβλίον). This seems to be a codex, the dominant type of book in late antiquity, and not a scroll.[34] Since it appears to be posited at a central point in the school, it is likely to be its main or only book. It is placed on a bookstand, a lectern (ἀναλογεῖον).[35] Both book and lectern evidence a setting with some material and cultural surplus: the former was a relatively rare and valuable object, and the latter a specialized object to be found only in some schools.[36] In

29. On toys in late antiquity/early Christianity, see Horn, "Children's Play," 97–105; also Uzzi, *Children in the Visual Arts*.

30. Ransom, *Couches and Beds*, 109; Richter, *Furniture of the Greeks*, 52–63, 105–10, esp. 52–53. It is from the description not possible to decide whether the bed is represented as Greek or Roman.

31. White, *Agricultural Implements*, 123–36; Rees, "Agriculture and Horticulture," 489–90.

32. White, *Agricultural Implements*, 136–37.

33. Hanson, "The Galilean Fishing Economy and the Jesus Tradition."

34. Gamble, *Books and Readers*, 49–66.

35. The word is rare in ancient texts. In TLG, it is not documented before the tenth century (here it is used of a stand on which a gospel book is placed), but occurs in the *Hermeneumata Ps.-Dositheana*, Greek and Latin school handbooks whose material may date as far back as the 3rd century, see Cribiore, *Gymnastics*, 15–17, 132–33, with references.

36. Bertelli, "The Production and Distribution of Books," 41; Cribiore, *Gymnastics*, 129–34.

addition, the teacher had something on which to write the alphabet (6:8; 13:1). This may have been a small papyrus codex (which was often used for taking down notes), a wax tablet (on which letters could be erased and rewritten), a wooden tablet, a piece of pottery (ὄστρακον), or possibly some kind of larger blackboard.[37] Generally, schools were sparsely equipped, but would occasionally have an armchair (θρόνος) for the teacher and stools (βάθρα) for the pupils.[38] No such items occur here, however.

Other objects described in IGT are a "noisy gong" and a "clanging cymbal" (6:8). Gongs were usually made of brass and cymbals of metal; thus they were precious items.[39] Although the phrase is a biblical loan (cf. 1 Cor 13:1; pp. 118–20), we may assume that IGT's audience was familiar with such musical instruments—playing an instrument occasionally formed part of school curriculum.[40]

The objects for household, food, clothing, and work (jar, cloak, bed, plow, yoke, lectern) are all likely to have been produced locally.[41] The familiarity with books, gongs, and cymbals, however, is evidence of some commercial and cultural exchange with the surrounding world.

Money is not mentioned. The economy is probably not only a barter economy, however: the rich man's hiring of Joseph, and Joseph's of the teachers, seem to presuppose a monetary system. Nonetheless, the impression is of a primarily self-supporting local community in which monetary exchange was limited. This may agree with a tendency in late antiquity, namely of diminished production and use of coins as compared to early imperial times.[42]

Some immaterial "objects" are also mentioned. Letters have a central role, especially the alpha (6:8—7:1). Obviously, IGT belongs within a setting that was at least partly literate. It is also clear that Greek was the

---

37. Cribiore, *Writing,* 57–72; ibid., *Gymnastics,* 147–59.

38. Ibid., *Writing,* 13–26; ibid., *Gymnastics,* 31–34.

39. See Mathiesen, *Apollo's Lyre,* esp. 170–71.

40. Such production in late antiquity was less industrialized than in the early Empire, see Rawson, *Children,* 170–72.

41. See relevant articles in Brogiolo, *Towns and Their Territories.*

42. Kent, "Monetary System," 568–85. However, Banaji, *Agrarian Change,* 216–21 underscores the importance of a developing monetary system as a presupposition for the prosperity in rural areas.

primary language: students learn the Greek alphabet, not the Hebrew.[43] This gives some indication of the story's geographical origin: in IGT's early stages (second–fifth centuries), Greek was taught and spoken in the eastern half of the Empire.

Names also play a part in IGT. Most are taken from biblical tradition (cf. pp. 126–27). The only exception is Zeno (9:3), which is a common Greek-Hellenistic name—compare the renowned Stoic philosopher Zeno of Citium.[44] The use of such a distinctively Greek name again situates the transmission of IGT within a predominantly Greek setting.[45]

Although objects spoken of or implied are relatively few, they support and complement the impression from the previous section. The picture drawn is of a community basing its subsistence primarily on barter economy, agriculture, and handiwork, and of a predominantly Greek-speaking social milieu with moderate means with regard to food, clothing, and utensils, but yet with capacity for cultural activities such as reading and music.

Characters

A broad range of characters appear in IGT. Persons of all ages are represented. Children constitute a large portion of its "population." Apart from Jesus, individuals included are Annas' son, the careless boy, Zeno, James, and the injured youngster. Children also show up in groups, together with Jesus by the river and on a roof, as "those his own age" and as orphans (2:3; 9:1; 11:2). Many adults also play a part, most of them in parental roles: Joseph, Mary, Annas, the parents of the careless boy and of Zeno. Elderly people also appear, with Zacchaeus, who characterizes himself as an old man (7:3), and more generally in the mention of the "old" and "elders" (6:2, γῆρας, πρεσβυτέρους).

Various other groups also participate: Jews (6:5), a crowd (10:1 etc.), the people (4:1 etc.), friends (2:5; 7:3), and unspecified (2:4; 10:2). These groups have only secondary functions, partly as responding au-

43. In Gb 7:1 (which, however, is a rather late variant, see p. 16), Zacchaeus is said to write the Hebrew alphabet; other variants and versions also occasionally deviate from this, cf. Hock, *Infancy Gospels*, 117.

44. Portrayed in Diogenes Laertius, book 7. But cf. also p. 127 (personal names).

45. It is used in all the Greek variants and even in versions, such as the Latin (Zeno/Sinoo).

dience (pp. 45–46) and partly as objects for Jesus' words and deeds (5:1; 8:2; 13:3).

Only a few occupations are mentioned. The most central is teacher (6–8; 13–14). The words διδάσκαλος ("master") and καθηγητής ("teacher") are used interchangeably in IGT; both are common terms for primary school teachers.[46] In addition, καθηγητής is often used of itinerant tutors, who made a living in rural areas distant from the large educational centers.[47] The fact that they are denoted καθηγητής and that no other pupils are mentioned might imply that the teachers are seen as private tutors, although the existence of a schoolroom as a locale for teaching groups indicates otherwise.

Joseph's craft is explicitly identified: he is carpenter (12; p. 66). Some religious professions are named, particularly in Jesus in the Temple: High Priest (3:1), Pharisee (2:5; 6:5; 17:4), teacher of the Law (6:5; 17:2), elder (17:2), and scribe (17:4).[48]

People from different economical levels are represented: Joseph makes repairs for a rich man and gives from the harvest to poor and orphans (12:1; 11:2). Although the mention to poor and orphans reflects biblical heritage (cf. p. 131), these groups were well-known in any demographic sample of a certain size.[49]

Thus, a considerable number of characters appear in IGT and from different human and social groups: persons of all ages, with children and parents being prevalent; both males and females take part; and the characters represent a relative variety in occupations and socioeconomic levels.

Nothing in this picture—except for the Jerusalem High Priest—contradicts the impression from the above of a rural, small-town setting. Nor does the absence of slaves, a large group in cities and on estates, or

46. The former title is used very broadly of teachers at various levels of education, the latter similarly, but particularly of private tutors, Cribiore, *Writing*, 163–67. The third teacher is only called καθηγητής, however; but this is likely to be incidental.

47. Ibid., *Gymnastics*, 51–54, esp. 53–54.

48. In Gd, Annas is not High Priest, but a scribe (3:1), and it is he himself who destroys the pools, not his son. Nevertheless, his parents turn up at Joseph's door to complain about Jesus; thus, Annas here appears to be depicted as a "child-scribe." In Gb too he is a scribe.

49. See Rawson, *Children*, 250–63.

of military personnel, who, however, could be stationed at select places in the countryside.[50]

Human Behavior

The actions and reactions of IGT's characters add color to its narrative world. A variety of actions takes place in the gospel. Several physical movements are described: forming and clapping (2:2, 4), walking and running (2:1; 4:1; 14:3; 15:2), bumping and leaping (4:1; 6:7), pulling and striking (5:2; 6:8; 13:2), embracing and kissing (10:2; 12:2), and sitting (14:2; 17:2). There also occur verbal modes of expression such as speaking and shouting (2:2; 2:4; 4:1; 6:5; 9:3), laughing and praying (8:1; 10:2). Jesus is the one to perform the broadest range of such actions.[51]

Personal interactions are both verbal and physical. Characters often converse, such as Joseph and the teachers. Jesus' interaction with others is mainly verbal. Only on two occasions does he touch others: when breathing on James' snakebite and in the healing of the injured foot (15:2; 16:2). All other physical contact is directed toward Jesus and on the initiative of others: often in a hostile manner (4:1; 5:2; 6:8; 13:2), occasionally in a friendly manner (10:2; 12:2). On his way to school he is led by hand (6:8; 14:1, 4).

Emotions play a central part in IGT. Reactions often come in the form of emotions: human feelings of many kinds are presented, and in various ways. They are identified explicitly, as marvel (2:5 etc.), hate (5:1), distress (5:3), vexedness and anger (6:8–9), fear, concern, and joy (10:2; 14:1), worry and grief (17:3). But emotions are also implied through actions: Jesus is accused (2:3); Joseph is rebuked (2:4); Jesus curses when offended (3:2; 4:1 etc.); Joseph pulls Jesus' ear (5:1); "no-one dared" (8:2); and Joseph embraces and kisses Jesus (12:2).

Jesus is depicted as having special insight into the minds of others, and what he reveals about them is sometimes their emotional condition: Joseph is distressed, but cannot cause Jesus grief (5:3; 12:1); the crowd is full of marvel and admires trifles (6:6, 7).

---

50. See Brunt, "Labour," 705–8; Trombley, "Epigraphic Data on Village Culture," 535–86, esp. 563–66.

51. In Gb's variant of Careless Boy (4), the boy also throws a stone!

Jesus himself displays a variety of feelings, from jocularity and joy (6:7; 8:1; 14:1) to anger and severity (6:8–9; 7:2), with the exception of fear. The same is the case with his parents, although with a somewhat different register: they are angry and distressed (5:2; 12:1–2), fearful, worried, and grieving (10:3; 17:3), full of loving and marvel (12:2; 13:1; 17:5). The teachers share much of the parents' register, except their concern: they marvel (6:1; 7:4), become irritated (6:8; 13:2), confused, and despairing (7:1–4), but also—in the case of the third teacher—react with fear, concern, and pleasure (14:1, 2). It is interesting to note the emotional correspondence between Jesus and the last, and successful, teacher: The boy "was glad" to go off with him to school, and the teacher in the same way "was glad" to hear him (14:2, ἡδέως). Thus, both conflict and harmony between characters are often displayed through emotions.

Except for these main characters, other persons are depicted as emotionally flat, depending on their narrative function in the story: the crowds marvel at Jesus' words and deeds, and parents of cursed children turn to Joseph and Jesus in anger (4:2—5:1; 9:2).

Thus, human behavior in IGT often involves actions: there is much walking and running, talking and shouting going on. Equally characteristic is the focus on emotions: this is generally the manner in which the characters express themselves. Verbal interaction is of a declaratory kind, and it is primarily positions and feelings that are being communicated and challenged. Rationality and logic have limited place—IGT is far from being a well-considered religio-philosophical tractate![52]

Much of the scholarly disregard of IGT has been rooted in these kinds of observations. Instead of criticism, however, it is in my view more apt to ask about the causes for the "emotionality" of the story. But this is a matter we must return to later (chaps. 11–12).

Social Activities

IGT presents a broad spectrum of social activities. Many activities have to do with meeting basic physical needs. Domestic work is executed: house management and baking, water and wood fetching, and wood

---

52. In Ga 3, Jesus abuses Annas' son: "You unjust and impious fool! What wrong have the water and the pools done to you?" (3:2). In Gb, the unfortunate boy is called "lawless" (παράνομος). In Gd, he is branded as "sodomite."

chopping (10:1; 15:1; 16:1). Agricultural work is undertaken: plowing, sowing, harvesting (11; 12:1). Joseph performs a craft: carpentry (12:1). The occupational specialization assumed is not high, however, since he has to handle different carpentry tasks (yoke, plow, bed), and also undertakes other jobs, such as agricultural work. In sum, these activities cover all kinds of tasks necessary for securing human survival, with the exception of fabrication of clothing.[53]

Beyond such fundamental activities, IGT devotes much space to social adaptation, particularly the socialization and formation of children. This is presented as the concern of both parents. In keeping with ancient practice, Joseph as *paterfamilias* emerges as having primary responsibility for Jesus' upbringing, but Mary also participates in this (see pp. 109–11). Other couples also cooperate: both mothers and fathers of the ill-fated boys go to blame Jesus for his misdeeds (4:2; 9:2).

IGT emphasizes formal education as central in children's formation (6–8; 13–14). The village has its own educational institution, with teachers to choose among. This indicates—given that we read these episodes as not only reflecting the narrative pattern-of-three—that IGT's implied village has a size and a cultural level to allow for more than one teacher.[54] According to Joseph and the teachers, the aim of primary education is that Jesus learn the letters, i.e. basic reading skills (6:2; 13:1; 14:1). In addition, he is to be instilled with a set of cultural values (see pp. 73–77).

IGT also mirrors customary pedagogical strategies: a teacher's primary means was to encourage a child, by flattering and admonishing it (6:8; 14:1, 2). But stricter measures were also close at hand: when Jesus disobeys, the two first teachers hit him (6:8; 13:2). Often, this was performed with a stick (ῥάβδος), although such an instrument is not mentioned here.[55] Children's play is referred to as a matter of course (2:1; 9:1).

IGT describes nothing else that would imply surplus wealth, such as waste, banquets, or the like. Again, the life conditions reflected are modest, yet ample enough not only to allow for basic activities (primary

53. In Jesus and the Dyer (see appendix 4), which occurs in many manuscripts, fabrication of clothing, i.e. dyeing, is a central issue.

54. On the organization of schools and their "two-track system", see Cribiore, *Gymnastics*, 36–44.

55. Ibid., *Writing*, 24–26; ibid., *Gymnastics*, 68.

industry), but also for cultural activities such as education (school) and leisure (play).

Social Institutions and Arrangements

In spite of its brevity, IGT reflects several of the main social arrangements and institutions of antiquity.[56] First, the story mirrors social and economic hierarchies of the time, with rich people and people living at subsistence level. The majority, however, appears to be in-between, as some kind of middle or lower middle class.[57] This is at least the case with the characters in IGT; other levels only appear at its fringes. Religious hierarchy also has a place, through leaders such as the High Priest, Pharisees, and scribes, and followers such as Mary and Joseph (17:1–5).

The most important social institution in IGT is the family. The picture presented is not that of a large household, however: virtually all families are of a nuclear type, consisting of parents and children (4:2; 9:2–4; 13). This corresponds with the general picture of late antiquity: although various family patterns existed (multi-generational, extended households etc.), the nuclear family seems to have been the most common.[58] Parent-child relations are central: Jesus assists each of his parents and even performs miracles for their benefit (10; 12). But sibling relations are also of importance. This is indicated in the joint action of James and Jesus in Snakebite (15). Other family members are only hinted at in Jesus in the Temple (17:2).

On a couple of occasions, IGT refers to the institution of friendship. In Sparrows, the Pharisee is said to report "to all his friends" (2:5). Since friendship in antiquity usually presupposed social equals, Pharisees or other religious dignitaries are probably intended (2:3).[59] Moreover, Zacchaeus twice appeals to his "friends" (7:3). It is not clear

56. Exceptions are slavery, voluntary associations, and patronage; however, the contact between Joseph and the rich man (12:1) may mirror a patron-client relationship.

57. I am of course aware of the problematic nature of the designations "class" and "high"/"low", but nonetheless find them viable here. For reflections on this, see Clarke, *Art in the Lives of Ordinary Romans*, 4–9.

58. Dixon, "Sentimental Ideal"; Aasgaard, *My Beloved Brothers and Sisters*, 43–45.

59. On ideas of friendship, see Fitzgerald, *Greco-Roman Perspectives on Friendship*.

who they are: they may be the anonymous "Jews" (6:5), the "many" who were gathered (6:10), or simply an undefined audience.

Other social arrangements are that of fictive siblingship and teacher/student relations. The former occurs in the Joseph/teacher dialogs. The latter, which—differently from friendship and siblingship—was highly asymmetrical, with a marked authority/obedience hierarchy, is central in 1–3 Teacher and in Jesus in the Temple. We shall return to both below (pp. 77–83).

Summary and Reflections

What kind of narrative world emerges from the analyses? The first reflection to be made is that the milieu depicted appears unexceptional and ordinary; there are no unusual or phantastic elements to signal that it is not meant to be a realistic world. Although information is limited, not least due to IGT's brevity, a fairly coherent picture emerges: we are presented with a village, placed in a rural landscape in close proximity both to cultivated land and to uncultivated areas, the latter consisting of different biotopes (river, woods, but no sea). Although few animals and plants are spoken of, indications are given of a fairly varied fauna and flora (wild and domestic animals, trees, bushes). The climate seems to be comfortable, neither very dry nor very wet.

The village portrayed is of a moderate size: it is clearly not a city, but not very small either—the presence of a school shows this. The village has some, but not a high, degree of specialization in architectural function. Dwellings, at least some, appear to be of a two to four storey type.

IGT's narrative world is inhabited by people covering the whole life cycle, but with focus on children and parents. A broad social spectrum is represented, from rich to poor, with the majority being in between. Characters are primarily described on the basis of their physical actions and emotional reactions; these are in IGT main means for human interaction.

The villagers are occupied with activities related to domestic work and primary industries, such as handiwork and agriculture. However, no fishing or other kinds of industry are mentioned. Although material resources are limited, there clearly also exists an economical and cultural surplus, evidenced by an educational system, specialized objects such as books, and a certain economical and cultural exchange beyond the village to the world at large.

Socialization and formation of children, both privately (in the household) and publicly (in school), play an important part and mirror current pedagogical strategies. Somewhat surprisingly, there are no references to religious activities other than Sabbath observance and Passover pilgrimage. Focus is on basic social relations and hierarchies in antiquity, particularly the nuclear family. But other relations, such as friendship, fictive siblingship, and teacher/student are also central.

What can these analyses tell us about the setting of IGT? As for traditional questions about location results are meagre. Little can be said about location in time beyond a late antiquity setting (cf. p. 13). A little more can be inferred about geography: the material points to a Greek-speaking, mainly Hellenistic setting, probably in the eastern half of the Mediterranean. This supports the verdict of a majority of scholars about IGT, but still leaves us with a vast area.[60] Despite some Palestinian scenery, IGT seems not to be rooted in a Jewish core or dominated area (cf. also p. 127).

More important, however, are what our observations signal on other matters; two merit special attention here. First, the picture painted in IGT is of a rural, village world. Although this of course is intended to be Nazareth, the data given do not limit it to this location at all. Except for the Biblical elements, which appear as garnish and among the least realistic in the story (e.g., the High Priest's son being in Nazareth), the picture is very much in accordance with another, but quite similar setting: the late antique countryside. As concerns biotope, community type, human resources, working life, and social patterns, there is nothing to contradict this as a plausible milieu for IGT and its transmission.

A brief survey of the picture given particularly in archaeological studies of the eastern Mediterranean countryside can serve to support this claim.[61] One important observation within recent research is that

60. See the discussion in Chartrand-Burke, "Infancy Gospel," 269–76.

61. For valuable surveys of recent research on the late antique countryside, see Bowden and Lavan, "Late Antique Countryside," xix–xxvi; Chavarría and Lewit, "Archaeological Research," 3–51. There has during the last two decades taken place "a substantial re-evaluation of rural developments," from a rather sombre to a much more positive view, see ibid., 3–4, with references. See also the contributions in Barker and Lloyd, *Roman Landscapes*. For a fairly similar picture of the western part of the Empire, see Dyson, *The Roman Countryside*, 103–6; also Bowes; "Rural Home."

the late antique world was very much a rural world. Although there were several big and medium-size cities in the Empire, most of the population lived in the countryside, i.e. in villages and their environs. Estimates suggest up to 90%.[62] This probably is too high, though; but there are good reasons to assume that far more than half of the population can be characterized as rural.[63] Recent research also indicates a growth in rural settlement, occupational opportunities, and levels of production at least from the second century on, resulting in general prosperity within agriculture and small industry.[64] Numerous villages seem to have been established and expanded, with a considerable number of free landowning peasants.[65] Large estates existed, though they appear to have been fewer than in the West.[66] The rich man having his bed repaired by Joseph can be seen as mirroring a local landowner or landlord (12:1).[67] Villages were in late antiquity far more common in the East than in the West, and are likely to have been the typical settlement pattern of the region—this also agrees well with the picture given in IGT. They would range from small hamlets to settlements with some industrial and com-

Regrettably, Bowden, *Social and Political Life in Late Antiquity* came to my attention too late to be taken into consideration here.

62. Brunt, "Labour," 701–3, 707.

63. Although no extensive attempt has been made to calculate the size and distribution of the rural population, several assumptions can be made on the basis of archaeological investigation, comparison with similar types of historical and modern agrarian societies, and demographic models. For this, cf. Lloyd, "Forms of Rural Settlement," 129–45; Morley, *Metropolis and Hinterland*, 33–54; Christie, *From Constantine to Charlemagne*, 401–96, esp. 491–96.

64. Chavarría and Lewit, "Archaeological Research," 3, 16–20, with references; Brandes and Haldon, "Towns, Tax and Transformation," 141–72; Banaji, *Agrarian Change*, esp. 213–21; Manning, "Industrial Growth," esp. 586–88. For a significant collection of articles, see Lefort, *Les Villages dans l'Empire Byzantin*. Important regional studies that support the general impression can be found in Bowden, *Recent Research*; cf. also Brogiolo, *Towns and Their Territories*.

65. See esp. Banaji, *Agrarian Change*, 101–33, also 134–70, and chapters on Italy, North Africa, Greece, and Albania in Christie, *Landscapes of Change*, but also Rees, "Agriculture and Horticulture," 483–85, who holds that there were considerable regional differences as concerns both developments and setbacks.

66. Chavarría and Lewit, "Archaeological Research," 16–17. For the role of such estates within the local and regional economy, see Sarris, "Rehabilitating the Great Estate," 55–71. On towns and villages in the West, see Drinkwater, "Urbanization in Italy and the Western Empire"; Dyson, *The Roman Countryside*, 90–96.

67. See Chavarría and Lewit, "Archaeological Research," 8–9.

mercial buildings, but with few public buildings. Formal street plans also seem to have been rare. Excavations show that houses were often made of stone. They frequently bear traces of having belonged to free peasant owners (such as IGT's Joseph?), with generally small differences between the dwellings of the poor and the more well-to-do.[68]

The late antique villages were often surrounded by agricultural areas and sometimes had walls, which seldom were used for defense purposes, however (cf. children's freedom in IGT to move around). Cultivation of grain (cf. 11; 15) and olives was important. Local pottery production was a thriving industry in rural districts between the third and sixth centuries (cf. 10:1).[69] Late antiquity may also have seen innovations in agricultural technology, with the introduction of use of metal for plows and harvesting equipment; though some hold that the technical improvement of plows took place later. In any case, the period would be a time of both challenge and promise for carpenter-peasants such as Joseph (12:1). The eastern Mediterranean also witnessed an increase in export of local products from the fifth century on (cf. economical exchange in IGT).[70]

In sum, many of the features emerging from the analyses above fit in with the findings in research on the eastern Mediterranean: it appears to have been a rural village world, inhabited mainly by a free, variously well-to-do, but overall thriving population—"middle class" people—occupied with agriculture and artisan work.[71] Keeping all provisos in mind (cf. pp. 54–55), this appears to be the milieu mirrored in IGT's narrative world—this is a hypothesis which I shall also follow up later (pp. 171–73 and 187–91).

The second matter that should be addressed is IGT's "anonymity." In spite of the analyses above, we are still left with considerable vagueness

---

68. In the eastern Mediterranean, many small dwellings and simple farms have been preserved, ibid., 16–17. See also Trombley, "Epigraphic Data on Village Culture," 73–101; Rees, "Agriculture and Horticulture," 497. For a comparison between urban and rural houses, and a wide-ranging presentation of housing throughout the Empire, see Ellis and Kidner, *Travel, Communication and Geography*, chap. 3, esp. 112–13.

69. On pottery production and export/import, see Vroom, "Late Antique Pottery," 281–331, esp. 324–26.

70. For this passage, see Chavarría and Lewit, "Archaeological Research," 11–17; Parker, "Trade within the Empire," 635–57.

71. For a presentation of central issues and the problem of diversity, see Christie, "Themes, Directions and Problems," 1–37, esp. 5–10.

concerning the place, time, and background of IGT/Gs. Analyses of the other variants may lead to similar results. Instead of considering this a problem, however, a more adequate approach is to see this as evidence of IGT's adaptability. Although the vagueness may pose a challenge for research, it signals one of the strengths of the story itself: it gives IGT a durability that enables it to cross boundaries in time, language, and culture. In this it has very much in common with other oral/written material: it contains a central and distinctive stock of elements, but is at the same time stripped of most of its less significant detail.[72] Thus, there is in IGT—both in its variants and in its general transmission— a balance between fluidity and fixity that makes the story sufficiently anonymous to be easily adapted to new contexts, yet preserves enough of its personality to make it attractive to ever new audiences.

72. Cf. Anderson, *Fairytale*, 164.

5

Cultural Concepts and Values

"Cultural concepts and values" is of course a very broad category.[1] In this chapter, focus will primarily be on concepts and values reflected in social interaction among IGT's main characters. One very important aspect, that of worldview and theology, will be reserved for later chapters (chaps. 8–10).

All societies build on a set of notions of how reality is shaped (concepts) and how they are to be assessed (values), a so-called cultural script or matrix.[2] Examples are individualism/collectivism, purity/impurity, and honor/shame. A number of such concepts and values are highlighted in IGT, and others are clearly presupposed without being made explicit. In the following, I shall first present the cultural concepts and values underlying IGT, and then analyze how some main characters relate to them, partly through social negotiation, partly by challenging them, but also by re-adapting to these values, however with some remnants of protest still remaining.

Basic Cultural Concepts and Values

One of the most explicit formulations of cultural concepts and values in IGT occurs in 1 Teacher, in Zacchaeus' justification of Jesus' need of education. In addition to learn reading, the aim is to

> learn to have affection for those his own age (στέργειν ἡλικιώτας), and respect the old (τιμᾶν γῆρας) and please elders (αἰδεῖσθαι πρεσβυτέρους), so that he can in his turn teach them

---

1. For discussons of these terms and concepts, see the discussions in Pilch and Malina, *Biblical Social Values*, and Per Bilde, "Introduction," 13–27.

2. Malina, *New Testament World*, 14–27.

to have a wish to become like children (ἀντεπαιδεύσῃ) in the
same way. (6:2)[3]

The cultural ideal emphasized first here is that one should nourish good
relations with equals, viz., to equals of age and—probably—of status:
στέργειν is often used of a close relationship, with focus on emotional
aspects.[4] The appeal to such love is probably occasioned by what has
taken place earlier, the cursing of Annas' son and of the careless boy.
However, it also clearly reflects a central value within IGT and within its
social setting—if not it would not have been emphasized.

The next ideal is reverence toward elders. However, this is not motivated by what has preceded, but anticipates what follows, viz., Zacchaeus'
conflict with Jesus: "I am an old man (γέρων) who has been overcome
by a child" (7:3). At the same time, this ideal too reflects current values
in the setting of IGT.[5] The importance of the ideal is underscored by the
double description "respect" and "please." The final words, "teach them
to have a wish to become," also emphasize reciprocity as a value. The
formulations here are rather enigmatic, however, and we shall deal with
them in more detail later (p. 140).

Surprisingly, however, IGT leaves out what was regarded as a central
educational aim in antiquity, namely to imbue students with reverence
toward ancestors and not least toward the deities. This is for example
formulated in the introductory lines of a writing presenting the basis
for moral teaching within the Pythagorean school: "First honor the
immortal gods, as the laws demands; . . . Then venerate the divinities
under the earth, due rites performing; then honor your parents, and all
of your kindred."[6] The reason for the omission may be that traditional
religion and deities were of little significance within IGT's cultural milieu (predominantly Christian?). Or, more speculatively, it can be that
such an injunction was not appropriate (for the implied audience) as
concerns Jesus, who had God as his father (17:3). Whatever the reason,

3. The last part of the saying ("so that he can . . .") is crookedly formulated and
makes the translation somewhat uncertain.

4. Liddell and Scott, *Greek-English Lexicon*, ad loc. Cf. Sir 27:17; Josephus *J. W.*
1.596; *Ant.* 8.249; *1 Clem.* 1:3; Ign. *Pol.* 4:2; also Rom 12:10; Aasgaard, *My Beloved
Brothers and Sisters*, 173.

5. The terms γῆρας and πρεσβυτέρους are here clearly used as characterizations
of age, and not of social authorities, such as village leaders or the like.

6. The translation is from Fideler, *The Pythagorean Sourcebook*, 163.

IGT seems fairly remote from the influences of current Greco-Roman religions.

Obedience emerges as an important value in IGT, both within the family and vis-à-vis other authority figures: Jesus is to obey his parents. His father is called upon to take action against his misdeeds (2:3). Jesus follows the orders of his mother (10:1). And he is expected to be subject to both of them (17:5). He is also supposed to show deference toward teachers; and if he, as a student, disobeys, teachers can employ physical punishment (6:8; 13:2).

Parent-child relations are, as noted (p. 67), central throughout IGT, and clearly hierarchical in nature: Joseph at home calls upon and commands Mary (13:3); she in turn has authority over Jesus (10:2).[7] Parents are expected to have control over and to teach their children (6:3). A father has the right and responsibility to correct his offspring (2:3; 14:3). Joseph does this by rebuking Jesus, by pulling his ear, and by confining him to the house (2:4; 5:1–2; 13:3)—all are punishments of a moderate kind.[8] Thus, parental authority in IGT is not exercised in a brutal way. Differently from the teachers, Joseph does not hit Jesus; and no other physical chastisement is mentioned.

Parents are also depicted as supportive (4:2; 9:2). Both Joseph and Mary caress Jesus, ask God to bless him, and are worried about him (10:2; 12:2; 17:3). In addition, Joseph is attentive to the child's mental skills and wishes him to develop his talents: "When Joseph saw his wise and sensible thinking he didn't want him to be unacquainted with letters. Thus he handed him over to another master" (13:1). In sum, child formation appears to be practised in a fairly "humane" way, with a positive evaluation of children and their potentials, and a balancing of elements of encouragement and chastisement. As compared to other parents and educators, Mary and Joseph belong within the positive range of the specter known from late antiquity.[9]

Furthermore, honor and shame are basic concepts in IGT. This has already been signalled in the ideal of respecting (τιμᾶν) elders and plays a role in several other episodes. It is broadly elaborated at the

7. On the relationship between Mary and Joseph, see pp. 109–11.

8. Saller, *Patriarchy*, 133–53; Laes, *Kinderen*, 123–31; also Laes, "Child Beating," 75–89.

9. For examples of a variety of parent-child relations, see Rawson, *Children*, 220–39; also Grubbs, "Parent-Child Conflict."

end of 1 Teacher: Zacchaeus is being utterly shamed both in the face of himself and others. He laments:

> Dear me! Dear me! I am totally baffled and miserable. I have caused and brought down shame (αἰσχύνην) upon myself. . . . I am troubled, friends, about my shame (αἰσχύνην) . . . I cannot any longer be seen in view of all, especially those who saw that I was overcome by such a very small child. (7:1–3)

To preserve one's honor one has to prevail in competition with others. In being overcome (7:3, νενίκημαι, ἐνικήθην) by an obvious inferior, a child, Zacchaeus has lost his honor in a most humiliating way. As a consequence, his lot is to be "grow weary and die, or have to flee from this village because of this child" (7:3).

A similar loss of honor has overtaken Jesus' family. Because of his cursing, they risk social ostracism: people come to hate them (5:1). They may even be forced to move: "Because you have this child, you can't live with us in this village. If you want to be here, teach him to bless and not to curse" (4:2).

Erudition is also regarded a value (though with some ambivalence, cf. below). This is seen in the focus on the power of words (2:1 etc.), in the interest in learning letters (6:2; 13–14), and in the fascination with their character (6:8—7:1). This fascination is developed in a striking way in Jesus' explanation of the "order" and "principles" of the alpha (6:10; 7:1; see pp. 143–46).

Death has a special role in IGT: it is viewed as the most fundamental threat to both children and adults. In the gospel, four children (Annas' son, the careless boy, Zeno, the injured youngster) and one adult die (the second teacher), and one child is on the verge of dying (James). The presence of orphans also attests to death as a common occurrence (11:2). Clearly, IGT mirrors a setting or an audience for which death, and in all age groups, was very much a reality. It is also worth noting that no illnesses are mentioned, except for blindness (5:1). This is markedly different from the canonical gospels: in them, almost all healings follow upon illnesses, and no such accidents as in IGT are reported.[10]

Some types of behavior are culturally disapproved, particularly cursing and hypocrisy (2:3; 4:2; 6:9). There also occur religious obligations: Sabbath observance and a visit to Jerusalem. However, these

---

10. The single exception is the youngster Eutychus who fell out of a window (Acts 20:9–12).

Jewish elements are introduced in contingent ways: the Sabbath only at the beginning of IGT (2:2–4; 3:1), the Passover only in the excerpt from Luke (17:2). Except for these, nothing is mentioned that might be related to special cultural constructions of time, such as calendars, festivals, and rituals. There is also no reference to special purity regulations; this is markedly different from the canonical gospels and can indicate a rather distant relationship to a Jewish setting.

Social Negotiation: The Case of Joseph

Even though the concepts and values above are seen as given, some social negotiation nonetheless takes place. Joseph is a prime example of this. In IGT, he emerges as a representative of a middle class man: he is an artisan with his own business, maybe even his own workshop. In addition, he has farmed land at disposal, whether as owner or tenant, and decides freely over its crops (11). He also has the necessary means to pay for his son's education.

Joseph's social bargaining can be observed in his interaction with the teachers. Although teachers in antiquity were often not very highly regarded, they would in a small-scale society such as a village have a certain status, being one of few specialized or learned professions. Possibly, they would rank somewhat above a carpenter or belong to the same social stratum.[11] If IGT's teachers are to be depicted as private tutors, this may place both them and (at least) Joseph in a middle class stratum, since he could afford such tuition for his son.

The social negotiation going on between Joseph and the teachers is apparent in the use of sibling language in 1 and 3 Teacher (cf. p. 68). It occurs only in direct speech (in the vocative ἀδελφέ, 6:2–3; 7:2–4; 14:1,3). At the beginning of 1 Teacher, Zacchaeus addresses Joseph as "brother," with Joseph responding similarly, and then the teacher again (6:2–3). When he has come into trouble with Jesus, he appeals twice to Joseph as a brother (7:2). Somewhat surprisingly, he then addresses the audience differently, namely as friends (7:3), but then in his final appeal again returns to addressing Joseph as brother (7:4). Thus, Joseph is never addressed as friend, only as brother. The reason for this change is

---

11. Cf. Chartrand-Burke, "Infancy Gospel," 342–44; Cribiore, *Gymnastics*, 59–65, 102–5, 108–14, 123; Rawson, *Children*, 164–65.

not evident, but it nonetheless verbalizes a shift from Joseph to a more indefinite group, and probably also a shift in closeness, with "brother" either being the more intimate (ingratiating) or the more formal (polite) address. In 3 Teacher, the mutual brother address is repeated, with the teacher approaching Joseph as "brother" and Joseph responding similarly (14:1). Finally, in his last words, the teacher again twice addresses Joseph as brother (14:3).

Clearly, the brother address at these points serves to regulate the relationship between Joseph and the teachers.[12] In both cases, it is the teacher who first addresses him. This can indicate that the teacher is the superior and thus the one to define their relationship as brotherly, with Joseph adapting to this. The context makes it more likely, however, that the pattern of address reflects a more balanced relationship already from the outset: both teachers are on the outlook for "customers" and appeal to Joseph in order to get a student in Jesus. Thus, the use of address signals a relationship in which they mutually aim at confirming their equality and (high) status.

Joseph's social status is also evidenced in that he has a rich customer (12:1; pp. 70–71). Although this may only be an occasional customer, it still witnesses to a position, and also a social climate, that lets him have contact with a social superior. At the same time, his status is not very high, since his problems with fixing the rich man's bed bring him into great distress (12:2). Failure may, in addition to the economical side, lead to social damage, not least the loss of honor, whereas success will secure his place or lift him up on the social ladder.

Joseph's ambitions are seen in his plans for Jesus, too: he wants to give his son an education, which would enhance his family's position (13:1). Although his taking Jesus to school can imply that he himself is illiterate, it is more likely to reflect his social ambitions.[13] Similar pretensions are visible in his relations to inferiors: his charitable attitude is shown in his distribution of the miraculous harvest to the poor (11). Probably, IGT primarily considers this an expression of altruism, as love of neighbor. But it also clearly reflects classical ideals of social

---

12. On the use of such kinds of address, see the analysis in Aasgaard, *My Beloved Brothers and Sisters*, chap. 14, and esp. 263–67, 283–84.

13. On literacy as a means for social climbing, see Cribiore, *Gymnastics*, 248–50. Hock, *Infancy Gospels*, 113, holds that Joseph takes Jesus to school because he himself is illiterate.

benefaction; such actions were intended to heighten the benefactor's honor and status.[14] Joseph's magnanimity is also underscored in that he appears to give the whole harvest away (11:2).[15]

Cultural Challenging: The Case of Jesus

Whereas the social flexibility evidenced in the Joseph figure is well within the range of conventional social interaction and status negotiations in antiquity, other features in IGT tend to threaten the given social order and hierarchy. Usually, it is Jesus who gives expression to this.

First, and most pronounced, is Jesus' disobedience toward his teachers. In the case of Zacchaeus, Jesus contradicts him, does not answer him, and instructs him (6:4, 9–10). As a result, the teacher breaks out in the lament about his own shortcomings: he has in every respect failed in his profession (7). In this long speech, Zacchaeus not only discloses his foolishness: the speech also functions as ridicule, with Jesus' revolt leading to his defeat (cf. p. 48). In 2 Teacher, the seriousness of the revolt is even greater in that the teacher falls dead (13:2).

The second, even more striking, kind of disobedience is against his parents. As for Joseph, Jesus gainsays him and acts against his will (2:4; 5:1–2), is unruly, and even gives him orders (6:3; 12:1). As a twelve year old, he disobeys and opposes both parents by remaining in Jerusalem and pronouncing God as his true father (17:1, 3). In addition, Joseph is made a comic figure: he displays his helplessness at work, with Jesus having to comfort and instruct him (12:1–2); and he behaves disgracefully with his running to rescue the third teacher (14:3).[16]

IGT's presentation of Jesus' conflicts with his father and teachers also signals differences in its evaluation of social relations. Whereas the teachers' punishment of Jesus leads to their public shame and death, Joseph's punishment only results in Jesus reprimanding him (7; 13). Although the offenses are equally grave (hitting in head, pulling of ear),

14. On benefaction in antiquity, and esp. in the NT, see Winter, *Seek the Welfare of the City*.

15. In Ga/Gd it is Jesus who harvests the grain, and who shares it with the poor (12:2). In Ga Joseph is said to own the field (χώρα), which also has an area for threshing (ἅλων).

16. On irresolution and running as disgraceful modes of behavior, cf. Gleason, *Making Men*, esp. 55–58, 61–62, with references to primary texts.

Jesus lets his father get off far more easily—he too could have been cursed to death! In addition, Jesus takes no action against his father, even though Joseph later confines him to the house (13:3). Implicitly, then, IGT regards loyalty bonds within parent/child relations to be stronger than that of teacher/student relations. At the same time, however, the difference can also attest to a greater acceptance of punishment within the family: a father was more than a teacher viewed to be in the right to punish his children, without risking revenge.[17]

Not only teacher/student and parent/child relations are challenged, however. There is in IGT also animosity toward other authorities: the first to be cursed is son of the High Priest. This information is unlikely to be only narrative finery; rather, it signals a polemical front. But against whom? There are several alternatives: the sting may be directed at Jewish religious authorities, represented by the High Priest's son and also by the Pharisee in the previous episode (2:3, 5). If so, it could reflect a heritage from the canonical gospels or a stock polemic against Jews and/or Judaism (cf. 6:5, the somewhat critical description of the Jewish crowd), and thus attest to tension with a Jewish cultural milieu. The latter is less likely, however, considering IGT's distance from such a setting (cf. pp. 125–27).

Alternatively, the polemic could be against religious authorities within IGT's own setting, for example a Christian establishment. Recent research has indicated that there were in the third to fifth centuries occasions of tension and rivalry between a Christian rural élite at the big estates and an urban-based ecclesial leadership, represented by bishops and other clergy.[18] It is worth noting in IGT that there is—as distinct from the religious élite—no visible tension in Joseph's interaction with his social superior, the rich man; what is in focus there is Joseph's potential loss of honor, and not any challenging of power structures. But it can also be that IGT here signals a protest against authorities more generally, and that these Jewish authority figures stand as representatives of them all.[19]

---

17. Cf. Saller, *Patriarchy*, 133–53.

18. Bowes, "Rural Home," esp. 163–69. See also ibid., *Private Worship*, esp. chap. 3.

19. Cf. the views within scholarship on anti-Jewish and/or gnostic (anti-orthodox) features in IGT; see for example Chartrand-Burke, "Infancy Gospel," 271–6. The issue of IGT's ideological setting will be developed particularly in chap. 10.

Cultural protest is also indicated in IGT's ambiguity toward book learning. On the one hand, Jesus is taken to school to learn reading, which implies that reading (and reading of books) is seen as valuable. On the other hand, we are told that when Jesus at his third school visit finds a book on the lectern, he "didn't read what was written in it," since—the author comments—"it wasn't from God's law" (ἐκ νόμου Θεοῦ, 14:2). "God's law" is here likely to refer to Scripture (or the Pentateuch), and shows that IGT regards it as a book of fundamental importance (see pp. 158–60). However, if IGT's portrayal of the biblical world had been sophisticated or historically true to a Jewish milieu, the book would very probably have been a biblical text. Instead, IGT's description reflects the setting of a pagan school. In such a setting the main textbook might have been a major classical work, such as Homer (ca. eighth century BCE, most likely the *Iliad*), or some kind of *florilegium* with excerpts from central authors.[20] Clearly, both the refusal to read and the motivation for it are viewed not only as pertaining to Jesus, but also to others: Jesus serves as a model for the audience of IGT. Interpreted this way, there appears in this milieu to have been a critical attitude to pagan books, maybe even toward the pagan curriculum as a whole.[21]

Instead of reading from the book, Jesus is said to utter (ἐπεφθέγξατο, 14:2) awe-inspiring words. The verb επιφθέγγομαι can mean "quote" or "express," "utter."[22] In the former case Jesus is citing Scripture, "God's law," by heart, thus witnessing to his learning (cf. 17:2). In the latter case the awe-inspiring words refer to statements similar to sayings elsewhere in IGT, such as Jesus' self-revelations and his interpretation of the alpha (6:4–10; 8:1). It is probably used in the latter sense here, since this is the most common usage, and thus functions to underscore the powerful nature of Jesus' appearance. Interpreted this way, the formulations can reflect a milieu in which prophetic or spirit-inspired gifts were highly regarded.

20. Cribiore, *Gymnastics*, 130–34, 138–42, 194–97.

21. This is also indicated by Chartrand-Burke, "Infancy Gospel," 402–3. For a brief presentation of Christian attitudes to the pagan curriculum, see Bakke, *When Children Became People*, 201–15. Sandnes, *Challenge of Homer* (part 2) has a detailed presentation of early Christian views and discussions about how to relate to the encyclical studies of their times. For an example, see *Didascalia Apostolorum* 2 (Syriac version); English text in Vööbus, *Didascalia Apostolorum*, esp. 14–15.

22. Liddell and Scott, *Greek-English Lexicon*, ad loc.

Very striking are also Jesus' breaches of the honor code, in particular the generally acknowledged prohibition against killing (3:3; 4:1; 13:2). In view of the trifling offenses that occasion them, the murders are manifestly dishonorable. Jesus also seems to bring shame on himself by his cursing and by improper behavior such as leaping and laughing (4; 6:8; 8:1–2; 13:2).[23]

In sum, the many offenses in IGT against social authorities (teachers, parents, religious leaders) and cultural values (educational ideals, school curriculum, honor code) serve to give the gospel a "rebellious" character.

Re-adaptation to Social and Cultural Values

Generally, the challenges in IGT against established authority structures and cultural values are not fundamental, however. Even though the gospel mirrors tensions with social and cultural givens, most are solved within the story: a re-adaptation takes place and on premises set by the existing socio-cultural order.

This is seen in a number of instances: Jesus' opposition at school is not a protest against teachers per se, but against ignorant teachers who do not recognize his greatness. The third instructor is, by dealing adequately with Jesus, able to restore proper order and respect toward teachers (14).

Jesus' disobedience toward his parents also ends with adjustment and harmony: in IGT's final words, we are told that Jesus "followed his mother from there, and was obedient to his parents" and that he "increased in wisdom and age and grace before God and humans" (17:5). With this, the cultural ideals presented by the first teacher of loving those one's own age and respecting parents and elders are re-affirmed (6:2).

Several of Jesus' actions affirm honor as a fundamental value. On more than one occasion, Jesus protects the honor of others. This is evident in 3 Teacher. Although Jesus has nothing to learn from him, the teacher is through his handling of the matter nonetheless depicted as honorable: he displays "fear and worry" toward Jesus, is "glad" to hear him and encourages him, with the effect that Jesus because of this even

23. See for example Gleason, *Making Men*, 56, 61–62.

"saves," probably revives, the second teacher (14:1–2, 4). And although Jesus repeatedly is on the verge of jeopardizing his family's honor, he safeguards and even enhances it by his deeds and words (4:2—5:1 etc.). Both his parents and others testify to this (6:5; 9:3; 10:2; 12:2). By miraculously fixing the uneven bed, Jesus follows up the cultural expectation implied in this episode: he saves not only Joseph's day, but also his honor (12). Mary too receives honor because of him: she is blessed, since "the Lord God has blessed the fruit of your womb" (17:4).

In addition, Jesus is depicted as protecting his own honor. Indirectly, this is shown in the defense of the pools and of his body, in Annas' Son and Careless Boy respectively (3–4). Even in the cases of his most serious breach of taboo, the murders, he manages to restore his honor: he revives the inflicted so that equilibrium is achieved again by the end of the story (8:2; 9:3; 14:4).

If there were a tension vis-à-vis religious authorities in IGT, this also seems to have disappeared in the final episode, cf. the scribes' and Pharisees' great satisfaction with Jesus' teaching (17:4). Here, IGT's positive attitude to Scripture is also affirmed, telling that Jesus "explained the main points of the law and the riddles and the parables of the prophets" (17:2).

Remnants of Protest?

Not all social and cultural tension in IGT is resolved, however—some traces of protest and offense remain. One such remnant is Jesus' general unpredictability and playfulness. Even though he is in the final episode said to adapt to the given order (17:4–5), this solution appears to be a heritage from Luke rather than from IGT itself. In spite of the attempt at creating ultimate harmony, the spirit of unruliness in IGT is not fully quieted. The instances of serious offense against social hierarchies and cultural codes are too many to be mended and forgotten by the end of the story. Examples of revolt, and their success, have been demonstrated, and remain for the audience a possibility, at least in fantasy. The protest is sometimes clothed in humor, but its seriousness cannot be concealed. Although it can be ascribed to and "excused" by Jesus' uniqueness, he nevertheless emerges in IGT as some kind of model person for its audience.

Despite the value ascribed to education and learning, Jesus' refusal to read pagan writings also signals cultural protest. His ridicule of people's failure to understand him, sometimes seen as evidence of IGT's gnostic leanings, can be interpreted this way. The crux also remains as concerns Jesus' brutality, which has been an offense to many: why is he depicted as cursing people to death? Arguably, should there not be more sympathetic means for displaying the greatness of Jesus? These, however, are matters that we shall return to below (pp. 86–102 and 160–62).

Summary and Reflections

The analysis has shown that IGT presupposes a number of basic cultural concepts and values shared across all social strata in late antiquity, such as good relations toward equals, respect and obedience toward superiors, acceptance of honor codes, and regard for learnedness. Together these features support and deepen the picture from the previous chapter and place IGT firmly within the cultural mainstream of the period. It is worth noting, however, that Jewish-biblical purity matters play no part in IGT. Instead, the issue of life/death has a central place, especially in the miracle episodes. Why this is so will be addressed later (pp. 163 and 208–9).

Social mobility emerges as important in IGT; this is clearly visualized in the Joseph character. This supports the impression of a middle class setting for the gospel, since this was the social stratum with the best potential for social improvement. It also fits in with a rural context for IGT: in the prosperity of the eastern Mediterranean countryside in late antiquity (cf. pp. 70–72), the economic and social climbing of a Joseph would be a realistic aim for a considerable part of the population.

IGT's rebellious features, with opposition against authorities and testing out of social and cultural boundaries, can point in a similar direction. These broad middle, or lower middle, class strata are likely to have had an interest in resistance against power figures such as school teachers and various types of leaders, particularly religious leaders. There may also within this social segment have been an impetus for establishing alternative authority regimes, for example of an anti-intellectualistic and anti-bookish, more charismatic, experience-based kind.[24] These are matters that will be touched on later (see chaps. 11–12). At large, however, tensions in IGT are settled, with conventional values, such as honor, loyalty, and subordination, being eventually re-affirmed. This is in agreement with the strong expectations about social harmony current in antiquity—also within a middle class stratum.

In sum, the narrative world to emerge from the analyses in chapters 4–5 is in several respects akin to that of many in late antiquity, the early Christians alike. The world of IGT would be recognizable as their world, with its middle class, small-town, rural milieu, with its social patterns and conflicts, with its adherence to traditional ideals and values, but also with a more or less hidden dream of overthrowing the powerful, or at least of making them objects of ridicule.

---

24. Similar ideas are also indicated in Chartrand-Burke, "Infancy Gospel," 364, 402.

6

JESUS AS A CHILD

Jesus is by far the most important, but also most problematic character in the *Infancy Gospel of Thomas*. On the one hand, he is depicted as a divine figure—or at least as a person with divine powers. He can perform healing miracles, vivify matter, and take and give life. All his words work miracles, he has "come from above" (8:1) and possesses superhuman wisdom. On the other hand, he is portrayed as human—in fact, he seems in some respects far too human. He appears emotionally imbalanced and outraged without due reason: he abuses the child who destroys his pools, pours his rage over the one bumping into him. When his father punishes him by pulling his ear, he is infuriated and scolds him too. He is disobedient, and corrects and ridicules his teachers. He provokes spectators by claiming to be co-existent with God, and then—unpredictably—wards it off by saying that he is making fun of them. He is not only aggressive, however: he can cease being angry and give comfort. He is also playful and humorous—though scorn seems close at hand (6:7).

Thus, Jesus emerges as an odd combination of divine and human elements, an enigmatic figure who behaves in ways seemingly improper both for a divine character and for an honorable human being. No wonder perhaps that IGT's Jesus has been characterized as "an *enfant terrible* who seldom acts in a Christian way" and even as a "hero of ridiculous and shabby pranks."[1] For how should these features be understood? This is the question to be addressed in this chapter. Here, focus will particularly be on the human element in Jesus. His "divine side" will be dealt with later (pp. 152–57).

---

1. Elliott, *Apocryphal New Testament*, 68, and Hervieux, *New Testament Apocrypha*, 106, respectively. Cf. also the verdict of Kelly, *Origins of Christmas*, 42, of Jesus as "a detestable little brat."

In the following, I shall present central scholarly views on IGT's Jesus, outline main features in children's life in late antiquity, and then argue in favor of a new understanding of Jesus in IGT.

Earlier Conceptions of the Personality of Jesus

Previous research has focused on the incongruous features in IGT's Jesus, often at the expense of other equally important matters. Several explanations have been given for Jesus' personality, some of them in combination.

An early approach was by means of history-of-religion parallels. This was particularly popular in the late-nineteenth century, but has also been repeated later.[2] It has been used both to explain the origin of the childhood stories in general and their odd portrait of Jesus in particular. Usually, apparent analogies in Indian childhood stories about Krishna and Buddha have been adduced. Scholars have also opted for Egyptian roots interpreting episodes in IGT as allegories of the Horus myth.[3] In later years, some have argued in favor of Jewish roots and brought to light stories with features similar to IGT.[4]

Such similarities are sometimes explained historically, suggesting that the stories were imported along trade routes from the East to the Greco-Roman world or from Egypt to the north, and then being adapted by the early Christians to the life of Jesus.[5] At other times, phenomenological explanations are given, considering IGT as parallel, but independent developments within other religions.[6] The parallels offered are usually vague, however, and although there may be occasional similarities, differences are very marked.[7] And more important is that links to such stories—even if they existed—only to a very limited

---

2. The view has been revived by Thundy, "Intertextuality, Buddhism and the Infancy Gospels"; also ibid., *Buddha and Christ*. I agree in the critical assessment of Thundy's work in Chartrand-Burke, "Infancy Gospel," 81–82. See also ibid., 37–40, 299–302.

3. Conrady, "Das Thomasevangelium."

4. Cf. particularly McNeil, "Jesus and the Alphabet," 126–28; Bagatti, "Nota sul vangelo," 484–85; Evans, *Noncanonical Writings*, esp. 234; Wilson, *Related Strangers*, 84.

5. See for example Conrady, "Das Thomasevangelium," 403–4.

6. See the presentation in Chartrand-Burke, "Infancy Gospel," 38–39.

7. For similar criticism, see Hock, *Infancy Gospels*, 98–99.

degree throw light upon the particular character of IGT's Jesus itself. For example, why should Christians take over such stories and adapt them to their own convictions? Why did this picture of the child Jesus prove so popular? What was its setting, its Sitz im Leben, within early Christianity? Answers to these questions can only be found by close attention to the material itself, and by then placing it within a theological and social context which is historically plausible.

Another related way of coming to terms with IGT's odd Jesus takes its point of departure from psychology-of-religion. Within this view, Jesus is seen as a trickster, a jester-like character meant to meet popular demands for a counter-figure, for someone who breaks rules and challenges authorities. Such examples are known from various religious settings and periods.[8] Clearly, there are features in IGT which support such a view (cf. pp. 82–85). But the idea also has its obvious problematic aspects. For example, it makes it difficult to account for the broad and long-lasting popularity of IGT: it is unlikely that such a trickster figure should be felt adequate as the main and only picture of the child Jesus. Thus, this idea can at the most only serve as a partial explanation of the special character of IGT's Jesus.

Occasionally, less credible explanations have been given, for example that the special character of Jesus is due to the crudity of its audience; no further justification of such a claim is offered, however.[9] At times, Jesus' "deviant" personality has been thought to reflect theological heresy; this will be touched on later (chap. 10).

Jesus in IGT: An Adult Clothed in a Child's Body?

In the last decade there has been a marked shift in approach to IGT's Jesus. Instead of focusing on remoter historical and religious counterparts, scholars have turned to material from the immediate context of early Christianity, especially from Greco-Roman and Jewish literature.[10] As model for IGT's Jesus they point to biographical accounts about miracle workers and political leaders. Such writings, which focused

8. Rebell, *Neutestamentliche Apokryphen*, 134–36.

9. For example Cowper, *Apocryphal Gospels*, xiv–xv.

10. Central examples are Hock, *Infancy Gospels*; and Chartrand-Burke, "Infancy Gospel," esp. 380–94.

on the hero's personal and moral qualities, were produced to enhance their fame. Usually, these writings expanded on their virtues (ἀρεταί), hence the label "aretalogical writings." Sometimes, however, they would instead—as frightening examples—depict the vices of evil men.

Antiquity is often seen as having little interest in issues of psychological development and change.[11] This is regarded as particularly typical of aretalogical writings: one of their aims was to show that their chief character's personality remained stable throughout a lifetime. When depicting their heroes' childhood, the biographers would point out similar virtues and deeds as were known from their public career. In this way, childhood foreshadowed what was to come, with the heroes' grandeur being present already at an early age. In this view, children were valued according to their display of adult qualities. [12]

Many classical sources, and among them aretalogical writings, also tend to depict children very much through the lenses of grown-ups: notions of childhood were shaped according to adult needs and ideals, not to what might be distinctive features of this stage of life itself. This could take different forms. Sometimes, children were idealized (as "innocent" and "pure") or sentimentalized (as "sweet" and "funny"). At other times, such as with famous persons or in cases of premature death, children could be characterized as equalling grown-ups, and even old people, in wisdom and rhetorical abilities.[13]

This idea has within scholarship often been termed the *puer senex* motif (the adult child). According to this, such children were particularly cherished, since they managed to live up to the cultural ideals of human maturity. Consequently, they were depicted as adults clothed in children's bodies. In the opinion of scholars such as Hock and Chartrand-Burke, IGT gives expression to such a motif: Jesus is there an idealized child.[14]

Chartrand-Burke has developed this view in greatest detail (cf. pp. 9–10). He sees the *puer senex* motif reflected in a broad range of

11. Cf. Malina and Neyrey, *Portraits of Paul*, 1–18.

12. See Wiedemann, *Adults and Children*, 55–80, for examples. Hock, *Infancy Gospels*, 96–97 lists examples of such notions in IGT.

13. See Chartrand-Burke, "Infancy Gospel," 366–67, 375–78, 392; also Rawson, *Children*, 45–53.

14. Hock, *Infancy Gospels*, 96–97; Chartrand-Burke, "Infancy Gospel," 381, 400–405.

material from antiquity, such as in biographies of Hellenistic heroes and divine men.[15] In his opinion, however, the most obvious model for IGT's Jesus is the Jewish holy man. Such figures occur both in the Old Testament and in early Jewish literature, for example in Josephus and in early rabbinic writings. Most important are the prophets Elijah and Elisha: they are both said to have blessed and cursed, and to have performed saving as well as punitive miracles. Other such figures are Moses and the more contemporary Honi (first century BCE). Many stories in the NT and in the apocryphal acts also mirror such a model. Within this tradition, apostles and others are depicted as eschatological holy men demonstrating "the greater power of God over the forces of evil." In Chartrand-Burke's view the early Christian creation of stories about Jesus' birth and childhood—such as that of IGT—is similar to the development among Jews of childhood stories about famous Old Testament figures.[16]

In order fully to understand IGT's Jesus figure, however, it is necessary to consider what view of childhood it is based on. In this respect, Chartrand-Burke holds that one is dependent on adult depictions of children. These are usually marked by disdain, since children were primarily valued as means for securing family income and succession and as provision for parents in their old age. There was in his opinion little respect for children's need for leisure and play, and discipline was upheld by physical punishment. Children were seen as lacking judgment, as being ignorant and quarrelsome, as speaking nonsense, and as physically frail and easy frightened. Parents' relations to children were also distant and reserved.[17] The most characteristic feature of childhood was "the push toward adulthood": it was a training ground for adult life, for becoming self-sufficient and productive.[18] In spite of some nuances, Chartrand-Burke paints a dire picture of children's life in antiquity.[19] In his view, early Christian children were not better off.

15. Examples of such figures are the miracle workers Apollonius of Tyana (Hellenistic, first century CE) and Ḥanina ben Dosa (Jewish, first century CE), cf. Chartrand-Burke, "Infancy Gospel," 299–315.

16. Ibid., 309–14. Cf. also *Jub.* 11:14–24.

17. Ibid., 330, 337–40, 342–45, 348, 350–53.

18. Ibid., 364–65, 367–68.

19. See for example ibid., 335–37, 345, 348, 380. Chartrand-Burke has a slightly more positive view as for "middle class" than for upper and lower class children, ibid.,

They may also more often have witnessed family conflict as a consequence of the new faith.[20]

Chartrand-Burke focuses strongly on the *puer senex* motif and its depiction of children as miniature adults. Rather than being derived from the classical writers' own experience, their childhood stories drew upon this cultural stereotype.[21] Thus, he posits a sharp contrast between the realities of antique childhood and the idealization reflected in the *puer senex* motif.

In Chartrand-Burke's opinion, such idealization was taken over by the early Christians.[22] In fact, IGT "reveals little, if anything, about the real experiences of children."[23] Rather, its Jesus conforms to an "ideal in which all childlike characteristics are absent." Indeed, IGT agrees with other sources in that it lacks what "one would expect to see associated with children—playfulness, innocence, impulsiveness, disobedience."[24] Such qualities are instead "replaced with those qualities valued in adults—wisdom, maturity, conformity, composure."[25] Like other famous classical figures, then, the child Jesus is depicted as having the same virtues and performing similar deeds as he would as an adult. And like other early biographical literature, IGT's aim is to extol the character, teachings, and deeds of its main character.[26]

As for IGT's problematic features, Chartrand-Burke sees them as reflecting the author's overall ideas about Jesus: the depiction was in

---

362. Occasionally, however, ancient letters and funerary inscriptions give glimpses of affection toward children, and late antiquity sources seem to reflect a development for the better, ibid., 345–48, 359–61.

20. Ibid., 353–61. However, he overstates the degree of family disruption both within early Christianity (cf. Balla, *Child-Parent Relationship* for a different view) and within IGT itself (cf. chap. 5 above).

21. Chartrand-Burke, "Infancy Gospel," 368–70. But he also suggests that their descriptions could be due to repression of their own bad childhood experiences (370).

22. Ibid., 379–80.

23. Ibid., 320. Although he often repeats the claim that adults were not interested in or unable to have insight into children's life (e.g., 316, 319–20, 337, 364–65), he presents no arguments in support of it.

24. Ibid., 316 and 366; also 404–5.

25. Ibid., 366. Although the Jesus figure has some realistic traits, he "is no ordinary child"; ibid., 400.

26. Ibid., 394–401. He also suggests that there may lie specific propagandistic motives behind the text, such as a front against adoptionism or an anti-Jewish polemic, but does not expand on this.

fact in agreement with what he thought the adult Jesus to be like. The portrait may be somewhat at odds with that of the NT and also repulsive to modern sensibilities—still, it is likely to have expressed the author's perception of Jesus.[27]

With its point of departure in the social and literary setting of antiquity the *puer senex* view is clearly more apt in its understanding of Jesus than are earlier views. In general, the history-of-religion and psychology-of-religion theories, and also others, are based on models whose relevance for IGT is hypothetical. Tracing such influences and parallels can put IGT in relief, but only to an extent contribute to the interpretation of the text itself and to a nuanced understanding of its Jesus figure.

But the *puer senex* view also fails to account sufficiently for IGT's Jesus portrait, both for its "normal" and its "deviant" features. The strong tension which Chartrand-Burke posits between the harsh everyday reality of children and adult idealization of them seems particularly problematic. Do the ancient sources support such a conflict? Is the very negative picture of children's life and of attitudes to children apt when held up against the antique material? And how well does the view come to terms with IGT's Jesus, i.e. with his all-too-human appearance, and the strange combination of human and divine features? Although Chartrand-Burke deals extensively with the life conditions of children and with perceptions on childhood, he—surprisingly—only to a very limited degree relates his discussion to IGT itself and what it has to say about children and childhood.[28] As I shall argue in the following, the *puer senex* view falls short both in its presentation of children in antiquity in general and in its understanding of Jesus in IGT in particular.

Children's Life in Late Antiquity

During the last two decades research on children in antiquity has flourished.[29] Since Philippe Ariès' influential seminal study *Centuries*

27. Ibid., 314–15, also 395. He also ascribes the incongruous features in IGT's Jesus to the genres of "burlesque and satire" (398), but without developing on the point.

28. In spite of his generally dire portrait of ancient childhood in chaps. 7–8 he is sensitive to a number of important aspects such as class, ethnicity and gender.

29. For a survey of research with an extensive bibliography, see Aasgaard, "Children in Antiquity." For updated presentations of children in antiquity and early Christianity,

of Childhood (1960), which painted a very dark picture of ancient childhood, research has become far more sophisticated and nuanced, giving
a multi-faceted and balanced view.[30] The use of a broader spectrum of
sources has contributed much to this effort: in addition to written and
archaeological material, art, epigraphy, and juridical documents are
now taken into account, thus integrating a broad set of variables against
which to study ancient childhood.[31] Here, only main features will be
sketched, and with particular attention to elements that can serve as a
contrast to the views presented above.

Generally, children's life situation in antiquity was of course demanding. Child mortality was high: a fourth died during the first year,
almost one half under the age of ten.[32] The many children's graves and
funerary inscriptions preserved is one indicator of the high mortality.[33]
Death rates meant that the number of children in a family reaching
maturity was low, about 2–3 in average.[34] Families were unstable, with
children being orphaned or adopted, experiencing divorce, and being
left on their own.[35] Nutrition and sanitary conditions were often defec-
tive. Children were exposed to maltreatment, with physical punishment
occurring at home, work and school, and sexual exploitation not being
infrequent. A majority of children did not go to school, although there
were regional differences. From early age, children were used as labor
force: they had to take part in household tasks or engage in work elsewhere in order to contribute to the survival and income of their fam-

see Rawson, *Children*; Bakke, *When Children Became People*; Laes, *Kinderen*; Bunge,
The Child in the Bible.

30. Ariès, *L'enfant*. Chartrand-Burke clearly stands in the tradition of Ariès. For
contributions that paint a very different and more positive picture, see for antiquity
Rawson, *Children*, and for Medieval times (with relevance for late antiquity) Shahar,
Childhood in the Middle Ages; Orme, *Medieval Children*. As for Medieval and later
times, Ariès' views have been largely refuted. As indicated in this chapter, they are not
tenable for the period of antiquity, either.

31. See the presentation in Aasgaard, "Children in Antiquity," 24–30.

32. Saller, *Patriarchy*, 25; Wiedemann, *Adults and Children*, 11–17; also Bradley,
"The Roman Child."

33. Rawson, "Family Life among the Lower Classes," 71–83; Saller and Shaw,
"Tombstones and Roman Family Relations," 147.

34. For this section, see esp. Parkin, *Demography and Roman Society*, 92–111
(mortality), 111–33 (fertility, marriage age).

35. Rawson, *Children*, 250–63.

ily. Often, loads were put on them which far exceeded their abilities.[36] Ethnic and cultural differences were small: Greek, Roman, and Jewish children had to cope with the same basic conditions. The situation of early Christian children is unlikely to have differed much from other children, although there probably were some shifts in emphases.[37]

So far, this appears to support the sketch of childhood given above. The picture needs, however, to be balanced. Despite challenging living conditions, children would not have been worse off than most other comparable groups, for example women and the elderly.[38] Slaves probably were in a considerably more unfavorable situation.[39] There is ample documentation of children engaged in leisure activities, such as playing with toys and pets, and performing sports.[40] Depictions and archaeological finds show children wearing a variety of clothing: they were dressed much in the same way as adults and in accordance with the social level of their parents.[41] There were also many limitations to the exercise of authority within the family, for example as concerns coercion and punishment—children had to be treated in a way that did not dishonor their family. Even the "push toward adulthood" (see p. 90) need not be seen primarily as a sign of disparagement of childhood as such, but as evidence of concern for children and their ability to handle future demands of life.

The living conditions of children also appear to have improved over time, particularly from the second century CE on, probably as a consequence of the relative social stability within the Roman Empire.[42] The thriving economy of rural areas, especially in the eastern Mediterranean, would also contribute positively to children's living conditions (see pp. 69–72).

36. For a broad presentation, see Laes, *Kinderen*, 133–98 (chap. 4).

37. Nathan, *The Family in Late Antiquity*, 133–59, esp. 158–59; Bakke, *When Children Became People*, 280–86; Tropper, "Children and Childhood."

38. Cf. Osiek and MacDonald, *A Woman's Place*; Parkin, *Old Age in the Roman World*.

39. For a presentation and discussion of slavery, see Harrill, *Slaves in the New Testament*.

40. See Neils and Oakley, *Coming of Age in Ancient Greece*; Uzzi, *Children in the Visual Arts*; Horn, "Children's Play," 97–105 (toys), 105–6 (pets).

41. See Croom, *Roman Clothing*, 120–22.

42. Rawson, *Children*, 69–70.

Adult attitudes to children were varied and complex. On the one hand, children were dealt with in a functional way: as means for securing family income and succession, for providing for parents at their old age, and for maintaining family interests and traditions.[43] Children were viewed as capricious and unfinished, and sometimes even as only humans in the making, with the mature male embodying the ideal. Examples of adult lack of insight into children's minds and the characteristics of childhood are also numerous.

On the other hand, there is much evidence of positive attitudes to children. As noted above, children were often described as "pure" and "innocent." Although this of course very much mirrored adult thinking, it nonetheless implied that children were perceived as being in need of help and protection. Children were sometimes also made symbols of happiness.[44] They could, due to their "undefiled state," even be used as mediators to the gods, for example as oracles.[45] Important deities such as Persephone and Demeter were regarded as protectors of children.[46] Commemorative art (e.g., sarcophagi) and epigraphy (epitaphs) often give voice to parents' deep grief at the loss of children.[47] There is a fairly broad consensus that parents in late antiquity and early Christianity were more responsible for their children's upbringing than earlier.[48] Several sources also speak of beneficence toward children.[49]

Many authors, such as Cicero (106–43 BCE), Plutarch (ca. 46–127 CE), Pliny the Younger (63–113 CE), and Augustine (354–430 CE) give vivid glimpses into the lives of children in the family, of parents playing with and coddling their children, and of mutual love and affection.[50]

43. For a survey, see Aasgaard, *My Beloved Brothers and Sisters*, 45–49, 59–60, 90–92.

44. See Rawson, *Children*, 64–66.

45. For example Price, *Religions of the Ancient Greeks*, 89–97. But cf. also the critical assessment of this in Chartrand-Burke, "Infancy Gospel," 392–93.

46. Price, *Religions of the Ancient Greeks*, 24–25.

47. See Rawson, "Death, Burial, and Commemoration of Children"; ibid., *Children*, 336–63.

48. Nathan, *The Family in Late Antiquity*, 133–59, esp. 158–59. According to Bakke, *When Children Became People*, 285–86, this can also have entailed that parents' control of their children's life was strengthened.

49. For example Rawson, *Children*, 59–64, 71–72.

50. For example Wiedemann, *Adults and Children*, 84–99; Rawson, *Children*, 82–88; also Augustine *Civ.* 19.12.

And ideas about children as "sweet" and "funny" need not only be seen as adult-centered sentimentality, but also as mirroring an appreciation of characteristics of childhood. John Chrysostom (347–407 CE) shows great interest in the upbringing of children, particularly in his *Address on Vainglory*, and he is very much concerned with how to adapt to children's level of social and mental development.[51] For example, he is sensible of the fears that children would often have toward teachers.[52] And Augustine, particularly in his *Confessions*, displays deep psychological insight into children's minds, in spite of his somewhat gloomy view of the human psyche in general.[53]

The rhetorician Quintilian (35–95 CE) can serve as example of such attitudes to children. He devotes considerable space in *The Orator's Education*, a fruit of his long experience in teaching, to a discussion of pedagogical ideas related to primary level education (*Inst.* 1.1–3). Although the work is concerned with rhetorical training of élite boys, its presentation clearly mirrors more general attitudes. The work was very influential in late antiquity, our period of interest.

Quintilian has a positive view of children's abilities. Most are "quick to reason and prompt to learn," and willingness to learn is characteristic of human nature (1.1.1). Teaching must begin as early as possible, since the early years are the most receptive, for example as concerns memorization (1.1.19). Quintilian underscores the vital importance of childhood experience, both for good and bad (1.1.5). Thus, his demands on those responsible for children's education are high: he appeals to the sensitivity of mothers and fathers alike (1.1.6–7), but also to nurses, slaves, and primary school teachers (1.1.4–5; 1.1.8–9). Family members are a child's most important role models, and it will from the very beginning try to emulate them in attitudes and behavior (1.2.7–8).

Quintilian is very attentive to differences in talents among children. Educators must respect this variation (1.1.2–3) and adapt their teaching

51. The full title is *Address on Vainglory and the Right Way for Parents to Bring Up Their Children*. The time of its writing is impossible to determine, cf. the extended discussion in Laistner, *Christianity and Pagan Culture*, 78–84. Cf. also the discussion of Chrysostom's ideas about childhood in Leyerle, "Appealing to Children"; Guroian, "The Ecclesial Family."

52. *Inan. glor.* 39. See also Leyerle, "Appealing to Children," 256, with references; Guroian, "The Ecclesial Family," 74–76.

53. See esp. *Conf.* 1.6–19; cf. also Stortz, "Augustine on Childhood," 82–87.

both to the precocious and to the slow-minded (1.3.1–7; 1.2.27–30). Children also have the potentials for learning very different things, even from an early age, and should not be underestimated in this. There is for example no reason why they should not learn reading as soon as they are able (1.1.15–19). However, one must not put pressure on them too early (1.1.20). Rather, learning is to be motivated positively: it should be fun like a game and be the result of encouragement and challenge, not of threats (1.1.5; 1.1.20). Children must also be given the chance to relax and play; the latter is a sign of healthiness (1.3.8–12).

Quintilian urges the right balance between gentleness and severity. A child needs boundaries; unless it will be spoiled or unable to adapt to its surroundings (1.2.4–6). But educators should not be too strict and punishment should only be moderate—flogging must for example be avoided (1.3.13–16).

He also underscores the importance of a learning milieu. Rather than being taught individually at home, children profit from going to school, where they can experience being on a level with others, compare themselves with others for sake of both emulation and competition, and receive social training (1.2).

Quintilian describes children in a way that displays empathy and insight into children's experience of the world:

> study also has its infancy, and, as the rearing of what will one day be the strongest bodies begins with breast feeding and the cradle, so the great speaker of the future once cried as a baby, tried to speak with an uncertain voice, and was puzzled by the shapes of letters. (1.1.21)

He is also sensitive to the needs of children. They are in need of protection, for example against adults using their authority to punish them:

> I blush to mention the shameful purposes for which evil men abuse their right to flog, and what opportunities the terror felt by these poor children sometimes give [. . .] to other persons also . . . no one ought to be allowed too much power over helpless and easily victimized young people. (1.3.17)

In sum, a child is to be educated by its parents with the same care as did Philip of Macedon when he let his son Alexander receive even his elementary instruction from the great philosopher Aristotle: "So let us imagine that an Alexander is entrusted to our care, that the child placed in our lap deserves as much attention (though of course every father thinks this of his son) . . ." (1.1.24). Although fatherly ambition is part of his thinking, Quintilian nonetheless gives evidence to a high valuation of children, and even from their earliest years.[54]

As argued here, the sombre picture of children's lives and of attitudes to children needs to be considerably nuanced. Generally, grown-ups in antiquity should be seen as able to relate to children in adequate ways. Parents would feel strong affection for their children and as far as possible show concern for their well-being. There is also no reason why adults should not be able to see in childhood a distinctive phase of life and as a period with—at least some—value of its own. Indeed, the repeated scholarly claim that the ancients had little interest in character development and limited ability of insight into children's minds and lives is weakly argued and little tenable.[55]

As noted, this claim has very much been based on sources such as the aretalogical writings (see pp. 88–89). However, this kind of material has clearly been shaped by its aim, namely to account for the honor of their heroes or the depravity of their villains. Thus, it is not surprising that basic character traits are highlighted at the cost of change and growth. Still, some such sources do in fact make attempts at analyses of psychological developments and complexities in their main characters. This is for example the case in several of Suetonius' emperor biographies.[56] And other sources, such as John Chrysostom's *Address on Vainglory*, clearly have an eye for the potential of personal development, even on the part of adults.[57] It can in fact be that a reading of the antique sources with attention to psychological change can lead to new insights, not least if other sources are taken into consideration.[58] The matter cannot be taken further here, however.[59] The point has been to indicate that ancient perceptions of children and childhood were richer

54. Cribiore, *Gymnastics*, 108–14 also adduces much (similar) material from Libanius, whom she considers "the Quintilian of the Eastern world."

55. For a similar view of the apostle Paul, see Aasgaard, "Paul as a Child," esp. 157–59; Aasgaard, "Like a Child."

56. *Julius* 74–77; *Augustus* 61–67; *Tiberius* 10–14, 30–33; *Claudius* 15, 38; *Nero* 1–19 vs. 20–57; *Vespasian* 11–17; *Domitian* 9–10.

57. See Laistner, *Christianity and Pagan Culture*, for example 58 (*Inan. glor.* 25).

58. For example literature on ancient medicine, such as that associated with Hippocrates, particularly *Affections, Nature of Man, Nature of the Child*.

59. As for comparison, modern literature often tends toward the other extreme, viz., to focus on mental development to the neglect of stability in character traits.

than has often been acknowledged. It will soon become clear that this has implications for how to interpret the Jesus of IGT.

Jesus as a Child in IGT

Previous scholarship has, as noted, dealt extensively with religious, literary, and social parallels to IGT's Jesus, but to a surprisingly little degree with the depiction of him in the story itself (pp. 87–92). Here, I shall pursue such an analysis, with attention to how Jesus is described as for looks, character traits, behavior, and kinds of social interaction. Although the material is limited, significant features appear.

First, as for physical appearance, Jesus is characterized as "a very small child" (7:3). His hands (2:4; 6:8), shoulder, and ear (4:1; 5:2), mouth and breath (14:2; 15:2) are referred to. Although this description is rather vague, it is no less specific than what is found in the canonical gospels. Like them, IGT appears to have little interest in Jesus' physical features per se. Whereas ancient rhetoric would often focus on a hero's physical features, such as beauty, strength, healthiness, and good posture, nothing is said about this as concerns Jesus—except possibly for his "severe look" (7:2).[60] It seems that IGT just imagines him as an ordinary child with no special traits. There is indeed very little of a docetic pseudo-human or a gnostic heavenly being in the description—Jesus even feels pain when Joseph pulls his ear (5:2).

IGT has considerably more to say on Jesus' personality. He is easily provoked when others act against his will or come too near him (3:2; 4:1; 13:2). He is angered when his father and teachers punish him (5:3; 6:8–9). When others speak ill of him he is vengeful (5:1). He seems to act on impulse and makes jokes on others (6:7). He laughs, in an apparently self-righteous way (8:1), and is impudent (6:8; 13:2). He is on several occasions unruly (2:4 etc.), but can also be helpful (10:1; 12:1), able of compassion (11:1), and obedient (17:5). Thus, an impression is given of a rather disharmonious, emotional, and unpredictable character. These are among the features that have caused puzzlement among scholars, and have both led to derision of IGT and given rise to the interpretations of Jesus as a jester, a gnostic figure etc. (cf. pp. 64–65).

---

60. There is a lacuna in Gs here, but it is probable that the words lacking are τὸ αὐστηρὸν. On ancient physiognomy, see for example Amberger-Lahrmann, *Anatomie und Physiognomie*, 13–18.

As has been argued, however, such views cannot adequately account for his special traits. Nor do these features fit well in with the *puer senex* view, according to which one would expect a more dignified portrayal of Jesus.[61]

Instead, a much simpler explanation of his character is at hand: Jesus is here—in his emotionality and unpredictability, but also with his compassion—simply described as a *child*, with the personality traits associated with ordinary children in antiquity. In fact, IGT's Jesus displays precisely such childish qualities as playfulness, impulsiveness, and disobedience that Chartrand-Burke holds to be replaced by adult properties "wisdom, maturity, conformity, composure"—such a view can only be upheld by neglecting a number of puerile features in IGT's Jesus.

My interpretation finds support in other aspects of IGT's portrait of Jesus: he is presented as engaged in typical children's activities. Play is central: he is playing near a small river, gathering water into pools, and forming playthings, sparrows, out of mud (2:1–2). Thus, two types of perennial activities for children are spoken of, viz., ordering and forming, and involving two basic materials for play, viz., water and mud. Later too Jesus is said to be playing with other children, now on a roof (9:1).

Play is also described as a social matter. Jesus is not an individualist, but mingles with others: "many children were with him" (2:2). The picture given is of a gang of children, sometimes playing at the outskirts of a village (stream), sometimes in its middle (roof), and with Jesus as integral member of the group.

Other activities associated with children are also described. A boy is running and bumping into Jesus (4:1). Jesus is clapping hands and leaping about (2:4; 6:7)—both evidence a lack of self-control acceptable for children, but disgraceful for adults.[62]

On several occasions, Jesus performs tasks expected of children in antiquity, such as fetching water for his mother, helping his father in the workshop and on the field, and assisting his brother in gathering wood (10–12; 15).

Furthermore, Jesus attends primary school (6–8; 13–14). Joseph's taking him to school is presented as a non-exceptional, matter-of-

61. On attitudes to anger in antiquity, also as concerns children, see the articles in Braund and Most, *Ancient Anger*.

62. Gleason, *Making Men*, 55–62.

course event, which implies that this within IGT's milieu was viewed as relatively common (6:1–2; 13:1). The broad place given to it supports the impression and also shows that school was sensed to be a central element in children's life.

The ways in which Jesus and other characters interact also support the interpretation above. With the exception of invoking a curse on others, Jesus relates to others in two ways. Vis-à-vis other children he always communicates through action (play etc.). Vis-à-vis adults, however, he primarily communicates through speech (discourse). But toward both groups he displays emotions. To state the matter simplistically, Jesus relates in a "childish" way toward same age persons; toward older persons, however, his behavior is a combination of "childish" and "adult."[63] Thus, the *puer senex* features manifest themselves solely in his relations to adults, and only in his verbal communication with them. In all other respects he relates to others like a child.

This is even clearer in how *others* relate to Jesus. With the exception of the awe shown toward him, all deal with him as with a child. Children play with him (2:2; 9:1), tease and provoke him (3:1; 4:1), and desert him when in peril (9:1). Adults command (10:1; 13:1), reprove (2:4; 5:1), and punish him (5:2; 6:8; 13:2), but also embrace and kiss him (10:2; 12:2). On a couple of occasions, he is led by hand, both by his father and by a teacher (6:8; 14:1). He is considered unruly and even given house detention (6:3; 13:3). Thus, there is in these descriptions nothing that makes him different from an ordinary child.

What, then, does this imply for our understanding of Jesus in IGT? It implies that the most adequate approach is to see in its Jesus a fairly true-to-life portrait of a late antiquity child—with the physical and mental traits, and the doings and relationships typical of such a child. Interpreted this way, IGT is not only a story about an exceptional child with a unique childhood; it also becomes very much a story about ordinary children living in an ordinary village environment.[64] The story is, of course, guided by the agenda of an implied author and such an author's perceptions of childhood. Nonetheless, its portrait of Jesus

63. I admit that these characterizations are simplistic. Nonetheless, I find them of value as heuristic tools; they also very much agree with stock attitudes in antiquity.

64. This is also hinted at in Hägg, "Evangelierna som biografier," 55. He suggests that IGT, in addition to presenting a coarse-cut reflection (of a more uncompromising variant) of the NT Jesus, also aims at depicting behavior typical of children; cf. also Osiek and MacDonald, *A Woman's Place*, 88.

incorporates numerous realistic elements and shows considerable insight into children's life. Even though we must of course beware not to mix up modern ideas about children with ancient notions, there is—as has been argued above—no reason why people in antiquity should not be able both to identify with children and to describe their lives in adequate ways. In chapters 4–5, I maintained that IGT reflects social conditions and cultural values representative of a late antique eastern Mediterranean rural world. In my opinion, IGT has in its Jesus given an equally realistic picture of a child in the area and period at issue.

Reflections and Conclusions

This true-to-life view of IGT's Jesus means that we have to regard the history-of-religion and psychology-of-religion interpretations above as of limited relevance. Nothing has so far supported ideas of a gnostic or docetic Jesus; the inadequacy of such views will be further confirmed later (chap. 10). Even the idea of a *puer senex* Jesus appears weakly grounded in the text. Although there are points of resemblance with this motif, cf. Jesus' wisdom, such a model does not sufficiently account for IGT's depiction of him. Instead, the special traits in his character are likely to have other roots. This will be addressed when we turn to the theology and thinking of IGT (chaps. 8–10).

In fact, lurking behind previous scholarly attempts at coming to terms with IGT's Jesus figure, whether recourse is made to the *puer senex* motif or to other concepts, is the problem of his childishness. This problem may, however, be a clue to an adequate understanding of this gospel's main character. Indeed, the verdicts about Jesus as an *enfant terrible* and "childish" are likely to be true, but in a sense quite different from what has been assumed.[65] As for his human side, Jesus is in IGT simply depicted as a child.

---

65. Currie, "Childhood and Christianity," 206–8, seems closer to truth than she realizes in saying that Jesus "also appears to be considerably worse-tempered than the average *puer senex*. There is something childish and uncontrolled about his irascible and violent behavior. One part of this Jesus conforms to the classical perceptions of the angry and passionate child."

7

⸎

JESUS FROM BOY TO MAN

The issue of gender has not been taken up in studies of IGT so far. However, it looms large in the writing: in the ideas and values reflected in it, in the figures involved, and not least in Jesus, its main character. Focus here will particularly be on the depiction of him: what notions are reflected in him as concerns male qualities? To what degree is he even as a child depicted as male? And do any changes occur from his early childhood as a five year old until he enters his next stage of life as a young adult of twelve?

In recent decades, matters of gender have received much attention within research on early Christianity, and lately the specific issue of masculinity has also come into focus.[1] Scholars have emphasized the strong duality between what was considered male/female character traits (psychology), male/female activities (work), and male/female social context (private/public), and have shown the very hierarchical nature of gender relations (socially and sexually). A fundamental feature of ancient masculinity seems to have been the notion of control: men were—in order to live up to the ideals of masculinity—to display dominance (control of others) and self-restraint (self-control). Males who did not conform to these standards were considered effeminate and soft.[2]

Research on ancient childhood has also taken questions of gender and gender socialization into account.[3] Here, however, I cannot enter

1. See Aasgaard, "From Boy to Man," which has a broader presentation and discussion of research on children/childhood and gender/masculinity in antiquity. Cf. also Moxnes, "Conventional Values"; Kuefler, *The Manly Eunuch*; Moore and Anderson, *New Testament Masculinities*; Larson, "Paul's Masculinity."

2. See, e.g., Malina, *New Testament World*, 46–48, 78; Halvor Moxnes, *Naturlig Sex*; Williams, *Roman Homosexuality*, 125–59.

3. For important examples, see Eyben, "Fathers and Sons"; Neils and Oakley, *Coming of Age in Ancient Greece* (esp. Shapiro, "Fathers and Sons," 85–111); also Harlow and Laurence, *Growing Up*.

into a discussion of the scholarly challenges and findings, and must only assume them as a basis for my presentation.

The IGT material will be analyzed from two complementary perspectives. First, the characterization of Jesus and his social relationships will be addressed. Here, I take my point of departure from dominance and self-restraint as basic notions (cf. above). For the benefit of analysis, I break the former down into more specific categories, namely strength, violence, persuasive speech, honor, and female exclusion.[4] Second, I shall analyze the narrative of IGT with a view to its notions of gender socialization, particularly as to how Jesus is adapted to his role as a male person of late antiquity. Here, focus will be on Jesus' ongoing socialization with growing age, and on the depiction of his relations to his parents.[5] Although my approach is methodologically unassuming, it will suffice to reveal basic features as concerns ideas of gender in IGT.

The Description of Jesus' Character and Social Relations

Let us now turn to the characterization of Jesus and his social relationships. We shall see that antiquity's stock expectations about maleness are generally fulfilled.

First, as for the category of strength: typical of IGT's Jesus is that he is described as powerful. Like the Jesus of the fourth gospel, he is portrayed as the one in charge, the one to take control of what happens.[6] He cannot be dominated (6:3, 7), he knows everything (6:6), and he has the power to do everything, even wake people up from the dead (8:2; 9:3). When violated by others, he does not whine, but takes action and repays offenses against him: he invokes curses upon children and teachers and reprimands his own father (3:2; 4:2). His strength is also evident in the emotions ascribed to him: when hit by the first teacher,

---

4. I have here developed the elements used by Clines, "Paul, the Invisible Man," 181–82. Although his categories can be seen as somewhat anachronistic, I find them useful, though primarily as heuristic tools. I have, however, added the "honor" category, which he mentions, but has not used. A similar analysis of Jesus in the gospel of John is made by Conway, "Behold the Man."

5. On gender socialization and the life cycle, see Rawson, *Children*, 134–45.

6. See Conway, "Behold the Man," 173–75.

he becomes vexed and angry (6:8–9), he laughs at him and others (8:1), and has a "severe look" (7:2).[7]

One aim of strength is to prevent others from threatening one's personal integrity or social position. The most visible expression of such strength is violence. A striking characteristic of IGT's Jesus is his violent behavior. When Annas' son destroys his pools, Jesus makes the boy wither away (3:3). The child bumping into Jesus suffers the same grim fate (4:1). And when Zacchaeus hits his disobedient pupil on the head, he too is cursed to death (13:2). Thus, Jesus appears as violent, and to a degree that cannot easily be justified from the offenses made toward him. Although the gravity of Jesus' reactions can be explained in other ways (cf. pp. 160–62), the important point here is that he nonetheless emerges as distinctively male. We should note, however, that Jesus' violence is defensive; he is always first provoked and does not use his strength to infringe upon the integrity or position of others.

A less physical, but still manifest expression of strength is rhetorical power. For antiquity this was a universally acknowledged value, and a male value. This is also a prominent feature in IGT's description of Jesus: he emerges as an unusually able speaker. His rhetorical power is most strikingly demonstrated in 1–3 Teacher. When Zacchaeus wants to teach him the alphabet, Jesus with his erudition and speaking ability drives him and the watching crowd to silence (6:7, 9), and finally Zacchaeus to despair (7:1–2). The second teacher displays even less understanding than the first (13:2). The third teacher, however, is presented as the ideal: he does not try to teach Jesus, but acknowledges his oratorical gifts by listening to his "holy words" (14:2). By the end of IGT, Jesus' rhetorical power is canonically endorsed in his encounter with the learned in the temple: although nothing is related from the conversation, it is clear that they are left awe-inspired, as is his mother (17:3–5).

Jesus' rhetorical power is most clearly displayed in the miracle stories, however. As appropriate for a being of divine origin, his words turn into reality: clay sparrows become alive and fly away only upon his word (2:4); the bumping boy is cursed to death; and he wakes the boy Zeno by saying his name (9:3).

---

7. Although such emotions are, for example, far from the Stoic ideal, they emerge as distinctively "male" (and very different from how Paul describes his weakness in his letters). But see ibid., 166–67.

Honor was, as noted earlier (chap. 5), regarded as a fundamental value in the ancient Mediterranean societies.[8] Jesus is accordingly presented as an honorable person: he protects what is his property, for example when his pools, his "area of dominion," are destroyed by the High priest's son (3:1–3), and when his physical boundaries are violated by the boy who bumps into him (4:1–2). When accused of causing Zeno's death, he defends his reputation by resuscitating the boy so as to invalidate the accusation (9:2). Jesus' honorable status is most explicitly voiced in 1 Teacher (7:1–3). And to the same degree as the teacher is shamed, Jesus is elevated as winner of honor competition. Jesus' claim to honor is finally confirmed in the temple episode: "we have never known nor heard such wisdom as his, nor such glory of virtue" (17:4).

The final category, female exclusion, means that relationships between males are highlighted, with focus on loyalty, exclusivity, and mutual commitment, whereas cross-gender relationships are minimized and female characters and roles marginalized.[9] Although Jesus in IGT is not an adult but a child, such patterns are largely confirmed. Indeed, the characters Jesus relates to throughout the gospel are almost exclusively male, at least as far as can be judged from indications of gender in the text. All children singled out are boys (3:1; 4:1; 9:3). Joseph, Jesus' father, has a very prominent role (2; 5–6; 11–14). The teachers—all central characters—are male. Other figures too are male, such as a Pharisee (2:3–5), the High Priest (3:1), a rich man (12:1), Jesus' brother James (15:1–2), and an anonymous young man (16). In fact, out of the fifteen individuals mentioned in IGT, fourteen are male.[10] The only exception to this male-dominated cast is Mary; she has a central position, and we shall return to her below. But we should also note that she in IGT has a far more modest role than in the canonical gospels. Except for Mary, female characters appear only twice and implicitly, viz., as mothers in parental couples (4:2; 9:2–4).

On one point, however, IGT's Jesus does deviate from ancient masculinity standards, namely in his limited self-restraint: he becomes vexed (6:8–9), seems to be capricious and unreliable (6:7), and repays offenses in ways dramatically out of proportion (3:3; 4:1; 13:2).

8. See Malina, *New Testament World*, 27–57, esp. 52–56.

9. See Clines, "Paul, the Invisible Man," 188, n. 12.

10. When groups of more than two are mentioned, gender distinctions are not noted. It may be that the groups of children are assumed to be gender mixed.

Although this behavior can—to an extent—be seen as an expression of strength (cf. above), it does nonetheless conflict with ancient attitudes about moderation and predictability of conduct as central male qualities. How can this deviation be explained? In my view, such behavior was acceptable for one particular group of males, namely young males, *i.e.* boys. Children were, as noted, regarded unstable and irrational. Even though such features were often negatively valued, they were acknowledged as typical of children and as something to be indulgent and even understanding to (pp. 95–99). Thus, what was not accepted in the case of adult masculinity could be approved in male children. In fact, this can be seen as a central differentiating factor—a factor that made boys' masculinity look different from that of their adult counterparts. Interpreted this way, Jesus in IGT emerges as true-to-life not only as a child, but also as a male child.

Jesus' Age and Gender Socialization

In IGT, a development in Jesus' activities and relationships occurs as he grows older.[11] In the first episodes he is five years old and is playing by a stream, building pools and forming clay birds (2). At this age he is also taken to school for the first time, which would make him an "early starter"—the starting time in antiquity would usually be about age seven.[12] The point seems to be to demonstrate Jesus' precocity, since his young age is repeatedly stated (5:1; 6:5).[13] The startling nature of his precocity is also underscored through the despair of the first teacher: he, an old man, has been "overcome by a child" (7:3). Some time later, but probably still at the same age, we encounter Jesus playing again, this time on a roof together with other children (9:1). Then at seven, Mary sends him off to fetch water (10:1).[14] An unspecified time later he is together with Joseph sowing seeds (11). In the next episode Jesus has become eight years old (12:1); here, he has joined Joseph in his work

11. This is against, for example, Hock, *Infancy Gospels*, 96, who holds that the order of the stories is not important.

12. Rawson, *Children*, 158–59. The age of seven was, according to ibid., 75, "perceived as a milestone in intellectual development." For ancient perceptions of stages of age, see ibid., 134–45; Wiedemann, *Adults and Children*, 143–70.

13. Rawson, *Children*, 159–60.

14. Here, Gabd and Lm have six years.

as a carpenter, fixing a bed. Now Joseph also thinks it high time to take Jesus to school again—with considerably more success than on the first occasion.

Thus, with increasing age there occurs a slow transformation in the life of Jesus: as a five and six year old, he is playing, together with other children. At seven, he is under the wings of his mother: she tells him to fetch water, a task carried out by females and children.[15] After this, play is not referred to any more. Instead, Jesus gradually becomes involved in household duties.[16] At this point, Joseph—as a representative of the male world—begins to take action, by performing the public task of bringing Jesus to school. Although in some cases schools were also open to girls, learning the skills of reading and writing was viewed as more requisite for boys.[17] After that, Joseph step by step introduces Jesus to male activities, first to sowing in the field and then to his own profession, carpentry.[18] Several male children would about this age—at eight—be engaged in various kinds of crafts, although the starting age for regular apprenticeship would normally be at ten to thirteen.[19]

In the following sections, the adaptation to the male world is completed. In the last two miracle episodes, Jesus assists his brother James in fetching wood in the forest (15), and heals a young man who is performing the male activity of splitting wood—and of splitting his foot (16). His introduction to the male world is finally confirmed in the temple episode, where Jesus as a youth, on the threshold of the male adult world, displays his religious and social maturity in the discourse with the learned and his mother (17).

Thus, what takes place in IGT as Jesus' grows up is his gradual gender socialization: from being occupied with small children's activities, such as playing and performing simple household duties up to the age of about seven, he is led into the male adult sphere, by going to school and by accompanying Joseph and other male family members in their

15. See for example White, *Farm Equipment*, 152; Wiedemann, *Adults and Children*, 153–54.

16. The age of seven was often viewed as an age for the child to take on more responsibility for "adult" tasks, cf. Wiedemann, *Adults and Children*, 152–54.

17. For a good presentation of the educational "system" in Roman antiquity, see Rawson, *Children*, 146–209; about girls, esp. 197–209.

18. Wiedemann, *Adults and Children*, 155–64.

19. Laes, *Kinderen*, 170–74.

male-gendered environment. Thus, Jesus develops from a less differentiated or female-coded state of being to a markedly male-coded. The picture given clearly reflects what would be common notions in late antiquity as concerns gender development.

Jesus' Relations to His Father and Mother

The other aspect, which slightly modifies the impression given above, is IGT's depiction of Jesus' relations to his father and mother. As in real life, these two persons emerge as the main dialog partners in the child's process of maturation.

Joseph is present as *paterfamilias* throughout the story: when Jesus is accused of breaking the Sabbath and of cursing a child to die, Joseph is made responsible for mediating between him and his opponents (2:3; 4:2), by defending him (2:3) or by defending others against him, particularly the teachers (6:2–4). But Joseph is also the one to correct and punish him (2:4; 5:1–2). In addition, he is the one often leading Jesus when they appear in public space (4:1), at important points in his life such as his first school day (6:8; also 6:2–4), and at work on the field and in the workshop (11:1–2; 12:1–2). Finally, Joseph is present in the temple episode, though only in the periphery (17:1, 4).

Thus, Joseph plays a prominent part as a father in IGT. His role is ambiguous, however. He is depicted as occasionally uncomprehending and critical toward Jesus, siding with his opponents (2:4; 5:1–2; 6:3–4; 14:3), and as falling short of him (as a carpenter, 12:1). But he is also able to see Jesus' potential: he takes him to school because of his "wise and sensible thinking" (13:1); and when witnessing one of his miracles, he embraces and kisses him, and even exclaims, "Blessed am I, since God gave me this child" (12:2). Thus, Joseph is presented as a nuanced figure, able to express emotions, understand and misunderstand, and to react in various manners—in sum, he emerges as a very lifelike figure.[20]

Mary plays a far less visible part in IGT than Joseph. She only appears in the last half of the story, when sending Jesus to fetch water (10:1). She is mentioned a second time when Joseph commands her to

---

20. Probably, this is very much on a level with general notions in late antiquity about the father role. A father was expected to display authority and firmness, but also to be understanding and relate positively emotionally toward his children, see for example Eyben, "Fathers and Sons," 112–43.

keep Jesus home (13:3). In both cases, she has a traditional female role, as administering female duties within the private sphere of the household, and in a position inferior to her husband. Her final, and major, appearance is in the temple episode. Here, she plays a part that goes beyond the expected and takes over the role elsewhere in IGT ascribed to Joseph, namely of correcting Jesus and of representing him in public (17:3–4).

Like Joseph, Mary is depicted as not fully understanding their son (10:2). Both she and Joseph are concerned about Jesus' well-being, but this concern is expressed in different ways, which reflect their respective gender roles. Whereas Joseph's perspective is that of the public sphere— he is anxious lest Jesus cause harm (14:2), Mary sees the matter from the private sphere—she is afraid that someone may "put a ban on him" (10:2). Mary and Joseph alike are presented as believing figures—both ask for God's blessing of Jesus (10:2; 12:2)—and thus serve as figures of religious identification, for Jesus (within the narrative) as well as for IGT's implied audience. Differently from Joseph, however, Mary's role in the story is—except for her sending of Jesus to fetch water—passive: she is obedient and does not respond to others, unless when being directly addressed (10:2; 17:4).

Thus, as a figure Mary leaves a much fainter impression than Joseph. Only on one point does she diverge from him: she does not, at least not explicitly, display doubts in Jesus or side against him. Instead, her reaction as concerns his singularity is entirely positive. Seeing his miraculous power, she kisses him, exclaiming, "Lord, my God, bless my child" (10:2). And in the temple episode, she is said to treasure up the words about Jesus, pondering "them in her heart" (17:5). Consequently, Mary appears as more of an ideal figure than does Joseph: she is the one to react adequately vis-à-vis their son. This, however, is her only point of precedence; in all other respects the focus is on Joseph.[21]

In sum, Mary and Joseph each have their distinctive profiles, which very much mirror ancient thinking. Stated in modern terms: Mary has the role of a supporting and protecting mother, Joseph of a controlling and advising father. But even though Mary is an ideal of trust in Jesus,

---

21. In Gb, Mary is mentioned from the start: as Jesus at five goes out to play, he leaves "the house where his mother was" (2:1). In Gd, Mary is called "Mother of God" (11:1–2, Θεοτόκος).

Joseph emerges as far more important for his socialization and for the male coding of IGT in general.

Reflections and Conclusions

The analysis above of Jesus' character and his relations to others reveals IGT's male focus. Its depiction of his personality, words, and actions conforms to conventional patterns of maleness in antiquity, and particularly to values such as strength, honor, and male exclusivity. To a surprising degree, this can be seen in the dominance of male figures in IGT, with men, except for Mary, holding all important roles. It is likely that this reflects the gender-segregated social world of late antiquity, and its prime preoccupation with the male (hemi)sphere of that world.

These features are confirmed in the analysis of the development that Jesus undergoes within IGT and of his parents' roles as catalysts of socialization. Here, the direction in Jesus' development is from the more open, less explicitly gender-coded activity of play, to the child and female activities of a household, and finally to the clearly male-marked tasks in the workshop and in the temple. His parents too act according to expected gender patterns, taking different roles. The prominent role of Mary in Luke 1–2 is in IGT replaced by Joseph: Jesus' father is, at her expense, made the main figure in the socialization of Jesus. IGT seems in this respect to mirror a narrative return to antiquity's traditional male-dominated gender patterns.

At the same time, the picture given is not of a single-track male-focused world. IGT is more nuanced than that. First, there is a distinct awareness in it as concerns the special character of the phases of childhood. Jesus and other children are given room for play, by the river, in the village, even on a roof—tasks and obligations only emerge by and by. Jesus is also allowed to have emotional outbreaks like that of an ordinary child, such as anger and joy, laughing and scorning.[22] Second, there is also in IGT a sensitivity to the processes of human growth and social adaptation. This is clear in the manner in which Jesus' development is described. And although IGT does not explicitly make a point of a mental maturing in the boy, there still seems to take place a change

22. But cf. Conway, "Behold the Man," 166–67, 173, who argues that such emotional outbursts can be signs of "proper anger" on the part of a wise man.

from a more unruly personality in the former half of the story to a more responsible in the latter, summarized in the temple episode, in which IGT joins in with Luke in stating that Jesus "increased (προέκοπτεν) in wisdom and age and grace before God and humans" (17:5). Both these elements appear to reflect realistic glimpses of children's lives in late antiquity, and thus to substantiate the view forwarded in the previous chapter (chap. 6).

Moreover, IGT bears witness to an openness as to how the male role was construed in antiquity. This is visible in the description of the teachers, but even more so in the case of Joseph. He is far from being a stereotype of a male or of male values. Rather, in his relationship to Jesus he is depicted as a round character, who moves within much of the role spectrum available to a male at that time: he can be stern, angry, and punishing, but also display weakness and bewilderment, tenderness and awe toward his little boy.

Finally, a similar openness can be seen in the Jesus figure, although he very much lives up to the ancient ideals of manliness. The only exception is that he appears not to be showing the self-restraint appropriate of a male. This can be accounted for, however, by the fact that IGT portrays him as a child: although he possesses several adult properties, such as wisdom and strength, he is in his activities and reactions depicted as a true-to-life child, and a male child at that. And whereas self-control was required from adult men, it was not expected to the same degree from male children.

To conclude: IGT gives us a picture of Jesus very much in accordance with what was likely to be the process of maturing and gender adaptation for a male child in late antiquity and early Christianity. As for these matters, there is little in the story to surprise us. In fact, this is one of the most important points emerging from my analysis: except for his divine origin and powers, there is nothing enigmatic or aberrant about Jesus at all. He is quite simply portrayed as an ordinary boy child of the time at issue. IGT's values are those of a male-focused culture. Jesus' social context is that of a male-dominated world. And his childhood reflects the customary development for a male: from being a small child belonging to a less differentially or female-coded sphere, Jesus is with growing age and at suitable points of time gradually socialized into a male adult world. Step by step, from age five to twelve, the boy Jesus makes it: he becomes a man.

8

INTERTEXTUALITY—REFLECTIONS OF
THE BIBLE

The *Infancy Gospel of Thomas* has often been judged lopsided and shallow in theology and thinking. In chapters 8–10 this issue will be studied more closely. Focus will be on three elements: intertextuality, "strange sayings," and main theological issues.

Critical views of IGT's theological substance have often been based on the scarcity of its biblical references, although the matter has not been studied in depth.[1] The most detailed analyses point to some dependency on the gospels of Luke and John.[2] For example, Chartrand-Burke argues that IGT only had Luke (and Acts) at its disposal, and that similarities with John are of a theological and not an intertextual character.[3]

The aim of this chapter is to trace the influence of Scripture on IGT, and to assess the extent and character of its use of biblical material. As will be shown, the influence is considerably stronger than has been previously observed. Some indication has already been given through IGT's similarity in genre with the NT gospels (p. 51). In the following, the impact will in some cases be evident, in other cases more remote or uncertain. Sometimes the biblical links seem intentional, at other times conventional and even coincidental. Thus, inferences must be done with caution. I shall pay special attention to which biblical writings

---

1. Most scholars hold that NT loans and influences are few, for example Chartrand-Burke, "Infancy Gospel," 268.

2. The most detailed analyses of intertextuality with the Bible is Hock, *Infancy Gospels*, 97–98, 150–52; Chartrand-Burke, "Infancy Gospel," 140–223 (apparatus), 251–54, 268–69, 309–15; also Cameron, *Other Gospels*, 220–24. None of them deal with it in depth and systematically, however. The term "intertextuality" is of course multivalent; I employ it here in a rather broad and general sense.

3. Chartrand-Burke, "Infancy Gospel," 269, 275.

(or part of) that can be linked up with IGT, but also to whether it appears to be reproduced from writing or memory (cf. pp. 27–31). I am of course very much aware that speaking of the "Bible" and the "Old" and "New Testament" is somewhat anachronistic in the case of IGT, since such a Christian canon was not established as early as the 2nd century, However, I still find the terms viable here, but use them as referring, in a loose sense, to writings that were fairly widespread and generally well regarded at the time, and most of which were later included in the canon of the churches.[4] And as will be seen, we shall also occasionally come upon material that did not find its way into this canon.[5]

The material will be grouped as follows: use of form-critical types; obvious biblical references; allusions to specific Bible texts; use of biblical words and concepts; use of place names, titles, and personal names; echoes of biblical accounts; and echoes of biblical narrative patterns and elements. The discussion will at times be detailed; in such cases, the material is presented in numbered lists, and can be read in a cursory way without loss of coherence.

Use of Form-critical Types

As noted above (p. 39), IGT mainly consists of two kinds of episodes: miracles and discourses. Although both have parallels in other classical literature, their closest precursors appear to be in the NT: their frequency and distribution very much correspond to the canonical gospels.

The miracles, which form a distinctive feature in IGT, are described with the same sobriety as are the NT miracles, and the main types are the same as in the canonical gospels. In relative number of miracles, IGT seems to come closest to Mark. As for contents, its nature miracles generally have little in common with those of the NT. In fact, they are more varied: whereas the NT have feeding and stilling of storm miracles, IGT miracles take place in a variety of contexts (village, river, field,

4. Another methodological problem must also be mentioned: since Gs is represented only by an eleventh-century manuscript, it is difficult to assess the degree and character of biblical influence at different stages during its transmission from the second century on. Thus, findings must be assessed critically, especially through comparison with different NT text types and with the oldest versions of IGT. Further study is clearly needed.

5. For such instances, see ibid., chap. 4 (synopsis), 299–315; Hock, *Infancy Gospels*, 154; also McNeil, "Jesus and the Alphabet."

workshop) and involve different materials (water, earth, wood, seed). As concerns health miracles, similarities are stronger, particularly in those dealing with healings. Curse miracles, however, represent a deviating type; but even this has NT parallels (see pp. 129–30 and 161–62).

Whereas IGT's miracles serve to display Jesus' power, the discourses communicate ideas that are important to IGT as a whole, primarily Jesus' teaching (6:4, 9; 7:1 etc.). Here, IGT has much in common with NT discourses, particularly Jesus' speeches in John, and his discussions with disciples and with Pharisees and scribes in the Synoptics.

Biblical Reference I: Luke 2:41–52

IGT has few obvious references to biblical writings. In such a short writing, however, we should not necessarily expect to find many direct references. As for comparison, there are strikingly few OT quotations in some NT writings, for example Mark, 1 Thessalonians, and 1 John, without that meaning that Scripture is of little importance in these writings.

Measured strictly, IGT quotes only two biblical texts. Most important is Luke 2:41–52, Jesus in Temple (17). It is not copied word-by-word, however: IGT has a mixture of identical wording and degrees of reformulation. Clearly, IGT knows the episode well and is basically faithful to it, even down to detail. Nonetheless, there is some deviation, which shows both a liberty toward it and a wish to adapt it to one's own ends. A closer look at the text will thus be rewarding.[6]

In 17:1 IGT reproduces Luke 2:41 nearly verbatim. Luke 2:42–44a, however, are rephrased: interestingly, IGT does not state explicitly that Jesus followed his parents to Jerusalem and also excludes the information about the festival being over. Clearly, the audience is expected to know these events, with IGT just summarizing them.[7]

17:2a follows Luke 2:44b–46 very closely: the parents' search for and finding of Jesus are retold in almost identical wording. 17:2b, however, deviates significantly from Luke 2:47. It does not only report the amazement about Jesus' understanding and answers, but expands upon

---

6. The most detailed treatment is Schmahl, "Lk 2,41–52 und die Kindheitserzählung," 249–58; however, he uses a composite and rather late text as the basis for his analysis. See also Chartrand-Burke, "Completing the Gospel" for a discussion of the passage.

7. The mention of Jesus' age is also moved to the start, probably to fit as an introduction, parallel to the indications of age in 2:1; 10:1; 12:1.

his teaching: "he examined (ἀπεστομάτιζεν) the elders and explained the main points of the law and the riddles and the parables of the prophets." The word ἀποστοματίζω is not used in the Septuagint and is very rare in Greek literature.[8] It occurs only once in the NT, in Luke 11:53. IGT's use of the term may be coincidental, but more likely signals familiarity with Lukan vocabulary in general, and maybe even with Jesus' discussion with the Pharisees and scribes in Luke 11:37–54. Interestingly, IGT also employs ἀποστοματίζω elsewhere (6:9); this can indicate that it aims at imitating Lukan—or biblical—style also apart from 17:1–5.

Other expressions in 17:2b are also of interest, and we shall return to them later ("main points," "riddles," "parables," see pp. 158–60). Here, it suffices to note three points: that IGT by its mention of "the law" and "the prophets" refers to the Old Testament as a unit, and thus is familiar with it as a collection of writings; that IGT by this expansion develops on Luke (Luke is silent on the contents of the conversation); and that IGT in doing this signals interest in the interpretation of Scripture.

In 17:3, IGT leaves out Luke's remark in 2:48a on the astonishment of Jesus' parents and instead underscores their worry.[9] In Luke 2: 48b–49, the episode core, IGT reproduces it with only slight changes.

17:4 has a major deviation from Luke: IGT says nothing about the parents' lack of understanding in Luke 2:50. This seems in keeping with IGT's depiction of their growing insight into Jesus' mission (cf. pp. 45–47). Instead, a dialog follows. When Mary has confirmed being Jesus' mother, the scribes and Pharisees say:

> Blessed are you, for the Lord God has blessed the fruit of your womb. For we have never known nor heard such wisdom as his, nor such glory of virtue.

The saying clearly summarizes central ideas in IGT, particularly about blessing and wisdom (pp. 47 and 154–55). Interestingly, however, the expression is not IGT's invention: the first half is a combination of Luke 1:42, Elisabeth's words to Mary, and Luke 11:27, a woman blessing Jesus. Thus, IGT here seems to memorize and conflate these texts. IGT's use

8. There are only four passages in Plato and one in Plutarch.

9. Cf. their "great anxiety and distress" (ὀδυνώμενοι λυπούμενοι). A reading with ὀδυνώμενοι καὶ λυπούμενοι is found in a few NT manuscripts (among them D). For a valuable assessment of text-critical and tradition-historical issues regarding the relationship between Luke and IGT here, see Chartrand-Burke, "Infancy Gospel," 252–54.

of them indicates that it is familiar with the annunciation in Luke 1 and with Jesus' exorcisms in Luke 11:14–28 (cf. also above on 11:37–54). The second half of the saying follows up what Luke has intimated in 2:47, but not developed.[10] It also employs terms used elsewhere in IGT and in Luke: "wisdom" and "glory."[11] "Virtue" (ἀρετή) does not occur in the NT gospels, but occasionally in the letters (Phil 4:8; 1 Pet 2:9; 2 Pet 1:3, 5). But it is more frequent in the Septuagint, especially in the Hellenistic-influenced 4 Maccabees (1:2, 8, 10 etc.), and it is widely used in other Greek literature. Thus, the wording here may point to Greek-Hellenistic influence on IGT rather than a narrowly Jewish.

In 17:5, IGT focuses on Mary rather than on Joseph: Jesus is said to follow "his mother" (Luke 2:51: "them").[12] IGT here stays very close to Luke 2:51–52. The most important change is a conflation: IGT has combined the first half of the expression in 2:51b, that Mary "treasured (διετήρει) all the[se] words," with the latter part of (the almost identical) Luke 2:19, that she "pondered (συμβαλοῦσα) them in her heart"— "pondered" is not in Luke 2:51.[13] This signals that IGT is familiar with the account of Jesus' birth, of which 2:19 is a part.[14]

IGT's way of dealing with Luke 2 can indicate that it is reproduced from memory rather than by copying. The following point in this direction: (a) the main structure is faithfully preserved; at the same time (b) parts are summarized (2:42b–43a, 47–48a); (c) core formulations are precisely reproduced (2:49, 51b–52); (d) changes and additions are in keeping with usage elsewhere in IGT (2:47–48a/IGT 17:4, v. 50); and (e) there are conflations with other texts (Luke 1:42; 2:19; 11:27). In addition, (f) the accumulation of certain stylistic features is more readily

10. Cf. Schmahl, "Lk 2,41–52 und die Kindheitserzählung des Thomas," 252.

11. Σοφία, 8:1; 14:3; 17:5 (Luke 2:52; 11:49 etc.) and δόξα, 6:8; 17:5 (frequent in Luke and the other NT gospels), respectively.

12. Somewhat awkwardly, the mention of Mary is moved to the beginning of the passage, so that it becomes grammatically less clear that the expression "treasured . . . in her heart" refers to her.

13. IGT has double, Luke 2:19 single *lambda*. In Luke 2:51, a number of manuscripts add ταῦτα (probably an influence from 2:19); no significant manuscripts add συμβάλλουσα, however.

14. Provided of course that the variant(s) available to IGT had a wording similar to 2:19 or 2:51b, i.e. a non-harmonized text. Another deviation in IGT is the lack of mention of Nazareth; this corresponds to its general geographical vagueness (see pp. 125–26).

explained by memorization than by transcription, such as changes in word order, verbal forms,[15] prepositions, conjunctions, and particles.[16]

In sum, the analysis of 17:1–5 shows that: (1) IGT in general follows Luke closely and loyally. (2) When it deviates, its expansions emphasize matters of importance for IGT, particularly about Jesus' parents' understanding of him (cf. p. 46), the interpretation of Scripture (pp. 158–60), and the role of Jesus himself (pp. 152–57). The expansions are not contrastive or polemical, however, but very much on a level with Luke, both as concerns style, vocabulary, and viewpoints. Thus, IGT appears to intend to unfold what is implicit in Luke. (3) The fact that IGT uses this episode as its rounding off indicates that Luke (and probably also other early Christian writings) has already attained considerable authoritative status. It has not, however, the kind of canonicity—at least not in IGT's setting—that requires verbatim reproduction: the author has much freedom in the adaptation of the passage.[17] (4) IGT is likely to reproduce Luke 2:41–52 from memory rather than by copying, which can support the oral/written approach promoted earlier (chap. 2). (5) IGT knows and makes use of other parts of Luke, such as the latter part of chapter 1 (cf. 1:42), the first half of chapter 2 (cf. 2:19), and most of chapter 11 (cf. 11:27, 53).

Biblical Reference II: 1 Corinthians 13:1

The other NT text cited in IGT is 1 Corinthians 13:1. The quotation, which occurs in 1 Teacher, is surprising, as it seems both unmotivated and misplaced.[18] When Zacchaeus has tried to teach Jesus the alpha and hit him on the head for not responding, the boy in 6:8 replies in anger:

---

15. The first and last of the verb forms in IGT (Luke 2:43, 45, 49) are used in variant readings, but there appear to be no special tendencies as to what manuscripts/recensions IGT has followed.

16. 1. εἶναι αὐτὸν for αὐτὸν εἶναι; 2. ἦλθαν for ἦλθον, ἀπέμεινεν for ὑπέμεινεν, ζητοῦντες for ἀναζητοῦντες, οἴδατε for ᾔδειτε; 3. εἰς for ἐν; 4. ἵνα τί for τί ὅτι; 5. omissions of δέ.

17. Cf. also the discussion in Chartrand-Burke, "Infancy Gospel," 275.

18. It is also used in Gad. Ibid., 268–69, esp. n. 47, believes the phrase to be a late addition to IGT since it has no parallel in the early versions (Syriac, Georgian, Ethiopic, Latin).

I want to teach you rather than be taught by you. For I know the
letters that you are teaching much more accurately than you.
To me this (ταῦτα) is like *a noisy gong or a clanging cymbal*
(my emphasis) which can't provide the sound (φωνὴν) or glory
(δόξαν) or power (δύναμιν) of insight (συνέσεως).

Why has IGT used this expression here? It is unlikely that the author
knew it as an independent maxim: such separate use is not documented, and it is too fragmentary and disconnected so as to have a life
of its own.[19] The expression is far more likely to have been taken over
directly from Paul; thus, we must take a closer look at its place within
1 Corinthians. In the letter, the verse serves as a bridge from Paul's discussion of spiritual gifts in chapter 12. Two of the most important gifts
are speaking in tongues and interpretation; both are mentioned at the
end of the chapter (v. 30). Then, in 13:1, Paul uses speaking in tongues
to introduce love, the more excellent gift: "If I speak in the tongues of
mortals and of angels, but do not have love, I am a noisy gong or a
clanging cymbal." And in v. 2 he goes on to compare love to other gifts,
such as "prophetic powers" and to "understand all mysteries" and "all
knowledge" (13:2).

In the context of 1 Cor 13:1, then, there are some elements
which appear to fit well with IGT 6:8–9, particularly cues such as
"speak"/"teach," "mystery," and "knowledge." Although it is not clear
what Jesus in IGT refers to (ταῦτα) as being like a "gong" or a "cymbal,"
it is probably the teacher's words, i.e. his teaching and repetition of the
letters. The following confirms this: both what he says (cf. φωνὴν) and
its—lack of—effect (cf. δόξαν, δύναμιν) show that he does not have real
insight (συνέσεως) into his own teaching.[20] Consequently, Jesus calls
him a hypocrite (6:9).

In IGT 6:9–10 the most important thing is not—as in Paul—love,
but to understand the mystical meaning of the letters. It is unlikely, however, that IGT by this intends to replace love with knowledge; the point
is rather to make use of Paul's somewhat tickling expression and its link
to speech and mystery. It may even—in its grandiloquence—have been

19. The expression is possibly Paul's invention, although there are some distant
parallels to it; see Collins, *First Corinthians*, 475.
20. The genitive συνέσεως, "of insight," is here likely to be related not only to
"power," but also to "sound" and "glory."

employed as means to impress its audience. Nonetheless, IGT's use of the phrase appears somewhat impenetrable and idiosyncratic.

The analysis implies that IGT was familiar with 1 Cor 12–13 and tried to make use of the verse in a meaningful way. Whether the author knew the rest of 1 Corinthians cannot be inferred from this; the famous passage can just as likely have been known through oral transmission (preaching?) or a *florilegium*. What should also be noted here is that IGT, by putting this Pauline phrase in the mouth of Jesus, gives it added authority: it is made into a dominical saying.

Allusions to Specific Biblical Texts

On several occasions IGT appears to allude to specific biblical passages, although the degree of resemblance varies. First, there are a number of similarities with the gospel of John. The most important are:

1. 4:1, the crowd's question "From where (πόθεν) was this child born (ἐγεννήθη)" is Johannine in wording and thought, cf. John 7:27–28; 8:14; 9:29–30; 19:9 etc.[21]

2. 5:3, when Joseph pulls Jesus' ear, the boy exclaims "let it suffice for you to seek (ζητεῖν) and find (εὑρίσκειν) me": the phrase echoes in wording and thought favourite turns in John, particularly 7:34–36.[22]

3. 6:4a, Jesus' reproach that Zacchaeus "do not, even though you are a lawyer, know the law" may—if not in wording, but in thinking—mirror John 3:10: "Are you a teacher of Israel, and yet yo do not understand these things."

4. 6:4b, Jesus' proclamation "When you were born, I existed (ὢν ἐγώ) and came to you . . ." is in thinking close to John 8:58: "Very truly, I tell you, before Abraham was, I am."

5. 6:5a, the crowd's statement that the "child is perhaps only five years old" may mirror John 8:57: "You are not yet fifty years, and have you seen Abraham?" Although it can be incidental, the similar age

21. But cf. Mark 6:2 par.; Luke 20:7 par.

22. E.g., John 7:34: "You will search for me, but you will not find me." But cf. *Gos. Thom.* 2; 38; 92; 94; *Gos. Mary* 8,20–21; *Gos. Heb.* 6b; *Dial. Sav.* 129,15.

specification is worth noting, with the age suggested in IGT being a tenth of that in John.

6. 6:5b, the crowd's reaction seems to combine John 7:46 ("Never has anyone spoken like this") and Matt 7:29/Mark 1:22.

7. 6:6, also 7:2, Jesus' statement has much in common with John 17:5 ("before the world existed") and 24 ("before the foundation of the world").[23]

8. 8:1a, Jesus' exclamation has elements in common with John 9:39: "I came into this world for judgment so that those who do not see may see, and those who do see may become blind."[24]

9. 8:1b, Jesus' explanation of his mission ("For I have come from above to rescue those below") comes very close to a number of places in John, e.g. 3:3, 7, 31 etc./8:23/4:34; 5:24, 37 etc.[25]

Together, these common features show that IGT is influenced by John. Even though some also are parallels with the Synoptics, others are exclusively dependent on John (IGT 6:4a; 6:4b; 6:5a). Indeed, the common features may stem from shared ideas rather than direct knowledge of John, but the similarities are so many that familiarity with John—in written or at least "heard" form—is the more likely (cf. also pp. 123–25).[26] The gospel is utilized in a less direct way than is Luke, though. But as will be seen later (p. 156), the similarities between IGT and John in theology is so marked that this too supports IGT's knowledge of John.[27]

23. But cf. 1:1–3; Col 1:15–16; Heb 1:2; Rev 3:14.

24. But cf. Matt 11:5, 25–27; John 3:3; 4:34; 5:19–23 etc.; also Isa 54:1–2; Gal 4:27.

25. Cf. "from above" (ἄνωθεν); "those below . . . above" (τοὺς κάτω . . . τὰ ἄνω); "the one who sent (ἀποστείλας) me to you." In this formulaic expression John has πέμπω instead of IGT's ἀποστέλλω, which, however, occurs elsewhere, see Matt 10:40; Luke 9:48/Mark 9:37; Luke 10:16). Thus, IGT in 8:1 seems to borrow extensively from John, but has replaced πέμπω with the Synoptic ἀποστέλλω.

26. This is contrary to some scholars' opinion, e.g., Chartrand-Burke, "Infancy Gospel," 269.

27. As can be seen from the list, the influence is the most evident in 6:1—8:2 (1 Teacher—but not only there!). If 1–3 Teacher belong to IGT's earliest layers (see p. 176), this can indicate that the influence from John was strongest in that stage of its development.

THE CHILDHOOD OF JESUS

IGT has few obvious parallels with the Synoptics beyond the material from Luke already discussed, and they are just as likely to reflect general biblical background as some specific gospel. However, IGT 6:4, Jesus' proclamation that "I am from outside of you, but I am also within you" can mirror sayings such as Matt 18:20; Luke 17:21 (also Luke 11:20); cf. also *Gos. Thom.* 3. In some cases IGT appears to reflect Matthew, particularly Matt 7:19; 10:40; 11:5, 25–27 (cf. 6:5b; 8:1a; 8:1b above).

There are only a few potential allusions to the letters of Paul:

1. 4:2, "to bless and not to curse" is in wording and thought likely to mirror the admonition in Rom 12:14: "bless and do not curse them"; cf. Matt 5:44; also Deut 11:26; 23:6 etc.[28]

2. 6:3, the phrase "do not be worried" (μή σοι μελέτω) is verbatim identical with 1 Cor 7:21. The "brother" (ἀδελφέ) address here may also reflect Pauline usage.[29]

3. 6:4, "noble birth in the flesh" (σαρκικὴν εὐγενίαν): the adjective σαρκικός is found six times in Paul (Rom 15:27; 1 Cor 3:3 etc.), but just once in the rest of the NT (1 Pet 2:11), and scarcely elsewhere in Greek literature. Thus, IGT here probably echoes Pauline usage.

The few points of contact do not mean that IGT shows little or no knowledge of Paul's letters, however. Since it quotes 1 Cor 13:1 and also may allude to other passages, particularly in Romans and 1 Corinthians, it appears more reasonable that IGT is at least superficially familiar with some of them. Besides, extensive use of Paul is not to be expected in a story that primarily deals with the life of Jesus.

There are very few allusions to specific sayings from the rest of the NT. The teacher's exclamation in 7:3: "I understand neither the beginning (ἀρχὴν) nor the end (τέλος)" can be an ironic play at Rev 21:6 (also 22:13; also IGT 6:9), but just as likely come from common Christian tradition.

There are in IGT no unequivocal references to the Old Testament, with the possible exception of the blessing/curse motif (see above, IGT 4:2).

---

28. Cf. also Prov 3:33; Sir 3:9; Neh 13:2; Ps 108:17; Jos 8:34.

29. For the sibling address, see Aasgaard, *My Beloved Brothers and Sisters*, esp. chap. 14; for the allusion to 1 Cor, cf. Chartrand-Burke, "Infancy Gospel," 269.

Use of Biblical Words and Concepts

IGT frequently utilizes biblical material in a more general way, particularly on the levels of terminology and style. Typical biblical words and concepts are:[30]

1. the christological titles "lord" (1:1; 9:3) and "the name" (6:4).

2. the soteriological terms "rescue" (ῥύομαι, 8:1), "save" (σῴζω, 8:2 etc.), "salvation" (σωτηρία 6:4 etc.), "blessing" (10:2 etc.), "glory" (δόξα, 6:8 etc.), and "grace" (χάρις, 14:3 etc.). Some have a strong Lukan colouring, and occur in Luke 1–2, cf. pp. 115–18.[31]

3. the anthropological terms "soul" (ψυχή, 16:3) and "flesh" (σάρξ, 6:4).

4. the epistemological terms "know" (γινώσκω, 5:1 etc.), "ignorance" (ἄγνοια, 5:3), "light" (5:3), "understanding" (ἐπιστήμη, 6:2), "insight" (σύνεσις, 6:8), "examine" (ἀποστοματίζω, 6:9; 17:2), "teaching" (παιδεία, 6:4; 7:1), "principle" (7:1), and "wisdom" (8:1 etc.); some are common in the NT, others rare.

5. the paraenetical term "exhortation" (παράκλησις, 6:8), which in the gospels occurs only in Luke-Acts (Luke 2:25 etc.), but frequently in Paul.

6. the missiological term "send" (ἀποστέλλω, 8:1).

7. the theological terms "god" (7:4) and "angel" (7:4), cf. John 6:14; 9:29–33.

8. the idea of Jesus as "not of this earth" (γηγενής, 7:2), cf. esp. John 3:31; 8:23; 18:36.

---

30. See also 9:3, "praised God and worshipped," cf. Matt 9:8; 15:31; 28:9, 17; Acts 3:13; Rev 7:11; 11:16; 19:4/10:2, "sign" (σημεῖον), cf. John 2:23 etc./10:2; 12:2; 17:4, "bless(ed) . . . ," cf. Luke 1:42; 11:27/14:1, "with much fear and worry," cf. 2 Cor 7:15; Eph 6:5; Phil 2:12; also Luke 1:13, 30; 12:32/14:2, "he opened his mouth," cf. Matt 5:2; Luke 1:64; Acts 8:35; 10:34/14:4, "testified true" (ὀρθῶς ἐμαρτύρησας): ὀρθῶς, cf. Luke 7:43; 10:28; 20:21, elsewhere in NT only Mark 7:35/μαρτυρέω, cf. John 1:7 etc.

31. Ῥύομαι only occurs twice in Matthew and once in Luke (1:74!), and otherwise primarily in Paul. Σωτηρία and χάρις are only used in Luke-Acts (particularly Luke 1–2), in the NT letters, and a few times in John (4:22/1:14, 16–17).

9. elements from Jewish tradition: Sabbath (2:2–4), Sabbath observance (2:3–4), Passover (17:1), temple (17:2), law (17:2; also 14:2),
prophets (17:2).

10. the Hebrew measuring unit *kor* (11:1–2), which in NT only occurs
in Luke 16:7 and elsewhere only a few places in the Septuagint
(e.g., Num 11:32) and Josephus (*Ant.*).

In many instances IGT seems to imitate biblical style. Most conspicuous are:

1. 1:1; cf. 6:2, "brother," which is typical of the NT letters.

2. 3:2, the curse on Annas' son, "Your fruit be without root," may
echo Luke 6:43–44 par.; Matt 21:18–19 par.; Luke 3:9 par.; also
Gos. Thom. 40.

3. 4:1; 5:1; 6:5; 14:2; 17:5, "word" (ῥῆμα), which is primarily used by
Luke (1:37, 38, 65; 2:15, 17 etc.) and John (3:34; 5:47 etc.).

4. 5:3, "behold," which occurs particularly in the gospels.

5. 6:4, "Jesus looked at them and said," which is identical with Luke
20:17. Matt 19:26 and Mark 10:27 differ slightly.

6. 6:5, "incredible (παραδόξου) miracle": similar outbursts are common in the gospels. The adjective παράδοξος is rare: in the Septuagint, it occurs a few times in late writings, e.g., 2 Macc 9:24;
Wisd 5:2. In the NT, it occurs only in Luke 5:26.

7. 6:6, "Why do you marvel" (τί θαυμάζετε): an identical question
occurs in Acts 3:12, cf. also John 5:28; 7:21. The verb is especially
frequent in Luke-Acts and John.

8. 7:1, "dear me" (οἴμοι) occurs several times in the Septuagint (as
οἴμμοι; e.g., Joel 1:15). It is not used in the NT, but has a parallel
in οὐαί ("woe"), which is especially frequent in Luke, Matthew,
and Revelation. Interestingly, Jesus' woe at the Pharisees occurs in
Luke 11.

9. 7:4; 14:3, "take him with salvation to your house" occurs twice in
IGT. It unites three NT elements: the imperative "take" (ὕπαγε,
typical of Matt/Mark, but not in Luke, and rarely in John); Lukan
vocabulary ("salvation," cf. above); and the phrase "to your house"
(εἰς τὸν οἶκόν σου, common in the gospels and Acts). Thus, IGT

here appears to combine elements from Luke and Matthew/Mark; in fact, the last two elements are found together in Matt 9:6/Mark 2:11. If IGT here imitates biblical phraseology, the expression here betrays familiarity with one or both of these gospels.

10. 9:3, "Jesus . . . cried out in a loud voice" is identical with Rev 19:17; cf. also 7:2 etc.; Luke 1:42; 4:33. The raising of Zeno may also reflect John 11:43 (and be modelled on the Lazarus story) or Matt 9:18, 23–26 par. (Jairus' daughter).[32]

This material shows that IGT is familiar with central theological concepts and often makes use of biblical phraseology. Reflections of specifically OT ideas and terms are few, however. Again, IGT's knowledge of Luke is confirmed. So is its familiarity with John: similarities in ideas and wording are too many to be coincidental. IGT can also reflect knowledge of Matthew and/or Mark, since there appear to be some conflations of Matthean/Markan and Lukan expressions.[33] Similarities with the rest of the NT are not many, but a few elements have parallels in the letters and Revelation.

Even though its style is sometimes clumsy, the impression given is that IGT attempts to imitate biblical idiom, possibly in order to give its story a more solemn air, or even to make it fit in with or follow up the NT story about the life of Jesus.

Use of Place Names, Titles, and Personal Names

IGT uses biblical nomenclature on several occasions. Bethlehem and Nazareth are spoken of in the prolog (1:1, cf. p. 40). The information is imprecise, however: Nazareth is called a village (κώμη) in the region (χώρα) of Bethlehem. Jerusalem and the temple are also mentioned (17:1), but no other locations. Thus, there is little to indicate knowledge of Palestinian geography, and the place names only seem to serve as narrative coloring and to be derived from tradition. In fact, if we exclude the secondary prolog and the Lukan temple episode, no geographical information is left at all.

---

32. Some other examples are also suggested in Chartrand-Burke, "Infancy Gospel," 268–69.

33. However, IGT may here be dependent on manuscripts of Luke which are more harmonized with Matthew and Luke than the main witnesses to the Nestle-Aland text.

A similar vagueness is apparent in the use of titles. "Pharisees" (2:5 etc.), "scribes" (17:4), "lawyer/teacher of the law" (6:4–5), and "High Priest" (3:1) are spoken of, but with no further notice. The likelihood for the son of the High Priest to be in Nazareth (3:1) is small indeed. In a couple of instances, ethnic terms are employed: Israelite (1:1, prolog) and Jew/Jews (2:3; 6:5). Like the geographical information, these too emerge as varnish and a heritage from biblical tradition.[34]

One feature is of special interest, however. The terms "lawyer" (νομικός, 6:4) and "teacher of the law" (νομοδιδάσκαλος, 6:5) occur in the NT gospels only in Luke: it has νομικός six times, three of them in chapter 11 (vv. 45, 46, 52), a passage that IGT already has shown knowledge of (pp. 117–18). It also occurs in Matthew 22:35, but which is uncertain on text-critical grounds, and in Tit 3:13. In the Septuagint, νομικός is used only once, in 4 Macc 5:4, and it is also rare in other Greek literature. Νομοδιδάσκαλος is extremely rare; in the biblical writings it occurs only in the NT, in Luke 5:17; Acts 5:34; 1 Tim 1:7. Outside the NT, it occurs only, and rarely, in a few church fathers. Again, these occurrences signal IGT's familiarity with Luke. In addition, the use of the terms in the Pastoral epistles (1 Tim, Tit) is worth noting.

As for IGT's use of personal names, the most interesting are Zacchaeus (6:1) and Annas (3:1). The former occurs in a single but famous NT passage: here he is not a teacher, however, but the rich tax collector addressed by Jesus. He appears only in Luke (19:1–10), and it is likely that this is IGT's source. The reason for IGT's borrowing of the name can be that this Lukan story was particularly treasured. But it can also be that the name was borrowed since both characters in the stories, a tax collector and a teacher, were power figures, but with an authority that was contested. It is also worth noting that Zacchaeus' words in 7:4: "take him with salvation to your house" may echo Jesus' words in Luke 19:9 that "today salvation has come to this house."

The name Annas is employed in a way closer to biblical usage and to historical reality: Annas, who is mentioned in Luke-Acts and John

---

34. It is worth noting that all Jewish/ethnic terms are located within the prolog (1:1), the first group of miracles (2–3), a small part of 1 Teacher (6:4–5), and in Jesus in Temple (17:4); it is also only here that Jewish customs and festivals are mentioned. Thus, all that links IGT up with a Jewish context is limited to these passages, which (except for the prolog) belong to its oldest layers. Cf. also chap. 5 in Chartrand-Burke, "Infancy Gospel," esp. 265–67. In Gd, Jesus is playing with "Hebrew children" or the "children of the Hebrews" (2:2).

(Luke 3:2; Acts 4:6; and John 18:13, 24), was High Priest in 6–15 CE at the time of Jesus' childhood and youth.[35] Surprisingly, this agrees chronologically with Jesus as a five-year-old. Although this may represent some kind of historical recollection, the fit is—considering IGT's general vagueness—very probably coincidental. Its occurrence is far more likely to reflect NT usage: Annas appears in Luke immediately after the Jesus in Temple episode. Thus, this again supports the claim about IGT's familiarity with the early chapters in this gospel. Worth noting, however, is that Annas' position is more prominent in John: here, he is the emeritus High Priest questioning Jesus in the passion narrative. Thus, this may support IGT's knowledge of John, and even of its passion narrative. IGT's use of the name can be due to Annas being one of Jesus' main opponents in the NT gospels.[36]

Other personal names yield less information. IGT clearly assumes that Thomas, Joseph, and Mary are well-known. Nothing is said about James being Jesus' brother (15:1); this too seems to be considered self-evident. Finally, the name Zeno is a Greek-Hellenistic and non-biblical name (see p. 62).[37]

The analysis, then, suggests that IGT has no knowledge of Palestinian geography beyond what can be found in the NT. Its use of titles and personal names are also derived from the NT, particularly from Luke, and maybe John. The persistence of the names Zacchaeus, Annas, and Zeno in the Greek manuscript—the names occur in all variants—is in agreement with the rules of oral transmission and its tendency to preserve this kind of narrative detail (see p. 26).

Echoes of Biblical Accounts

IGT appears to reflect specific biblical accounts on a more structural level, namely by echoing their basic narrative patterns. In fact, IGT

---

35. He is also mentioned *in Prot. Jas.* 15:1 (here, however, he is a scribe); also *Gos. Nic.* 1. Richard Bauckham, "Imaginative Literature," 797, holds that IGT owes its use of the name from *Prot. Jas.* Considering the otherwise few points of contact between the stories, it is more likely that they draw on common traditions in which the name could be used in different contexts and of different characters.

36. The cursing of Annas' son can, admittedly speculatively, be seen as IGT's way of taking revenge on him.

37. It is, however, found in a few variant readings of 2 Tim 4:19 and in *Acts of Paul and Thecla* 3:2.

explicitly signals such knowledge: as already noted (3.3), the crowd toward the end of IGT exclaims that Jesus "will go on saving all the days of his life" (16:3)—a statement that clearly betrays knowledge of accounts from the life of the adult Jesus. The most plausible reverberations of, or maybe even allusions to, specific biblical stories are:[38]

1. 2:1–4 reflects Gen 1–2. The disturbed, unclean water (Gen 1:2) is ordered, i.e. gathered into pools (Gen 1:6–10) and made clean through Jesus' word (Gen 1:3 etc.; John 1:1–3). The sparrows are made out of clay and given life, like man (Gen 2:7). The placing of the episodes at IGT's start supports such an interpretation: they serve as its creation narrative, recalling the OT account.[39]

2. 3:1–3 can be interpreted as a parallel to Gen 3 with its serpent in the paradise: the boy is presented as a criticizing intruder (Gen 3:1) and as the evil one who upsets the created order (Gen 3:4–5) by destroying the pools. The Pharisee in 2:3 may also play a similar part, in his criticism of Jesus' work (as creator) on the Sabbath.

3. 3:3, the cursing of Annas' son can be a parallel to the cursing of the serpent in Gen 3:14–15. If so, IGT 2:1—3:3 can be read as a pastiche on Gen 1–3. However, this cursing can also mirror the cursing of the fig tree in Matt 21:18–19 (cf. also Mark 11:12–14, 20–21). In both IGT and Matt the cursed object withers immediately. Thus, IGT may here be reflecting a NT episode and even to develop on it: what is in the NT a miracle related to nature (tree) is in IGT transformed to the area of humans; and what is in the NT presented as a symbolic event happens in IGT in reality, i.e. to a human being.[40] We should note that Luke has omitted the passage or possibly given it as a parable (13:6–9). If the IGT event is derived from the gospels, it seems more dependent on Matt/Mark than on Luke.

38. A few scholars have briefly brought attention to some parallels, Baars and Helderman, "Neue Materialien" (parts I–II); Hock, *Infancy Gospels*, 97–98; also Chartrand-Burke, "Infancy Gospel," 268–9.

39. Cf. Bauckham, "Imaginative Literature," 797; Baars and Helderman, "Neue Materialien" (part I), 205–11.

40. The withering (ἐξηράνθη) boy may echo the withered (ἐξηραμμένην) hand in Mark 3:1 par.

4. 11:1–2 clearly mirrors the parables of the sower in Mark 4:3–8 par. Interestingly, IGT again (cf. above) seems to develop a NT motif: it spells out in reality what the gospels only have in parable (cf. also *Gos. Thom.* 9; *Ap. Jas.* 8,16–27; *Pap. Eg.* 4).

5. 14:1–3 can reflect Luke 4:16–22, Jesus' rejection at Nazareth. The many common elements suggest that this Lukan passage has served as model for IGT.[41]

6. There appear to be some resemblance between miracle episodes in IGT and OT accounts (in 1–2 Kings) about Elijah and Elisha, who were highly esteemed as prophets in early Judaism/Christianity and who also have a special place in Luke (4:24–27; cf. also Matt 16:4 par.).[42] The influence may even go beyond mere Lukan mediation and betray more direct (oral?) knowledge in IGT of the OT accounts about them.

7. Whereas other antique biographical writings usually have nativity and childhood in combination, IGT focuses only on Jesus' childhood. This can imply that the author of IGT was familiar with the NT nativity accounts, at least Luke 1:5—2:40, and did not see a need to reproduce them itself.[43]

Several interesting features emerge from these structural similarities: first, evidence of IGT's knowledge and use (though limited) of Old Testament material is strengthened, by its references to Genesis 1–2 (and

---

41. Such as geographical location (Nazareth); the scene (a place for teaching: synagogue/school); a strong focus on Jesus; the central role of a book; reading from the word of God versus not reading from another book; powerful speech; encouragement/expectation that Jesus should say more; a present crowd; and the amazement at Jesus' words. In addition, both episodes serve as climaxes within the narrative: in Luke it marks Jesus' first public appearance, in IGT it is the peak episode in 1–3 Teacher.

42. (a) Both prophets perform miracles: resuscitations (1 Kgs 17:17–24; 2 Kgs 4:18–35; cf. IGT 8:2; 9:3; 14:4) and feedings (1 Kgs 17:8–16; 2 Kgs 4:42–44; cf. IGT 11:1–2). Elisha performs healings (2 Kgs 5:8–14; 13:20–21, cf. IGT 15:2; 16:2) and purifies water (2 Kgs 2:19–22; cf. IGT 2:1). (b) This they enact primarily through speech (cf. IGT 2:1, 4; 3:2 etc.) or touch (cf. IGT 15:2; 16:2). (c) Like Jesus in IGT, they proclaim curses (1 Kgs 21:17–24; 2 Kgs 1:9–12; 5:25–27). Worth noting is Elijah's cursing in 2 Kgs 2:23–24 of children who insult him; this has similarities with IGT 4:1, as has the blinding of the Aramean army in 2 Kgs 6:18 with the blinding in IGT 5:1. (d) Luke has a special interest in these prophets and is the only NT writer to mention Elisha explicitly (4:24–27). See also Evans, "Luke's Use of the Elijah/Elisha Narratives," 75–83.

43. This is also the opinion of Chartrand-Burke, "Infancy Gospel," 397–98.

possibly 3) and to the passages on Elijah and Elisha in 1–2 Kings. Second, the use of Genesis 1–2(–3) as a model for 2:1–4 supports the claim about IGT as a consciously structured narrative (cf. see p. 45). Moreover, IGT's knowledge of Luke is again supported by its reflection of Luke 4:16–22, 24–27, and possibly also of 1:5—2:40. Furthermore, IGT's knowledge of Matthew is suggested through its parallel with the account of the fig tree (Matt 21:18–19). And finally, IGT not only alludes to specific biblical passages, but occasionally also develops on them, both by echoing them (creation and Elijah/Elisha) and by transforming symbolic actions (cursing of the fig tree) and parables (the sower) into events in the life of Jesus (Pools/Sparrows, Annas' Son, Harvest). This is done through various typological-like interpretations of the biblical texts.

Echoes of Biblical Narrative Patterns and Motifs

In several instances IGT seems to reflect biblical narrative patterns and elements in a more general way. The most important are:[44]

1. 2:2, the number twelve as reflecting the forefathers/tribes of Israel, or the apostles.

2. 2:3, accusation against Jesus for violating the Sabbath, cf. Mark 2:24.

3. 2:3; 5:1; 9:2, the accusations remind of the accusations against Jesus in the NT, particularly in the passion narratives.

4. 6–8, 13–14, 1–3 Teacher seems a variation of the OT/NT turning-of-tables motif.

5. 6:4, 8; 13:2, Jesus' encounters with the teachers have features in common with the process against Jesus in the NT, for example his silence at the interrogators and the hitting of his head.[45]

44. Others are 2:1—3:3, intertwining of episodes, Mark 5:21–43 par./2:2, the sparrows, Matt 10:29–31 par., possibly Matt 6:26; 13:32 par./2:3, criticism of Jews and Pharisees, e.g., John 3:25–30/4:1; 5:1, word becoming deed, e.g., Ps 32:9 (LXX)/4:2, expulsion from hometown, Luke 4:24 par./5:1, blinding as curse, 2 Kgs 6:18; Acts 13:6–12; also Luke 6:39 par.; John 9:1–38/6:7, silencing of others, e.g., Luke 20:26/6:10, interpretation of secrets, Mark 4:1–29 par./10:1, carrying water in cloak, Prov 30:4/11:2, love of neighbor/13:3; 14:4; also 7:4, Luke 1:23, 56, etc. Cf. also Chartrand-Burke, "Infancy Gospel," 268/14:4, saved because of others, Matt 9:1–8 par.

45. Cf. particularly Jesus' silence at his interrogators, cf. Matt 26:62–63; Mark 14:60–61; Matt 27:12–14; Mark 15:4–5; John 19:9–10; Luke 23:9/the striking of Jesus

6. 9:1, Jesus deserted by the other children. This resembles the disciples' flight in the passion narratives in Matt 26:56/Mark 14:50—a detail not mentioned by Luke.

7. 9:1–4 may have a parallel in Acts 20:9–12, the boy who fell out of a window.

8. 11:2, poor and orphans are in the Bible frequently viewed as receivers of beneficence. The groups are mentioned together in Ps 81:3 (LXX).

9. 12:1, Joseph as a carpenter (τέκτων) is biblical heritage.[46] This is mentioned in Matt 13:55 and Mark 6:3, but not by Luke and John.

10. 15:1, the "miscreant" snake who bit James may have its forefather in the serpent of Eden, Gen 3:15, or in the snake who bit Paul on Malta, Acts 28:3–6.[47]

The select list of examples indicates that IGT draws on a general and fairly broad reservoir of biblical material. Although some may reflect common thinking in antiquity, most of them have parallels in the Bible, particularly in the gospels, and thus contribute to IGT's biblical coloring.

The patterns and motifs are utilized in a variety of ways. Sometimes they are applied in contexts that appear relevant, for example the turning-of-tables motif in 1–3 Teacher and the beneficence toward poor and orphans. At other times they are employed in ways that are less lucid and even seem casual. For example, the number twelve in 2:2 appears to have no specific meaning beyond creating a biblical aura.

Some patterns and motifs resemble what can be found in Luke. But there are others that seem dependent on other gospels, most frequently Matthew, or gospel tradition more generally, e.g. the information about

---

before the High Council, in IGT the teacher hits Jesus in the head; in Matt 26:67–68; Mark 14:65; John 18:22 Jesus is hit in the face; in Luke 22:63–64 he is only said to be hit/Jesus' self-conscious and provocative answers at his interrogators, cf. Matt 26:64 par.; John 18:19–23, 33–37.

46. Joseph's occupation as a carpenter became firm tradition in early Christianity. *Prot. Jas.* develops this idea (9:1; 13:1), but does not use the word τέκτων.

47. The Greek παλαμναῖος ("miscreant") occurs only seven times in Greek literature, in Sophocles (twice), Euripides, Plutarch, Xenophon, Apollonius Rhodius, and Aeschylus.

Joseph's occupation (12:1). A few motifs may also have roots in the OT (Snakebite) and in Acts (Zeno).

Of special interest are IGT's reverberations of the NT passion narratives. Although there is a risk of pushing similarities too far, they seem too many to stem from coincidence. The common motifs, which occur at various points in IGT, are (1) accusations against Jesus, (2) his silence under interrogation, (3) the striking of him, (4) his defense, and (5) the flight of his playmates. Together, these motifs indicate that IGT had some knowledge of Jesus' passion story. In fact, the NT passion narratives appear to an extent to be employed as a soundboard for the adversity against Jesus in IGT. These are important observations since there is nothing in IGT (i.e. Gs) that explicitly refers to this—for the NT so crucial—part of Jesus' life. The seeming lack of such references has been a central reason for the critique of IGT as being devoid of biblical foundation and theological depth. IGT does not, however, seem to be influenced by a specific variant of the passion story, since the information reflected is of a rather general nature. Thus, IGT's knowledge of the passion may just as well come from oral/aural as from literary familiarity with the story (cf. p. 24).

Reflections and Conclusions

IGT's use of biblical material is more extensive than has been acknowledged and ranges from similarities in genre via references, quotations and allusions to textual detail. Even given that some similarities can be coincidental, there remains more than enough to support the claim that IGT reflects a fairly broad and close knowledge of such material. The degree and kind of familiarity need to be clarified, however.[48]

It is obvious that the gospel of Luke is a primary source for IGT. In the analysis, knowledge of extensive parts of Luke 1–4 and 11 has been documented. In addition, there are many other reflections of characteristic Lukan narrative patterns, expressions, and stylistic elements. Together, this indicates that IGT has a considerable degree of familiarity with Luke as a whole. The nature of this familiarity is not clear, however. There is little to indicate that IGT has copied directly from it. Rather,

---

48. These are matters that need further study, both in the case of Gs and in the case of the other main manuscripts and variants.

most of the material seems to be reproduced from memory, cf. the many instances of imprecision and conflation. Even the temple episode can have been memorized. Although IGT has dealt relatively freely with the gospel, the many common features nonetheless mirror that it must have had special access to it, whether as written text or through it being frequently read in IGT's milieu. As concerns Acts, however, evidence is far from clear. Potential references to it can all have other sources.

What is said about Luke can also be said about John. Even though no particular passages are reflected in IGT, the numerous other links show equal familiarity with it, particularly through the many common terms and concepts. The similarities are so strong that it presupposes knowledge of John at least as a heard, if not as a written, text.

As for Matthew and Mark, the evidence is more ambiguous. Little or no evidence is exclusively Markan; thus, IGT may not have known Mark, or has not used it. As for Matthew, there are clearer indications of knowledge, as some detail information may be derived from it, in particular from its passion narrative. But the familiarity seems rather general and distant, at the most based on occasional hearing.

One may also speculate whether IGT's knowledge of Jesus' life can be based on some kind of gospel harmony, for example Tatian's *Diatessaron*, which had a firm and lasting footing in the eastern Mediterranean.[49] This is unlikely (at least as for Gs and the other Greek variants), however, since the influence of Luke and John is in wording and thinking far stronger than that of Matthew and Mark, and thus presupposes accessibility to them as discrete gospels.

IGT is familiar with the apostle Paul, at least with parts of 1 Cor 12–13. Some potential links to other letters also occur, for example Rom 12:14, but they are sparse and uncertain. In a story like IGT, not many references to Paul are to be expected, however. This makes the matter-of-course quotation from 1 Cor 13:1 the more striking.

References to the Pastoral epistles and the Catholic letters are rare. None are compelling in favor of use of these letters, although IGT may have had some knowledge of them (see p. 126). Interestingly, there are some pointers to Revelation, cf. Rev 3:14; 17:6; 19:17; 21:16. Although they do not explicitly link IGT up with Revelation, the similarities may go beyond mere communality of words and ideas.

49. Metzger, *Early Versions*, 10–36.

IGT knows the Old Testament as a collection of writings and refers to it as the Law and the prophets (17:2). The common NT term for Scripture, ἡ γραφή, is not used, though. IGT's ties with the OT are generally few and considerably weaker than with the NT. In itself, this is a strong testimony for IGT's distant relations to Judaism or Jewish influenced Christianity. The distance, however, seems to come from limited familiarity with/irrelevance of Jewish tradition rather than from animosity (see also pp. 80 and 159). Still, the analyses have indicated some OT links, particularly the many parallels with Genesis 1–3 in narrative patterning, with 1–2 Kings and their prophet figures, and very occasionally with passages in poetic and sapiental writings such as Psalms (32:9; 81:3; 108:17), Proverbs (3:33; 9:18; 30:4), Sirach (3:9; 13:26; 43:25) and the historical writings 2 Maccabees and 4 Maccabees.

In addition, there appear to be a few similarities with early Christian non-canonical material, such as the *Gospel of Thomas*, *Gospel of Mary*, and *Gospel of the Hebrews* (see IGT 3:2; 5:3; 11). The points of contact, however, are so vague that similarities likely come from shared traditions rather than from direct influence. Interestingly, there is—apart from a common interest in Jesus' early years and some similarity in genre—no clear textual interchange between IGT and *Prot. Jas.*

The impact of non-Christian and non-Jewish literature on IGT also appears very limited, although this has not been in focus here. The impression is that IGT is a type of popular material with little or no relation to the literature of the more educated (cf. the scepticism voiced in 14:2; see pp. 80–81).

To summarize: the main biblical influence on IGT comes from Luke and John, very occasionally from Paul, and possibly from Matthew and Revelation. But IGT is also familiar with some other biblical writings, or at least select NT/OT passages. Much of the knowledge can stem from hearing, possibly preaching. Knowledge of non-gospel material can also be drawn from *florilegia* or the like. Influence is generally of a kind that supports the impression of primarily orally based transmission.

IGT reflects no knowledge of biblical prolegomena other than what can be extracted from the mentioned writings, and it even appears to have a very limited grasp of—or interest in?—data otherwise easily available in its sources, for example about Palestinian geography.

Can these observations tell us anything about the age or geographical provenance of IGT? It has been assumed that the scarcity of Biblical, especially NT, references indicates an origin already in the second century, at a time when these (collections of) writings had not yet been widely dispersed.[50] Although this may have something to it, the argument is not very strong, since there is—as I have shown—more of biblical influence in IGT than has been acknowledged. In addition, the impact of the NT writings varies in Christian sources in the second and third centuries, and IGT is not the kind of material in which one need expect such influence. As for geographical provenance, there may be a little more to say. The gospels of Luke and John appear to have had a strong position in Asia Minor in the second century, and IGT's special familiarity with them makes this one of the most plausible places of origin.[51]

Equally important as charting biblical influence on IGT, however, is seeing how it makes use of such material. Some characteristic features emerge:

IGT aims at creating a biblical atmosphere in the story, primarily by drawing on words, concepts, and stylistic elements from Luke and John. It shows considerable familiarity with the material and ability in its use of it. It also employs other biblical material, sometimes in ways that seems arbitrary, and maybe even less skilled. In a surprising way, however, IGT is congenial with its predecessor Luke: just like Luke, in form and content, is writing a sequel to the OT, particularly in the story of Jesus' birth, IGT is a continuation of Luke in its telling of Jesus' childhood story, indicated most explicitly in its inclusion of Luke 2:41–52.

IGT has in several instances managed to develop on biblical narratives in ways that are both literarily creative and theologically advanced. This may especially be the case with passages such as Gen 1–3 (creation), 1–2 Kings (Elijah and Elisha), Matt 21:18–19 (cursing the fig tree), and Mark 4:3–8 (parable of the sower).

IGT utilizes its biblical sources in a manner loyal to them. When it develops on them, this is done in a restrained way. The individual episodes are for example told with a sobriety similar to the NT gospels, and there is no extensive or fantastic elaboration of biblical references, such as found in gnostic material.

---

50. See particularly Chartrand-Burke, "Infancy Gospel," 132–34.

51. Ibid., 133–34, suggests Asia Minor or Syrian Antioch. If we are to make an inference from the rural landscape reflected in IGT's narrative world, the city of Antioch appears less plausible as a place of origin for the story.

Nevertheless, IGT deals relatively freely with its sources, in ways that appear autonomous and reveal special emphases. This is visible in its development of biblical parables into events (3:2–3; 11) and in Jesus in the Temple (17), with its focus on Mary and Joseph's reaction, the interpretation of Scripture, and the role of Jesus. Some of these matters will be expanded on later (chap. 10).

9

⊰◈⊱

Strange Sayings

On some occasions Jesus and others express themselves in ways difficult to comprehend. These sayings have been a key reason for the claims about the gospel's heretical leanings. Modern readers are not the only ones to have problems with deciphering them. IGT's early audiences appear to have had similar problems: the fact that many sayings differ considerably in the manuscripts is evidence of this. In this chapter, I shall deal with some of these sayings in order to establish their meaning and function within IGT. In this, the chapter will also serve as preparation for the theological discussion in chapter 10.

The causes for obscurity in the sayings can vary. In addition to the "heresy option," the obscurities can be due to some kind of corruption in transmission of the material. The scribes or storytellers can, for example, have misunderstood what was being said. They may also have had limited proficiency in Greek. The opacity can also reflect awkwardness, idiosyncrasy, or failing capability of expression on their part. But the problem can also be that we as modern interpreters lack information needed to understand the sayings. And it can even be that some of the sayings were intended to be unfathomable and incomprehensible. Thus, we may in some cases come up with plausible explanations, in some have to guess, and in other cases have to give up finding a sense at all.[1] Since Gs/H is our default text, I focus on the sayings in their form there and interpret them primarily within the context of this variant.

---

1. In this matter, it is clearly necessary to study each manuscript (or at least variant) individually and in detail in order to uncover their specific character, idiosyncrasies, and possible ideological/theological leanings. For some other preliminary work, see Baars and Helderman, "Neue Materialien" (parts I–II); Chartrand-Burke, "Strange New Sayings," sections 2–4.

But since other IGT variants and language versions may also be of help, we shall also occasionally take side glances to them.[2]

Curse on a Careless Boy (4:1)

In Careless Boy, Jesus responds to the boy's bumping by cursing his "ruling power." The word employed, ἡγεμών, can in Greek refer to an external element ("ruler," "leader," "chief," "guiding spirit") or to an internal factor guiding one's life ("will," "principle").[3] If the former is meant, some evil power, possibly the devil, can be intended. But this is uncertain, since no such powers are hinted at elsewhere in IGT. Thus, the latter is also possible: the boy is cursed because of his own bad attitudes. In any case, the meaning is not very different: the boy acts ruthlessly because he lacks control of himself. The expression has a solemn tone, but appears at the same time somewhat stilted—like an awkward or jocular way of hitting a high pitch of style. The other Greek variants have a completely different and more sensible wording: "You shall not go your way."

Joseph Rebukes Jesus (5:1–3)

After Jesus' curse in Careless Boy Joseph reproaches him for making others hate them. Jesus' response has a solemn air similar to the previous saying. His first statement, "you know wise words" (5:1), appears to acknowledge his father's wisdom. The text is ambiguous, however, with other interpretations being possible. The other Greek variants also differ considerably from Gs/H, and some versions imply that Jesus here instead refers to his heavenly father.[4]

---

2. For surveys of the sayings in the Greek variants and in the versions, see the notes in the translation by Chartrand-Burke, "Infancy Gospel," 224–44. In addition to the "strange sayings" dealt with in the following, there are also several other textual problems in Gs/H, but these are less relevant here.

3. For the former, Liddell and Scott, *Greek-English Lexicon*, ad loc. In the latter case, it can refer to the usually Stoic idea of τὸ ἡγεμονικόν as a ruling principle in a person, cf. Aetius 4.21.1–4 (Greek and English text in Long and Sedley, *The Hellenistic Philosophers*, sec. 53H).

4. Cf. Chartrand-Burke, "Infancy Gospel," 227.

The following words, "you are not ignorant where your words came from: they were spoken about a five-year-old (ἐπὶ πέντε διήγισαν)," is also difficult to decipher and make sense of, although it seems to reflect Johannine style (see p. 121). In my translation the first sentence states that Joseph knows that his words are given him from above, from God, and the second sentence demonstrates the truth in this, with a small child being able to do such extraordinary things as cursing other people to death. But the saying can also mean that Jesus utters the curses on behalf of his heavenly father in order to show his foes whom they are encountering.[5]

Since they do not recognize who Jesus is, he blinds his opponents, and as a consequence Joseph pulls his ear to punish him. Considering the gravity of Jesus' deed, his father's reaction is minimal, and the scene appears to be painted with more than a touch of humor. And again Jesus responds to his father in lofty, rather inscrutable words, and with biblical echoes: "Let it suffice for you to seek and find me. . . ." (5:3; cf. p. 120). Here, Jesus reproaches Joseph, but also comforts and excuses him: he has "a natural ignorance" and does "not see with light," but at the same time knows that he cannot really "distress" Jesus. In most other variants and versions Jesus is more reproaching and less comforting than here.[6]

Jesus' final statement in the episode is also enigmatic: "For I am yours and have been put in your hands"; the last words can alternatively be translated "been handed over to you" or "been made your captive" (πρός σε ἐχειρώθην). The saying has been taken to reflect gnostic thinking, of Jesus being a "captive" in the world. Such an idea, however, does not readily suggest itself from the wording per se, and is also nowhere else expressed in IGT—neither matter nor persons are seen as fundamentally evil. A more probable and straightforward reading is that Jesus, since he is only a child and has been entrusted to Joseph (by God?), should not be punished in such a way.[7] This part of the saying is also special to Gs/H and can reflect an idiosyncrasy in it.

---

5. Cf. ibid.

6. Cf. ibid., 228–29. The words "with light" may reflect a biblical idiom or simply be a current expression for "clearly."

7. Another matter is that this saying is open to allegorization in a gnostic direction, especially if it is seen together with 13:3 in which Joseph confines Jesus to the house!

First Teacher (Dialog) (6:2–7)

Several of the strange sayings occur in 1 Teacher (6–8). Why this is so is not clear. It can be that the episode belongs to IGT's oldest layers (see pp. 38 and 175–76) and that the sayings during transmission have suffered more distortion than later material. Or it can be that the passage had a theological stamp, a level of reflection, or other characteristics that caused problems for the tradents.

The first difficulty occurs in Zacchaeus's statement about the aims of Jesus' education: he is to be enabled to teach others to "have a wish to become like children in the same way" (εἰς τέκνα πόθον κτήσηται ἕξειν ὁμοίως αὐτὰ ἀντεπαιδεύσῃ) (6:2). The phrase is syntactically intricate and grammatically next to unintelligible. Again, Gs/H seems to try to strike a high note in style, but without being quite able to keep it firm. The phrase, which has no close parallel in the Greek variants, is hard to make sense of. In my (admittedly vague) translation, Zacchaeus states that Jesus should be made able to teach other children "to be good" too. However, the text can also be rendered "acquire a desire to be among children, also teaching them in return"; some of the versions convey such an understanding, especially the Syriac: "have the love of children and again so that he may teach them."[8] The point in Gs/H and most other texts can be that Jesus learn to socialize with other children and to become a model and teacher to them.

When Joseph hands Jesus over to Zacchaeus, he warns him about his unruliness, and states that the teacher should "not regard him to be a human in miniature (μικροῦ ἀνθρώπου εἶναι)" (6:3). The phrase is ambiguous and can also be translated "to be almost a man" or "not to be a little man." The meaning appears to be that Jesus is not only an ordinary human being, but should also be considered divine. However, it can also mean that the boy has shown himself so far from being a responsible (adult) person that the challenge will be more than Zacchaeus can handle.[9]

---

8. See Chartrand-Burke, "Infancy Gospel," 229 n. 49 for this translation and for a survey of formulations in other versions.

9. Gd and the Syriac have instead "a small cross" and the Ethiopic "a big cross." Whereas several of the Greek variants and the versions mention the cross, thus probably hinting at Jesus' crucifixion, this is never referred to in Gs.

According to Jesus, Zacchaeus is despite his cleverness "a stranger to the name by which he names [you]" (6:4). It is not clear who "he" refers to, but probably it is to Joseph with his warning (6:3). Thus, "the name by which he names" is likely to be Jesus, the meaning being that the teacher, despite Joseph's words, is unable to realize who he is. This interpretation is supported by some of the other variants; in them, however, it is Jesus who is a "stranger" because he does not fit in with the human description ("name") given of him.[10] Nonetheless, what is underscored is Jesus' uniqueness, with the expression "the name . . . names" being an attempt at a solemn or mysterious reference to Jesus. In addition, it may also allude to the biblical idea of Jesus as the "name" (e.g., 3 John 7; p. 123).

The precise meaning of Jesus' next words, "I am from outside of you, but I am also within you because of my noble birth in the flesh" is not clear, although it has much in common with expressions in other variants and versions.[11] The "noble birth in the flesh" (σαρκικὴν εὐγενίαν) is unlikely to reflect gnostic or docetic ideas, since the expression does not evince any devaluing of Jesus' body. On the contrary, it appears to upgrade his birth and material existence, and thus to aim at describing his human nature in a dignified way.[12] It is also not clear what is meant by Jesus being "from outside (ἔξωθεν) of you" and "from within (ἔνδοθεν) you." Probably it is an attempt at expressing the incarnation: his divinity (pre-existence and/or otherness) and his being ("real presence") in the world. Ἔνδοθεν may imply that Jesus somehow dwells "within" people, or also as meaning "among," "in your midst"— in either case, the formulations cannot be turned to account of some particular theological view. It seems clear, however, that IGT here imitates biblical style (Matt 18:20; Luke 17:21; see p. 122).

Jesus then ends his brief speech in 6:4 by addressing his father, telling him that he "will take on the saving name" (τὸ σωτήριον ὄνομα βαστάσεις), or possibly "the name of salvation." This saying occurs only in Gs/H and is evidence of its interest in soteriology (pp. 155 and 162–63). It appears to refer back to the "name" above and to imply that

10. Cf. Chartrand-Burke, "Infancy Gospel," 230.

11. Cf. ibid.

12. It may also refer to Jesus as son of Joseph and as belonging to a "good family," cf. the status of Joseph as a free artisan-peasant (see pp. 77–79). There is no mention in IGT, at least not in Gs, of Jesus' birth from a virgin.

Joseph will gain salvation when, or if, he realizes who Jesus is, and understands his teaching.

In his response to the crowd's amazement, Jesus presents himself as omniscient: "I—and he before the world was created—know accurately (οἶδα . . . καὶ ὁ πρὸ τοῦ τὸν κόσμον κτισθῆναι)" when those present and their forefathers were born (6:6). The formulation here is special to Gs/H and must be corrupt; probably some letters or words have been omitted.[13] A plausible way of emending the text is adding "who existed," thus: "I—and he who existed (i.e. God) before the world was created—know accurately."[14] According to this, the saying can be interpreted on a level with formulations in other IGT variants of Jesus having omniscience equal to that of God, the creator.[15]

Jesus' demonstration of his omniscience leaves the crowd speechless. This makes him leap about (ἐσκίρτα) and say "I was playing (ἔπαιζον) with you, for I know that you are easily impressed and small-minded" (6:7). Both his leaping and his statement about "playing" with them are somewhat surprising, but have parallels in Ga/Gd. It is unlikely that ἔπαιζον should mean that Jesus is first joking and then retracts what he has said about himself—such a logic has no support in the context of the saying. The statement makes much more sense if it is taken to imply that Jesus is trying the others out and is shown to be in control—he is able to twist them round his finger. Interpreted this way, the words are a criticism of their failure to understand who Jesus is.

But why does Jesus "leap about" when saying this? According to antique standards, such kind of behavior was regarded improper (p. 82). As noted (p. 88) there is little to support the idea of Jesus here being a jester figure; more likely, he is depicted as behaving like a child (pp. 100–102), jumping with joy for having scored on the others. A similar description occurs in John Chrysostom's *Address on Vainglory*, in which children "rejoice and leap with pleasure" at the recognition

13. H has ὁπρωτοῦτὸνκόσμονκτησθῆναι.

14. Cf. Chartrand-Burke, "Infancy Gospel," 168 and 231 emends ὁ πρῶτον κόσμον κτισθείς, and translates "the one created before this world." Both the emendation and the translation are problematic, however (Chartrand-Burke has later revised them). It is unlikely that God is here spoken of as created, or that the formulation can be taken to support gnostic ideas of a demiurge, a divine figure who is himself created—nothing of this kind is hinted at elsewhere in Gs/H. For my emendation, see p. 223.

15. For the formulations in the other Greek variants and in the versions, see ibid., 231.

of a Bible story because they know "what the other children do not know" (p. 203).[16] It is also worth noting that the gospel of Luke makes similar use of the verb in the case of Elizabeth, pregnant with John the Baptist: when meeting Mary, she greets her by saying that "the child in my womb leaped (ἐσκίρτησεν) for joy" (Luke 1:44).

First Teacher (Alpha Lesson) (6:10)

Jesus' exegesis of the alpha in 1 Teacher has by several scholars been taken as evidence of IGT's gnostic character (pp. 174–76).[17] At closer scrutiny, however, there is little to link it up with such an origin. Letter and number speculation of different kinds and often of great complexity was widespread in antiquity and is documented at all levels of society.[18] In addition, it was often linked up with magic.[19] The phenomenon was also common within early Christianity.[20] Thus, it is not surprising to find such speculation in IGT. Indeed, its interest in the alpha very much reflects general fascination in expounding the hidden meaning of letters.[21]

The fact that the explaining of the alpha takes place in the setting of a school is not surprising either. Similar pedagogical strategies often formed part of the introduction to reading in early education. Numerous exercises are preserved, for example, in which each letter is tied up with a maxim, usually beginning with that particular letter.[22] Often, specific

16. *Inan. glor.* 41.

17. See Vielhauer, *Geschichte*, 676; also Baars and Helderman, "Neue Materialien" (part II), 2–5, 8–11, who, however, do not ascribe to it a gnostic origin exclusively, but also point to parallels with Osiris and Buddha legends.

18. For discussions and examples, see Dornseiff, *Das Alphabet in Mystik*; Fideler, *Jesus Christ, Sun of God*; Cribiore, *Writing*; Morgan, *Literate Education*; also Baars and Helderman, "Neue Materialien" (part II), 5–8.

19. See for example Ankarloo and Clark, *Witchcraft and Magic in Europe*; Janowitz, *Magic in the Roman World*; Mirecki and Meyer, *Magic and Ritual in the Ancient World*.

20. Numerous examples can be found in the books listed in the previous note. Cf. also Aland, "Das Rotas/Sator-Rebus." A very interesting, but later (probably sixth century) example is dealt with in Bandt, *Der Traktat "Vom Mysterium der Buchstaben."*

21. It may, however, be that the kind of letter exegesis found in IGT had its roots within lower, less educated strata of the population.

22. See Hock, *Infancy Gospels*, 102, for a fourth-century alphabet akrostikon meant for moral instruction in school. Morgan, *Literate Education*, 120–51, has also

meanings were attributed to each letter of the alphabet—examples of this are known from various contexts.[23]

The way reading is taught in IGT also conforms to standard procedures in antiquity, with repetition and imitation of pronunciation and writing, and with the letters being taught individually in alphabetical order. Only after having learned all letters, the pupils would learn to combine them in words.[24] Phrases could be joined in acrostics as aid for memory.[25] Sometimes difficult words were gathered in lists for rote learning.[26] For exercise, letters, syllables, and words could be combined in new ways and even in meaningless patterns, often in order to improve pronunciation.[27] Even Quintilian supported pupils learning nonsensical combinations of syllables by heart.[28] Teachers would also use these—often contraproductive—teaching strategies as power tools against their pupils.[29] Such lists could easily be turned into virtual jingles, just like more modern hocus-pocus and abracadabras. To some, such phrases and fragmentary maxims would also function as doors into a world of supernatural knowledge.[30]

For the illiterate and beginners in reading the mere forms of the letters could take on special meaning. For example, the writer Athenaeus in *The Deipnosophists* (late second century CE) refers to an illiterate man trying to visualize to others the writing of the Greek name Theseus. The man says:[31]

---

many examples. For a still valuable analysis with several primary text references, Hofmann, *Leben Jesu*, 218–27. For medieval times, see Orme, *Medieval Children*, 161–62, 254–61.

23. See for example Hofmann, *Leben Jesu*, 220–21; also Dornseiff, *Das Alphabet in Mystik*.

24. Cribiore, *Gymnastics*, 160–76; also ibid., *Writing*, 38–49, 139–52. For a detailed presentation of common pedagogical strategies, see Quintilian *Inst.* 1.1.24–37.

25. Cribiore, *Gymnastics*, 167.

26. Ibid., 39–41.

27. For presentations of such lists, see Morgan, *Literate Education*, 101–5; Cribiore, *Gymnastics*, 164–75; also Orme, *Medieval Children*, 261–70.

28. *Inst.* 1.1.30.

29. Cf. Morgan, *Literate Education*, 1998, esp. 102–3; Cribiore, *Gymnastics*, 162.

30. Cf. Cribiore, *Gymnastics*, 179, 183–84.

31. Athenaeus *Deipn.* 10.454d (Gulick, LCL). Athenaeus, who is fairly contemporary with IGT, here reproduces some lines from the fifth century BCE tragic poet Agathon's *Telephus*. Athenaeus also has other similar examples in this passage.

The first part of the writing was a circle with a navel in the centre;

Θ

then two upright rules yoked together

H

while the third was like a Scythian bow.

C

After that lay adjacent a trident on its side;

E

then mounted on one rule were two slanting lines.

Y

And as was the third, so also was the last again.

C

In my view, Jesus' exegesis of the alpha should be interpreted on the basis of such pedagogical strategies and experiences—this is far more likely than attempts at extracting gnostic or some esoteric meaning out of the passage. Parts of Jesus' exposition clearly refer to the form of the letter alpha, either written as the uncial A ("sharp lines," "a middle stroke," "sharpening," "joining," "equally-measured") or as cursive α ("dancing," "intersecting"). Other parts seem to play on numbers and words ("three-marked, double-edged," "same-formed, same-placed, same-kinded"), with some words being virtually unintelligible. Some terms may also refer to diacritical signs, such as dots and ligatures ("creeping out, drawing back, elevated").[32]

Interpreted this way, Jesus' exegesis emerges as a jingle consisting of a series of meaningful, half-sensical, and non-sensical words. It appears to be organized in patterns that make it easy to memorize: it has an inclusio ("how it has sharp lines" – "such lines does the alpha have"), similar word beginnings (ὁμο-, ἰσο-), and endings (-μένους, -οντας), alliteration (β-/τ-/δ-, ε-/α-/ο-), and elements of rhyme (-πολεῖς, -γενεῖς) and rhythm. These features can very much account for the similarities among the variants, and also for the combination in Gs of fragments from Ga and Gd (see p. 21).[33] The jingle is a form which easily allows for inclusion and exclusion of such elements.

32. Interestingly, some of the examples given by Athenaeus (see the previous note) contain some of the same linguistic elements as the exposition of the alpha in IGT, such as ἰσο-, κανών, three-, counting, and some rare or difficult words.

33. A fuller analysis of this passage (and its variant parallels) needs to be made, but cannot be done here. Hofmann, *Leben Jesu*, 222–23 makes an attempt at a theological (trinitarian) analysis of the passage.

In this interpretation, the passage can also be seen as a distortion and parody of reading exercises familiar to anyone having attended the antique school and—as a popular jingle—also to others. It would have been an easily memorable piece, well fit for being recited and performed, and with much playfulness in its formulations.[34]

From this the function of the passage within 1 Teacher (6–8) becomes clearer. Within the narrative, Jesus' explanation of the alpha leaves the teacher and others overwhelmed as for his wisdom: they are unable to understand and explore the depths of his words. As a result, they are put to shame, as is shown in Zacchaeus' subsequent lament (7:1–4). For the real-life audience of IGT, however, the passage will have functioned differently. For most of them, it would be obvious that this was a parody, and that its series of words was only partly, or not at all, comprehensible—they could boast of having a knowledge that the poor teacher lacked. They would sense what Jesus was at and could amuse themselves with the shortcomings of such an authority figure. Here, a teacher falls pray to teachers' own strategies—one of their power tools, the neck-breaking word exercise, is now applied on one of their own kind, to his great detriment. And even for those in IGT's audience who might not perceive the raillery, the alpha exegesis would appear entertaining, serve as a curiosity-inspiring riddle, and encourage admiration of Jesus' learning (p. 154).[35]

First Teacher (Exclamation) (8:1)

Jesus' laughter at the end of 1 Teacher, as he exclaims "let the unfruitful bear fruit" (8:1), has sometimes been interpreted as a gnostic feature.[36] The view above, however, offers a far more obvious and less strained explanation: his laughter at Zacchaeus' bewilderment and defeat simply reflects the probable reaction of IGT's audience to this comic scene. Clearly, humor is a central element in the episode, as it is elsewhere in IGT (e.g., 6:7, pp. 142 and 207); this is a feature that has been very much

34. For similar examples, see Cribiore, *Gymnastics*, 209–10.

35. Cf. also Leyerle, "Appealing to Children," 256, with references.

36. Baars and Helderman, "Neue Materialien" (part I), 215; ibid., "Neue Materialien" (part II), 16–17. On laughter within Gnosticism, see Gilhus, *Laughing Gods*, esp. 69–77. The laughing Jesus has also been linked up with docetism, see Stroumsa, "Christ's Laughter."

neglected in earlier, mostly deadly serious, analyses of the story.[37] And Jesus' exclamation—which resembles statements in the NT gospels (Matt 11:5, 25–27; John 9:39; see p. 121)—is not a revelation of some secret knowledge, but a response to Zacchaeus' incipient recognition that Jesus might be "a god, and angel, or whatever else"—as a result of which Jesus immediately heals those who had been cursed.[38]

Conclusion

The analyses have indicated that the obscureness of the sayings above are of different origin and are also often best explained with attention to their context in IGT itself, and not to external factors. On some occasions the sayings aim at hitting a high pitch of style (Careless Boy, Joseph's Rebuke, 1 Teacher [Dialog]). This may betray insufficient ability of expression on the part of the author(s). But the clumsiness can also be intended: both in these and other cases humor plays a considerable part (1 Teacher [Alpha and Exclamation]). Some of the sayings very much echo biblical expressions, and can be explained as attempts at imitation, both in form and content (Joseph's Rebuke; 1 Teacher [Dialog and Exclamation]). Jesus' exegesis of the alpha, with its many half- and nonsensical words, more than anything emerges as a jingle, taking the form of a popular parody on a school lesson in reading. In some cases, the problems with understanding the text seem due to idiosyncrasy on the part of Gs/H or to corruption in the transmission of the story (Joseph's Rebuke, 1 Teacher [Dialog and Alpha]).

On a very few occasions, the sayings could be taken to reflect "heretical" theological positions. Jesus' final comment in Joseph's Rebuke about being a "captive" in the world and his laughter in 1 Teacher (Exclamation) can be interpreted as gnostic traits. However, they are

---

37. On humor in the Bible and in antiquity, see for example Jónsson, *Humour and Irony in the New Testament*; Bremmer and Roodenburg, *A Cultural History of Humour*; Halsall, *Humour, History, and Politics*. Joking about teachers was a common feature in ancient humour. Laughter can in many cases be interpreted as reflecting opposition against social and religious authorities; cf. Gilhus, *Laughing Gods*, 68–69.

38. In Ga/Gd the second teacher says that he wants Jesus first to learn the Greek letters, then the Hebrew (14:1). Gb 7:1a states that Zacchaeus wrote down the alphabet in Hebrew (ἑβραϊστί); nonetheless, he is said to teach Jesus the Greek *alpha*, not the Hebrew *aleph*. Gb also says that Jesus recited all 22 letters of the alphabet—the Hebrew alphabet has 22, the Greek 24 letters.

better explained from the textual contexts, with Jesus being entrusted in the hands of Joseph, and Jesus laughing (with the implied audience) at the foolishness of the teacher and others. The negative attitude within Gnosticism toward the body and the material world is not reflected in any of IGT's strange sayings; IGT also as a whole has a positive view of materiality.

As a whole, none of these difficult sayings deviate in contents perceptibly from what is already found in the New Testament. This impression will be further substantiated as we now turn to a systematic theological analysis of IGT.

10

MAIN THEOLOGICAL ISSUES

IGT has been considered theologically superficial and naïve,[1] and even lacking Christian substance.[2] Its theological profile has been said to be heretical, occasionally anti-Jewish, and even non-theological.[3] Because of this negative evaluation, scholars have by and large refrained from studying its theology in detail. Even Chartrand-Burke, who has the most extensive discussion, primarily bases his analysis on a comparison with literary and historical parallels (pp. 89–92). Clearly, in-depth study of IGT's theology is needed, and will be pursued in the following.

In the analysis, I shall present the main theological issues of IGT. It will become evident, however, that it addresses a limited number of such issues. There is for example no mention of a synagogue or other religious locations, except for the temple. Nothing is said about sacraments, rituals, or "followers" of Jesus. Justification and eschatology go unmentioned. Other central theological issues are also only assumed and subsidiary, and appear to be of secondary interest. Still, this does not mean that IGT is theologically deficient. On the contrary, it can—in spite of its timid appearance—in some respects be viewed as theologically well gifted. In the following, we shall deal with IGT's Christology, epistemology and hermeneutics, ethics, and theology of creation and anthropology.

---

1. The verdict of Schneider, *Evangelia Infantiae*, 37 is particularly unmerciful: IGT is "theologisch unerhört banal." Van Voorst, *Jesus Outside the New Testament*, 205 states that it has a "crude emphasis on miracles." Cf. also Rebell, *Neutestamentliche Apokryphen*, 125.

2. Cameron, *Other Gospels*, 123.

3. For an anti-Jewish profile, see p. 7; also Hurtado, *Lord Jesus*, 451. If there is such hostility in IGT, it appears far less virulent than in some NT writings, for example the gospels of Matthew and John. For a non-theological agenda in IGT, see Ehrman, *Lost Christianities*, 204–6.

Christology in Earlier Scholarship

Christology is the most important theological issue in IGT and has received attention from several scholars. Usually, their focus has been on the problematic features in IGT's portrait of Jesus and not on its Christology in general.[4] Some scholars see in IGT the result of a negative historical development: it reflects a degeneration of elevated NT Christology into shallow entertainment and folklore.[5] The view is more of a value judgment than the outcome of actual analysis, however. Chapter 8 showed that IGT's biblical heritage is richer than has been assumed and the same point will be argued here as concerns its Christology.[6]

Other scholars allow for more specific christological interests in it. Some detect docetic tendencies (p. 3) and see in Jesus' maturity and superhuman character evidence of this.[7] However, this does not fit well with IGT's Jesus: he is depicted as fully human both in appearance and actions; he has a material body, shows emotions, feels pain, and moves and behaves like a human being (pp. 100–101). In brief, there is little docetic about him. Consequently, a few scholars also hold an opposite view, that IGT presents an anti-docetic polemic.[8] But this too is mere speculation: there are no traces of such an apologetic front in the text. And the fact that the material can be used to argue opposite positions suggests that such an approach is misleading.[9]

More scholars have held that IGT's Christology is gnostic. Within this view, IGT's Jesus is seen as modeled upon a gnostic redeemer figure.[10] This has proven a long-lived opinion and has even led scholars

4. Chartrand-Burke's criticism of different views is much to the point, see esp. his assessments in "Infancy Gospel," 95–99.

5. For example Vielhauer, *Geschichte*, 675–77; Schindler, *Apokryphen*, 439.

6. Among the few so far to speak in favor of IGT's theological sophistication is Gero, "Infancy Gospel," 69.

7. See the survey in Cullmann, "Infancy Gospels," 391–92; also Nicolas, *Études*, 333–35. The view is repeated in Currie, "Childhood and Christianity," 206–7.

8. Cf. the references in Chartrand-Burke, "Infancy Gospel," 296–97.

9. I here agree with ibid., 297–98.

10. For example Santos Otero, *Das kirchenslavische Evangelium*, 172–78; Schneider, *Evangelia Infantiae*, 37–38. For a discussion and rejection of this view, see Chartrand-Burke, "Infancy Gospel," 67, 70–71. Recently, van Aarde has argued that IGT reflects ebionite Christology; his arguments are weak, however (see p. 10 above). His default text (Cod. Sin. Gr. 453) may have such a coloring, although I question this. The text of Gs/H gives no support to the view.

to extensive allegorization of individual episodes in IGT.[11] The view has often been based on external evidence, primarily the church father Irenaeus (130–202 CE) who linked 1–3 Teacher up with the Marcosians, a gnostic group. In spite of the weak basis for Irenaeus' view (cf. pp. 174–76), it has held much research in a firm grip and led to the many strained tradition-historical theories about gnostic addition/orthodox expurgation.[12]

Gnostic attribution of IGT has of course also been based on a study of the material itself. But the arguments have been weak. For example, terms such as "bear fruit" (8:1), IGT's descriptions of the amazement caused by Jesus (2:5; 6:1, 6), and its notions about wisdom and about Jesus as all-knowing revealer and savior, have been taken as signs of such a background.[13] However, these terms and ideas are also well-known from the NT and are not used by IGT in typically gnostic ways. IGT's alpha speculation has been read in the same light, but on insufficient grounds (cf. pp. 143–46). In addition, the view is often argued on the basis of outdated or too rigid perceptions of Gnosticism and its historical developments.[14] Thus, elements that have been regarded gnostic are more readily understood as reflecting common—yet variable—early Christian christological heritage. Finally, the view is also methodologically problematic, since it has been based on a faulty textual basis, viz., on texts that are composite and thus unfit for such analysis.[15] Gnostic influence in some IGT traditions can of course not be ruled out, but must in the future be explored in each variant and manuscript (pp. 23 and 33).

11. For an example, Baars and Helderman, "Neue Materialien" (parts I–II). I agree with the criticism by Chartrand-Burke, "Infancy Gospel," 88; see also the research history in ibid., e.g. 66, 70, 97, 99. For an allegorizing approach, see van Aarde (cf. p. 10 above).

12. In addition, the early mixing up with *Gos. Thom.* has strongly contributed to preserving the idea of a gnostic Jesus, even after the publication of this gospel (see pp. 3–6).

13. Cf. also the use of "sons of the bridal chamber" in the Church Slavonic version. However, the expression is also used in the NT (Matt 9:15 par.) and often in the early church fathers.

14. Cf. the criticism in Chartrand-Burke, "Infancy Gospel," 88–89; also King, *What Is Gnosticism?*

15. With the exception of Baars and Helderman, "Neue Materialien" (parts I–II), which analyzes a Syriac manuscript, but which is burdened by other methodological problems.

Chartrand-Burke is the only scholar to deal with Christology in IGT at length, seeing in its Jesus a reflection of the Jewish holy man in combination with elements from the NT Jesus. Although the latter is in my view correct, the former is more questionable (see pp. 132–34, 90, and 101–2). In his presentation, however, he primarily bases his view on a comparison with sources outside IGT and only to a limited degree on an in-depth study of the text itself.[16] However, to get a satisfactory picture of IGT's Jesus it is again necessary to turn to the story itself, and in some detail.

Christology in IGT

At first glance, even Christology seems to have a limited place in IGT. For example, the death and resurrection of Jesus, so central for example in the theology of Paul, is at the most only hinted at (cf. pp. 44 and 132). Christological titles are used very occasionally and with little emphasis: Jesus is called Christ only in the secondary prolog (1:1), and Lord (κύριος) only in the prolog and in Zeno (9:3). Even with Zeno it is not clear whether it functions as polite address or as a confession. But the latter seems to be the case, since the address follows after Jesus has resuscitated him; it also appears unnatural that a child should address another child as "lord." Titles such as son of God, son of David, son of Man, and Messiah do not occur.

On a second look, however, the Jesus portrait turns out to be richer in nuances. This is seen in some implicit references to christological titles. IGT appears to be familiar with Jesus as Alpha and Omega, "the beginning and the end" (Rev 21:6; 22:13): at his failure in teaching Jesus letters, Zacchaeus concedes that he himself falls short in understanding the alpha and confesses that he knows "neither the beginning nor the end" (7:3; cf. p. 122). In addition, IGT obviously considers Jesus to be the Son of God: the idea of Jesus in the temple being in his "Father's house" is without reservation taken over from Luke (17:3; cf. pp. 79 and 116).

The prominent place of Christology is more visible in other ways, however. First, Jesus is portrayed as a miracle worker. Since miracles

---

16. Thus, he speaks of a Christology "behind" the text; Chartrand-Burke, "Infancy Gospel," 292.

occupy considerable space in IGT, this emerges as a central feature. Clearly, it also reflects its central place in the NT depiction of Jesus, particularly in Mark (see pp. 114–15). And although IGT's description also has elements in common with OT and other antique miracle workers, the NT gospels seem to be IGT's main sources (cf. pp. 129 and 132–34).[17]

As in the NT the miracles in IGT underscore Jesus' divine power. This is clear from the spectators' responses: they see it as coming from God (9:3; 10:2; 12:2; cf. Luke 5:17–26 par.). Differently from the Synoptics, however, the miracles do not signal the presence of the kingdom of God: the expression is never used in IGT. With its focus on the role of Jesus, IGT's depiction owes far more to the gospel of John: Jesus is no ordinary miracle worker; rather, he may be "a god, an angel, or whatever else" (7:4; see pp. 120–21 and 123).

Characteristic of IGT's miracle worker is his power to curse (3:2; 4:1–2; 8:2; 13:2). This feature, however, is also well-known from the Bible (cf. pp. 122 and 129). Even Jesus is portrayed in the NT as having such ability, as are other NT figures: in the Synoptics, Jesus curses the fig tree (Matt 21:18–22 par.), disbelieving towns (Luke 10:13–15 par.), and the scribes and Pharisees (Matt 23:13–36; Luke 11:39–52). In John, he proclaims his curse over those who reject him (8:31–58). Disciples are allowed to curse (Luke 9:5; 10:10–12 par.). In addition, in Acts Peter causes Ananias and Sapphira to die (5:1–11), and Paul blinds the prophet Bar-Jesus (13:6–12).[18]

Moreover, Jesus is presented as teacher in IGT. He is not an ordinary teacher, however, but one who outdoes all others (1–3 Teacher; Jesus in Temple). Like the adult Jesus of Matthew and John (e.g., Matt 5:17–21; John 1:17–18), he is teacher par excellance: he has supreme knowledge (6:5; 7:1). He does not need to be taught, but is the one to teach (6:4, 9; 7:2). He sticks to the law, not wanting to read anything but "God's law" (14:2). At the same time, he also—like the NT Jesus—stands above the Law, with the right to perform miracles on the Sabbath (2:3). His divine powers are manifested in his teaching: spectators are left speechless

17. In Injured Foot, Gd characterizes Jesus as the "healer of sicknesses, our Lord Jesus Christ" (10:2). Gd appears to emphasize Jesus as healer: at the end of the temple episode, he is said to be healing the sicknesses of all (Gd 19:5/Gs 17:5).

18. Similar instances also occur in other early Christian literature: Acts Pet. 2; 32; Acts Paul 4–5; Acts Thom. 6–8; Acts John 37–45.

(6:7), in awe (17:2), and even in despair (7:1–4), and his words become deed (2:1; 4:1).

As part of his teacher role, Jesus is revealer. He has insight that is not acquired from any human source: he knows the secret principles of each and every letter (6:8, 10; 7:1, 3). He speaks what is unknown to humans (8:1). Instead of reading from a book, he by himself utters awe-inspiring words (14:2). He is also able to explain "the riddles and the parables of the prophets" (17:2). In brief, he teaches "a teaching . . . no one else knows or is able to teach" (6:4).[19]

Central to Jesus' teaching is that he brings wisdom: he states himself that he has come to let "the foolish in heart become wise" (8:1). The third teacher confirms this by saying that he "is full of much . . . wisdom" (14:3). Jesus is to "let the unfruitful bear fruit" (8:1), which may mean to make people come to faith or to live in accordance with their faith. He is also "full of much grace" (14:3; also 17:5). The linking of "wisdom" and "grace" in 14:3 seems to reflect 17:5/Luke 2:52, and thus emphasize the centrality of these concepts in IGT's understanding of Jesus.

Not much is said about the contents of Jesus' "wisdom" (or "fruit," "grace"). Two things are important to note, however. First, there seems to be a point in the very unintelligibility of Jesus' sayings. His interpretation of the alpha was, as argued above (pp. 145–46), probably an abracadabra to IGT's author and audience alike. At the same time, this row of strange words can have served to show Jesus' otherworldly character and his overwhelming wisdom. IGT shares this sense of enigma as concerns parts of Jesus' teaching with the NT gospels, but puts less effort in explaining this wisdom than they do (cf. Mark 4:1–34 par.; John 6:22–65).

Second, IGT's "wisdom" is closely associated with Jesus' mission. This is most explicitly expressed in his statement at the end of 1 Teacher:

> Now let the unfruitful bear fruit, the blind see, and the foolish
> in heart become wise. For I have come from above in order to
> rescue those below and call them to what is above, just as the
> one who sent me to you ordered me. (8:1)

19. This way of thinking has much in common with the gospel of John (3:11–12; 7:28–29 etc.). On the use of riddles in antiquity and in John, see Thatcher, *The Riddles of Jesus in John*.

Here, the wisdom that "the foolish in heart" are to find is that Jesus has "come from above" and that he acts on behalf of God, "as the one who sent me . . . ordered me." To embrace wisdom thus means to realize who Jesus is and to receive him. As indicated (pp. 120–21), this has much in common, both in wording and thinking, with the gospel of John. Although "wisdom" is a favorite word within Gnosticism, such terminology is also common in NT writings, particularly the gospels, Paul's letters, and the Deutero-Paulines. And the little that is said about wisdom in IGT has close parallels in the canonical texts and probably has its main roots there.

Furthermore, central to Jesus' mission in IGT is that he is savior: he has come to "rescue (ῥύσωμαι) those below," by calling them "to what is above" (8:1). He saves (σῴζω) those who have come under his curse (8:2). The second teacher is "saved" on account of the third teacher (14:4). And at a crucial point in the story, at the end of the last raising miracle and before the final episode, the crowd summarizes much of the morale of the story concerning Jesus: "he has indeed saved ([ἔσω]σεν) many souls from death. And he will go on saving (ἔχει σῶσαι) all the days of his life" (16:3). Jesus' saving activity here comprises both the healing of bodily ills (blindness and death) and the eternal blessings given to human "souls." Even his mere presence brings salvation. For example, Zacchaeus says to Joseph: "Take him with salvation (σωτηρία) to your house" (7:4; also 14:1, 3). Although the expression "with salvation" can be interpreted as being a greeting only, its repeated use and at central places in the episodes, point to a deeper meaning.

Finally, and also important, is IGT's presentation of Jesus' relation to God. In addition to having God as father (17:3) and being his gift (12:2; 17:4) and ambassador (8:1), Jesus is equipped with a number of divine qualities. He is superhuman, "not of this earth" (γηγενής, 7:2).[20] This notion is also found in the NT, especially in John (see p. 124). Furthermore, Jesus is omniscient: whereas others repeatedly betray their limited understanding (4:1; 5:3 etc.), Jesus knows people's minds (6:7), human history (6:6), the meaning of the letters (6:8), the solution to problems (10:2; 12:1–2), the Law (6:4; 14:2), and even God's will (8:1)—in brief, his knowledge equals God's. Again, this has much in common with the all-knowing Jesus in John (e.g., John 4:18; 6:64). IGT's

20. The Greek word does not occur in the NT, but in the LXX (Ps 48:3; Prov 9:18; Wis 7:1) and in Greek literature (Herodotus and Plato).

Jesus also has the same unshakable nature: he does not let himself be unduly influenced by other people (2:4; 5:3; cf. John 2:4; 10:17–18).

Moreover, Jesus is almighty: he has the power of a divine creator. IGT's creation story presents a micro-cosmos (2–3): Jesus orders the water into pools and purifies it "only by means of a word" (2:1; pp. 128 and 162–63). He also has the power to give and take life (2:2–4; 4:1 etc.). He can change the laws of nature (10:2; 11:2; 12:2). And he has the right to perform judgment (3:2; 4:1 etc.). Thus, IGT presents Jesus as closely related to God and with a number of features associated with him—a description similar to the high Christology of John (e.g., 1:1–18), but also to the NT christological hymns.[21] We should note, however, that Jesus is not—despite his nearness to God—made identical with him. There are obvious differences: he is for example sent by God, under his command (8:1), and blessed by him (17:4).

In sum, Jesus emerges in IGT as a divine figure: he is miracle worker, teacher, revealer, bringer of wisdom, savior, and co-equal with God. This picture is neither one-sided nor heretical in character, and can in no way be said to go beyond what we find in central NT writings. In fact, the depiction appears very much dependent on the NT, especially the gospels, and follows them loyally without retouching the picture. It is also evident that IGT's divine Jesus owes particularly much to the gospel of John.[22]

What we have in the Jesus of IGT, then, is a portrait of Jesus as a divine figure, but also as the all-too-human child described earlier (p. 102). As noted (pp. 87–92), scholars have had great difficulties in combining these two sides into a coherent whole and have tried to come to terms with it through various strategies of interpretation. In particular, they have attempted to evade the problem by disputing Jesus' divine and human side respectively: in the former case by denigrating IGT's theology or by giving it a heretical brand, in the latter case by weakening Jesus' humanity by seeing him as an idealized child.[23]

---

21. Cf. John 1:1–18; Eph 1:3–14; Phil 2:6–11; Col 1:15–20.

22. Cf. also Chartrand-Burke, "Strange New Sayings," subchapter 5 (conclusion). There also are similarities between IGT and John in how Jesus' emotions are presented, cf. Voorwinde, *Jesus' Emotions in the Fourth Gospel*.

23. Chartrand-Burke, "Infancy Gospel," 314 holds that "any assessment of the Christology behind the text must be made without thought to the fact that Jesus is here presented as a child."

In my opinion, such views underrate the theological reflection in IGT and thus fail in dealing adequately with its depiction of Jesus. Instead, the story gives evidence of radical theological reflection, of Jesus as God incarnated (see pp. 141–42): IGT's Jesus is no less divine than the one found in the NT and no less human than a true-to-life late antiquity child. Jesus is in IGT not fully divine/partly human or partly divine/fully human, he is fully divine and fully human. To put it squarely, but precisely: in the *Infancy Gospel of Thomas*, Jesus is not only true God and true human, he is true God and true child.

Epistemology and Hermeneutics:
Ways and Aims of Understanding

The words "faith" and "belief" are never used in IGT. Disbelief is only hinted at (6:6, ἀπιστεῖτε). Not even the NT chief interpreter, the Spirit, is spoken of; thus, pneumatology at least in a narrow sense appears to play no role.[24] Nonetheless, the issue of understanding and interpretation is markedly present in IGT. This is shown in its rich epistemological vocabulary, particularly terms such as ἐπιστήμη, γινώσκω, οἶδα, παιδεία, σύνεσις, and σοφία. This is a feature that has contributed to the gnostic labeling of IGT, but unjustly, since it is also typical of many biblical writings, such as the OT wisdom literature and the Johannine and Pauline writings (see pp. 123–25).

IGT emphasizes the need for understanding. Insight is praised, and can make good things happen. For instance, Jesus credits Joseph for having some—though limited—understanding of his words (5:1). Zacchaeus' confession of ignorance makes Jesus save those previously cursed (7:1—8:1). The wisdom of the third teacher saves his predecessor (14:4). Lack of insight is similarly blamed: Joseph has a "natural ignorance" and does "not see (εἶδες)" (5:3). Zacchaeus does not understand what he should understand (6:4). And the Jews have "never known such words" as those of Jesus (6:5).

The epistemological process itself is also of interest for IGT: understanding primarily comes about by being taught. The first teacher needs to be instructed about the alpha (6:9). Joseph is to be "taught a teaching"

---

24. In 3 Teacher, Jesus in Ga/Gd speaks in the Holy Spirit and teaches the law (Ga/Gd 15:2; Gs 14:2).

(6:4). Joseph needs to "see with light" the relationship between Jesus and himself (5:3); the expression can imply that he has to be "enlightened" by Jesus or God. Through teaching one is able to "know" (6:2; 6:9) and to acquire "understanding" and "wisdom" (ἐπιστήμη, 6:2; σοφία, 8:1). Jesus of course possesses such an understanding (6:6; 7:2; 17:4), which enables him to call people "to what is above" (8:1).

IGT emphasizes three aims of understanding. First, and central, is that people acknowledge who Jesus is (cf. pp. 154–55). This is presented as a matter of life and death: some who fail in this die (3:3; 4:1; 13:2). Such understanding is attainable, however. This is demonstrated in the growing recognition of Jesus in the last half of IGT (cf. pp. 45–47). The author also clearly presupposes that its implied audience has an adequate understanding of Jesus.

The second aim is to understand the "order" (6:10) and "principles" (7:1) of the first letter. This, however, is unattainable for all characters in the story, except for Jesus—it is his privilege alone. In fact, it is not even expected from IGT's audience (cf. pp. 145–46).

The third aim is to be able to interpret Scripture. The importance of this is shown in the somewhat illogical shift that takes place within the story: whereas 1–2 Teacher focus on learning letters and their mean-ing (6–8; 13), attention is in 3 Teacher directed toward reading and understanding Scripture ("God's law," 14:2; cf. p. 81). This is presented as a special ability in Jesus, the interpreter par excellance (14:2–3; cf. pp. 153–54). Implicit in this, however, is that the interpretation of Scripture is an important matter also for IGT's audience.

The issue of Scripture interpretation is taken further in Jesus in Temple (17), in which Jesus is again presented as the unique teacher. Differently from Luke, IGT 17:2b not only reports the amazement at Jesus' insight and answers, but also summarizes his teaching:

> he examined the elders and explained the main points (τὰ κεφάλαια) of the Law and the riddles (τὰ σκολιὰ) and the parables (τὰς παραβολάς) of the prophets.

Several points deserve notice here (see also pp. 81 and 116–17). First, IGT shows familiarity with the OT here as an entity and takes its two-fold division—the law and the prophets—for granted. Furthermore, Jesus' preaching is—as in Luke—basically related to the interpretation of the Old Testament. Apart from focusing on his own role and on the meaning of the alpha, Jesus in IGT does little to express the contents of his message. Thus, IGT's interest in Scripture is the more striking, also considering its few OT references. This supports the impression that the issue of Old Testament interpretation was of special concern—IGT is groping with problems related to this. But in what ways and for what reasons? Its characterization of Scripture in 17:2b may give some hints.

The issue of interpretation is first signalled in the word κεφάλαια, which in Greek literature is common for "main points"; for instance, Philo uses the term frequently.[25] The term occurs in a similar sense only in Dan 7:1 in the Septuagint and in Heb 8:1 in the NT; however, it is not linked up with the Law in any of them. It also occurs in *Shepherd of Hermas*, as summarizing the word pair "commandments" (ἐντολάς) and "parables" (παραβολάς).[26] The uncommon use of the term may reflect uncertainty on the part of IGT's author and audience about the position of the Law and a need of assistance in sorting out its central elements.

The challenge of interpretation is more visible, however, in the description of the prophets as containing "riddles" and "parables." The term σκολιά does not occur in the NT in a substantival sense. The Septuagint employs it several times, but mainly as an adjective and in a derogatory sense, meaning "crooked" or "perverse" (cf. Prov 23:33; Hos 9:8). In IGT, σκολιά appears to be used more neutrally, of something difficult or enigmatic.[27] The term παραβολάς, which can also be translated "proverb" or "oracle" (cf. Num 23:7; 1 Kgs 5:12; Sir 13:26), should probably be understood similarly. Although the term is frequent in the Synoptics (but never in John), its use in connection with the prophets is uncommon.

Together, these two terms indicate that IGT tries to deal with a situation in which the Old Testament has become less intelligible: neither the Law nor the prophets are clear in meaning. The need for interpretation has become stronger. This is a need which Jesus is in a position to handle, but which IGT itself does nothing to remedy, neither here nor elsewhere—possibly because its author was unable to do so.

---

25. See Borgen, *Philo Index*, 178.

26. Herm. *Vis.* 5.1.5(-6).

27. See also Liddell and Scott, *Greek-English Lexicon*, ad loc; Thatcher, *The Riddles of Jesus in John*.

These analyses indicate, then, that IGT reflects a situation in which the Old Testament is still central Christian heritage, but also has come to pose considerable problems of interpretation. This agrees well with the overall impression that IGT belongs within a non-Jewish context.[28]

Ethics: An Unchristian Jesus in IGT?

Ethics has a limited place in IGT. For example, although the "law" (17:2) and "God's law" (14:2) are mentioned, they are not developed on as sources for ethics and morality in particular. Still, it is not true—as has been stated—that IGT and its Jesus are immoral or amoral.[29] As shown (pp. 73–85), the story is very much concerned with issues related to attitudes and behavior: it presupposes and promotes positive values such as love of those one's own age, respect toward the older generation, obedience, helpfulness, and generosity toward people on the margins. Thus, criticism of IGT's ethics has been too fixed on its potentially problematic aspects. Instead, its morality should be seen as fundamentally of a traditional and far from unchristian kind.

IGT is fundamentally also very much in agreement with the "turning the tables" motif that frequently appears in the OT (cf. Gen 37–50 [the Joseph cycle]; and Isa 52:13—53:12) and in the NT (cf. Jesus' many sayings and parables about the least and the greatest; cf. also p. 130). Such upheaval of the given order is a leitmotif throughout IGT and particularly in the episodes about Joseph and the teachers (see pp. 79–84).

We should note that IGT does not touch on any of the morality issues that were important in contemporary Christian literature, such as asceticism, celibacy, virginity, and martyrdom. Some of them are for instance central in the *Infancy Gospel of James'* story about Mary, and in the apocryphal acts' accounts about the lives of the apostles. Although such issues are of course not likely to be focused in a story about Jesus' childhood, they may nonetheless be expected to surface or at least to be hinted at. However, IGT shows no interest in such issues at all. Very

---

28. The vague way of dealing with Scripture can signal a social and theological milieu somewhat at a remove from the main centers of learned early Christian exegesis (which were located in big cities such as Alexandria, Antioch, Ephesus, and Rome). Again, this may point in the direction of a non-elite, non-urban setting for IGT.

29. Cf. Elliott, *Apocryphal New Testament*, 68, on a Jesus who "seldom acts in a Christian way" (see p. 86 above).

likely, this is because they were of little relevance for its author and audience (cf. p. 211). This feature also sets IGT off clearly from its "twin," the *Infancy Gospel of James*.

One special feature need to be addressed here, however, not least since it has been considered problematic and even repulsive, namely Jesus' cursing. Why does he act so destructively so as to curse children and adults alike, even causing them to die? As noted, scholars have tried to explain this by means of various history of religion parallels or by the crudity of IGT's audience (p. 88). However, the embarrassment should be countered in other ways.

First, it should be explained theologically: despite IGT's generally positive morality, the main emphasis of its story is not ethical. It may even miss the mark to measure the gospel on the basis of certain notions about morality and how Jesus should act—not least if they reflect modern and not ancient concerns. In fact, IGT itself shows awareness of the problematic nature of Jesus' cursing: Joseph gives expression to this, when he states that his behavior makes people "suffer and hate us" (5:1; also 4:2). Instead, the cursing should be seen as reflecting IGT's strongly christological focus: the gospel aims at demonstrating Jesus' superiority and power. The point of departure for the author is that Jesus is different from and beyond other human beings. And as a divine person he has the sovereign right to give and take life. This does not mean that he acts arbitrarily. On the contrary, his cursing is just. For IGT, the problem is not on the part of Jesus, but on the part of those being cursed: they should already at the outset have realized who he is and thus not have challenged him.[30] Stated in narrative terms: this is what the implied author and readers already know, and what the characters of the stories should have known. And when they fail to do so, the outcome is often fatal. Thus, theological concerns take the lead over moral interest: ethics is made subordinate to Christology.

Second, Jesus' cursing should also be explained by IGT's roots in folktale tradition and its narrative laws (see pp. 25–31 and 52). Here, a fundamental principle is: all's well that ends well. IGT sticks to this rule: Annas' son (3:3), the careless boy (4:1), the blinded accusers (5:1)—all are healed. As IGT later takes care to tell: "immediately all those who had fallen under his curse were saved" (8:2). The teacher

---

30. Cf. Bauer, *Leben Jesu*, 91–92.

who dies is also vivified (13:2; 14:3). This even takes place "some days after" (14:1). The indication of such a time interval probably serves to emphasize the greatness of the miracle. But it also signals that we here move within the time frame of legend. And within it such an illogical element (the teacher should according to custom have already been buried) poses no problem—this is the world of magical realism. Thus, IGT adheres to the rule, so that by the end of the story all problems are solved.[31] Things have turned out fine, thanks to the wonderboy Jesus.

There is one conspicuous exception to this, however: the child Zeno. Surprisingly, Gs states that Jesus after waking him up makes him return to death by saying: "Fall asleep" (9:3). Why this happens, is far from clear. It can be that his death was regarded natural or nonsensational, despite that it was an accident. It is worth noting, however, that Zeno in the other Greek variants remains alive (see p. 29). Thus, his fate appears to reflect some idiosyncrasy in Gs or in its process of transmission.[32]

True, these explanations does not take away all sense of offense as concerns Jesus' cursing. To an extent, we are in IGT left with a special portrait of Jesus. But it is a portrait that clearly has roots in the NT and that need not be more challenging than some of the depictions of him found there. And even if IGT's Jesus should suit our modern taste less than desired, he may nonetheless have made very good sense to IGT's early Christian audience.[33] Probably, this Jesus was fundamentally in keeping with their perceptions both of childhood and of divinity, thus presenting to them a fully credible portrait of Jesus, true God and true child. With this, we are in any case left with a picture of Jesus far less problematic than that which has, with few exceptions, been offered within IGT research.

Theology of Creation and Anthropology

A theology of creation does not have a central position in IGT. Nevertheless, a view of creation is implied and serves as a necessary supposition for theological issues more central to IGT. Clearly, God is creator, and in IGT's cosmology the world is seen as created by him

31. See the story of Job (42:10–17) for a biblical example.

32. Ga/Gd occasionally appear to be more apologetic on the part of Jesus' behavior than Gs (9:2–3; 14:4; 17:3).

33. Cf. also Chartrand-Burke, "Infancy Gospel," 314–15.

(7:2, κοσμοποιΐα; also 6:6), [34] with 2:1–3 being a typological counterpart to Genesis 1–2. God is the giver of life: the child Jesus is his gift to Joseph (12:2). He is also the provider of life's blessings (10:2; 17:4) and of wisdom and grace (17:5). Obviously, God and the creation are seen as fundamentally good: God is no gnostic demiurge and the world no evil substance. God is also the source of a more special revelation, the law (14:2). For all he has given, human beings are supposed to praise and glorify him (9:3; 17:5).

Thus, although IGT does not focus on theology of creation per se, God has a matter-of-fact place in the story, and the picture given is traditional and in no way theologically deviant.

Little is said about anthropology, i.e. of the identity structure, the social role, or the existential state of human beings. What is stated is generally inconspicuous: humans are described as "souls" (16:3, ψυχὰς) and as lacking in knowledge of the divine (5:3; 6:7 etc.). Sin is not spoken of, nor are evil forces such as demons. Nonetheless, human beings are seen as being in need of rescue, "salvation" (8:2; 14:4; 16:3). And what they primarily have to be saved from is death. In IGT, this is presented as the only, but very serious, threat against human beings (cf. p. 76). In fact, all health miracles—both cursing and healing miracles—revolve around the issue of life/death (except for the blinding in 5:1). Thus, IGT almost exclusively focuses on miracles of the most drastic kind. Although such miracles also occur in the NT, IGT's repertoire is nonetheless far narrower.

What can be the reason for this focus? The single, rather unconvincing, explanation offered has been that it reflects a vulgarizing of taste from the first Christian generation to the post NT period. [35] There must, however, be better and less disparaging reasons for this focus—but this is a matter that we shall return to later (pp. 208–9). [36]

---

34. On the reading of 6:6 (probably corrupt), see p. 142.

35. See for example Cullmann, "Infancy Gospels," 416–17, 442.

36. One—admittedly rather speculative—way of accounting for it is to see in it a reflection of a general emphasis in Eastern theology, cf. IGT's provenance, on death being characteristic of the human lot (rather than sin).

Conclusion: The Theological Profile of IGT

Chapter 8 showed that there is more of biblical legacy in IGT than has been assumed, and in chapter 9 it was demonstrated that IGT (Gs), despite some idiosyncrasy, does not represent deviation, but is compatible with commonplace early Christian thinking. The analyses in the present chapter have confirmed the impression of its unexceptional, "mainstream" character: nothing can be said to differ from what is already found within central NT writings.

IGT takes up a broader specter of theological matters than has been held, despite the fact that many are not touched on. Considering its special subject, IGT cannot be expected to present a "complete" theology; still, it manages within its brief format to deal with several such issues.

Furthermore, IGT is more theologically reflected than has been acknowledged. Its theology is not formulated through reasoning, however, such as in the letters of Paul. Nor can it be distilled by means of some kind of allegorical reading, as has been attempted (cf. pp. 150–51). Instead, theology is in IGT—apart from the brief speeches and a few sayings—expressed in historical-narrative form, through Jesus' actions and reactions, often with emotional coloring. It is theology narratively patterned and transmitted. This does not make IGT theologically inferior or shallow, as many critics have held by measuring it against some alien, often intellectual, standard. Rather, IGT should be read on its own terms: it is shaping and communicating its message through its own special and powerful medium, namely storytelling. It performs this in a way similar to for instance the gospel of Mark, and not necessarily less competently than it.

IGT clearly also has a theological profile of its own, with both major and minor theological emphases. Among the latter are ethics, creation theology, and anthropology, which all fall well into line with biblical tradition, as does the turning-of-tables motif. The same is the case with the major issues Christology and epistemology. As for the interest in the latter, this can partly be occasioned by a need in IGT's milieu to come to terms with problems of hermeneutics. In addition, it serves to put focus on Jesus: he is the only to have perfect understanding and consequently the only to be fully able to interpret Scripture.

Obviously, Christology occupies the main role in IGT's theological shooting script; this is seen in the centrality of Jesus. But it also becomes clear in the manner in which other theological issues are linked up with it. They do not only serve to direct attention to IGT's Jesus figure; it also works the opposite way round: Christology contributes to solving problems within other theological areas. With his perfect understanding Jesus can interpret Scripture, even if others are unable to do so. And the problem of his immorality (almost) dissolves when one realizes who Jesus is: the one sent by God. Thus, both epistemology and ethics are made subject to Christology.

As has been shown, Jesus emerges in the Christology of IGT as a combination of a divine Christ and a true-to-life child. Little indeed has been found to support the idea of a docetic or a gnostic figure. The disastrous stumbling stone of heresy should be put aside, or placed at an extreme outpost, in future research. The theology of IGT is fundamentally based on NT heritage and moves well within the range of early Christian mainstream thinking and faith. It may indeed be a worthy representative of such a theology.

11

A Popular Tale from Early Rural Christianity

What was the aim of IGT? And who was its audience? These are two closely interconnected questions to be dealt with in this chapter. Some ideas of how they can be answered have been hinted at earlier (esp. chaps. 4–5). Now, however, I shall synthesize and develop more systematically on the matter.

It has been an assumption in previous chapters to see in IGT's narrative world a reflection not primarily of first-century Palestine, but of the setting in which the story was transmitted, namely late antique Christianity—although the differences between the two need not be exaggerated. Nothing has so far made this assumption improbable. On the contrary, the biotope emerging from the analyses appears to have much in common with what has been portrayed in research on the late antique countryside and its population (pp. 69–72 and 84–85). Nor has there been any indication of a distance or tension between IGT's implicit audience and what may have been its historical addressees—IGT seems narratively quite unsophisticated in this matter.[1] Thus, I will in this and the next chapter pursue a similar reading of IGT.

Whereas focus up to this point has primarily been on text-internal elements, this chapter will also draw on more external material. The objective will be to collect evidence as to what can plausibly have been IGT's aim and audience, but also to present a more general sketch of

1. Treu, "Der antike Roman und sein Publikum," 186–89, discusses in what way the audience is reflected in the Hellenistic novels, *i.e.* whether these stories depict the actual world of the addressees, their everyday life, or the opposite, a world of longings and dreams, and concludes with the latter. In the case of IGT, the former is more probable, as I have argued on several occasions in this book.

IGT's dispersion and reception. I shall first develop on the issues of *Sitz im Leben*, communication settings, and social location, and then turn to IGT's reception history, chronological and geographical dispersion, and position in the manuscript tradition.

The *Sitz im Leben* of IGT

Research has so far dealt only superficially with the question about IGT's *Sitz im Leben*. Often, it has been the object of guess work; at other times more qualified approaches have been attempted. Many scholars have, as noted, relegated IGT to the fringes of early Christianity. The analyses above have given no support to such views. A few scholars have suggested that IGT served polemical aims, for example as criticism of Jews and Judaism.[2] However, IGT has at best a distant relationship to Judaism, and it is not possible to discern such a cutting edge; indeed, tensions of this kind appear considerably higher in many NT writings. Nor has it been possible to see in IGT criticism of other Christians, whether gnostic, docetic, or other.[3] Missionary purposes have also been proposed, but have no support in the text itself.[4] Other functions could also be considered, particularly the apologetic and the kerygmatic. It is, however, difficult to envisage settings in which it would serve as apology vis-à-vis outsiders or be used in preaching.[5]

Several scholars have advanced a "filling-the-gap" theory about IGT, with human curiosity being the impetus for its creation: Christians were eager to hear more about the life of their hero and particularly periods not dealt with in the canonical gospels.[6] Thus, IGT was produced in order to make up for this lacuna and meet such a need. This theory clearly has something to it and finds support in similar material, for

2. Chartrand-Burke, "Infancy Gospel," 32–33, 43–44, 398–99.

3. Ibid., "Authorship and Identity," 27–43, esp. 34–37, argues that IGT was part of an internal-Christian discussion on Christology, viz., between Johannine and Thomasine Christians, possibly within a Syrian milieu. However, in ibid., "Infancy Gospel," 82, he self-critically rejects his earlier view.

4. So Cameron, *Other Gospels*, 123.

5. Rather unfounded, Chartrand-Burke, "Infancy Gospel," 264, considers IGT to be "a historical allegory," with Jesus personifying Christian claims of superiority against threats from outsiders.

6. See for example Cullmann, "Infancy Gospels," 416–17; Klauck, *Apocryphal Gospels*, 64.

example the NT infancy stories and other ancient biographical writings (see pp. 87–92), and also in similar developments in other apocryphal material. But beyond pointing to possible psychological presuppositions, the theory does not contribute much to a deeper understanding of IGT's aim and audience—I shall below be presenting a more plausible explanation for this interest in Jesus' early years (see pp. 209–10). Implicitly, however, this theory serves to normalize the gospel as a product of general human inquisitiveness rather than of some "esoteric" religious attitude.

Occasionally, IGT has been seen as a story primarily for entertainment.[7] This too has something to it. As I have argued, IGT has many such qualities, for example humor, liveliness, and drama—in this it has much in common with the Hellenistic novels, one of whose functions clearly was to entertain.[8] But this is still saying too little about it. It is a universally accepted insight within the study of literature that no stories are only entertaining: they always aim at imparting a message in their audiences, whether of ethical, ideological or other character. And there is no reason why IGT should be an exception to this.

Within this spectrum of potential function for IGT, the last two seem the most appropriate, viz., the informative and the entertaining. One more function, however, should be added, namely the edifying. Although a few scholars have suggested this, it has not been developed. But as I have shown, IGT is concerned with mediating a positive message, both directly (esp. Christology) and indirectly (e.g., cultural values). Considering its form (narrative) and its central topic (Jesus and his childhood), the story emerges as well-suited for Christian edification. In this it has much in common with other early apocryphal material, although IGT's focus on Jesus and on Christology is stronger than in most of these writings.

From this the following picture emerges: IGT's purpose was to serve as both entertainment and edification for early Christians. Through this combination the story would further its message in a powerful way. In addition, it can have served to meet a demand for data about Jesus' early life, whether this information was considered factual or not.

---

7. See Schindler, *Apokryphen*, 439; Ehrman, *Lost Christianities*, 206.

8. On the audience of the Hellenistic novels, see Stephens, "Who Read Ancient Novels," 405–18; Hägg, *The Novel in Antiquity*, 91–101; also ibid., *Parthenope*, chap. 4.

The Audience of IGT: Settings of Communication

The question about IGT's audience has rarely been discussed with any precision. Here, it will be expedient to distinguish between the settings in which the story can have been communicated, and the people to whom it may have been directed; the former will be addressed in this section.

A variety of such settings can be envisaged, and storytelling is known to have taken place in all of them.[9] One such setting is early Christian meetings. It is quite unlikely, however, that IGT was used on a regular basis as readings in church services—and especially not after the canon had been firmly established. The lack of ecclesial art and church decoration related to IGT is an indication of this: whereas scenes from *Infancy Gospel of James* are found on several early altarpieces and paintings, none is known to come from IGT.[10] And nothing in the story itself, at least not in Gs, signals that it had its basis in the context of a Christian community.[11] Occasionally, IGT may have been told in less formal Christian meetings, however.

Family and household gatherings appear more likely as settings for the transmission of IGT. At home, stories were told at various points through the day, for example at meals, at times of relaxation, during routine activities, and in the twilight hour.[12] IGT is in both format and content well fit for such situations and for the audiences present there, whether the family was of a core or an extended type with more generations, servants, and slaves. The place given in IGT to family activities and values makes such a setting plausible (see chaps. 4–5).

9. For surveys of settings, see Anderson, *Fairytale*, 3–4; Shiner, *Proclaiming the Gospel*, chap. 2; Buxton, *Imaginary Greece*, 18–44. On early Jewish (and Christian) storytelling, see also Wire, *Holy Lives*.

10. For *Prot. Jas.*, see Cartlidge and Elliott, *Art and the Christian Apocrypha*, chap. 2. Interestingly, there are a few artistic depictions of IGT in eleventh- to fifteenth-century material, see ibid., 106–16.

11. This is against Chartrand-Burke, "Infancy Gospel," 264, who assumes that there was some kind of community behind the gospel, but without substantiating it.

12. For example John Chrysostom *Inan. glor.* 39–40; cf. Leyerle, "Appealing to Children," 255. See also Bowes, *Private Worship*, which regrettably appeared too late to be consulted in full for this book.

Places of work were also important contexts for storytelling, as diversion during monotonous activities in a workshop, on the field or during transport—all situations that are dealt with in IGT.[13]

A central occasion for storytelling, particularly among men, was the party (συμπόσιον, *triclinium*). This is well documented in sources such as Plato's (427–347 BCE) *Symposium*, Plutarch's *Banquet of the Seven Sages*, Petronius' (27–66 CE) *Satyrica*, and Apuleius' (123/125–ca. 180 CE) *The Golden Ass*.[14] Several of the stories told in them, some of which can be classified as fairytales, are also known from other types of literary sources.[15] This may also have been a setting for IGT, but possibly not a main setting.

Storytelling also occurred in public settings, such as at marketplaces, fairs, and taverns. Here, local storytellers would gather many eager listeners. Occasionally, itinerant professionals offered their services to those willing to hear and pay for a good story.[16] IGT may very well have been part of the repertoire of such persons too.

Finally, IGT can also have been used for individual reading. Such a setting, in which persons read themselves or were read for, is well-known from antique literature and art. Hellenistic novels, apocryphal acts and martyr stories were obviously used on such occasions. Often, the audience would be among the elite, since such reading presupposed a more than minimum level of literacy and also the presence of books.[17] Given its popular and distinctively oral shape, this is not likely to have been a main setting for IGT, though it may have been an occasional context for it. It has also been suggested that the story was used as leisure reading in the early monasteries.[18] This too can be possible, but nothing suggests this to be its primary context.

13. Cf. for example Ovid *Metam.* 4.39.

14. For more (and more specific) references, see Anderson, *Fairytale*, 11.

15. Cf. ibid., 3–11.

16. Pliny the Younger *Ep.* 2.20.1; Dio Chrysostom *Or.* 20.10; see also Anderson, *Fairytale*, 4, 8–9.

17. See Bowie, "Readership of Greek Novels," 435–59; Hägg, *Parthenope*, 109–40 (who in a critique of Bowie argues in favor of a fairly broad, popular, and not necessarily literate audience); ibid., *The Novel in Antiquity*, 91–101.

18. Gero, "Infancy Gospel," 75. He makes only very general assumptions in favor of such a setting, and there is nothing in IGT itself to promote values highly regarded in monastic circles, such as continence, celibacy, or otherworldliness.

In sum, the most probable setting for IGT appears to be the early Christian household, since it could offer many occasions for storytelling, a social context very similar to that found in the story itself, a varied audience, and a multi-generational milieu that would further its transmission—this view will be expanded on below (chap. 12). It is also plausible, however, that places of work, less formal community gatherings and even public storytelling could serve as secondary, yet occasionally important, settings for the performing and handing on of the story.

The Audience of IGT: Social Location

The chapters above have given several indications of what can have been the primary social context and place for IGT's main audience: a plausible scenario to emerge from the analyses is that of an early Christian middle class milieu, situated within an eastern Mediterranean rural village setting.[19] A variety of evidence has been presented in support of this: chaps. 2–3 argued in favor of an oral basis for IGT and of a popular, common folk, character of its narrative. Its plain style and its genre-mixture of legend and gospel indicated the same (pp. 47–52)—in this, it appears to reflect a lower socio-cultural level than writings such as *Infancy Gospel of James* and the Hellenistic novels.[20]

The analyses in chapters 4–5 of IGT's narrative world, its social relations and cultural values are also in agreement with such a scenario: by and large, the story conforms to what is likely to have been the lived world and attitudes of an early Christian rural population. This is also the case with the element of opposition against authorities: IGT's challenging of hierarchies (pp. 77–84) supports the idea that its audience is to be located within a middle/lower class stratum. Such opposition is a feature well-known from other popular classical material, for example *Life of Aesop*, and from a Christian writing such as the Revelation of John.[21] IGT's emphasis on emotions—which it shares with the gospel

19. This follows up the brief suggestions made by early scholars (Nicholas, Variot, Meyer) and recently by Chartrand Burke (see pp. 4 and 10), but argues and develops on the idea in far more detail.

20. For discussions of the novels, see Treu, "Der antike Roman und sein Publikum," 185–86, 192–96.

21. See for example Shiner, "Creating Plot," 162–63. IGT can of course have appealed

of Mark—may also situate it within such a social stratum, as does its anti-intellectual tendencies (pp. 84–85).[22]

Chapter 6 showed IGT's notions about children and childhood to be more nuanced and true-to-life than has been assumed. This can have agreed very well with attitudes shared by such a group of early Christians. In a similar way, the ideas about gender presented in chapter 7 reflect perceptions typical of such an audience.

It is of course problematic to assume some specific connection between character of ideology and social location.[23] Nonetheless, a number of features in IGT's theology and thinking can have had an affinity to a middle/lower class setting (chaps. 8–10). First, this is suggested by the charismatic character of Jesus and his preaching, with his claim of superior knowledge independently of established religious authorities. Besides being a heritage from the NT gospels, particularly John, it also suits well with other early Christian material of popular origin, such as the *Shepherd of Hermas*. Second, IGT focuses on the spectacular elements of Jesus' deeds, viz., his miracles, thus very much presenting him as a wonderworker, and maybe a magician. This is a feature which IGT particularly shares with the gospel of Mark, and which may have had a broad appeal, also given late antiquity's strong interest in magic (cf. p. 143).[24]

Furthermore, similar features are seen in early Christian art, which can serve as an alternative window on the world of early Christianity, and often on a more popular, less literate form than the written

---

to people from different social levels. The written variants of IGT presuppose a certain educational level at least on the part of its transmitters. See Hägg, "A Professor and His Slave," 184–86 for a brief discussion on the level of the readership of such material.

22. On Mark, see Voorwinde, *Jesus' Emotions*, esp. appendixes 5 and 7; Kannaday, *Apologetic Discourse*, 132, also 129–39; also Shiner, *Proclaiming the Gospel*, chaps. 3 and 9. Although this is a matter of speculation, such emotionality can have been more acceptable from the perspective of the lower/middle class than from the social élite, for which Stoic ideals of equanimity would often have been an ideal; cf. Gleason, *Making Men*, and several of the articles in Braund and Most, *Ancient Anger*.

23. See for example the caveats in Hägg, "A Professor and His Slave," 186.

24. See for example Kannaday, *Apologetic Discourse*, 119–29. IGT's Jesus also seems to correspond to a tendency in early Christianity to focus on high Christology. This can be observed in the inclination of early scribes to heighten the christological level when copying NT manuscripts, and thus to blur the lines between the Father and the Son. In spite of their literacy, scribes would usually belong among the lower/middle class stratum rather than the élite; cf. ibid., 78–82.

material.[25] In this art, which spans from painting and mosaic to epigraphy and graffiti, Jesus is presented both as a very elevated figure and as a young miracle worker, a deliverer from sickness and death—elements that are in keeping with IGT.[26] Most of the motifs especially cherished in early Christian art are also found in IGT: Jesus as healer in its many miracle accounts; the Resurrection of Lazarus in its numerous vivifications; the Multiplication of loaves and fishes in the Harvest episode; and Jesus as teacher in 1–3 Teacher and Jesus in Temple.[27] Christ helios, a central motif in early art, is not in our variant of IGT; however, the association of Jesus with the sun occurs in the Sunbeam episode of some versional manuscripts.[28] The final main motif, the wise men, is not in IGT. This is not surprising, since the story deals with an other period in Jesus' life. However, the motif occurs in *Prot. Jas.* 21. Thus, although the similarities between IGT and early Christian art are not in every case very close, the repertoire of motifs is nonetheless much the same.

The lack of concern in IGT about matters more closely associated with the Christian ecclesial and social élite, such as asceticism and celibacy (cf. p. 160), can also indicate a popular base for IGT's theology.[29]

Finally, IGT's focus on only a limited number of theological issues, and on Christology in particular, can also point to a non-learned and popular social setting. Its portrait of Jesus, which may seem jarring in comparison to the canonical gospels, can have made perfectly sense to an audience of commoners.

---

25. See the discussions in Jensen, *Understanding Early Christian Art*, chaps. 1–2; also ibid., *Face to Face*, 131–72. On the place of art in the lives of common people in late antiquity, see Clarke, *Art in the Lives of Ordinary Romans*.

26. According to Snyder, *Ante Pacem*, 110, the Christology of this early art is more in keeping with the hero Jesus in Mark than with the crucified Christ in Paul. Early Christian art does for example not employ the cross symbol. The cross is not mentioned in Gs, but in Gabd.

27. Ibid., 107–26; see also Jensen, *Face to Face*, esp. 33 and chap. 5. Exceptions are Baptism of Jesus, Fisherman, and Woman at the well; the absence of these motifs in IGT is unsurprising.

28. Chartrand-Burke, "Infancy Gospel," 51, 54, 132.

29. Cf. also Bowes, *Private Worship*, esp. chap. 3.

Reception History

It is now time to turn to the external evidence about IGT and examine what it can say about its aim and audience. Focus will primarily be on its second to fifth-century references (see appendix 6).[30]

There are four second-century testimonies to IGT. In his *Dialogue with Trypho*, Justin Martyr describes Jesus' baptism in Jordan (ca. 150 CE, Ephesus or Rome). In defense of his human nature, he states that Jesus was "said to be son of the carpenter Joseph, and was himself said to be a carpenter, for he worked . . . doing carpentry, making plows and yokes . . ."[31] In the anonymous *Epistle of the Apostles*, reference to IGT is more detailed (*Ep. Apos.*, middle second century, Asia Minor or Egypt). The writing is a revelation discourse probably written to combat gnostic gospels advancing secret teachings by the risen Christ.[32] The passage runs:

> This is what our Lord Jesus Christ did, who was delivered by Joseph and Mary his mother to where he might learn letters. And he who taught him said to him as he taught him, "Say Alpha." He answered and said to him, "First you tell me what Beta is." And truly (it was) a real thing which was done.[33]

Third, Irenaeus in *Against Heresies* (before 180 CE, Lyon) sharply criticizes gnostic opponents, *in casu* the Marcosians, for presenting "an untold multitude of apocryphal and spurious writings, which they have composed to bewilder foolish men." He exemplifies their falsifications with the following:

> When the Lord was a child and was learning the alphabet, his teacher said to him—as is customary—"Pronounce alpha." He answered: "Alpha." Again the teacher ordered him to pronounce "beta." Then the Lord answered: "You tell me first what alpha is, and then I shall tell you what beta is." This they explain in

30. Ibid., 11–19 presents these texts, but without analyzing them systematically; however, see 277–79, 284–85. Other references to a "Gospel of Thomas" in the early sources are probably to *Gos. Thom.*, not to IGT; cf. the list in Chartrand-Burke, "Infancy Gospel," 18–19.

31. *Dial.* 88 (my translation).

32. Schneemelcher, *New Testament Apocrypha: Gospels and Related Writings*, 250–51.

33. *Ep. Apos.* 4. Cf. Schneemelcher, *New Testament Apocrypha: Gospels and Related Writings*, 253.

the sense that he alone understood the Unknowable, which he revealed in the figure of alpha as in a type.[34]

Finally, IGT appears to be hinted at in the gnostic, possibly Valentinian, *Gospel of Truth* (140–180 CE, Egypt or Rome). The text presents Jesus as revealer and teacher, and states that

> he became a guide, restful and leisurely. In schools he appeared
> (and) he spoke the word as a teacher. There came the wise in
> their own estimation, putting him to the test. But he confound-
> ed them because they were foolish. They hated him because they
> were not really wise. After all these, there came the little chil-
> dren also, those to whom the knowledge of the Father belongs.
> Having been strengthened, they learned about the impressions
> of the Father.[35]

Although this passage may refer to Jesus in the Temple, the reference is more likely to the teacher episodes (cf. the mention of schools and the failure of the wise). Scholars have suggested that this text can in fact be Irenaeus' source, since he later in *Against Heresies* speaks of a "Gospel of Truth."[36] But his rendering of the story is more detailed than that of *Gos. Truth*; thus, it is more probable that they share a common knowledge of the material.[37]

These four references are important for a number of reasons. First, the attestation is geographically very varied, from the East (Egypt/Asia Minor) to Rome and to the West (Lyon).[38] Second, they show knowl-

34. *Haer.* 1.20.1–2; translation by Unger and Dillon.

35. *Gos. Truth* I 19, 17–32; translation in Attridge and MacRae, "Gospel of Truth," 41. Rome is a possible place of origin, since some scholars have suggested that *Gos. Truth* is written by Valentinus himself (he lived in Rome ca. 136–160 CE and died in the early 160s, possibly on Cyprus).

36. Attridge and MacRae, "Gospel of Truth," 38.

37. *Gos. Truth*'s mention of "little children" is also interesting, since it can reflect allegorical use of IGT, in which Jesus' playmates are interpreted as the true believers in the Father, the children of God. This is admittedly rather speculative, but can give some support to the notion that IGT was (also) used by gnostics. The passage can also refer to Jesus as an adult teacher, with "the little children" being his disciples or others.

38. The value of these geographical indications is somewhat limited, however, since the provenance of *Ep. Apos.* is contested, and since both Irenaeus and Justin did several travels during their lifetime: the former grew up in Asia Minor and visited Rome; the latter grew up in Palestine (but did not become a Christian before in his thirties) and lived both in Ephesus and Rome. It is thus uncertain where they had come across the IGT material. In spite of this, the geographical diversity indicated is conspicuous.

edge of IGT material at a very early time (middle of the second century), although the extent of their knowledge is uncertain. Third, it is Jesus' encounter with the teacher(s) that is best attested, which shows that this historically belongs to IGT's core material. Although most seem to refer only to one teacher episode, *Gos. Truth* may betray knowledge of more (cf. "schools" in plural). In addition, Justin's reference to Jesus "making plows and yokes" can refer to other IGT material (cf. 12:1).[39]

It is also worth noting that it is only Irenaeus who attributes the material to gnostics—he even holds that they have produced it. His view appears weakly grounded, however, since it is far from clear—despite the reference given in the gnostic *Gos. Truth*—what source he bases his claim on. Instead, his statement can very much be read as a wholesale rejection of all writings that might for him, as an eager polemist and spokesperson for the episcopal office, be associated with deviance and heresy. And even provided that IGT were used among gnostics, this does not mean that the material itself is deviant—gnostics employed a variety of material for their own purposes, also the NT writings. In fact, *Ep. Apos.* appears to hold a position contrary to Irenaeus: it regards the teacher episode to be historical and employs it in order to underscore this as a real event in Jesus' life: "And truly (it was) a real thing which was done." Thus, a gnostic verdict basing itself on Irenaeus builds on shaky foundations indeed.

Finally, we should note that the data given in these sources are floating in character: whereas they have some features in common with IGT, they vary much in degree and matters of detail, for example with *Ep. Apos.* having both Joseph and Mary sending Jesus to school. And in Justin it is not only Joseph who is called a carpenter, but even Jesus (cf. Mark 6:3). The fluidity and variation can imply that *Ep. Apos.* and Justin, and probably also *Gos. Truth*, can be dependent on oral rather than written tradition.[40]

---

39. Irenaeus discusses Jesus in Temple immediately after the Teacher episode(s) and thus seems to be the only to indicate knowledge of IGT as a collection of stories; see *Haer.* 1.20.2. But the sequence of the two episodes can be incidental. It can also be that Irenaeus here sticks to a biographical chronology, not necessarily that he knows the stories from a common source, since he in the same passage refers to several other NT texts.

40. This is also suggested by Chartrand-Burke, "Infancy Gospel," 267.

From the third century there is only one reference to IGT. This is in *Acts of Thomas* (early third century, probably east Syria), which states that Jesus "taught his own <teacher>, for he is the teacher of truth and the wisest of the wise"—again a reference to the Teacher episodes.[41]

There are a couple of references to IGT from the fourth century. In *Gospel of Bartholomew* (possibly Egypt fourth century or later) Mary says to the apostles that "[i]n your likeness God formed the sparrows and sent them to the four corners of the world"—the earliest explicit reference to the Sparrows episode.[42] Of considerable interest is a passage in *History of Joseph the Carpenter* (Egypt, fourth–fifth centuries), which has Joseph on his deathbed say to Jesus:

> Do not for this cause wish me evil, O Lord! for I was ignorant of the mystery of your birth. I call to mind also, my Lord, that day when the boy died of the bite of the serpent. And his relations wished to deliver you to Herod, saying that you had killed him; but you raised him from the dead, and restored him to them. Then I went up to you, and took hold of your hand, saying, "My son, take care of yourself." But you said to me in reply, "Are you not my father after the flesh? I shall teach you who I am."[43]

The passage clearly mixes elements from a number of episodes (4:1; 5:3; 6:8; 9:3; 15), and thus betrays knowledge of substantial parts or the whole of IGT. By its freedom in adapting the material and in adding new elements (e.g., Herod), it also attests to the fluid character of IGT's transmission.

Although these third and fourth-century writings are sometimes considered gnostic, the passages display no special dogmatic or polemical concerns: the IGT elements are referred to as matter-of-fact information and as familiar to its authors and audiences.

This is also the case with Epiphanius of Salamis' IGT reference in *Panarion* (374–377 CE, Cyprus), a work that aims at refuting nearly eighty different heresies.[44] Here, Epiphanius employs the childhood

---

41. *Acts Thom.* 79; Schneemelcher, *New Testament Apocrypha: Writings Related to the Apostles*, 370.

42. *Gos. Bart.* 2:11; Schneemelcher, *New Testament Apocrypha: Gospels and Related Writings*, 544.

43. *Hist. Jos. Carp.* 17; the translation of Elliott, *Apocryphal New Testament*, 116–17.

44. Also called *Refutation of All Heresies*. Epiphanius was born in Judea and was for many years a monk in Egypt, before becoming bishop in Salamis on Cyprus.

miracles in order to criticize adoptionist views of Jesus as not becoming the Christ until his baptism. Although Epiphanius is reluctant as to the historicity of these miracles, his approach is striking: he employs them in defense of orthodoxy. He states:

> For John does not say that Christ went to a wedding before the temptation, or that he worked any of his miracles <before> he started preaching—except, perhaps the ones he is said to have performed in play as a child. (For he ought to have childhood miracles too, to deprive the other sects of an excuse for saying that "<the> Christ," meaning the dove, came to him after [his baptism in] the Jordan . . .). They say this because of the sum of the letters alpha and omega, which is [the same as the sum of the letters of] "dove," since the Savior said, "I am Alpha and I am Omega."[45]

The first after Irenaeus to criticize IGT explicitly is John Chrysostom, two centuries later. In *Homilies on John* (386–398 CE, Antioch) he says:

> Thence, in short, it is plain to us that those miracles which some ascribe to Christ's childhood are false, and merely products of the imagination of those who bring them to our attention. If He had worked miracles beginning from His early youth, neither would John have failed to recognize Him, nor would the rest of the crowd have needed a teacher to reveal Him.[46]

The reason for Chrysostom's critical attitude is that IGT emerges as historically untruthful, not that it is heretical: since the Gospel of John holds that Jesus did his first miracle in the wedding at Cana (John 2:11), this excludes the possibility of any earlier miracles—something that Epiphanius, however, allows for.

The references from the fifth to seventh centuries are of special interest since they are of a different and probably more popular kind than those in Epiphanius and Chrysostom. A fifth-century pair book cover in the cathedral of Milan shows two reliefs of Jesus in school, made by an anonymous artist.[47] And in his *Itinerarium* as pilgrim to the Holy Land,

---

Interestingly, this is also the place of origin of H (Saba 259)! He also traveled to Antioch and Rome, and thus had a broad ecclesial network.

45. *Pan.* 51.20.2–3; translation from Williams, *The Panarion of Epiphanius*, 45.

46. *Hom. Jo.* 17; translation by Goggin.

47. The reliefs may, however, depict Jesus in Temple. They are printed in Morey, *Early Christian Art*, pl. 142, and p. 283.

Antoninus Placentinus (ca. 570 CE) describes his visits in Nazareth and to the church of St. Mary (between Jordan and Jericho) with evident references to the Teacher and Harvest episodes (or variants of these stories), and without second thoughts as to their historicity:

> But from Tyre we came to the village of Nazareth, in which there are many miracles. Here is also exhibited the book in which the Lord put the A B C. In this synagogue is also placed the beam where he used to sit with the other children. This beam can be moved and lifted by Christians, but Jews are in no way able to move it, nor does it let them carry it out.[48]
>
> And in front of the church is an area, the Lord's field, which the Lord sowed with his own hand so that it carries about three measures of grain. This is gathered and never sown again; still the field produces seed grain by itself.[49]

Some sixth- and seventh-century canon lists also mention certain "childhood deeds of Jesus" and count them among writings to be regarded false. The lists are the *Decretum Gelasianum* (sixth century, with fourth-century roots),[50] Anastasius Sinaita's *Hodegos* (ca. 640–ca. 700),[51] and an apocrypha list interpolated into Timothy of Constantinople's *De receptione haereticorum* (late sixth century)[52]—all are representatives of ecclesial authorities with a strong wish of purging the church of heresy and of keeping the canon clean.

In the seventh century, the Qur'an (611–632) refers indirectly to IGT as a story and explicitly to Sparrows, although the Qur'an only speaks of one bird. In telling about God's sending of Jesus, it says:

---

48. *Itin.* 5, my translation, on the basis of the second recension of the text, see Antoninus Placentinus, "Antonini Placentini Itinerarium," 196–97.

49. *Itin.* 13, my translation, see ibid., 201–2. The construction "an area, the Lord's field" is somewhat strange (in both Latin recensions: "campus ager Domini"). There may here be a mistake in the copying of the text (perhaps as a result of dictation/error of hearing), so that a more original text should be *campus sacer Domini* ("the Lord's sacred field").

50. The work, which is of sixth-century south Gallic origin but can in parts reflect fourth-century Roman material (perhaps from the church strategist Damasus' papacy, 366–84 CE), mentions a "liber de infantia salvatoris," cf. Schneemelcher, *New Testament Apocrypha: Gospels and Related Writings*, 38–39.

51. *Hodegos* 17; cf. PG 89:229/230B–C.

52. PG 86:21/22C.

He will speak to people in his infancy and in his adulthood . . .
He [God] will send him as a messenger to the Children of Israel:
'I have come to you with a sign from your Lord: I will make the
shape of a bird for you out of clay, then breathe into it and, with
God's permission, it will become a real bird.'[53]

Despite its relative sparseness, the third to seventh-century external evidence supports the impression from the second-century witnesses of IGT's broad geographical dissemination and of its basis in oral/written transmission (cf. the variation in rendering of central passages). In addition, IGT is from the third century on also attested by a broader variety of sources, also of a popular kind.

Importantly, we should note that throughout the whole period the approach toward IGT material is generally matter-of-fact and favorable, with several sources regarding it to be historically reliable.[54] Only Irenaeus and Chrysostom are critical, but on different grounds: the former is the only one to associate the material with heresy; the latter is negative because IGT appears to conflict historically with the canonical gospels. It is not surprising to find reservedness and occasional suspicion from the theological élite toward material of this kind. However, the overall attitude in the sources seems to have been acceptance and even appreciation. Ecclesial censoring appears to have increased only in the sixth and seventh centuries with the canon/apocrypha lists. In fact, Antoninus Placentinus may be a contemporary representative of notions which were shared by a majority among late antiquity Christians, but which the theological élite would regard problematic.

Chronological and Geographical Dispersion

IGT is found in a considerable number of manuscripts, both Greek and versional.[55] Here, I shall present a brief survey of them and their transmission history in order to give an impression of the dispersion of the material (see appendix 5).

---

53. Qur'an 3:46 and 49; translation by Haleem in *The Qur'an*, 38. For some later references to IGT, cf. Chartrand-Burke, "Infancy Gospel," 17–19.

54. So also Chartrand-Burke, "Infancy Gospel," 245–46.

55. Ibid., 101–33, 245–64, 277–88 has a detailed survey with information about each individual manuscript.

IGT clearly originated within a Greek setting somewhere in the eastern Mediterranean (pp. 71–72). Since the preserved Greek manuscripts are rather late, they are of course of limited help for locating the early IGT traditions geographically. Still, the fact that the manuscripts come from quite diverse contexts can attest to its broad dissemination: the manuscripts are for example related to Crete (D), Cyprus (H), mainland Greece (Mt. Athos, V), Samos (L and M) and Sinai (C and S).[56] How far these manuscripts have traveled from their Vorlagen is impossible to say, but it may in several cases not have been so far. It is also interesting to note that most of these places are rural and small-town areas, with a low degree of urbanization and centralization.

The fourteen manuscripts of IGT in Greek (see pp. 15–16) are few in comparison to *Prot. Jas.*, which is found in at least 140 manuscripts; this, though, is extraordinary for a writing of this kind.[57] If we instead compare the Greek IGT manuscripts with other relevant material, such as *Life of Aesop* and the Hellenistic novels, the number is not so small; these writings are in fact preserved in fewer manuscripts than IGT.[58] And if manuscripts with IGT as part of larger story collections are included (cf. the combined form), the number appears fairly large. There is in any case no indication that the limited number of manuscripts is due to any kind of ecclesiastical dislike or censoring.

Compared to the Greek, the abundance of manuscripts in other languages is striking.[59] IGT was very early translated into Latin. There are three main variants: the oldest, Lv, is represented by a single fifth-century fragmentary manuscript.[60] This is the earliest witness to IGT's story, predating Gs/H by six centuries. The manuscript appears to mix variant forms of episodes and thus to presuppose a prior transmission

---

56. For a discussion on the matter of manuscript provenance, see Epp, "Issues in New Testament Textual Criticism," 61–70; also ibid., "Oxyrhynchus New Testament Papyri."

57. Cf. Hock, *Infancy Gospels*, 29–30.

58. See Stephens, "Who Read Ancient Novels?" 409–16, esp. 415–16; Stephens and Winkler, *Ancient Greek Novels*, xiii; and appendixes A and C. The manuscripts are generally older, though.

59. See the presentation of this material in Chartrand-Burke, "Infancy Gospel," 116–33.

60. Vindobonensis 563, see Philippart, "Fragments Palimpsestes." It is fragmentary, but appears to follow the short form of IGT.

process of some duration.[61] Together with Irenaeus' mention, this indicates that IGT was known in the Latin West as early as the late second or early third centuries. After being translated into Latin, probably no later than in the third to fourth centuries, it also seems to have been popular and widespread already by the fourth century (cf. also the fifth-century Milan book cover and the mention in *Decretum Gelasianum*).[62]

The second Latin variant, Lm, occurs in a large number of late manuscripts of the *Gospel of Pseudo-Matthew* (eleventh century on). This early seventh-century infancy gospel, which combines *Prot. Jas.* with other infancy material, also very often includes IGT.[63] Thus, the oldest manuscripts of Lm are contemporary with Gs. *Pseudo-Matthew* was very popular in early Medieval times: at least 185 manuscripts are preserved, of which a great number contain IGT.[64] The third Latin variant, Lt, is a longer edition of IGT. It is found in about fifteen manuscripts dating from the eleventh to the fifteenth centuries; most of them too form part of *Pseudo-Matthew*.[65]

As early as 700 CE, IGT was translated from the Latin Lv variant into an Irish versified paraphrase (Ir), a form typical of folklore material. The Latin IGT version was in Medieval times also translated into German, Danish, Provençal, and Old English, usually as part of *Pseudo-Matthew*.[66]

IGT was very early translated into Syriac (Syr).[67] At least four manuscripts are preserved. Two of them date from the fifth and sixth centuries; this makes them together with Lv the oldest witnesses to the story. Some IGT material is also incorporated elsewhere, for example in a *Life of Mary* story, an indication of its popularity. The antiquity of

61. Chartrand-Burke, "Infancy Gospel," 116–17, building on Philippart, considers it a composite text based on three separate archetypes, cf. Philippart, "Fragments Palimpsestes," 403. However, the text has not been analyzed in detail and not from an oral/written perspective.

62. See the discussion in Chartrand-Burke, "Infancy Gospel," 277–78. The argument about the book cover of course presupposes that it was produced in the Latin West and was not imported there.

63. Lm appears to be dependent on Lv, cf. ibid., 117, 287.

64. Gijsel and Beyers, *Libri de Nativitate Mariae*, 94–96.

65. See Chartrand-Burke, "Infancy Gospel," 121–22, with references to and discussion of the presentation in Gijsel and Beyers, *Libri de Nativitate Mariae*.

66. See Carney, *Poems of Blathmac*, esp. xv–xviii.

67. Chartrand-Burke, "Infancy Gospel," 124–29.

the Syriac version is supported by its lack of chapters 1, Gs 16/Ga 10, and Ga 17–18, and by the reference to it in *Acts of Thomas* (see p. 177). From this, it is clear that IGT had reached Syriac-speaking areas no later than the third to fourth centuries, almost contemporary with its spread to the Latin West.[68]

IGT was introduced into Armenian-speaking areas at least as early as the sixth century: Nestorian missionaries are said to have brought with them a story about the "Infancy of the Saviour" about 590.[69] No Armenian IGT is preserved, however, but it probably served as the basis for *Armenian Gospel of the Infancy* (*Arm. Gos. Inf.*). It is preserved in various manuscripts; the oldest is from the thirteenth to fourteenth centuries, but much older in origin.

About the same time, in the sixth to seventh centuries, IGT was translated into Georgian, probably through Armenian.[70] It is preserved in one manuscript (Geo, tenth century), which begins with chapter 2; very likely, it had the short form. Regrettably, the last part is lost (from 7:3 on).

IGT appears to have been introduced into Ethiopia well before the seventh century.[71] The Ethiopic version (Eth) follows the short form and was either translated directly from Greek or from Syriac or Arabic. It is preserved as one chapter of a large and popular compilation of material, *Ta'amra 'Iyasus* (*Miracles of Jesus*), into which it was added at a very late point of time.[72]

In the eighth or ninth century, IGT episodes were combined with parts of *Prot. Jas.* and other infancy accounts, thus producing the *Arabic Gospel of the Infancy* (*Arab. Gos. Inf.*). It is likely that IGT material was well-known in Arabic even earlier, so as to become incorporated into this gospel.

About the tenth century, IGT was translated into Slavonic (Sl). Its popularity is indicated by a considerable number of manuscripts (16) and versions in the Slavonic languages. Although all manuscripts are late (fourteenth to nineteenth centuries), the oldest—in Middle Bulgarian,

---

68. Some scholars have even held that IGT was originally composed in Syriac. For a survey and rejection of this, see ibid., 248–50. I support his view.

69. Ibid., 130–31.

70. Ibid.

71. Ibid., 131–33.

72. See Witakowski, "Miracles of Jesus," 279–80.

Serbian, Croatian, and Russian—show IGT's broad dispersion in the High Middle Ages.[73]

The diversity of languages into which the material was spread and the fairly high manuscript number in some versions attest to IGT's broad appeal.[74] The quick and broad dissemination of the short form also supports this. Already in the third to fourth centuries it had spread from Greek to Latin (West) and Syriac (East), and was by the fifth to sixth centuries known in Armenian and Georgian (North-East) and Ethiopic (South). And it was well-known in reworked and combined forms in Irish and Arabic in the seventh to early eighth centuries. IGT seems for example to have been spread (at least) as quickly and widely as its close temporaries the apocryphal acts.[75] As sign of its popularity, it is worth noting that IGT was translated into these vernacular languages fairly contemporaneously with or only a short time after the New Testament—IGT appears to have followed closely in the rear of its parents, the canonical gospels.[76]

The broad and lively dispersion of the material is also apparent in the episodes that sometimes occur independently of IGT, sometimes as part of it (see appendixes 4 and 7).[77] For example, the Sunbeam episode, which lacks in the Greek material, can be found in so different contexts as the versified Irish version, the Ethiopic version, and *Arabic Gospel of the Infancy*—clearly, this was material much in demand and on the move.

73. The Slavonic version is dependent on the long form of IGT and appears to have much in common with Greek Ga, thus showing that Ga dates back well before the oldest preserved Greek manuscript (Gs/H). Comparatively much research has been devoted to the Slavonic material, cf. Rosén, *Slavonic Translation*, and Santos Otero, *Das kirchenslavische Evangelium*.

74. If we regard the written remains as only the tip of an iceberg in an oral/written transmission, this becomes even more striking. The fact that there seems to exist independent translations, for example into Slavonic (cf. Chartrand-Burke, "Infancy Gospel," 53), also supports such an impression.

75. See the introductions in Schneemelcher, *New Testament Apocrypha: Writings Related to the Apostles*; also the introductions in the volumes in the series Studies on Early Christian Apocrypha.

76. See the dating of NT versions and manuscripts in Aland, "Significance of the Chester Beatty Papyri," 108–21; Metzger, *Bible in Translation*, esp. chaps. 3 and 4.

77. Moffatt, "Gospels," 485–88 has a synopsis of chaps. 4–5 of Gab, Lt and SyrW; cf. Voicu, "Notes," 126–30.

The malleable character of the IGT material is evident in its integration into larger units, especially *Ps.-Mt.*, *Arm. Gos. Inf.*, and *Arab. Gos. Inf.*, but also the Syriac *Life of Mary* and the Ethiopic *Miracles of Jesus*. Such compilations attest to a gradual, but rather late, transition from an orally based and freer transmission to one written and probably more controlled.

In sum, this indicates that IGT enjoyed great popularity and was spread swiftly and across large areas. There is no sign that the material was the reserve of some special theological milieu; rather, it appears to have been embraced and forwarded by early Christianity at large.

The Position of IGT in the Manuscript Tradition

What place does IGT have in the manuscripts? What texts does it appear together with: biblical writings, church fathers, apocryphal texts, or other material? What level of quality do the manuscripts have? How do the scribes deal with IGT: with care or scorn? Such and other questions can be of help for assessing how the story was treated and valued.[78] Here, however, a few spot tests among the Greek manuscripts must suffice.[79]

In H, the oldest Greek manuscript, IGT is placed among homilies and hagiographical texts. Its original eleventh-century scribe, probably a monk named Gerasimos, has acknowledged its value by adding an invocation at the beginning: "give your blessing, Lord." A marginal note of a much later hand characterizes the text as heretical, and rejects it for

78. There are of course problems involved in such an approach, e.g.: (1) the occurrence of IGT in manuscripts does not necessarily mean that the scribes or the owners sanctioned the story. On the other hand, by copying it they are likely to have seen at least some value in it. (2) The manuscripts are generally late and may not reflect early Christian attitudes to IGT. One the other hand, manuscripts were often copied as a whole, or in the main, from Vorlagen that can have been very old. (3) The manuscripts to have been preserved, and the inclusion of IGT in them, can have been incidental. On the other hand, the manuscripts appear to be many and diverse enough to be relatively representative.

For similar discussions of the relationship between manuscripts and audiences, see Treu, "Der antike Roman und sein Publikum," 189–92; Stephens, "Who Read Ancient Novels?" 409–15; Epp, "Issues in New Testament Textual Criticism," 61–70.

79. A more systematic study of these matters will probably be of use. In addition to my own work on some of the manuscripts (in microfilm, photography and photocopied form), the presentation in Chartrand-Burke, "Infancy Gospel," 101–33, has here been of much help.

the reason that Jesus did not perform any miracles before the wedding at Cana (cf. Chrysostom's criticism, see p. 178).

In W, IGT is found among New Testament excerpts, homilies, sermons, and other miscellaneous writings. Here, too, an invocation occurs after the title: "Lord, give your blessing." A later reader has crossed out the entire text in the manuscript, possibly out of dislike with it.

In V, IGT is placed among texts by Ephrem the Syrian (ca. 306–373 CE) and John Chrysostom (one of IGT's critics!), together with a part of the apocryphal *Pilate's Letter to Tiberius*. As in the manuscripts above, there is an invocation after the title: "Lord, give your blessing." In addition, there is a doxology at the end (V ends with Ga 16): "our God be honored forever, amen."

In P, IGT occurs at the end of a manuscript that otherwise only contains a commentary on Revelation by Andrew, archbishop of Cesarea (fl. seventh century). Here, it is added by a second hand, probably to fill in the remaining folios of the manuscript.

D features a large number of texts, among them *Prot. Jas.* In S, IGT follows a collection of writings on Saint Anthony (251–356 CE). In C, it is placed among various lives of saints. In T, it is found together with texts by Ephrem and Chrysostom, and with *Prot. Jas.*[80]

From this can be seen that IGT is usually placed among non-contested texts in the manuscripts. In fact, it is in many instances found with material held in high esteem, for example from the New Testament and from church fathers such as Ephrem and Chrysostom. Frequently, IGT is associated with non-canonical writings that were considered edifying, such as *Prot. Jas.* Only rarely is it found with texts that could be regarded problematic, such as *Pilate's Letter to Tiberius.* The scribal invocations sometimes occurring at IGT's heading also show reverence toward it. Some signs of disapproval with the text (marginal comments and crossing out of text) can be observed, but generally, it seems, by late hands.

80. As for the Latin versions, IGT is in Vindobonensis 563 (representative of Lv) placed together with the gospels of Matthew and of Nicodemus, cf. Philippart, "Fragments Palimpsestes," 399–403. The numerous manuscripts of Lm usually have IGT appended to or as part of *Ps.-Mt.*, occasionally also with *Assum. Vir.* and *Gos. Nic.* In many Lt manuscripts IGT is part of *Ps.-Mt.* In the Syriac manuscript SyrG (ca. sixth century) it is preceded by *Prot. Jas.* and followed by *Assum. Vir.*, in SyrP appended to *Arab. Gos. Inf.* In Arabic and Ethiopic versions it is integrated into compilations such as *Miracles of Jesus.*

In sum, there is not much to imply that IGT was regarded theologically suspect or the like, whether by the manuscript owners or by the scribes. On the contrary, its position in the manuscripts indicates that IGT was usually considered unproblematic and even valued. The impression of it as a story seen as fit for Christian edification is thus strengthened (cf. p. 168).

Reflections and Inferences

The external evidence adduced as concerns IGT's reception history, its chronological and geographical dispersion and the manuscripts in which it occurs, substantiates the idea that the story enjoyed widespread popularity within early Christianity. The material also supports the view that IGT's aim was to combine entertainment and social and religious edification for believers of a "mainstream" cast, not to bolster some special group's theological or ideological views. In this it seems to have been very similar to that of other contemporary Christian literature such as the apocryphal acts and *Infancy Gospel of James*.[81] Considering its style and contents, however, IGT appears to have been directed at a less educated audience than these writings.

In addition, the analyses above of the story itself have pointed to a rural setting (see chap. 4). This comports well with the picture of the ancient world as largely agricultural, with a major part of the population living in rural areas and with social differences less marked than in the cities, at least in the eastern Mediterranean. As noted, the countryside with its numerous old and new village centers experienced in late antiquity a time of economical expansion and social prosperity (pp. 70–72). Christians too are likely to have been noticeably present in rural areas and also to have benefited from general developments there—there is no reason why the Christian movement should be exceptional in this respect.

Unfortunately, the presence of the new faith in such areas has not been very systematically studied, at least not as concerns the first to third centuries.[82] Instead, focus has very much been on the urban Christians,

81. Cf. Treu, "Der antike Roman und sein Publikum," 192–6; Stephens, "Who Read Ancient Novels?" 406–9, 414–15.

82. However, there has during the last years been a marked increase in such research, especially as the late third to sixth centuries are concerned, see especially the

with the impact of Christianity on the countryside being overlooked or minimized.[83] However, there are signs that the new faith spread early and took lasting root in many rural districts—thus providing the socio-cultural setting for material such as IGT. Although this book obviously is not the place to take up a discussion of this, some examples from the first three centuries can make plausible that the countryside may have been a fertile biotope for the story.

First, there is the mention in 1 *Clem.* 42:4 (Rome, ca. 95 CE) that the apostles after Jesus' resurrection preached "both in the country (κατὰ χώρας) and in the towns (πόλεις) and appointed their first converts . . . to be bishops and deacons of future believers." It is of interest to note that both countryside and town are specified—the intention appears to be to underscore the all-inclusive spread of Christian belief. It is also worth noting that the χῶραι are listed first, which suggests that the gospel was actively propagated in such settings, and that the mention is not for the purpose of rhetorical amplification, but reflects an perception on the part of both the author and the addressees of 1 *Clement.* Finally, the reference is very early, viz., late first century, and the formulations presuppose that the letter did not simply have the Palestinian countryside in view: it states that the preaching took place after the resurrection and that the apostles appointed bishops and deacons—a remark that makes historically sense only if (a larger part of) the Greco-Roman world is included.

A second example is Pliny the Younger's famous letter to Trajan, written in 112 CE during his time as governor in Bithynia and Pontos. This is a rural area in northern Asia Minor, one potential candidate as the place of origin for IGT. When asking the Emperor about how to deal with the growing number of Christians there Pliny states:

> The matter seemed to warrant me to consult you, particularly because of the number endangered. For many persons of every age and class (*ordinis*), and also both sexes, are—and will con-

---

bibliography in Bowes, *Rural Home*, 146–50, 169–70; ibid., *Private Worship*, chap. 3; also Knight, *End of Antiquity*, chap. 6.

83. An early, important example of this "urban focus" is Meeks, *First Urban Christians.* Frend, *Rise of Christianity*, 421–24, holds that Christianity was slow to make an impact on rural populations, but does little to substantiate this; see also Frend, *Town and Country*, 1–14, 34–42. This is a view that needs new scrutiny, cf. also the comments in Dyson, *The Roman Countryside*, 98–102.

tinue to be—brought to trial. For this contagious superstition has spread not only to the cities (*civitates*), but also to the villages (*vicos*) and the countryside (*agros*).[84]

Although Pliny here makes use of his rhetorical abilities to underscore the seriousness of the problem, his comment about Christianity reaching even to the "villages and the countryside" is unlikely to be only an invention. Instead, it can be seen as an indication of a marked development taking place in the area—why should he otherwise go into such detail in his description? Since Pliny also elsewhere in the letter appears to be well-informed about this "contagious superstition," there is no reason that he should be less updated on the point about dispersion.

Furthermore, similar developments seem to have taken place further south, in central Asia Minor, documented in second–third century "Christian for Christians" epitaphs located in the rural parts of Phrygia.[85] The Montanist movement, which sprang up in the mid-second century, also had a rural basis. With its charismatic and establishment-critical attitudes it had several social features in common with what we have observed in IGT.[86] Another example of the spread of Christianity is reflected in the building of many monasteries in rural areas of Egypt, Palestine, and elsewhere from late antiquity on.[87] The Donatist movement of fourth–fifth century Northern Africa, with its social roots in earlier times, can also be seen as mirroring a rurally based form of early Christianity.[88] In Gaul too Christianity was well established during the same period.[89]

If these examples are taken as indicative, there appears in late antiquity to have existed a growing rural Christian population, a population which as argued can have been a central audience for IGT. Although this does not help us further in the geographical placing of the story, it can in other ways advance our understanding of the gospel's demographical and socio-cultural location. In particular, IGT may provide us

84. *Ep.* 10.96.9 (my translation).

85. Gibson, *"Christians for Christians" Inscriptions*; Snyder, *Ante Pacem*, 302–3.

86. See esp. Mitchell, "Why Family Matters," 39–40, with references; Tabbernee, *Montanist Inscriptions*, 555–69; Trevett, *Montanism*, esp. 15–26, 223–24.

87. For a survey, see Stewart, "Monasticism"; also Brenk, "Monasteries as Rural Settlements"; Patrich, "Monastic Landscapes."

88. Frend, *Donatist Church*, esp. 32–59.

89. See Knight, *End of Antiquity*, 112–27.

with a view into a milieu that—at least as concerns the first to the early third century—has received limited interest, especially within early Christian studies. To an extent, this deficit mirrors the sources: much of the written remains from classical antiquity, and late antiquity, have a strong focus on the urban world, particularly the major cities—the sources are by and large urbanocentric in their concerns.[90] Although descriptions of rural life exist, such as handbooks on agronomy, they are very often the product of the élite's praise of the otiose life as seen from their countryside estates.[91] The same focus is found in much early Christian material: its space is often cities such as Antioch, Rome, and Alexandria. As noted, however, the world of a large portion of the late antique population, probably the majority, was not these urban centers, but the big in-betweens: the rural areas.[92] The urban, and élite, provenance of most of the ancient written sources, including the Christian, has served to give a lopsided picture of the ancient world. And with its strong emphasis on this urban world, modern research on the first three centuries of early Christianity has not done much to correct this impression.[93]

IGT may, however, be one significant sample of material to interfere with this urbanocentric focus and to open a window into the lives of a large but neglected segment of early Christianity. The analyses above have indicated that the world depicted in IGT is neither that of the historical Jesus nor of some particular group of believers, but that of early Christian rural common people. Read this way, IGT can give access to socio-cultural milieus sparsely documented elsewhere and provide special, maybe even alternative, glimpses into matters of anthropology, gender, and theology within early Christianity. Indeed, IGT is likely to

90. The urban focus also seems to be characteristic of the Hellenistic novels, cf. Saïd, "The City in the Greek Novel."

91. For instance Cato Agriculture; Pliny the Elder Natural History; Varro De Re Rustica; also the example from Ausonius in Bowes, Rural Home, 143–46. Cf. Rees, "Agriculture and Horticulture," 481–82.

92. Partly, this is indicated in the relatively larger quantity of later sources, especially early Byzantine material, depicting rural settings (e.g., hagiographies), cf. Bowden and Lavan, "Late Antique Countryside," xxiv–xxvi, with references.

93. Our own times are marked by strong urbanization, with scholarly concerns to a considerable extent being influenced by an urban regime—this probably is one reason why so much energy has been put into the study of the urban aspects of early Christianity.

be a rustic produce of a milieu deserving far more attention than it has received. In my view, the *Infancy Gospel of Thomas* is an unadorned, yet precious gem handed down to us from the heritage of the first rural Christians.

12

⊰◇⊱

CHRISTIANITY'S FIRST CHILDREN'S STORY

The picture to emerge from the above of IGT's audience is that of an early Christian rural and common people population. But is there more to say about its audience? In my opinion there is, and I shall in the following argue in favor of a more specific target group for IGT, namely *early Christian children*. To my knowledge, this has not been argued earlier.[1] Such a view does of course not exclude that adults too could belong to IGT's audience; the point here, however, is the claim that children should be regarded its *main* target group.

Evidence of both external and internal kinds will be adduced to argue this. As for external evidence, I shall present material that shows that: storytelling for children was a common phenomenon; that various kinds of stories for children existed, with some such material also being of a Christian character. The aim of this is to sketch a cultural framework that makes my claim plausible. The purpose of my analysis of the internal evidence in IGT itself is similar: to read it with a view to children's place in the story and their reception of it, i.e. how it can have appealed to them. My focus will be on: IGT's format, contents, structure, and style: location and characters; events; chronological framework; and socio-cultural values and theology.

There are, admittedly, a number of problems inherent in such an approach to this material. For example, do we know enough about children in antiquity in general? How much can we say about what they thought and felt, and about what kind of narrative material that might have appealed to them? Is it possible to speak of a children's culture of

1. It has been suggested only by Meyer, "Erzählung des Thomas," 64, who states that the material in IGT may have been "zur Lust für grosse und kleine Christenkinder," and by Bovon, "Évangiles canoniques," 25–26, who as reason for the coming into existence of IGT "propose une hypothèse: curiosité des enfants," and that this was because second-century Christians wanted to have it as "un pendant aux Evangiles réservés aux adultes." However, neither of them develops the idea further.

this kind in antiquity? And so on. In spite of these and other objections, some of which we shall touch upon later, I believe that we possess enough information and methodological sobriety to undertake such a "child perspective" reading of the material (cf. pp. 92–99).[2] After all, other similar approaches to the ancient sources, for instance feminist and socio-rhetorical readings, are wrought with the same challenges, without that preventing us from applying them, and applying them successfully.

Evidence of Storytelling to Children in Antiquity

Little research has been done on children and storytelling in antiquity and early Christianity, and much remains to be done.[3] Clearly, however, children were told stories and would have had an engagement similar to modern day children in hearing them. Although the boundaries between tales for children and for adults probably were far from distinct, inter alia because of the generally low educational level, there must have been stories which were more aimed at children than at adults. And although there may have been no children's culture in the sense that is spoken of today, adults could nonetheless be very sensitive to the special demands on storytelling to children. This is, for example, evident in the advice given by Quintilian in *The Orator's Education* on storytelling.[4] It is also prominent in the strong awareness in Chrysostom's

2. Cf. Aasgaard, "Children in Antiquity," 24–26, 36–37. See also Aasgaard, "Uncovering Children's Culture." My interpretation will of course be informed by various notions about what may have appealed to children. In my view, we are justified in making some inferences from modern psychological insights on children and also from what we know about the literary likes and dislikes of adults in antiquity and early Christianity. Modern research on children's stories and literature also has much to say on children's stories and child perspective readings, see esp. Benton, "Readers, Texts, Contexts," and the articles in Hunt, *Children's Literature*, esp. those by Chambers (1:354–74), Bottigheimer (1:114–29), Tabbert and Wardetzky (2:21–37), Benton and Fox (2:125–46), Hunt (2:263–79), and Nodelman (2:384–95). The four volumes are a goldmine of contributions on children's literature and also include material on orality, fairytales, and folktales.

3. The issue is occasionally touched on in Leyerle, "Appealing to Children"; Anderson, *Fairytale*; Bakke, *When Children Became People*, chap. 5; Buxton, *Imaginary Greece*, 16–26. Far more has been written about storytelling in antiquity and early Christianity in general, especially by scholars involved in oral studies; for a survey, see Hearon, *Mary Magdalene Tradition*.

4. *Inst.* 1.2.

Address on Vainglory of the need to adapt stories to children's level of understanding. In his opinion, stories should be made agreeable, be told in a simple language, be introduced piecemeal depending on the children's age, be related to their everyday context, and be repeated in order to be remembered.[5]

There is considerable evidence in the ancient sources of the telling of stories to children. This is attested in non-Christian sources throughout the period. For example, Aristophanes (448–380 BCE) in *Lysistrata* lets the chorus speak about "a tale that once I heard when but a lad."[6] Plato in *Laws* mentions tales that children have heard since being nursed by their nurses' or their mothers' milk.[7] Later, within a Latin-speaking context, Tibullus (ca. 54–19 BCE) exhorts his beloved Delia to listen to "little stories" (*fabellas*).[8] Ovid (40 BCE—17 CE) relates a story known from Roman mythology told among non-Romans in the form of a popular tale.[9] In his *Satirae*, Persius (34–62 CE) describes situations in which fairytales were told.[10] Celsus, the famous late second-century critic of Christianity, refers to stories that old women "sing in order to lull a child to sleep."[11] And Philostratus the Elder (early third century CE), who in his *Imagines* depicts a situation in which a ten-year-old child is asked to study a series of pictures from various fairytales, refers to such a tale as something the child must surely have heard from his nurse.[12]

Christian sources contain similar evidence: Tertullian (ca. 155–230 CE) in *Against the Valentinians* relates of stories told to a child as "cure for sleeplessness."[13] Lactantius (ca. 240–ca. 320 CE) in *Divine Institutes* speaks of stories that are of a kind "fabricated" by "old women without enough to do, for an audience of gullible children."[14] The practice of

5. *Inan. glor.* 39–43, 52.

6. *Lysistrata* 782–783(–818).

7. *Leges* 887D; also *Respublica* 377B.

8. Tibullus 1.3.84 (my translation).

9. *Epistulae ex Ponto* 3.2.97. Ovid does not present it as a children's story, however, but as a story about young people.

10. *Satirae* 2.37.

11. Origen *Contra Celsum* 6.34 (my translation from Marcovich, *Origenes*, 411).

12. *Imagines* 1.15.1.

13. *Against the Valentinians* 20.3 (inter somni difficultates).

14. *Divine Institutes* 3.18.16.

storytelling is particularly well evidenced in John Chrysostom, notably in his *Address on Vainglory*, but also in his homilies.[15]

According to the ancient sources, storytelling could serve various purposes.[16] A central aim was simply to delight: in *The Golden Ass*, Apuleius refers to "pretty stories" told for diversion.[17] And in his *Orations*, Julian the Apostate (331/332–363 CE) holds that many stories were told simply for pleasure, but added that many also could serve as instruction.[18] Plutarch states in his *Moralia* that stories involving bogeymen, monsters, or ghosts could be used to scare children or to stop them from getting up to mischief.[19] He also states, however, that they could be used for encouragement.[20]

Occasionally, telling of stories would function as peace offerings: Dio Chrysostom (ca. 40—ca. 120 CE) speaks of nurses that, "after giving the children a whipping, tell them a story to comfort and please them."[21] Obviously, storytelling was an important means in exerting social control over children. This is also reflected in Maximus of Tyre (late second century CE), who holds that souls in earlier times needed to be guided and controlled "by the use of myths, just as nursemaids keep children in hand by telling them stories."[22]

Many different kinds of people are described as telling stories to children. Although the sources do not very often state this, parents—both fathers and mothers—would clearly have served as storytellers.[23] Nurses and slaves are frequently mentioned, as are pedagogues and guardians.[24] The sources speak particularly often of old women—this implies that these women, who would often have more time at hand

15. *Inan. glor.* 36–53. Cf. Leyerle, "Appealing to Children," 255–56.

16. Anderson, *Fairytale*, 3–4 offers a number of illuminating examples as concerns fairytales.

17. *Metam.* 4.27 (my translation).

18. *Oration* 7.207A.

19. *Mor.* 1040B; also John Chrysostom *Inan. glor.* 52. For other references, see Anderson, *Fairytale*, 3–4.

20. *Theseus* 23.

21. *Orationes* 4.74.

22. *Orationes* 4.3; translation by Trapp (p. 35).

23. John Chrysostom *Inan. glor.* 39. For surveys of various categories of storytellers, see Hearon, *Mary Magdalene Tradition*, appendixes A–D.

24. Tibullus 1.3.84 (*custos*, woman guardian); John Chrysostom *Inan. glor.* 37–38.

than the younger, were central in such cultural transmission.[25] In many instances, they may have been grandparents.[26] School teachers would obviously also function as storytellers for children—but probably not a story like IGT![27]

There were, as noted (pp. 169–71), a number of settings in which storytelling took place. For children the central arena for this would be the household. This was their main place of formation: here, they would receive their basic intellectual, social, religious, and cultural schooling, and here they would also be told stories that reflected their cultural heritage. In addition to occasions such as family dinners and hours of leisure, children's bedtime was an important occasion (cf. the reference in Tertullian above). Cicero also reports about such bedside storytelling.[28]

Children would, however, also experience storytelling at places of work. In large households, small children often stayed in the women's quarter, where the women would spend time during handiwork telling stories. In the men's workshop older boys would be an attentive audience. Children were also present at public places such as the market and the tavern, and would there get chances to hear stories, also stories of a more daring kind.

This brief look at occasions for storytelling highlights the fact that there were no sharp distinctions between audiences of children and of adults. The generations lived closely together and cultural traditions were handed over in multi-age settings, in which stories would float back and forth being transformed in the process (pp. 198–99). Whereas this makes it more, but not very, problematic to speak about children's stories in antiquity, it can explain the preservation of such material. With children generally being unable to put it into writing, its survival would depend on adults handing it over to posterity. The preservation

25. Dio Chrysostom *Orationes* 1.52–58; John Chrysostom *Inan. glor.* 38; Apuleius *Metam.* 4.27; cf. also the examples above.

26. Such transmission of stories from the grandparent generation to children is also a well-known phenomenon within the fields of folkloristics and cultural anthropology.

27. Cf. Cribiore, *Gymnastics*, 178–80.

28. *De natura deorum* 1.34.94. Leyerle, "Appealing to Children," 255, however, holds that dinner time was a more central occasion for storytelling than bedtime. But cf. the skepticism about common mealtimes in Nielsen, "Roman Children at Mealtimes," 56–66.

of a story like IGT is due both to the fact that adults served as oral and literary transmitters *and* that they too were captivated by these stories.

We should note that storytelling, and particularly of a popular kind, was very often devalued by ancient writers. Aristophanes in *Wasps* describes stories told to children as being nonsense and unimportant.[29] In *Dialogus de oratoribus*, Tacitus (ca. 56–ca. 117 CE) advises the sound orator to reject the fables told by nursemaids:

> Nowadays . . . our children are handed over at their birth to some silly little Greek serving-maid . . . It is from the foolish tittle-tattle of such persons that the children receive their earliest impressions, while their minds are still green and unformed . . .[30]

Christian writers also speak of traditional storytelling in a derisive way. According to Lactantius, this is what "old women without enough to do" engage in.[31]

Chrysostom advises against children hearing "frivolous and old wives' tales: 'This youth kissed that maiden. The king's son and the younger daughter have done this.' Do not let them hear these stories." This does not mean that he disapproves of storytelling; however, the stories should be "simply told with no elaboration" and introduce "nothing that is untrue but only what is related in the Scriptures."[32] According to Chrysostom, IGT would probably meet the first requirement, but clearly not the second. His statement may even be directed at popular non-scriptural stories such as that of the infancy gospels and the apocryphal acts (cf. p. 178).

Christian sources often present women as agents of storytelling and frequently with contempt. The description in the NT Pastoral epistles of "talkative" women (διαβόλους: 1 Tim 3:11 and Tit 2:3; φλύαροι: 1 Tim 5:13) and "old wives' tales" (γραώδεις μύθους: 1 Tim 4:7) reflects such negative attitudes to a female activity that probably also involved

---

29. *Vespae* 1174–1196. A "homely story" (τοὺς κατ' οἰκίαν) about a mouse and a cat is mentioned in 1182–1186 (cf. p. 200 below).

30. *Dialogus de oratoribus* 29.1.

31. *Divinae institutiones* 3.18.16. Arnobius of Sicca (died ca. 330 CE) also voices opinions very similar to those of Lactantius and Chrysostom, see the reference to him (and others) in Bremmer, "Performing Myths," 124–26.

32. *Inan. glor.* 38–39.

storytelling.[33] The reference in 2 Tim 1:5 to Timothy's mother Eunice and grandmother Lois gives a more favorable picture, however: the two figures—whether they are historical or not—seem to be viewed by the author not only as models of faith, but also as central mediators of Christian heritage. In the letter, they emerge as multi-generational females engaged in religio-cultural transmission. As a whole, the Pastorals appear to follow a specific strategy as concerns such transmission: it should take place in a way controlled by the individual household, with its male head (1 Tim 3:2–5). Whereas female social and cultural exchange between the households are to be restricted (1 Timothy; Titus), it is emphasized as an ideal when taking place from generation to generation within the hierarchy of the household (2 Timothy).

Two centuries later, John Chrysostom appears to follow a similar strategy. He emphasizes the importance of having the right persons in charge of storytelling: fathers are themselves to tell their children stories instead of leaving it to more or less responsible servants, tutors or nurses.[34]

The critical stance of these writers against storytelling is due partly to moral disapproval of some of the material, partly to an élite downgrading of people coming from social strata below themselves.[35] But it is also likely that their condemnation was based on a wish to maintain social, cultural, and ideological, including theological, control (cf. also p. 180).

From this we see that storytelling for children was established practice. There were persons of various kinds performing storytelling and acting as transmitters. And there were a cultural climate and a number of social settings in which such transmission could take place.

Evidence of Children's Stories in Antiquity

What kinds of stories were told to children? Answering this question encounters some problems. The problem of distinguishing between types of audiences—adults or children—has already been noted. A

---

33. For a discussion of this material with references to primary sources and updated bibliography, see Kartzow, "Female Gossipers"; also Hearon, *Mary Magdalene Tradition*, chap. 2, esp. pp. 25 and 27. If the Pastoral epistles are to be dated to the early second century, they predate IGT only by a few decades.

34. *Inan. glor.* 37–38.

35. So also Anderson, *Fairytale*, 4.

similar challenge exists as concerns genre, i.e. with distinguishing between different types of stories.[36] The greatest challenge, however, comes from lack of systematic research on the matter. Scholars studying related material have almost always focused on other issues than that of audience, and when they do, the matter is discussed in cursory ways or the audience is—explicitly or implicitly—depicted as adult. The fact, however, that children are not thought of as potential addressees reflects scholarly neglect more than anything else. In the cities of late antiquity children probably constituted no less than one third of the population, and in rural areas possibly half of it.[37] Their sheer number makes it highly probable that many children's stories were in circulation, and also that several instances of such material would have survived in written or oral-written forms.[38]

In spite of the lack of research, it is nonetheless possible to offer examples of material with children as main, maybe even *the* main addressees. Here, this can only be hinted at and will also include other kinds than strictly narrative material.

Stories in the form of fables were clearly very popular, the *Life of Aesop* being the most famous.[39] For example, Philostratus states in *Life of Apollonius* that Aesop's fables consist of "frogs . . . donkeys, and nonsense for old women and children to chew on."[40] Quintilian is far more positive as concerns fables: not only should young children learn about them in school, they should even "learn . . . to tell" them and to do so in a "pure and unpretentious language."[41]

Many fairytales were in circulation and were frequently adapted for use within other literary settings, for example the Hellenistic novels.[42] The ancient terms applied to such and related stories varied; however,

36. Cf. the interesting discussion in ibid., 15–23.

37. Parkin, *Old Age*, 36–56, 280–81 and Laes, *Kinderen*, 21–22 calculate that 33% of the population of Rome was children (0–15 years). Given the special character of Rome with its often unfavorable environments for children, e.g. sanitation, the percentage in other cities was probably higher, and even more so in rural areas.

38. On Medieval times, see Orme, *Medieval Children*, 274–94.

39. See Laes, "Children and Fables," 898–914, esp. 912–14; also Gibbs, *Aesop's Fables*, ix–xxix; Cribiore, *Gymnastics*, 15, 202–3.

40. *Vita Apollonii* 5.14.1.

41. *Inst.* 1.9.2.

42. For a major work on fairytales in antiquity, see Anderson, *Fairytale*. See also ibid., *Folklore*.

μῦθος was common in Greek, *fabula* and *fabulla* in Latin. Negative epithets were quite often added, such as γραῶν or γραώδεις μῦθοι and *aniles fabulae* (old women's tales).[43] In a more neutral tone, Quintilian speaks of such stories as *fabula nutricularum*, "nurses' stories."[44]

Fairytales are often hinted at in classical sources. For example, Aristophanes in *Wasps* speaks of stories "about mice and cats," which are an insult to tell to grown-ups, clearly implying that they were regarded purely for children.[45] Fairytale motifs are also found in other popular works, such as in Petronius' *Satyrica*; here, he alludes to and retells a number of fairytales, which in topic and outline have very much in common even with fairytales documented in modern times.[46]

Fables and fairytales incorporated a number of extraordinary features, such as miracles, transformations, illogical events, and talking animals. For example, Minucius Felix (third century CE) would in *Octavius* refer condescendingly to such stories as "fiction of folk-lore" finding "willing ears," but not worth remembering: "Why recall old wives' tales of human beings changed into birds and beasts, or into trees and flowers."[47] In a similar way, Tertullian speaks of children's stories about apples growing in the sea and fishes on trees, and John Chrysostom of "fairytales about sheep with golden fleeces."[48]

Stories from Greek and Roman mythology were also popular. Children are said to have heard the Greek myths at the knees of their mothers and nurses.[49] Many of these myths were given a written form by Ovid in his *Metamorphoses*. Mythological stories also formed part of both primary and secondary school curricula.[50] Plato advises against

43. See Plato *Theaetetus* 176B; *Gorgias* 527A; *Respublica* 350E; *Hippias maior* 286A; 1 Tim 4:7; Epictetus *Diatribes* 2.16.39–40; Strabo *Geography* 1.2.3 (C 17); Lucian *Philopseudes* 9; cf. Anderson, *Fairytale*, 195, n. 8; Cicero *De natura deorum* 3.5.12; Horace *Sat.* 2.6.77–78; Quintilian *Inst.* 1.8.9; Apuleius *Metam.* 4.27; Minucius Felix *Octavius* 20.4; also Tibullus 1.3.84.

44. *Inst.* 1.9.2.

45. *Vespae* 1181–86.

46. *Satyrica* 38.8; 77.6; cf. Anderson, *Fairytale*, 1–2.

47. *Octavius* 20.4.

48. Tertullian *Against the Valentinians* 20; John Chrysostom *Inan. glor.* 39 (probably a reference to the Greek myth about Jason).

49. See for example the reference in Price, *Religions of the Ancient Greeks*, 129.

50. Cribiore, *Gymnastics*, 178–80, 194–205; Rawson, *Children*, 167–69; also Morgan, *Literate Education*.

unsuitable stories being told to children.[51] And Julian the Apostate holds that whereas "the fable with a moral" aims at adult people, the "myth . . . is addressed to children."[52]

Hero stories obviously appealed to the children of antiquity. Such stories materialized particularly in Homer's *Iliad* and *Odyssey* and in Virgil's *Aeneid* (70–19 BCE), which were often used in school exercises and regarded morally improving for children.[53] Within Jewish and Christian contexts such tales were supplemented with, and sometimes replaced by, biblical stories.[54] John Chrysostom gives a fascinating example of pedagogical adaptation to children of the stories about Cain/Abel and Esau/Jacob, which in his opinion should serve as morally edifying example stories.[55]

In addition to such narrative material, children also learned songs and rhymes—although this matter has seldom been discussed.[56] Chrysostom admonishes parents not to "spend leisure on shameful songs and ill-timed tales."[57] The saying in Matthew 11:16–17 par. about children "sitting in the marketplaces and calling to one another, 'we played the flute for you, and you did not dance; we wailed, and you did not mourn'" probably refers to songs employed in children's games of wedding and burial.[58] In the famous episode leading up to Augustine's conversion in *Confessions*, a voice—probably a child's—is said to be repeatedly singing *tolle, lege* ("take and read"), which may be a fragment of a children's song or rhyme.[59]

Riddles and jokes surely also were part of children's cultural repertoire, many of which are incorporated into fable collections such as

51. *Respublica* 377.

52. *Oration* 7.207A.

53. Quintilian *Inst.* 1.8.4–5; Augustine *Confessiones* 1.13–16. See also Cribiore, *Gymnastics*, 194–97; Rawson, *Children*, 167–69.

54. Cf. the discussions in Bakke, *When Children Became People*, 174–201; Barclay, "The Family as the Bearer of Religion," 68–78.

55. John Chrysostom *Inan. glor.* 39–46. See also Leyerle, "Appealing to Children," 262.

56. For a brief treatment, see Horn, "Children's Play," 109–12. Orme, *Medieval Children*, 130–57 gives many (early) Medieval examples.

57. *Inan. glor.* 34.

58. Cf. Harrington, *Gospel of Matthew*, 157; Luz, *Matthew 8–20*, 146–47.

59. *Confessiones* 8.12.

that of Aesop. Similar material is probably reflected in the play with numbers and letters and in the nonsense verses found in many classical sources—an example of which we have in IGT's letter jingle (cf. pp. 145–46). Question-answer games are also known.[60]

Children and Stories in Early Christianity

Such, we may imagine, was the literary-cultural heritage received by children in late antiquity, a heritage that most early Christian children would share. But Christian children undoubtedly also had their own stories. In addition to Old Testament examples such as those mentioned by John Chrysostom, children must have been be introduced to a number of gospel stories about Jesus and to tales about apostles and other Christian heroes. Chrysostom in the same passage as he warns against "shameful songs" also recommends that children sing hymns to God; he can here refer to biblical psalms, early Christian hymns, or the like.[61] Although such material was not primarily intended for children, much of it would be well fit for them.

Very probably, early Christian children were told stories about other children whom they could identify with or admire. Tales about children martyrs can have been of such a kind.[62] The most attractive would be, however, if children could hear of their main hero as a small boy, namely about Jesus and his childhood years—and IGT may have been material of precisely such a kind.

The most important settings for the transmission of such material to children would be home and church. At home children were introduced to a variety of material, depending on the socio-cultural background of the family, and IGT—as argued above (pp. 169–71)—very probably had its main place here.[63] In church or community gatherings, stories from the Old Testament and from the commonly accepted Christian writings would dominate and serve to create a common cultural heritage and to secure ideological-theological stability. The

60. Quintilian *Inst.* 1.3.11.

61. *Inan. glor.* 34.

62. See e.g. the examples of such tales presented by Horn, "Fathers and Mothers Shall Rise up against Their Children."

63. On settings for storytelling, see Hearon, *Mary Magdalene Tradition*, 39–40, and appendixes A–D. For Medieval times, see Orme, *Medieval Children*, 204–13.

boundaries between the two settings would not always be sharp, however. This is documented by the many examples of artistic depictions in churches from the *Infancy Gospel of James* (p. 169). Although few (if any) such early works of art are known in the case of IGT, the story nonetheless contains elements that serve to bridge home and church: in particular, many children would be familiar with IGT's Jesus in Temple from church readings.[64] Interestingly, John Chrysostom speaks about the great pedagogical value of interaction between home and church: children who have been introduced to a biblical story at home will at church, in his words,

> pay heed particularly when this tale is read aloud. Thou wilt see him rejoice and leap with pleasure because he knows what the other children do not know, as he anticipates the story, recognizes it, and derives great gain from it. And hereafter the episode is fixed in his memory.[65]

IGT, then, can be regarded as comparable to other ancient children's stories, and as a supplement or an alternative to the contemporary pagan canon. It is improbable indeed that children within the steadily growing Christian movement should lead a storyless life or be left only with tales and myths that were felt to be increasingly irrelevant and even impious.[66] Instead, they would be given new stories, stories that they could adopt as their own. Adult Christians had stories to complement the pagan and Christian canons: they had variant accounts of Jesus' passion (*Gospel of Peter*), stories about his descent to the infernal world (*Gospel of Bartholomew*), and about his communications with disciples after his resurrection (e.g., *Gospel of Mary*). They even had moving stories about Jesus' family (*Prot. Jas.*), his apostles (e.g., *Acts of Andrew*), and others of his faithful (e.g. *Passion of Perpetua*). In sum, these were enough to satisfy adult curiosity as for their hero's life and deeds. Who, then, would be particularly interested in stories about Jesus' childhood, if not those who were the most curious about persons of such an age, namely the children themselves?

---

64. See Origen *Homiliae in Lucam* 18–20; Ambrose (340–397 CE) *Expositio Evangelii secundum Lucam* 2.63.

65. *Inan. glor.* 41.

66. Cf. Augustine's reaction in *Confessiones* 1.13–14 toward the pagan canon that he had to learn in school.

Format, Contents, Structure, Style

We now turn to a "child perspective" reading of IGT itself, starting with its format, contents, structure, and style. As for format, IGT is in its basic form a brief story of about 6–8 modern book pages, much shorter than for example the *Infancy Gospel of James*. If performed orally, the telling of the whole story would take 20–30 minutes, a size well suited for a variety of occasions and also for keeping the attention of children, for example at the table or at bedtime. As noted, smaller units of IGT were probably also transmitted separately at an early stage, cf. 1–3 Teacher. IGT's other triplet episodes (2–3; 11–13) also indicate that IGT can have been performed piecemeal. The several episodes that have been handed down individually (cf. appendix 4) attest to the same.

As for contents, IGT is unique among antique biographical stories in that it is restricted to telling only about the childhood of its hero. In all other comparable writings from antiquity the time of childhood is only given a brief and preparatory place, with emphasis on the mature period of the main character. Even if an adult audience would have some interest in Jesus' childhood, the group more taken up with such a period of life is far more probable to have been the children.

Structurally, IGT consists of narratives interspersed with discourses. The narratives, with their brief reports of Jesus' actions and spectators' reactions, give a high level of tension to the story: something is going on all the time. The discourses—both dialogs and speeches—serve to communicate ideas that are important within the gospel as a whole, particularly about Jesus' divinity, and stand out as climactic points in the story. In form and function, they are very similar to discourses in other classical and early Christian writings, for example in the Hellenistic novels, the gospel of John, Acts, and the apocryphal acts. At the same time, IGT's discourses are generally much briefer than in these writings, and brief enough so as not to tire children (and impatient adults). The frequent alternation between narrative and discourse also provide variation in a way that keeps concentration up right to the end.

It is also worth noting that the most stable parts in the story of IGT are the narrative elements, such as the information given about characters and events (cf. chap. 2). Thus, a central aim of IGT appears to be to communicate good stories. There is much more variation among its manuscripts as concerns the sayings of Jesus; the differences are particularly striking in the "difficult" sayings (cf. chap. 9). Thus, the preservation of many of these individual sayings does not appear to be a central concern in IGT—more important is the character and impact of what Jesus says: that he is speaking with authority and wisdom in a way superior to other human beings. Again, this seems well adapted to children: IGT is shaped so as to give them memorable stories about Jesus, and through his sayings to imbue them with an idea of his divinity.

As for style, IGT also appears well suited for children: as noted (pp. 48–49), the variants Gs, Ga, and Gb all have a plain, oral character. Their style is generally colloquial and simple, with very few difficult terms—but also with words and sayings very much eliciting curiosity and admiration (cf. pp. 138–46).[67]

Location and Characters

The location of IGT very much reflects children's environment. Differently from the Hellenistic novels and the apocryphal acts, which have considerable parts of the ancient world as their scene, IGT's locale is limited to everyday surroundings. Its narrative space is taken up by a home, a workshop, houses, public places, a school, a brook, fields, and woods—in fact, this is the domestic, small-town, rural setting that would be familiar to a majority of late antiquity children. Such a setting would be of little interest to adults; theirs was the bigger world of the novels and the acts. But for children this would be the biotope which they would recognize, identify as their own, and find pleasure in. This was their world, and the world in which they would also like to see Jesus, their special hero.

Children have a prominent position within the world depicted in IGT; in fact, it is teeming with them. The most important child is of course Jesus, who is characterized in a varied and vivid way (pp. 100–101). Although there is not much of development in his personality, he nevertheless displays a broad range of emotions and reactions: he laughs, is scornful, and becomes angry—just like ordinary children do. Jesus emerges as a round character, with IGT being more focused than the canonical gospels on giving a psychological sketch of his personality. In this way, IGT invites its audience to identify with their hero in a different, more emotional, manner than the NT texts in general.

67. See also Bovon, "Évangiles canoniques," 26.

Apart from Jesus, the central characters—excepting his parents and teachers—are also children: Annas' son, the careless boy, Zeno, and James. Much of Jesus' interaction is with children: they play (2:3; 9:1), quarrel (3:1–2), and harass one another (4:1). Jesus is even betrayed by his playmates (9:1). Nearly all of Jesus' miracles are performed on children. Thus, there are a number of central figures in IGT to whom an audience of children could relate, both positively and negatively.[68]

Adults hold only two main roles in the story: those of parents and teachers, both of which are very much related to children. Other adult roles are largely conditioned by their function in the narrative: the High Priest Annas' primary role is as a father, and the notice about Joseph being a carpenter mainly serves to prepare for the bed miracle. As parents, adults primarily appear through their children, cf. Annas' Son, Careless Boy, and Zeno (9). Jesus' interaction is first with children: they serve as primary cast and identification figures for the audience. It is only at the second stage of conflict that parents enter. Thus, parents stand at the fringes of the story and are almost only involved when it is necessary for the resolution of conflict.

Jesus' parents are more central, particularly Joseph (see pp. 78–79 and 109–11). He is depicted as both strong and weak, and may from the perspective of a child serve as a foil for its own father, both as concerns function and authority: he defends Jesus, but also corrects him; he takes him to work and school, and is in dialog with the teachers. Thus, Joseph is and does what a child might expect from a father.

At the same time, however, the father role is challenged, particularly when Jesus commands Joseph in the workshop (12:1–2), when Joseph is ridiculed in 3 Teacher (14:3, running and despair), and in Jesus' protest when being pulled in the ear (5:2–3). But the challenging is only slight, with proper relations being re-established in the end. Thus, some concession is made to children's wish for revolt, but within strict limits and without at all jolting parent-child relations (pp. 82–84).

---

68. The fact that all children who are specified by gender are male can also indicate that the story would have had a special appeal to male children—IGT here very much emerges as a boys' story. Cf. also Anderson, *Fairytale*, 158–59. According to Anderson comparable literature would often have a female audience in mind.

In Gb, children appear to have more active roles than in the other variants, e.g., by telling on Jesus to adults. In Gd, it is Jesus' playmates (in Gb a single child), not a Pharisee, who tell Joseph about Jesus' forming sparrows on the Sabbath (2:3).

The revolt against adult authority is stronger in Jesus' conflict with his teachers (pp. 79–80). This is understandable given their often harsh treatment of pupils, with physical punishment being common (cf. 6:8).[69] Similar protests are well-known from other sources, such as Aesop's fables (pp. 48 and 171–72).[70] They are even more understandable by the discontent among many early Christians with the pagan school curricula.[71] Not finding "God's law," but some other—pagan—book on the lectern must have been problematic for many (14:2).[72] The aspect of protest is evident in the travesty of 1 Teacher. It is not difficult to imagine the enthusiasm with which the performing of such a daring account would be met from an audience of children! With its elements of drama and comedy, particularly in the teacher's speech: "Dear me! Dear me! I am totally baffled and miserable. I have caused and brought down shame upon myself . . ." (7:1–4), it must have been a perfect occasion for a storyteller to excel in character portrayal, in a form well suited to children—and to others as well.[73] But here too adult authority is eventually confirmed, with the insight of the third school teacher and the teachers in the temple.

Throughout IGT, characters—both children and adults—are described in varied ways: they argue, display a broad range of feelings, walk in and out of the classroom, strike one another, and fall dead—all features that add liveliness to the story, and thus make it more appealing to a young audience.

69. See e.g. Rawson, *Children*, 175–79; Cribiore, *Gymnastics*, 65–70; Laes, *Kinderen*, 126–31. The problem is addressed at some length by Quintilian in *Inst.* 1.3.

70. See e.g. Shiner, "Creating Plot," 162; Hägg, "A Professor and His Slave," esp. 196–97.

71. So Chartrand-Burke, "Infancy Gospel," 402; also Bakke, *When Children Became People*, 201–15.

72. See p. 81 above. Cf. also Origen *Contra Celsum* 3.55 (Greek text in Marcovich, *Origenes*, 196–97): "But whenever . . . [Christian activists, acc. to Celsus] get hold of children in private, and some stupid women with them, they let out some astounding statements as, for example, that they must not pay any attention to their father and school teachers, but must obey them . . ." (translation by Chadwick, *Origen: Contra Celsum*).

73. Cf. Shiner, "Creating Plot," 163–66.

Events

The ways in which central events are described also indicate that IGT is well adapted to an audience of children. The activities of Jesus and his playmates are of a character with which they would identify. For example, the forming of clay birds is a typical children's activity (2:2–4). Their vivification may reflect the fantasy world of children, with the wish of being able to perform the extraordinary, to create something true-to-life. The episode with Annas' son destroying Jesus' pools (3) shows a typical conflict between children in which a child would sense that its spatial boundary was being violated. The next episode, Careless Boy (4), also depicts an incident in which a child would feel harassed, more seriously than in the previous case: now even its physical boundary, its body, is being infringed upon. And in both cases, the wishful thinking of children of having one's enemies drop dead comes true. [74]

The episode about Jesus being sent by his mother for water and then breaking the jar (10) relates an event that would seem insignificant for an adult, but a tragedy for a small child. Again, however, wishful thinking saves the day: Jesus' cloak is able to hold the water.

The episodes about Jesus being taught the letters would not only fascinate the many more or less illiterate adults of antiquity, but even more so the children. Thus, IGT's speculations on the alpha would probably appeal very much to them, especially since several themselves would be on the verge of being initiated into the mystic world of reading and writing.

The miracles in IGT also match with children's perspective. Many of the miracles take place in central everyday settings for children: family activities (water fetching, woodworking, harvest), social interaction (play, work, school), and related to basic elements: nourishment (water, bread, heating) and rest (bed). The miracles also reflect a variety of threats familiar to children: deadly animals (15:1, snake) and accidents (9:1, fall; 16:1, axe blow).

The many healing miracles are worth special notice, with their drastic character and thematically narrow focus: deaths and vivifications.

---

74. In Gabd 3:2 Annas' son is not cursed because he offended Jesus, but because he did harm to the pools ("What harm did . . . the pools do to you?")! In these variants something inanimate is made human in what seems a projection of Jesus' (and every other child's?) feeling of being hurt—a way of thinking that from a modern point of view appears to reflect a psychologically "childish" attitude.

Rather than seeing in this a vulgarizing of taste in early Christianity (p. 163), a more reasonable explanation is that this is a kind of miracle of special appeal to an audience of minors. Life/death miracles, which are also prominent in fairytales, would probably be the most impressive for such an audience. Children at the age of about five were at a stage of life in which they became conscious and reflective of the phenomenon of death.[75] In addition, children were in antiquity exposed to much higher death rates than adults.[76] Indicative of such awareness is also the fact that all persons but one raised from the dead are children. It is not unreasonable to think that children would generally be the ones most interested in hearing about children being resuscitated, whereas adults would more likely prefer adults.

The overall picture emerging from central events in IGT is that they are very much related to children. In what happens to Jesus, in his actions and reactions, and in the descriptions of life conditions, the fate and feelings of a young audience are reflected: they would recognize their own everyday world, and sense the same joys and fears. They would identify with Jesus' anger, sympathize with his wish for revenge, dream of having similar powers. This is formulated in ways which for adult interpreters may seem exaggerated and even offensive, but which could put a voice to the experiences of the children themselves.

Chronological Framework

As shown (pp. 107–9), the indications of Jesus' age in IGT conform very much to ancient ideas about the socialization and gender formation of children, with Jesus at five playing and going to school, at seven taking part in female activities in the household, at eight in male tasks in the workshop, and finally at twelve in the temple on the threshold to the adult world. Thus, his gradual enculturation leaves an impression of authenticity and is consequently likely to reflect and resonate with experiences of an audience of late antiquity children.

75. On the strong presence of death in children's life, see Rawson, *Children*, 336–63.

76. Saller, *Patriarchy*, 25; also Fox, "Health in Hellenistic and Roman Times," 59–82, esp. 65–66; Laurence, "Health and the Life Course at Herculaneum," 83–96, esp. 86–88. Cf. also Osiek and MacDonald, *A Woman's Place*, 80. For Medieval material, see Orme, *Medieval Children*, chap. 3, "Danger and Death."

It is also worth noting that the chronological distribution within this age five to twelve year span is very uneven. With the exception of Jesus in the Temple, IGT focuses on a very limited period, from age five to eight. And there are even within this span evident focal points, at five (2–9) and eight (12–16), with only two brief passages depicting him at seven (10–11). This interest in age and in specific years is striking. The reason for the foci on ages five and seven/eight can be that these were particularly important and demanding transitional points in children's socialization, and thus considered of special interest in the life of Jesus (cf. also p. 108).[77]

This narrow time span in IGT clearly weakens the filling-the-gap theory employed to account for the creation of the infancy stories: that the stories served to satisfy human curiosity about the blank spots in Jesus' biography (pp. 167–68). And even if we allow for such a curiosity factor, IGT does very little to fill the big time gaps within its own narrative. The theory is also contradicted by the fact that we have no stories at all that aim at filling the large gap in Jesus' life from age thirteen to twenty-nine. Such material might have been expected, and its absence strongly suggests that the main rationale for producing the infancy stories lay elsewhere.[78]

Thus, rather than being a product of human curiosity in general, IGT's interest in Jesus' early life is more readily understood with the question of audience as starting point. With its focus on Jesus' childhood and on central stages within this period of his life, IGT attempts to deal with matters of special concern to its main addressees: children in early Christianity.

Socio-cultural Values and Theology

IGT is, as argued in chap. 6, to a considerable degree adapted psychologically and pedagogically to the level of children. It does not idealize its characters, but gives—though in a brief format—a fairly realistic picture of childhood and of Jesus as a child in late antiquity. As argued in chap. 5, IGT also confirms contemporary values, and values very

---

77. On the notions of age division of childhood in antiquity, see Rawson, *Children*, 134–45, esp. 136, 139–41; Laes, *Kinderen*, 67–87.

78. So also Bovon, "Évangiles canoniques," 26.

much related to children, such as loyalty and obedience to parents and accommodation to honor codes—but at the same time with some concession to a wish for revolt.

Worth special notice is that IGT is sensitive to children's need of social and psychological affirmation. In the interaction between Jesus and his parents, both Mary and Joseph show their love for him by hugging and kissing him (10:2; 12:2). Such descriptions of intimate physicality do not occur in the infancy narratives of the canonical gospels. In comparison, IGT may on this point have had a more immediate appeal to children. It is also free of adult concerns that are central in other early Christian material, such as asceticism, virginity, and marriage (cf. p. 160). If children were IGT's main audience, the absence of such interests is little surprising.

Family conflict is a central issue in IGT; this is visualized in Jesus' encounters with his parents. This is a feature which it shares with much other similar literature, for example apocryphal acts and the Hellenistic novels. But as distinct from the acts, conflict is not due to differing beliefs among adults (e.g., parents and grown-up children), but reflects tensions typical of children vis-à-vis their parents (disobedience). In a way similar to the novels, IGT can be viewed as a story dealing with social-familial adaptation (conflict and reconciliation). But as distinct from them, IGT is about the adaptation of children, not of youngsters and adults.

Characteristic of IGT is the recurring turning-of-tables motif (p. 164). This is a motif which would attract children in particular, given their vulnerable social position. In addition to its biblical roots the motif is also central in ancient fairytales and fables—and in much modern children's literature alike.[79]

IGT reflects few of the issues at stake in early Christian theological controversies, whether doctrinal, polemical or apologetic. Instead, Christology is its main concern, with the aim to present a picture of Jesus credible to its audience. In this respect too, IGT appears well suited for children. By addressing Christology, it deals with a central matter indeed, for Christian theology probably the most central. By focusing so consistently on one issue, it has the pregnancy needed to get its message through. And by being mediated mainly through narratives

---

79. Cf. Zipes, *Breaking the Magic Spell*, esp. chaps. 2 and 7.

and dialogs, its theology is given an easily memorable shape—though not without passages also suited for reflection. Thus, theology in IGT is formulated in ways much likely to appeal to those it addresses—pointedly stated: it is theology for children.

Reflections and Conclusions

As argued in this chapter, there are many kinds of evidence that give credence to my claim about IGT being a children's story. This does not gainsay that IGT also had an adult audience—in fact, without this IGT would not have survived. Clearly, adults must have found the story attractive and important enough to perform it to children and to write it down at certain points of time (cf. pp. 196–97).[80] Nor does the critical attitude to IGT from church leaders such as Irenaeus and John Chrysostom (pp. 174–76 and 178) contradict my view. It is not to be expected that they should regard the material as intended for children. Their concerns were different: the former was taken up with rebutting anything that could be associated with heresy, the latter with safeguarding the canon historically.

The interests of children are of course not all-pervasive in IGT. It is also colored by adult concerns, such as keeping the honor code. In spite of this, IGT testifies to an impressive ability in taking children's perspective; the gospel indicates that one should not think little of adult people's capability in antiquity of insight into their minds and lives (cf. pp. 98–99).

Interpreted this way, IGT can offer a special glimpse into ancient child pedagogy, and in particular into how early Christians communicated religious beliefs to their children. Whereas other sources present examples of theoretical approaches, cf. Quintilian's and Chrysostom's reflections on children's formation, IGT may be offering a case of applied pedagogy: the story can be seen as the kind of material employed to introduce Christian beliefs to children. With its entertaining and edifying narrative about Jesus as child, IGT will have been a powerful means in the transmission of early Christian faith.

---

80. It can also be that IGT's various variants may have had an appeal to different groups. It is for example possible that *Ps.-Mt.* would suit an adult audience better than children.

The idea argued here is likely to be met by objections of a more general kind. First, are not the special traits in IGT's Jesus, his cursing in particular, after all too problematic for children to be its target group? For our modern taste, this may be so. However, what is problematic for us need not have been so for the early Christians. The Jesus of IGT can have been a figure with whom most of them were comfortable: this was in fact their view of him and a view they saw as natural to hand on also to their children.

Second, is not the unhistorical character of IGT problematic? Is it likely that the early Christians would tell their children fictional stories about Jesus? In fact, we cannot know whether IGT's story was perceived to be historical or not. Indeed, many (or most) early Christians may have regarded it historical. And even if they did not, this may still not have been felt problematic: many would be familiar with other Christian stories that were considered fictional, and would interpret such tales as edifying in their own right.

Finally, why has not the idea of IGT as a tale for children been developed on earlier? In my view, this is not due to lack of evidence of such material from antiquity or to lack of indications within IGT itself. Rather, it is due to general neglect within modern scholarship. Traditionally, scholars of early Christianity have focused on matters related to dogma, heresy, gender, and social relations. All are important matters indeed, but the study of them has shared the same bias: the adult bias. IGT has also fallen victim to this, with a number of little credible theories made to account for its existence and character. We now need to widen our scope. It is time to read this material from a different angle. IGT may very well be Christianity's first children's story.

13

CONCLUSIONS

In this book, I have made use of a number of old and new approaches to the *Infancy Gospel of Thomas*. I have given support to some earlier insights, but also argued that many ideas held about it need to be radically revised and even abandoned. In addition, fresh hypotheses have been presented as to how this story is to be interpreted. It is now time to reflect briefly on the challenges that the findings pose for the understanding of IGT and also for the study of early Christianity.

The synoptic comparison of IGT passages have shown that their variant forms are best accounted for as reflecting a combination of oral and written transmission of the story. This makes the quest for an original IGT both more difficult and less meaningful than has been previously assumed. It also implies that the establishing of a stemma for IGT variants and manuscripts must be done with much caution and with due attention to the oral element in the transmission process. Such a view agrees well with observations within similar studies of other early Christian material, for example of the Sayings Source (Q), the Synoptic Gospels, and the apocryphal acts.

Rather than being an obstacle for IGT research, however, the oral/ written approach opens new avenues. In particular, it means that each IGT variant, version, and maybe even manuscript, can be viewed as independent performances of the story and as mirroring their own particular place within early Christianity. Just like the canonical gospels have been read with much profit as for the characteristics of their individual geographical, social, and theological settings, the no less disparate IGT variants can be studied with similar aims in mind. This book has primarily focused on the Greek Gs variant, with occasional side glances at other IGT material. However, such investigations are also possible in the case of other variants, whether Greek or versional. So far, little of this has been done, and such research is likely to provide valuable insight into this manifold—and for early Christianity, and maybe even for antiquity, fairly unparalleled—material.

The analyses have also shown that there is far more of narrative sophistication in IGT than has been held. This sophistication is not of an élite and literary kind, however, but reflects the means and manners of popular-oral storytelling. This is what gives the story the qualities that make it rhetorically effective and attractive to its audience. And it is on the basis of such premises that IGT should be studied and assessed.

The former verdict on IGT as being historically peripheral and theologically aberrant has also turned out to be unfounded. Instead, the material should be seen as reflecting ideas within mainstream early Christianity: it shares the social and cultural values current in late antiquity, such as honor codes and perceptions of gender. Likewise, its theology is of a non-exceptional kind, with focus on central issues, especially Christology, and with evident biblical roots, particularly in the NT gospels. Rather than having its origin in the material itself, disparagement of IGT has usually come from misguided research: the gospel has been judged according to wrong standards, sometimes through an over-intellectual approach, sometimes through readings intending to display its heretical roots. My analyses have shown, however, that IGT—at least in the case of Gs—must first be interpreted on its own terms before it is allotted some particular historical or theological place within early Christianity. Whether other IGT variants and versions will differ from Gs in this must be made the object of further research.

Few scholars have dealt with the social setting and audience of IGT. Some of these have, however, loosely placed the story within a common people context. The analyses above have supported and developed on this view: the IGT material experienced wide dissemination among early Christian middle/lower class people. As such, the material becomes important for a number of reasons. In particular, it can give access to social strata from which there is otherwise limited material preserved. Interpreted this way, IGT offers precious testimony to the social life, cultural values, and theological thinking of a substantial number among the early Christians. Thus, its value for the understanding of early Christianity deserves to be considerably upgraded.

Similarly important, IGT should be seen as an example of material reflecting a rural setting, with the countryside being the habitat of a majority of the population in late antiquity, and very likely also of the early Christians. Given the urbanocentric bias of the ancient sources, and also of modern research, the value of the IGT material is evident. Whereas modern archaeology has already for some time focused on life in the late antique countryside, this has not been the case of much other research. Thus, IGT—but also other early Christian sources—should be further studied with a view to their testimony to this rural world.

In addition to this, however, IGT has been exposed to another misjudgment: it has fallen victim to adultocentrism, or—more specifically—to the adult bias within scholarship. This has not only been the lot of IGT, but also of much other classical and early Christian material. Considering the fact that children are likely to have formed the majority of the population at the time—and at most other points of time in human history—the scholarly neglect is obvious indeed. Although issues on children and childhood have been increasingly dealt with in research, particularly on the classical field, the sources have not been studied systematically enough as to what they can reveal about children's own culture, literature (in a broad sense), and experiences. But just as there has been much gain in approaching the ancient material from the perspectives of gender and social status, it can be equally profitable to do so on the basis of the criterion of age. Thus, the sources should be explored with a view to children, and from the perspectives of children. The ancient material is in this respect likely to yield far more than has been detected until now. And given the modern awareness of the importance of childhood and of children's living conditions and rights the need for such a quest is more than evident.[1]

As for IGT, the adult bias within scholarship has clearly contributed to its marginalization: it has been regarded too banal for serious study, and even as too childish. By such a verdict, however, scholars have been closer to truth than they have realized, but at the same time missed the mark in most respects. As I have tried to show, IGT is a story for children about Jesus, true God and true child. It is a story about a Jesus with whom they could identify, a story with both seriousness and humor, and a story well fit both to entertain and to edify. It presents—with considerable narrative skill—a contextualized Jesus, a

---

1. See also Aasgaard, "Liberating Childhood."

Jesus living in the household-village-rural world shared by most of its audience: early Christian children.

Very likely, history has in the case of the *Infancy Gospel of Thomas* committed the crime of adult appropriation. As adults we have always had our stories. It is now time to let the children have their stories back.

APPENDIX 1

Greek Text

Codex Sabaiticus 259, folios 66r – 72v (H)[1]
+ episodes 01–02/Ga 17–18

[f. 66r] Τὰ παιδικὰ μεγαλεῖα τοῦ δεσπότου ἡμῶν καὶ
σωτῆρος Ἰησοῦ Χριστοῦ

Prolog

1 Ἀναγκαῖον ἡγησάμην ἐγὼ Θωμᾶς Ἰσραηλίτης γνωρίσαι πᾶσιν
τοῖς ἐξ ἐθνῶν ἀδελφοῖς ὅσα ἐποί[f. 66v]ησεν ὁ κύριος ἡμῶν Ἰησοῦς
ὁ Χριστὸς γεννηθεὶς ἐν τῇ χώρᾳ ἡμῶν Βηθλεὲμ κώμῃ Ναζαρέτ.
῏Ων ἡ ἀρχή ἐστιν αὕτη.

Cleaning of Pools

2¹ Τὸ παιδίον Ἰησοῦς πενταετὴς[2] ἦν, καὶ βροχῆς γεναμένης ἔπαιζεν
ἐπὶ διάβασιν ῥύακος. Καὶ ταράσσον τὰ ὕδατα τὰ ῥυπαρὰ ὄντα

---

1. The manuscript is marked by frequent itacisms, di-/monophthong and quantity
confusions. I have in the text adapted the spelling to the koine standard. The most
common changes I have made are: αι → ε, ε → αι, η → ει, ει → η, η → ι, ι → η, ι → ει, οι
→ υ, ο → ω, ω → ο, ου → ο. The nasal ν in final position is often omitted in the manuscript, but has been added. There also occur misspellings and confusion of single and
double consonants. Most of all these changes have not been noted below. Nomina
sacra and other abbreviations also occur but are here written in full: ἄνθρωπος, Θεός,
Ἰερουσαλήμ, Ἰησοῦς, Κύριος, μήτηρ, πατήρ, πνεῦμα, σωτηρία, σωτήριος, υἱός, Χριστός.
Since I employ a diplomatic approach (see pp. 31–32), I have been very reserved toward making insertions of text from other manuscripts. In some cases I agree with
Chartrand-Burke, "Infancy Gospel" (see below) in his—sensible—corrections.

2. H: πενταέτιν.

συνήγαγεν εἰς λάκκους, καὶ ἐποίει³ αὐτὰ καθαρὰ καὶ ἐνάρετα τῇ καταστάσει λόγου μόνον καὶ οὐκ ἔργῳ⁴ ἐπιτάξας αὐτοῖς.

Vivification of Sparrows

2 Εἶτα ἄρας ἐκ τῆς ὕλεως⁵ πηλὸν τρυφερὸν ἔπλασεν ἐξ αὐτοῦ⁶ στρουθία ιβ′. Ην δὲ σάββατον ὅτε ταῦτα ἐποίει, καὶ πολλὰ παιδία ἦσαν σὺν αὐτῷ. **3** Ἰδὼν δέ τις Ἰουδαῖος τὸ παιδίον Ἰησοῦν μετὰ τῶν ἄλλων παιδίων ταῦτα ποιοῦντα, πορευθεὶς πρὸς Ἰωσὴφ τὸν πατέρα αὐτοῦ διέβαλεν⁷ τὸ παιδίον Ἰησοῦν λέγων ὅτι σάββατον πηλὸν ἐποίησεν, ὃ οὐκ ἔξεστιν, καὶ ἔπλασεν στρουθία ιβ′.

4 Καὶ ἐλθὼν Ἰωσὴφ ἐπετίμα αὐτὸν λέγων· Διὰ τί τὸ σάββατον ταῦτα ποιεῖς; Ὁ δὲ Ἰησοῦς συγκροτήσας τὰς χεῖρας μετὰ φωνῆς ἐπίταξας τὰ⁸ ὄρνεα ἐνώπιον πάντων, καὶ εἶπεν· Ὑπάγετε, πετάσθητε ὡς ζῶντες.⁹ Τὰ δὲ στρουθία πετασθέντες ἀπῆλθαν κεκραγότα. **5** Ἰδὼν δὲ ὁ Φαρισαῖος ἐθαύμασεν καὶ ἀπήγγειλεν πᾶσιν τοῖς φίλοις αὐτοῦ.

Curse on Annas' Son

3¹ Ὁ δὲ υἱὸς Ἄννα τοῦ ἀρχιερέως λέγει αὐτῷ· Τί ποιεῖς οὕτως ἐν σαββάτῳ; Καὶ λαβὼν κλωνὸν ἰτέας κατέστρεψεν τοὺς λάκκους, καὶ ἐξέχεεν τὸ ὕδωρ ὅνπερ συνήγαγεν ὁ Ἰησοῦς. Καὶ τὰς συ[f. 67r]ναγωγὰς αὐτῶν ἐξήρανεν. **2** Ἰδὼν δὲ ὁ Ἰησοῦς τὸ γεγονὸς εἶπεν αὐτῷ· Ἄριζος ὁ καρπός σου καὶ ξηρὸς ὁ βλαστός σου ὡς κλάδος ἐκκεόμενος¹⁰ ἐν πνεύματι βιαίῳ.¹¹ **3** Καὶ εὐθέως ὁ παῖς ἐκεῖνος ἐξηράνθη.

3. H: ποιῇ.
4. H: ἔργων.
5. H: φύλεως.
6. H: αὐτῶν.
7. H: διέβαλλεν.
8. H: ἐπετάσαν|τα.
9. H: ἐζῶντες.
10. H: ἐκκομένος.
11. H: τιμίῳ(?).Voicu and Chartrand-Burke guess βιαίῳ, and I agree with them.

Curse on a Careless Boy

4¹ Ἐκεῖθεν πορευομένου αὐτοῦ μετὰ τοῦ πατρὸς αὐτοῦ Ἰωσὴφ καὶ τρέχων ἐκεῖνος ἐρράγη εἰς τὸν ὦμον¹² αὐτοῦ. Καὶ λέγει αὐτῷ ὁ Ἰησοῦς· Ἐπικατάρατός συ ὁ ἡγεμών σου. Καὶ εὐθέως ἀπέθανεν. Καὶ εὐθὺς ὁ λαὸς ἐβόησαν ἰδόντες ὅτι ἀπέθανεν, καὶ εἶπαν· Πόθεν τὸ παιδίον τοῦτο ἐγεννήθη¹³ ὅτι τὸ ῥῆμα αὐτοῦ ἔργον ἐστίν; ² Οἱ δὲ γονεῖς τοῦ ἀποθανόντος παιδίου θεασάμενοι τὸ γεγονὸς Ἰωσὴφ τὸν πατέρα αὐτοῦ ἐμέμφοντο λέγοντες· Ὅθεν¹⁴ τὸ παιδίον τοῦτο ἔχων οὐ δύνασαι οἰκεῖν μεθ' ἡμῶν ἐν τῇ κώμῃ ταύτῃ. Εἰ θέλεις εἶναι ἐνταῦθα, δίδαξον αὐτὸν εὐλογεῖν καὶ μὴ καταρᾶσθαι. Τὸ γὰρ παιδίον ἡμῶν ἐστερήθημεν.¹⁵

Joseph Rebukes Jesus

5¹ Καὶ λέγει τῷ Ἰησοῦ ὁ Ἰωσήφ· Ἵνα τί τοιαῦτα λαλεῖς; Καὶ πάσχουσιν αὐτοὶ καὶ μισοῦσιν¹⁶ ἡμᾶς. Καὶ εἶπεν τὸ παιδίον τῷ Ἰωσήφ· Φρόνιμα ῥήματά συ εἰ γινώσκεις ἄν,¹⁷ πόθεν ἦν τὰ ῥήματά σου οὐκ ἀγνοεῖς. Ἐπὶ πέντε διήγισαν.¹⁸ Κἀκεῖνα οὐκ ἀναστήσονται,¹⁹ καὶ οὗτοι ἀπολήψονται τὴν κόλασιν αὐτῶν. Καὶ εὐθέως οἱ ἐγκαλοῦντες αὐτὸν ἐτυφλώθησαν. ² Ὁ δὲ Ἰωσὴφ ἐπελάβετο τοῦ ὠτίου αὐτοῦ καὶ ἔτιλεν²⁰ σφόδρα. ³ Ὁ δὲ Ἰησοῦς εἶπεν αὐτῷ· Ἀρκείτω²¹ σοι τὸ ζητεῖν με καὶ εὑρίσκειν, μὴ πρὸς τούτῳ[f. 67v] καὶ μωλωπίζειν²² φυσικὴν ἄγνοιαν ἐπιλαβόμενος, καὶ οὐκ εἶδες²³

12. H: ὄνομον.
13. H: ἐγενήθη.
14. H: πόθεν.
15. H: ἐσταιρήθημεν.
16. H: μισῶσιν.
17. H: ἐγεινώσκησαν.
18. H: Ἐπίπεπτε διήγισαν. The Greek text is easily readable, but makes no sense (misspelling?).
19. H: ἀναστήσοντε.
20. H: ἐτί ἄλλεν.
21. H: ἀρκετώ.
22. H: μόλοπηζὴν.
23. H: ἴδες.

μετὰ φῶς τί σοῦ εἰμι. Ἴδε, οἶδας μὴ λυπεῖν με. Σὸς γάρ εἰμι[24] καὶ πρός σε ἐχειρώθην.[25]

First Teacher

First Teacher (Dialog)

6[1] Καθηγητὴς δέ, οὗ τὸ ὄνομα[26] Ζακχαῖος, ἑστὼς ἀκούσας τοῦ Ἰησοῦ ταῦτα λέγοντος πρὸς τὸν πατέρα αὐτοῦ Ἰωσὴφ ἐθαύμασεν σφόδρα. [2] Καὶ εἶπεν τῷ Ἰωσήφ· Δεῦρο, δὸς αὐτό, ἀδελφέ, ἵνα παιδευθῇ γράμματα καὶ ἵνα γνῷ[27] πᾶσαν ἐπιστήμην καὶ μάθῃ στέργειν ἡλικιώτας καὶ τιμᾶν γῆρας καὶ αἰδεῖσθαι[28] πρεσβυτέρους, ἵνα καὶ εἰς τέκνα πόθον κτήσηται ἔξειν ὁμοίως αὐτὰ ἀντεπαιδεύσῃ.[29]

[3] Ὁ δὲ Ἰωσὴφ εἶπεν τῷ καθηγητῇ· Καὶ τίς δύναται τὸ παιδίον τοῦτο κρατῆσαι[30] καὶ παιδεῦσαι αὐτό; Μὴ μικροῦ ἀνθρώπου[31] εἶναι νομίζῃς, ἀδελφέ. Ὁ δὲ καθηγητὴς εἶπεν· δός μοι αὐτό, ἀδελφέ, καὶ μή σοι μελέτω.

[4] Τὸ δὲ παιδίον Ἰησοῦς ἐμβλέψας αὐτοῖς εἶπεν τῷ καθηγητῇ τοῦτον τὸν λόγον· Καθηγητὴς ὢν εὐφυῶς[32] ἐξῆλθες,[33] καὶ τὸ ὄνομα ᾧ[34] ὀνομάζει ἀλλότριος[35] τυγχάνεις. Ἔξωθεν γάρ εἰμι ὑμῶν.[36] Ἔνδοθεν δὲ ὑμῖν δι' αὐτὴν σαρκικὴν εὐγενίαν ὑπάρχων. Σὺ δὲ νομικὸς ὢν τὸν νόμον οὐκ οἶδας.[37] Πρὸς δὲ τὸν Ἰωσὴφ λέγει· Ὅτε ἐγεννήσω[38]

---

24. H: ἡμῖν.
25. Voicu guesses ἐχειρίσθην.
26. H: ὄνομα (probably misspelling).
27. H: γνώς.
28. H: ἐδήσθαι.
29. H: ἀνταπαιδεύσι.
30. H: κρατείσε.
31. Chartrand-Burke exchanges with μικρὸν σταυρόν, "small cross" (cf. Gd).
32. H: ἐμφὺως (probably misspelling).
33. H: ἐξῆχθες(?).
34. H: ὄνοματο(?).
35. H: ἀλλότριως.
36. H: ὑμῶ(†).
37. H: οἶδες(?).
38. H: ἐγέννηως (misspelling).

ὧν ἐγώ σοι παρειστήκειν³⁹ ἵνα, πάτερ, παιδευθῇς ✝✝✝⁴⁰ παιδείαν⁴¹
παρ᾽ ἐμοῦ ἣν ἄλλος οὐκ οἶδεν οὐδὲ διδάξαι δύναται.⁴² Καὶ τὸ
σωτήριον ὄνομα βαστάσεις.
5 Ἀνεβόησαν δὲ Ἰουδαῖοι μέγα[f. 68r] καὶ εἶπαν αὐτῷ· Ὦ
καινοῦ καὶ παραδόξου θαύματος. Τάχα πενταετὴς ἦν τὸ παιδίον,
καὶ ὦ ποῖα φθέγγεται ῥήματα. Τοιούτους λόγους οὐδέποτε οἴδαμεν,
οὐδένος εἰρηκότος, οὐδὲ νομοδιδασκάλου οὐδὲ φαρισαίου τινος ὡς
τοῦ παιδίου τούτου. **6** Ἀπεκρίθη αὐτοῖς τὸ παιδίον καὶ εἶπεν· Τί
θαυμάζετε; Μᾶλλον δὲ τί ἀπιστεῖτε ἐφ᾽ οἷς⁴³ εἶπον ὑμῖν ἀληθῶς
ἐστιν; Ὅτε ἐγεννήθητε ὑμεῖς καὶ οἱ πατέρες ὑμῶν καὶ οἱ πατέρες
τῶν πατέρων ὑμῶν, οἶδα ἀκριβῶς καὶ ὁ <ὢν> πρὸ⁴⁴ τοῦ τὸν κόσμον
κτισθῆναι. **7** Ἀκούσαντες δὲ πᾶς ὁ λαὸς ἐφιμώθησαν, λαλῆσαι
μηκέτι δυνηθέντες πρὸς αὐτόν. Προσελθὼν δὲ αὐτοῖς ἐσκίρτα καὶ
ἔλεγεν· Ἔπαιζον πρὸς ὑμᾶς ἐπειδὴ οἶδα μικροθαύμαστοί ἐστε⁴⁵ καὶ
τοῖς φρονίμοις ὀλίγοι.

First Teacher (Alpha Lesson)

8 Ὡς οὖν⁴⁶ ἔδοξαν παρηγορεῖσθαι ἐπὶ τῇ παρακλήσει τοῦ παιδίου,
ὁ καθηγετὴς εἶπεν τῷ πατρὶ αὐτοῦ· Δεῦρο, ἄγαγε αὐτὸ εἰς τὸ
παιδευτήριον, κἀγὼ διδάξω αὐτὸ γράμματα. Ὁ δὲ Ἰωσὴφ
ἐπιλαβόμενος τῆς χειρὸς αὐτοῦ ἀπήγαγεν αὐτὸν εἰς τὸ παιδευτήριον.
Καὶ ὁ διδάσκαλος κολακεύσας αὐτὸν ἤγαγεν αὐτὸν εἰς τὸ
διδασκαλεῖον. Καὶ ἔγραψεν αὐτῷ ὁ Ζακχαῖος τὸν ἀλφάβητον καὶ
ἤρξατο ἐπιστοιχίζειν⁴⁷ αὐτῷ. Καὶ λέγει τὸ αὐτὸ γράμμα πλεονάκις.
Τὸ δὲ παιδίον οὐκ ἀπεκρίνατο αὐτῷ. Πικρανθεὶς δὲ ὁ καθηγετὴς
ἔκρουσεν αὐτὸ εἰς τὴν κεφαλήν. Τὸ δὲ παι[f. 68v]δίον ἠγανάκτησεν
καὶ εἶπεν αὐτῷ· Ἐγώ σε θέλω παιδεῦσαι μᾶλλον ἢ⁴⁸ παιδευθῆναι

---

39. Η: παριστήκεν.
40. Two or more illegible letters, Η: μίαν(?).
41. Η: ἦν παιδία(?). I here concur with Chartrand-Burke.
42. Η: δύνατε.
43. Η: ἐφ᾽(ὅ?)ις.
44. Η: πρω. For the emendation, see p. 142 above.
45. Η: ἔσται.
46. Η: ὥσοῦ(ν).
47. Η: ἐπιστυχίζην.
48. Η: εἰ.

παρὰ σοῦ. Ἐπειδὴ οἶδα τὰ γράμματα ἃ σὺ[49] διδάσκεις ἀκριβῶς
πολλοὺς κρειττοτέρους σου. Καὶ ταῦτα ἐμοί εἰσιν ὥσπερ χαλκὸς
ἠχῶν ἢ κύμβαλος ἀλαλάζον ἅτινα οὐ[50] παρίστησι τὴν φωνὴν ἢ τὴν
δόξαν οὔτε τὴν δύναμιν τῆς[51] συνέσεως.

9 Παυσάμενον δὲ τῆς ὀργῆς τὸ παιδίον εἶπεν ἀφ᾽ ἑαυτοῦ τὰ
γράμματα πάντα ἀπὸ τοῦ ἄλφα ἕως τοῦ Ὦ μετὰ πολλῆς ἐξετάσεως[52]
καὶ τρανῶς. Ἐμβλέψας τῷ καθηγητῇ εἶπεν αὐτό· Ἄλφα μὴ εἰδὼς τὸ
κατὰ φύσιν, τὸ βῆτα πῶς διδάσκεις ἄλλον;[53] Ὑποκριτά, εἰ οἶδας
πρῶτον δίδαξόν με τὸ ἄλφα καὶ τότε σοι πιστεύσω[54] λέγειν τὸ βῆτα.
Εἶτα ἤρξατο ἀποστοματίζειν τὸν διδάσκαλον περὶ τοῦ α στοιχείου.[55]
Καὶ οὐκ ἴσχυσεν[56] αὐτῷ εἰπεῖν.

10 Ἀκουόντων δὲ πολλῶν λέγει τῷ καθηγητῇ· Ἄκουε, διδάσκαλε,
καὶ νόει τὴν τοῦ πρώτου στοιχείου τάξιν. Καὶ πρόσχες ὧδε
πῶς[57] ἔχει
κανόνας ὀξεῖς[58] καὶ χαρακτῆρα μέσον,
οὓς ὁρᾷς
ὀξυνομένους, διαβαίνοντας, συναγομένους,[59]
ἐξέρποντας, ἀφελκομένους,
ὑψουμένους,[60] χορεύοντας, βεληφοροῦντας,[61]
τρισήμους, διστόμους,
ὁμοσχήμους,[62] ὁμοπολεῖς, ὁμογενεῖς,

49. H: σου or σοι.
50. H: vid. ἀτιναοῦν.
51. H: τ††.
52. H: ἐξέστως. I agree with Chartrand-Burke's correction.
53. H: ἄλον.
54. H: πιστεύειν.
55. H: στυχίου.
56. H: ἴσχυεν.
57. ὧδε πῶς. H has πῶς δὲ (probably misspelling).
58. H: ὥδυς. I agree with Chartrand-Burke's correction.
59. H: συναγωμένας.
60. H: ὑψουμένος.
61. H: βελεφετούτας (misspelling?), but see the next note.
62. ὁμοσχήμους ... ἐπαρτικούς. The words are hardly intelligible. H seems to have ὁμοσχέμους, ὁμοπαλῆς, ὁμοπαγενῆς, ἐπαρτοῦχους. I generally follow Chartrand-Burke, who partly borrows words from other variants, partly exchanges the terms for similar, but more comprehensible words. Probably, there are no ways to make sense of the phrase. For an interpretation of the passage, see pp. 143–46.

ἐπαρτικούς, ζυγοστάτας,
ἰσομέτρους, ἰσομόρους
κανόνας ἔχων τὸ ἄλφα.

First Teacher (Lament)

7¹ Ἀκούσας δὲ ὁ καθηγητὴς τὴν τοιαύτην προσηγορίαν[f. 69r]
<καὶ>⁶³ τοὺς τοιούτους κανόνας τοῦ πρώτου γράμματος εἰρηκότος
τοῦ Ἰησοῦ, ἠπορήθη ἐπὶ τὴν τοιαύτην διδασκαλίαν καὶ ἀπολογίαν⁶⁴
αὐτοῦ. Καὶ εἶπεν ὁ καθηγητής·
Οἴμοι⁶⁵ οἴμοι. Ἠπορήθην ὁ ταλαίπωρος ἐγώ, ἐμαυτὸν αἰσχύνην
παρέσχον ἐπικατασπασάμενος. ² Τὸ παιδίον τοῦτο ἆρον ἀπ᾽ ἐμοῦ,
ἀδελφέ. Οὐ γὰρ φέρω <τὸ αὐστηρὸν>⁶⁶ τοῦ βλέμματος αὐτοῦ οὐδὲ
τὸ⁶⁷ τρανὸν τῶν λόγων αὐτοῦ. Ἁπλῶς τὸ παιδίον τοῦτο γηγενὴς οὐκ
ἔστιν, τοῦτο δύναται καὶ τὸ πῦρ δαμάσαι. Τάχα τοῦτο τὸ παιδίον
πρὸ τῆς κοσμοποιΐας ἦν; Ποία γαστὴρ τοῦτο ἐγέννησε ἢ ποία μήτηρ
ἐξέθρεψεν; Ἐγὼ ἀγνοῶ. Οἴμοι, ἀδελφέ, ἐξηχεῖ με. Οὐ παρακολουθῶ
τῇ διανοίᾳ μου. Ἠπάτησα ἐμαυτόν, ὁ τρισάθλιος ἐγώ. Ἡγούμην
ἔχειν μαθητήν καὶ εὑρέθην ἔχων⁶⁸ διδάσκαλον.
³ Ἐνθυμοῦμαι, φίλοι, τὴν αἰσχύνην μου ὅτι γέρων ὑπάρχω
καὶ ὑπὸ παιδίου νενίκημαι. Καὶ ἔχω ἐκκακῆσαι⁶⁹ καὶ ἀποθανεῖν
ἢ φυγεῖν τῆς κώμης ταύτης διὰ τὸ παιδίον τοῦτο. Οὐ δύναμαι
γὰρ οὐκέτι ὁραθῆναι εἰς ὄψιν πάντων, μάλιστα τῶν ἰδόντων
ὅτι ἐνικήθην ὑπὸ παιδίου πάνυ⁷⁰ μικροῦ. Τί δὲ ἔχω εἰπεῖν ἢ
διηγήσασθαί τινι περὶ ὧν προσέθηκέν⁷¹ μοι κανόνας τοῦ πρώτου
στοιχείου;⁷² Ἀληθῶς ἀγνοῶ, φίλοι. Οὔτε γὰρ ἀρχὴν οὐδὲ τέλος

63. καὶ added. The scribe has probably forgotten the word when changing to a
new page.
64. H: ἀπολογία.
65. H: οἴμμοι (x 2).
66. H has probably omitted some words. The words are added, as a "repair," from
Gad.
67. H: τὸν.
68. H: ἔχοντα.
69. H: ἐκκίσαι (probably misspelling). The text is adjusted to Gad.
70. H: πάνοι.
71. Or: προέθηκέν (possibly misspelling).
72. H: στυχίου.

ἐπίσταμαι. **4** Τοιγαροῦν,⁷³ ἀδελφὲ Ἰωσήφ, ὕπαγε αὐτὸ μετὰ σωτηρίας εἰς τὸν οἶκόν σου. Τοῦτο γὰρ[f. 69v] τὸ παιδίον τί ποτε μέγα ἐστίν, ἢ θεὸς ἢ ἄγγελος ἢ τί εἴπω, οὐκ οἶδα.

First Teacher (Exclamation)

8¹ Τὸ παιδίον Ἰησοῦς ἐγέλασεν καὶ εἶπεν· Νῦν καρποφορείτωσαν τὰ ἄκαρπα καὶ βλεπέτωσαν οἱ τυφλοὶ καὶ φρονείτωσαν⁷⁴ οἱ ἄσοφοι τῇ καρδίᾳ, ὅτι ἐγὼ ἄνωθεν πάρειμι ἵνα τοὺς κάτω ῥύσωμαι⁷⁵ καὶ εἰς τὰ ἄνω καλέσω, καθὼς διεστείλατό με ὁ ἀποστείλας με πρὸς ὑμᾶς. **²** Καὶ εὐθέως ἐσώθησαν πάντες ὑπὸ τῆς κατάρας αὐτοῦ πεπτωκότες,⁷⁶ καὶ οὐδεὶς ἐτόλμα παροργίσαι αὐτὸν ἀπὸ τότε.

Raising of Zeno

9¹ Πάλιν δὲ μετὰ ἡμέρας πολλάς ἔπαιζεν ὁ Ἰησοῦς μετὰ καὶ ἑτέρων παιδίων ἔν τινι δώματι ὑπερῴῳ.⁷⁷ Ἐν δὲ τῶν παιδίων πεσὼν ἀπέθανεν. Ἰδόντες⁷⁸ δὲ τὰ ἄλλα παιδία ἀπῆλθον εἰς τοὺς οἴκους αὐτῶν. Κατέλιπον δὲ τὸν Ἰησοῦν μόνον. **²** Καὶ ἐλθόντες οἱ γονεῖς τοῦ τεθνηκότος παιδίου ἐνεκάλουν⁷⁹ τῷ Ἰησοῦ λέγοντες· Σὺ κατέβαλας τὸ παιδίον ἡμῶν. Ὁ δὲ Ἰησοῦς εἶπεν· Ἐγὼ οὐ κατέβαλα αὐτό. **³** Ἐκείνων δὲ ἐμμαινομένων⁸⁰ καὶ κραζόντων κατέβη Ἰησοῦς ἀπὸ τοῦ στέγου καὶ ἔστη⁸¹ παρὰ τὸ πτῶμα καὶ ἔκραξεν φωνῇ μεγάλῃ⁸² λέγων· Ζῆνον, Ζῆνον (τοῦτο γὰρ τὸ ὄνομα αὐτοῦ), ἀνάστα καὶ εἰπὲ εἰ ἐγώ σε κατέβαλον. Καὶ ἀναστὰς εἶπεν·⁸³ Οὐχί, κύριε.

73. H: τί γὰρ οὖν.
74. H: φρονέσατα.
75. H: ῥύσωμε(ν).
76. H: πεποιθότες. I agree with Chartrand-Burke's correction.
77. H: ὑπερῴων.
78. H: ἰδών.
79. H: ἐνεγκάλουν.
80. H: ἐμμενῶντω. I agree with Chartrand-Burke's correction (cf. Gd).
81. H: ἔστι.
82. H: φωνὴν μεγάλην.
83. H: εἶπε.

Καὶ ἰδόντες ἐθαύμασαν. Καὶ λέγει αὐτῷ πάλιν ὁ Ἰησοῦς· Καὶ κοιμοῦ. Καὶ οἱ γονεῖς τοῦ παιδίου ἐδόξασαν τὸν Θεὸν καὶ προσεκύνησαν τὸ παιδίον Ἰησοῦν.

Carrying Water in a Cloak

10¹ Ἦν δὲ τὸ παιδίον Ἰησοῦς ὡς ἐτῶν ἑπτὰ καὶ ἐπέμφθη⁸⁴ ὑπὸ τῆς μητρὸς αὐτοῦ Μαρίας γε[f. 7or]μίσαι ὕδωρ. Ἐν δὲ τῇ ὑδρείᾳ ἦν ὁ ὄχλος πολύς, κρουσθεῖσα⁸⁵ ἡ κάλπη ἀπέρραγεν.⁸⁶ ² Ὁ δὲ Ἰησοῦς ἁπλώσας τὸ παλλίον⁸⁷ ὃν βεβλημένος,⁸⁸ ἐγέμισεν τὸ ὕδωρ καὶ ἤνεγκεν τῇ μητρὶ αὐτοῦ. Μαρία δὲ ἰδοῦσα ὃ ἐποίησεν σημεῖον ὁ Ἰησοῦς, κατεφίλει αὐτὸν λέγουσα· Κύριε ὁ Θεός μου, εὐλόγησον τὸ τέκνον μου.⁸⁹ Ἐφοβοῦντο γὰρ μή τις αὐτῷ βασκάνῃ.

Miraculously Great Harvest

11¹ Ἐν δὲ τῷ καιρῷ τοῦ σπόρου σπείροντος τοῦ Ἰωσὴφ ἔσπειρεν καὶ τὸ παιδίον Ἰησοῦς ἕνα κόρον σίτου. ² Καὶ ἐθέρισεν ὁ πατὴρ αὐτοῦ κόρους ρʹ μεγάλους. Καὶ ἐχαρίσατο πτωχοῖς καὶ ὀρφανοῖς. Ἦρεν δὲ ὁ Ἰωσὴφ ἀπὸ τοῦ σπόρου τοῦ Ἰησοῦ.

Miraculous Repair of a Bed

12¹ Ἐγένετο δὲ ὡς ἐτῶν ὀκτώ. Καὶ τοῦ πατρὸς αὐτοῦ τέκτονος ὄντος καὶ ἐργαζομένου ἄροτρα καὶ ζυγούς,⁹⁰ ἔλαβεν κράβαττον παρά τινος πλουσίου ἵνα αὐτὸν ποιήσῃ μέγα πάνυ⁹¹ καὶ ἐπιτήδειον. Καὶ τοῦ ἑνὸς κανόνος τοῦ καλουμένου κολοβωτέρου ὄντος καὶ μὴ ἔχοντος τὸ μέτρον, ἦν λυπούμενος ὁ Ἰωσὴφ καὶ μὴ ἔχων⁹² τί ποιῆσαι.

84. H: ἐπεύθη. I agree with Chartrand-Burke's correction.
85. H: κρουσθούσα.
86. H: ἀπόραγεν.
87. H: παλίον.
88. H: βεβλημμένος.
89. H: μας.
90. H: ζυγὰ.
91. H: πάνοι.
92. H: ἔχοντος.

Προσελθὼν τὸ παιδίον τῷ πατρὶ αὐτοῦ λέγει· Θὲς κάτω τὰ δύο
ξύλα καὶ ἐκ τοῦ⁹³ σου μέρους ἰσοποίησον αὐτά. ² Καὶ ἐποίησεν ὁ
Ἰωσὴφ καθὼς εἶπεν αὐτῷ ὁ Ἰησοῦς. Ἔστη δὲ τὸ παιδίον ἐκ τοῦ
ἑτέρου μέρους καὶ ἐκράτησεν τὸ κολοβὸν ξύλον καὶ ἐξέτεινεν αὐτό.
Καὶ ἴσον ἐποίησεν μετὰ τοῦ ἄλλου ξύλου. Καὶ εἶπεν τῷ πατρὶ
αὐτοῦ· Μὴ λυποῦ ἀλλὰ ποίει⁹⁴ ὃ θέλεις. Ὁ δὲ Ἰωσὴφ περιλαβὼν[f. 70v]
κατεφίλει αὐτὸν λέγων· Μακάριός εἰμι ἐγώ, ὅτι τοῦτον⁹⁵ παιδίον
ἔδωκέν μοι ὁ Θεός.

Second Teacher

13¹ Ἰδὼν δὲ Ἰωσὴφ τὸ φρόνιμον καὶ νουνεχὲς αὐτοῦ ἠβουλήθη⁹⁶
μὴ εἶναι αὐτὸ ἄπορον γραμμάτων, ἀλλὰ παρέδωκεν αὐτὸν ἕτερον
διδάσκαλον. Καὶ ὁ διδάσκαλος γράψας αὐτῷ τὸν ἀλφάβητον ἔλεγεν·
Εἰπὲ ἄλφα. ² Τὸ δὲ παιδίον λέγει· Σύ μοι⁹⁷ πρῶτον εἰπὲ τί ἐστιν τὸ
βῆτα, κἀγώ σοὶ⁹⁸ ἐρῶ τί ἐστιν τὸ ἄλφα. Πικρανθεὶς δὲ ὁ καθηγητὴς
ἔκρουσεν αὐτό. Καὶ κατηράσατο αὐτὸν ὁ Ἰησοῦς, καὶ ἔπεσεν ὁ
καθηγητὴς καὶ ἀπέθανεν.

³ Καὶ τὸ παιδίον ἀπῆλθεν εἰς τὸν οἶκον αὐτοῦ πρὸς τοὺς
γονεῖς αὐτοῦ. Καὶ Ἰωσὴφ καλέσας τὴν μητέρα αὐτοῦ παρήγγειλε⁹⁹
αὐτῇ· Μὴ ἀπολύσῃ¹⁰⁰ αὐτὸν ἀπὸ τῆς οἰκίας ἵνα μὴ ἀποθνήσκωσιν οἱ
παροργίζοντες αὐτόν.

Third Teacher

14¹ Καὶ μεθ' ἡμέρας τινὰς πάλιν ἕτερος καθηγητὴς εἶπεν τῷ πατρὶ
αὐτοῦ Ἰωσήφ· Δεῦρο, ἀδελφέ, δός μοι αὐτὸ εἰς τὸ παιδευτήριον ἵνα
μετὰ κολακείας δυνήσωμαι αὐτὸ διδάξαι γράμματα. Ὁ δὲ Ἰωσὴφ
εἶπεν αὐτῷ· Εἰ θαρρεῖς, ἀδελφέ, ἄγαγε αὐτὸ μετὰ σω[τηρί]ας. Καὶ

93. H: τω.
94. H: ποίω.
95. H: οὗτον.
96. H: ἠβούλη. The reading is taken from Gad.
97. H: μου(?).
98. H: σὺ.
99. H: παρέγγιλεν.
100. H: ἀπολύει.

ὁ διδάσκαλος λαβόμενος τὸ παιδίον ἐκ τῆς χειρὸς ἀπήγαγεν μετὰ φόβου καὶ ἀγῶνος πολλοῦ. Τὸ δὲ παιδίον ἡδέως ἐπορεύετο.

2 Καὶ εἰσελθὼν ἐν τῷ διδασκαλείῳ¹⁰¹ εὗρεν βιβλίον ἐν τῷ ἀναλογείῳ κείμενον. Καὶ λαβὼν αὐτὸ οὐκ ἀνεγίνωσκεν¹⁰² τὰ γεγράμμενα διὰ τὸ μὴ εἶναι αὐτὰ ἐκ[f. 71r] νόμου Θεοῦ, ἀλλὰ ἀνοίξας τὸ στόμα αὐτοῦ ἐπεφθέγξατο¹⁰³ ῥήματα φοβερὰ ὥστε τὸν καθηγητὴν ἄντικρυς καθιζόμενον ἡδέως πάντα¹⁰⁴ ἤκουει¹⁰⁵ αὐτῷ καὶ παρεκάλει αὐτὸ ἵνα πλείονα εἴπῃ.¹⁰⁶ Τὸν¹⁰⁷ δὲ παρεστῶτα ὄχλον ἐκπλήττεσθαι ἐν τοῖς ὁσίοις ῥήμασιν αὐτοῦ.

3 Ὁ δὲ Ἰωσὴφ ταχέως ἔδραμεν εἰς τὸ διδασκαλεῖον ὑπονόησας μήκετι οὗτος ὁ καθηγητὴς ἄπειρός ἐστιν καὶ πάθη.¹⁰⁸ Εἶπεν δὲ ὁ καθηγητὴς τῷ Ἰωσήφ· Ἵνα οἶδας, ἀδελφέ, ὅτι ἐγὼ μὲν τὸ παιδίον σου¹⁰⁹ παρέλαβον μαθητήν, αὐτὸ πολλῆς χάριτος καὶ σοφίας μεστόν ἐστιν. Τοιγαροῦν, ἀδελφέ, ἄπαγε α[ὐτὸν] μετὰ σωτηρίας εἰς [τὸ]ν οἶκόν σου.

4 Ὁ δὲ εἶπεν τῷ καθηγητῇ· Ἐπειδὴ ὀρθῶς ἐλάλησας καὶ ὀρθῶς ἐμαρτύρησας, διὰ σὲ¹¹⁰ καὶ ὁ πληγεὶς σωθήσεται. Καὶ παραχρῆμα ἐσώθη κἀκεῖνος ὁ καθηγητής. Ὁ δὲ λαβόμενος τὸ παιδίον ἀπήγαγεν εἰς τὸν οἶκον αὐτοῦ.

Healing of James' Snakebite

15¹ Ὁ δὲ Ἰάκωβος ἀπήγαγεν εἰς τὴν νάπην¹¹¹ τοῦ δῆσαι φρύγανα ἵνα ἄρτοι γίνωνται. Ἀπήγεν καὶ ὁ Ἰησοῦς μετ' αὐτοῦ. Καὶ συλλεγόντων αὐτῶν τὰ φρύγανα ἔχιδνα παλαμναῖα ἔδακεν τὸν Ἰάκωβον εἰς τὴν χεῖραν αὐτοῦ. **2** Κατατεινομένου δὲ αὐτοῦ καὶ

---

101. H: διδασκαλίον.

102. H: ἀπεγίνωσκεν.

103. H: ἐπεφθέξατω.

104. H: πάνοι. I agree with Chartrand-Burke's correction.

105. H: ἀκούη(?).

106. H: εἴπει.

107. H: τὸ.

108. H: πάθει.

109. H: παιδίονονσου (dittography?).

110. H: δι' ἐσε. I agree with Chartrand-Burke's correction.

111. H: τηνάπην (haplography?).

ἀπολλυμένου προσέδραμεν τὸ παιδίον Ἰησοῦς πρὸς τὸν Ἰάκωβον[112] καὶ κατεφύσησεν τὸ δῆγμα. Καὶ παραχρῆμα ἰάθη τὸ δῆγμα, καὶ τὸ θηρίον ἀπενεκρώθη, καὶ Ἰάκωβος ἐστάθη.

Healing of an Injured Foot

16[1] Πάλιν σχίζοντος ξύλα ἐν ἴσῳ νεωτέρου[113] τινός, καὶ ἔσχισεν τὴν βάσιν τοῦ[f. 71v] ποδὸς αὐτοῦ καὶ ἔξαιμος γενόμενος ἀπέθνησκεν. [2] Θορύβου γεναμένου ἔδραμεν ὁ Ἰησοῦς. Καὶ βιασάμενος διῆλθεν διὰ τοῦ ὄχλου καὶ κρατήσας τὸν πόδα τὸν πεπληγότα, καὶ εὐθέως ἰάθη. Καὶ εἶπεν τῷ νεανίσκῳ· Ὕπαγε, σχίζε τὰ ξύλα σου. [3] Ἰδόντες δὲ οἱ ὄχλοι ἐθαύμασαν καὶ εἶπαν· Πολλὰς γὰρ ψυχὰς [ἔσω]σεν ἐκ θανάτου, καὶ ἔχει σῶσαι πά[σας] τὰς ἡμέρας τ[ῆς] ζωῆς αὐτοῦ.

Jesus in the Temple

17[1] Ὄν[τος] δ[ὲ] τοῦ Ἰησοῦ δωδε[καετοῦς] ἐπορεύοντο [οἱ] γονεῖς[114] αὐτοῦ κατὰ τὸ ἔθος εἰς Ἱεροσόλυμα εἰς τὴν ἑορτὴν τοῦ Πάσχα. Ἐν δὲ τῷ ἐπιστρέφειν αὐτοὺς ἀπέμεινεν Ἰησοῦς εἰς Ἱερουσαλήμ. Καὶ οὐκ ἔγνωσαν οἱ γονεῖς αὐτοῦ νομίσαντες εἶναι αὐτὸν ἐν τῇ συνοδίᾳ. [2] Ἦλθαν ἡμέρας ὁδὸν καὶ ἐζήτουν[115] αὐτὸν ἐν τοῖς συγγενεῦσιν καὶ ἐν τοῖς γνωστοῖς αὐτῶν. Καὶ μὴ εὑρόντες αὐτὸν ὑπέστρεψαν εἰς Ἱερουσαλὴμ ζητοῦντες αὐτόν. Καὶ μετὰ ἡμέρας τρεῖς εὗρον αὐτὸν ἐν τῷ ἱερῷ καθήμενον ἐν μέσῳ τῶν διδασκάλων καὶ ἀκούοντα αὐτῶν καὶ ἐπερωτῶντα αὐτούς. Ἐξίσταντο δὲ οἱ ἀκούοντες αὐτοῦ πῶς ἀπεστομάτιζεν τοὺς πρεσβυτέρους καὶ ἐπιλύων τὰ κεφάλαια τοῦ νόμου καὶ τῶν προφητῶν τὰ σκολιὰ καὶ τὰς παραβολάς. [3] Καὶ εἶπεν πρὸς αὐτὸν ἡ μήτηρ αὐτοῦ· Τέκνον, τί ἐποίησας ἡμῖν;[116] Ἰδού, ὀδυνώμενοι λυπούμενοι ἐζητοῦμέν σε. Καὶ εἶπεν

112. H: Ἰάκωβος πρὸς τὸν Ἰησοῦν. The scribe of H has here confused the sequence of the names. This is clear from the textual context and is also in agreement with Ga and Syr.

113. H: ἐνίσυνεωτερου (misspelling: -υν- should have been -ων-?).

114. In this area the manuscript is worn, but the reconstruction is likely to be correct.

115. H has ὁ before ἐζήτουν.

116. Chartrand-Burke adds τοῦτο (cf. Gad); Luke 2:48 has οὕτως.

αὐτοῖς ὁ Ἰησους· "Ινα[f. 72r] τί ἐζητεῖτέ με; Οὐκ οἴδατε ὅτι ἐν τοῖς τοῦ πατρός μου δεῖ εἶναί με;

4 Οἱ δὲ γραμματεῖς καὶ οἱ Φαρισαῖοι εἶπαν τῇ Μαρίᾳ· Σὺ εἶ ἡ μήτηρ τοῦ παιδίου τούτου; Ἡ δὲ[117] εἶπεν· Ἐγώ εἰμι. Εἶπαν δὲ πρὸς αὐτήν· Μακαρία εἶ σύ, ὅτι ηὐλόγησεν κύριος ὁ Θεὸς τὸν καρπὸν τῆς κοιλίας σου. Τοιαύτην γὰρ σοφίαν ἐνεστώς καὶ δόξαν ἀρετῆς οὐδὲ εἴδαμεν[118] οὔτε ἠκούσαμέν ποτε.

5 Ἀναστὰς δὲ ἐκεῖθεν ὁ Ἰησοῦς ἠκολούθησεν τῇ μητρὶ αὐτοῦ καὶ ἦν ὑποτασσόμενος τοῖς γονεῦσιν αὐτοῦ. Καὶ διετήρει πάντα τὰ ῥήματα ταῦτα συμβαλοῦσα ἐν τῇ καρδίᾳ αὐτῆς. Καὶ ὁ Ἰησοῦς προέκοπτεν σοφίᾳ καὶ ἡλικίᾳ καὶ χάριτι παρὰ Θεῷ καὶ ἀνθρώποις. Ὦ ἡ δό[f. 72v][ξα] . . .

01-02/Ga 17-18 (episodes lacking in Codex Sabaiticus 259)[119]

Raising of a Dead Baby

01¹ Ἐν τῇ γειτονίᾳ τοῦ Ἰωσὴφ νοσῶν τι νήπιον ἀπέθανεν, καὶ ἔκλαιεν ἡ μήτηρ αὐτοῦ σφόδρα. Ἤκουσεν δὲ ὁ Ἰησοῦς ὅτι πένθος μέγα καὶ θόρυβος γίνεται, ἔδραμεν σπουδαίως. Καὶ εὑρὼν τὸ παιδίον νεκρὸν ἥψατο τοῦ στήθους αὐτοῦ καὶ λέγει αὐτῷ· Σοὶ λέγω, βρέφος, μὴ ἀποθάνῃς ἀλλὰ ζῆθι.[120] Καὶ εὐθέως ἀνέστη καὶ προσεγέλασε. Εἶπεν δὲ τῇ μητρὶ αὐτοῦ· Ἆρον τὸ τέκνον σου[121] καὶ μνημόνευέ μου.

2 Ἰδὼν δὲ ὁ ὄχλος ὁ παρεστὼς ἐθαύμασεν καὶ εἶπον· Ἀληθῶς τοῦτο τὸ παιδίον ἢ θεὸς ἢ ἄγγελός ἐστιν, ὅτι πᾶς λόγος αὐτοῦ ἔργον γίνεται. Ἐξῆλθεν δὲ ὁ Ἰησοῦς πάλιν καὶ ἔπαιζεν μετὰ τῶν παιδίων.

---

117. H: ἰδε(?).

118. H: οἴδαμεν.

119. I here follow Codex hist. Gr 91 (manuscript W), with some slight changes (partly adaptations to Chartrand-Burke, Hock, and Tischendorf A).

120. Greek family α (see p. 15) and the Slavonic translation (see pp. 183–84) add: καὶ ἔστω μετὰ τῆς μητρός σου.

121. Greek family α adds: καὶ δὸς γάλα.

Raising of a Dead Laborer

02 Μετὰ δὲ χρόνον τινὰ οἰκοδομῆς γενομένης ἔπεσεν ἄνθρωπος ἀπὸ τοῦ ἀναβαθμοῦ κάτω καὶ ἀπέθανεν. Συνδρομῆς δὲ γενομένης καὶ θορύβου μεγάλου ἵστατο τὸ παιδίον ὁ Ἰησοῦς καὶ ἀπῆλθεν ἕως ἐκεῖ. Ἰδὼν δὲ τὸν ἄνθρωπον κείμενον νεκρὸν ἐπελάβετο τῆς χειρὸς αὐτοῦ καὶ εἶπεν· Σοὶ λέγω, ἄνθρωπε, ἀνάστα, ποίει τὸ ἔργον σου. Καὶ εὐθέως ἀναστὰς προσεκύνησεν αὐτόν.

English Translation

The Great Childhood Deeds of our Lord and Saviour Jesus Christ[1]

Prolog

1 I, the Israelite Thomas, have considered it necessary to make known to all the Gentile brothers the things that our Lord Jesus Christ did after being born in our region Bethlehem in the village of Nazareth. This is how it begins:

Cleaning of pools

2[1] The child Jesus was five years old and was, after a shower, playing at the ford of a rushing stream. He collected the flooding water, which was unclean, into pools. And he made it pure and fresh; he commanded it only by means of a word and without any deed.

Vivification of Sparrows

2 Then he took soft clay from the mud and formed twelve sparrows from it. It was Sabbath when he did this, and many children were with him. 3 But a Jew, who saw the child Jesus doing this with the other children, went to his father Joseph and accused the child Jesus saying: "He

---

1. In the translation, I have aimed at being concordant particularly as concerns central terms and phrases. The very frequent conjunctive δέ and καί have been variously translated "and," "but," and "then," depending on context; sometimes the words have also been omitted in translation. When Sabaiticus 259's and Luke's Jesus in the Temple are in verbatim agreement, the wording has been held as close as possible to the translation of NRSV. On several occasions, the manuscript is difficult to decipher; some are noted here, some are also commented on in chap. 9.

has made clay on the Sabbath, which isn't allowed, and formed twelve sparrows."

4 When Joseph came he rebuked him, saying: "Why do you do this on the Sabbath?" But Jesus clapped his hands and commanded the birds with a cry in front of all. And he said: "Go, take flight like living beings." And the sparrows took off and flew away twittering. **5** But when the Pharisee saw this he marveled and told it to all his friends.

Curse on Annas' Son

3¹ Then the son of the High Priest Annas said to him: "Why do you do this on the Sabbath?" And he took a willow bough and destroyed the pools, and let the water that Jesus had collected run out; he dried up the pools he had collected. **2** But when Jesus saw what had happened, he said to him: "Your fruit be without root, and your shoot withered like a branch let off by a strong wind!" **3** And immediately that child withered away.

Curse on a Careless Boy

4¹ When he left there with his father Joseph, someone running bumped into his shoulder. And Jesus said to him: "Cursed be your ruling power!" And immediately he died. When the people saw that he died, they at once cried out and said: "From where was this child born, since his word becomes deed?" **2** But when the parents of the dead child noticed what had happened, they blamed his father Joseph, saying: "Because you have this child, you can't live with us in this village. If you want to be here, teach him to bless and not to curse. For our child has been taken away from us."

Joseph Rebukes Jesus

5¹ And Joseph said to Jesus: "Why do you say such things? They suffer and hate us." And the child said to Joseph: "Since you know wise words, you are not ignorant of where your words came from: they were spoken about a five-year-old.² And since they are unable to raise them [i.e. the

---

2. Gs is here difficult to read and make sense of.

children] up, they too shall receive their punishment."³ And the ones accusing him were immediately blinded. **2** But Joseph grabbed hold of his ear and pulled it hard. **3** Then Jesus said to him: "Let it suffice for you to seek and find me, and not also to torment me by having a natural ignorance. You do not see with light why I am yours. Behold! You know that you cannot distress me. For I am yours and have been put in your hands."

First Teacher

First Teacher (Dialog)

6¹ A teacher named Zacchaeus who stood listening to Jesus saying this to his father Joseph, marveled very much. **2** And he said to Joseph: "Come, give him [to me], brother, so that he can be taught letters, and so that he can have all understanding, learn to have affection for those his own age, and respect the old and please elders, and so that he can in his turn teach them to have a wish to become like children in the same way."

3 But Joseph said to the teacher: "Who is able to control and teach this child? Do not regard him to be a human in miniature, brother." But the teacher said: "Give him to me, brother, and do not be worried."

4 But the child Jesus looked at them and said this word to the teacher: "Since you are a teacher, you have shown yourself to be clever.⁴ But you are a stranger to the name by which he names [you].⁵ For I am from outside of you, but I am also from within you⁶ because of my noble birth in the flesh. But you do not, even though you are a lawyer, know the law." And to Joseph he said: "When you were born, I existed and came to you so that you, father, could be taught a teaching by me which no one else knows or is able to teach. And you will take on the saving name."⁷

5 And the Jews cried out loud and said to him: "Oh, what a new and incredible miracle! The child is perhaps only five years old, and

3. Gs is here difficult to read and make sense of.
4. Gs is here difficult to make sense of.
5. Gs is here difficult to make sense of. For an interpretation, see p. 141.
6. Or "from/in your midst", "among you", see p. 141.
7. The formulation is unique to Gs, see pp. 141–42.

oh, what words he utters. We have never known such words. No one, neither a teacher of the law nor a Pharisee, has spoken like this child." ⁶ The child answered them and said: "Why do you marvel? And why do you even not believe that I have told you what is true? In fact, I—and he <who existed> before the world was created[8]—know accurately when you and your fathers and your fathers' fathers were born." ⁷ All the people listening were put to silence and were no longer able to talk to him. But he went up to them, leaped about and said: "I was playing with you, for I know that you are easily impressed and small-minded."

First Teacher (Alpha Lesson)

⁸ Thus, as they seemed to be soothed by the child's exhortation, the teacher said to his father: "Come, bring him to school and I shall teach him the letters." And Joseph took him by the hand and led him to school. And the master flattered him and brought him into the classroom. Then Zacchaeus wrote the alphabet for him and began to instruct him, repeating a letter to him many times. But the child didn't answer him. The teacher became irritated and hit him in the head. And the child became angry and said to him: "I want to teach you rather than be taught by you. For I know the letters that you are teaching much more accurately than you. To me this is like a noisy gong or a clanging cymbal which can't provide the sound or glory or power of insight."

⁹ When his anger had ceased, the child said by himself with much care and clarity all the letters from the alpha to the omega. He looked at the teacher and said to him: "When you do not know the nature of the alpha, how can you teach another the beta? Hypocrite! If you know, teach me first the alpha and then I will trust you to talk about the beta." Then he began to examine the master about the letter A. But he couldn't answer him.

¹⁰ With many listening he said to the teacher: "Listen, master, and be mindful of the order of the first letter, and pay close attention
    how it has
    sharp lines and a middle stroke,
    which you see
    sharpening, intersecting, joining,

8. Gs is here difficult to make sense of, cf. pp. 142 and 223. The phrase can also be translated "the one existing before."

creeping out, drawing back,
elevated, dancing, missile-bearing,[9]
three-marked, double-edged,
same-formed,[10] same-placed, same-kinded,
raised, balanced,
equally-measured, equally-proportioned—
such lines does the alpha have."

First Teacher (Lament)

7[1] When the teacher heard Jesus make this exposition on these principles of the first letter, he was baffled by such teaching and his defense. And the teacher said:

"Dear me! Dear me! I am totally baffled and miserable. I have caused and brought down shame upon myself. [2] Take this child away from me, brother! For I can't bear his severe look or clear speech. The child is simply not of this earth—he is even able to tame fire. Perhaps this child existed before the creation of the world? What kind of womb bore him? What kind of mother raised him? I really don't know. Dear me, brother, he outdoes me! My mind can't comprehend this. I have deceived myself, thrice unhappy as I am. I thought to have a student but ended up having a master.

[3] I am troubled, friends, about my shame, since I am an old man who has been overcome by a child. And I shall grow weary and die, or have to flee from this village because of this child. For I cannot any longer be seen in view of all, especially those who saw that I was overcome by such a very small child. But what can I say or explain to anyone about the principles of the first letter that he presented to me? Truly, friends, I don't know. For I understand neither the beginning nor the end. [4] Thus, brother Joseph, take him with salvation to your house. For what great thing this child is—whether a god, an angel, or whatever else—I don't know."

9. The word is difficult to make sense of; see the Greek text.

10. This and the following three words are difficult to make sense of. See the Greek text with note and my interpretation of the passage in p. 145.

First Teacher (Exclamation)

8[1] The child Jesus laughed and said: "Now let the unfruitful bear fruit, the blind see, and the foolish in heart become wise. For I have come from above in order to rescue those below and call them to what is above, just as the one who sent me to you ordered me." [2] And immediately all those who had fallen under his curse were saved. And no one dared to make him angry after that.

Raising of Zeno

9[1] And again, many days later, Jesus was playing with some other children on the roof of an upstairs room. And one of the children fell and died. When the other children saw this, they went off to their houses. And they left Jesus alone. [2] Then the parents of the dead child came and accused Jesus, saying: "You pushed our child down." But Jesus said: "I didn't push him down." [3] And as they were in a rage and shouting, Jesus went down from the roof, stood beside the body, and cried out in a loud voice saying: "Zeno, Zeno (for this was his name), stand up and say if I pushed you down." And he stood up and said: "No, Lord."

When they saw this, they marveled. Then again Jesus said to him: "Fall asleep!" And the child's parents praised God and worshipped the child Jesus.

Carrying Water in a Cloak

10[1] When the child Jesus was about seven years old, he was sent by his mother Mary to fill water. But there was a big crowd at the water outlet, and the pitcher was knocked and broke. [2] Then Jesus spread out the cloak he was wearing, filled it with water, and carried it to his mother. But when Mary saw the sign that Jesus had done, she kissed him saying: "Lord, my God, bless my child." For she feared that someone might put a ban on him.

Miraculously Great Harvest

11[1] Then at the time when Joseph was sowing seeds, the child Jesus also sowed one measure of grain. [2] And his father harvested one hundred great measures, and he gave it to the poor and the orphans. But Joseph took it from Jesus' seeds.

Miraculous Repair of a Bed

12^1 Then, as he was about eight years old, his father, who was a carpenter making plows and yokes, received a bed from a rich man in order to make it very big and suitable. But since one piece called the sideplank was too short[11] and didn't have the [right] length, Joseph became distressed and didn't know what to do.

But the child went to his father saying: "Put the two boards down and align them from your end." ^{2} And Joseph did as Jesus told him. Then the child took place at the other end, grasped hold of the short board and stretched it. And he made it equal to the other board. Then he said to his father: "Do not be distressed but do what you want." And Joseph embraced and kissed him saying: "Blessed am I, since God gave me this child."

Second Teacher

13^1 When Joseph saw his wise and sensible thinking he didn't want him to be unacquainted with letters. Thus he handed him over to another master. And the master wrote down the alphabet for him and said: "Say alpha!" ^{2} But the child said: "You tell me first what the beta is, and I shall tell you what the alpha is." But the teacher became irritated and hit him. Then Jesus cursed him, and the teacher fell and died.

^{3} And the child went to his house to his parents. Then Joseph summoned his mother and instructed her: "Don't let him go outside the house lest those who annoy him end up dead."

Third Teacher

14^1 Then some days after another teacher again said to his father Joseph: "Come, brother, give him to me to school so that I may with flattery be able to teach him letters." And Joseph said to him: "If you dare, brother, lead him off with salvation." Then the master took the

11. The expression is difficult to make sense of. Some words may have been omitted. Ga has "But since one plank called the crossbeam was too short . . ."

child by hand and led him away with much fear and worry. But the child was glad to go.

2 And when he entered the classroom, he found a book lying on the lectern. And he took it, but didn't read what was written in it, since it wasn't from God's law. Instead, he opened his mouth and uttered words so awe-inspiring that the teacher sitting opposite was glad to hear all he said and encouraged him to say more. And the crowd standing there was highly impressed by his holy words.

3 But Joseph ran quickly to the classroom suspecting that this teacher was now in trouble and suffered. But the teacher said to Joseph: "Please know, brother, that I took your child as a student; however, he is full of much grace and wisdom. Therefore, brother, take him with salvation away to your house."

4 Then he [i.e. Jesus] said to the teacher: "Since you have spoken true and testified true, the one struck down shall also be saved because of you." And straight away that teacher also was saved. And he [i.e. Joseph] took the child and led him away to his house.

Healing of James' Snakebite

15¹ James went out into the forest to tie up sticks to use for baking bread. And Jesus went with him. And while they were gathering the sticks, a miscreant snake bit James on his hand. **2** As he was wracked with pain and dying, the child Jesus ran to James and blew on the bite. Then straight away the bite was healed, the snake was destroyed, and James stood up.

Healing of an Injured Foot

16¹ Then again, as a young man was splitting wood into equal pieces, he split the bottom of his foot, and died from loss of blood. **2** There was a commotion and Jesus ran there. And he forced his way through the crowd and grasped hold of the stricken foot. And it was immediately healed. And he said to the young man: "Go, split your wood."

3 When the crowd of people saw this, they marveled and said: "He has indeed saved many souls from death. And he will go on saving all the days of his life."

Jesus in the Temple

17¹ When Jesus was twelve his parents as usual went to Jerusalem for the festival of the Passover. But when they returned, Jesus stayed behind in Jerusalem. And his parents did not know it, assuming that he was in the group of travelers.

² They went a day's journey and searched for him among their relatives and friends. When they did not find him, they returned to Jerusalem to search for him. And after three days they found him in the temple sitting among the teachers, listening to them and asking them questions. And those who heard him were amazed how he examined the elders and explained the main points of the law and the riddles and the parables of the prophets.

³ And his mother said to him: "Child, what have you done to us?[12] Look, we have been searching for you in great anxiety and distress." But Jesus said to them: "Why were you searching for me? Did you not know that I must be in my Father's house?"

⁴ Then the scribes and the Pharisees said to Mary: "Are you the mother of this child?" And she said: "I am." Then they said to her: "Blessed are you, for the Lord God has blessed the fruit of your womb. For we have never known nor heard such wisdom as his, nor such glory of virtue."

⁵ Then Jesus stood up and followed his mother from there, and was obedient to his parents. And she treasured all these words and pondered them in her heart. And Jesus increased in wisdom and age and grace before God and humans. To him be the glory [forever, amen].

Translation of 01–02/Ga 17–18 (episodes lacking in Gs)[13]

Raising of a Dead Baby

01¹ In the neighborhood of Joseph a baby fell ill and died. And its mother cried terribly. But as Jesus heard the great mourning and noise

---

12. Or, if the text is adjusted to Luke 2:48 or Gad: "why have you treated us like this?"

13. These episodes primarily occur in the Greek Gad manuscripts; see appendix 5.

going on, he ran there quickly. When he found the child dead, he touched its chest and said to it: "I tell you, little child: you shall not be dead. Instead, live!"[14] And immediately it stood up and smiled. And Jesus said to its mother: "Take your child,[15] and remember me."

2 When the crowd present saw this, they marveled and said: "Truly, this child is a god or an angel! For everything he says comes to pass." But Jesus went out again to play with the other children.

Raising of a Dead Laborer

02 Some time later, during the construction of a building, a man fell down from the staircase and died. There was great commotion and noise, and the child Jesus got up and went off to the place. As he saw the man lying dead, he took hold of his hand and said: "I tell you, man: stand up, and go back to your work!" And immediately he stood up and worshipped him.

14. The Greek family α and the Slavonic translation add "and be with your mother."

15. The Greek family α adds "give it milk."

APPENDIX 3

The Structure of Ga/Gb/Gd

The following is a simplified outline of Ga, Gb (which lacks episodes 12 and 14–19), and Gd:

Ga/(Gb)/Gd			Gs
1	Heading/Prolog		1
2–3	Three Miracles		
	2:1	Cleaning of Pools	2:1
	2:2–5	Vivification of Sparrows	2:2–5
	3	Curse on Annas' Son	3
4–5	A Miracle and the Responses to It		
	4	Curse on a Careless Boy	4
	5	Joseph Rebukes Jesus	5
6–8	Teacher Discourse/First Teacher		
	6:1–7	Dialog	6:1–7
	6:8–10	Alpha Lesson	6:8–10
	7	Lament	7
	8	Exclamation	8
9–10	Two Miracles and the Responses to Them		
	9	Raising of Zeno	9
	10	Healing of an Injured Foot	16
11–13	Three Miracles		
	11	Carrying Water in a Cloak	10
	12	Miraculously Great Harvest	11
	13	Miraculous Repair of a Bed	12
14–15	Teacher Discourses		
	14	Second Teacher	13
	15	Third Teacher	14

16–18   Three Miracles
      16   Healing of James' Snakebite   15
      17   Raising of a Dead Baby   –
      18   Raising of a Dead Laborer   –
19   Final Discourse (Epilog)
      19   Jesus in the Temple   17

APPENDIX 4

Designations of Individual Episodes

The naming of individual episodes within IGT research vary considerably. In order to make reference easier and more consistent, the following titles are proposed and employed in this book.[1]

The numbering of main episodes follows Gs, since its sequence and selection probably is older than the other Greek, not least since it is very close to that of the ancient versional manuscripts.[2]

Episodes with a varying and evasive place in the infancy story tradition are designated with zero (0) before the number. Some of them are clearly variations over more established episodes (e.g. 06, 08, 018). The list is not complete, and primarily includes episodes related to Jesus' childhood, i.e. his age level in IGT, not to his birth or being a baby.[3]

Since some variants have episodes which differ much from the standard type, the titles will sometimes be less precise. For instance, in variants of episode 3, Annas' name is not given. When necessary such differences can be signified by adding (var.), for example Annas' Son (var.).

1. They have been developed with an eye to the works of Gero, Hock, Chartrand-Burke, and Elliott.

2. See pp. 14–15. For example episodes 01 and 02 which usually are included in modern translations of IGT occur primarily in the Greek Gad and rarely in any of the versions, and not at all in the earliest versional manuscripts.

3. It can be expanded by adding numbers also for other episodes. The present numbering first follows the sequence of episodes in *Ps.-Mt.*, then of *Arab. Gos. Inf.*, and then some of the other versions.

APPENDIX 4

Gs	Full title	Short title
1	Heading/Prolog	Prolog
2a	Cleaning of Pools	Pools
2b	Vivification of Sparrows	Sparrows
3	Curse on Annas' Son	Annas' Son
4	Curse on a Careless Boy	Careless Boy
5	Joseph Rebukes Jesus	Joseph's Rebuke
6–8	First Teacher	1 Teacher
6:1–7	First Teacher (Dialog)	1 Teacher (Dial.)
6:8–10	First Teacher (Alpha Lesson)	1 Teacher (Alpha)
7	First Teacher (Lament)	1 Teacher (Lam.)
8	First Teacher (Exclamation)	1 Teacher (Exclam.)
9	Raising of Zeno	Zeno
10	Carrying Water in a Cloak	Water in Cloak
11	Miraculously Great Harvest	Harvest
12	Miraculous Repair of a Bed	Bed
13	Second Teacher	2 Teacher
14	Third Teacher	3 Teacher
15	Healing of James' Snakebite	Snakebite
16	Healing of an Injured Foot	Injured foot
17	Jesus in the Temple	Jesus in Temple

Other Episodes in the Childhood Tradition

01	Raising of a Dead Baby	Dead Baby
02	Raising of a Dead Laborer	Dead Laborer
03	Playing with Lions	Lions
04	Making Joseph Raise a Dead Man	Joseph Raises Dead
05	Sharing a Meal with His Family	Family Meal
06	Healing a Snake-poisoned Boy	Poisoned Boy
07	Jesus and the Dyer	Dyer
08	Miraculous Repair of King's Throne	King's Throne
09	Children Made Goats	Goats
010	Children Make Jesus King	Jesus King
011	Riding the Sunbeam	Sunbeam
012	Children Made Swine	Swine
013	Healing of a Blind Man	Blind Man

014	Jesus and the Blacksmith	Blacksmith
015	Healing of Man with Serpent	Man with Serpent
016	Healing of Boy on an Ass	Boy on an Ass
017	Making Dead Fish Come Alive	Fish
018	Healing of Child's Snakebite	Snakebite (child)
019	Healing of Man with Serpent	Man with Serpent

APPENDIX 5

SURVEY OF GREEK VARIANTS AND THE VERSIONS[*]

Greek

Variant	Century	Subgroup	Manuscript	Date of Manuscript	Origin/ Place[1]	Contents (cf. app. 4)[2]
Gs	4th–7th c.	–	H	1089/1090	Cyprus	1–17
Ga	9th c.	W	W	14th–15th c.	?	1–17, 01, 02
		VPO	V	14th–16th c.	Mt. Athos	1–16
			P	1422/1423	?	1–5, 6 (parts), 07†
			O	before 1455	?	1–2a, 2b†
		Family α	B	15th c.	?	1–5, 6 (parts), 7–17, 01, 02
			L	15th c.	Samos	
			M	15th c.	Samos	
			D	16th c.	Crete	

* The detailed presentations in Chartrand-Burke, "Infancy Gospel," 101–33, and Elliott, *Synopsis*, 132–70, have been of much value for making this survey. See also pp. 15–16 and 180–85 above.

Variant	Century	Subgroup	Manuscript	Date of Manuscript	Origin/ Place[1]	Contents (cf. app. 4)[2]
Gd	11th c.	–	T	13th c.	?	10–15†, 16†, 17†, 01†, 02†[3]
			R	15th c.	?	1–2a, 2b†[4]
			A	15th c.	?	1–17, 01, 02[5]
Gb	15th c.	–	S	14th–15th c.	Sinai	1–5, 6 (parts), 7–10, 12, 16
			C	15th–16th c.	Sinai	

Versions

Language	Time	From	Variant	Manuscript	Ms. date	Contents[6]
Latin	3rd c.	Gr.	Lv	Vindob. 563	5th c.	2†, 5†, 7–9†, 13†, 17†
			Lm	In *Ps.-Mt.*	11th c. on	2–15
			Lt	Ca. 15 mss.	11th– 15th c.	1–16, 01[7]
Syriac	3rd c.	Gr.	–	SyrG	5th–6th c.	2–3, 4–7 (parts), 8–12, 15, 17 (parts)
				SyrW	6th c.	2–5, 6–8 (parts), 9–15, 17
				SyrB[8]	13th– 14th c.	4, 6–7, 10–15, 09, 010, 016, 017, 018, 019
				SyrP	1622/ 1623	5–8+

Language	Time	From	Variant	Manuscript	Ms. date	Contents[6]
Armenian	6th c.	Gr.?	Arm.Gos. Inf.	Some mss.	1240 on	6, 9, 12, 07
Georgian	6th c.	Arm.	–	A 95, Tblisi	10th c.	2–6, 7†
Ethiopic	6th c.	Gr.?	Mir. of Jes.	Many mss.	17th c. on	2–9, 11–15, 17, 07, 011
Irish	ca. 700	Lat.	–	G 50, Dublin	17th c.	2–12
Latin[9]	7th c.	Gr.	Ps.-Mt.	Many mss.	11th c. on	2–4, 10–15, 03, 04, 05
Arabic	8th c.	Syr.	Arab.Gos. Inf.	Several mss.	1299 and other	2–10, 12, 15, 17, 07, 08, 09, 010, 012, 013, 018
			Indep. transl.	G 11, Milan	Undated	2–5, 6–7 (parts), 8–9, 10–15, 17, 07, 012
Slavonic	10th c.	Gr.	–	16 mss.	14th–19th c.	Much of IGT, 07, 011, 012, 013, 014
Other	Mediev.	Lat.	–	Many mss.	Mediev.	Derived from Ps.-Mt.

Table Notes

1. The manuscripts located to Mt. Athos and Sinai (St. Catherine) may have other geographical origins.

2. Sequence of episodes can differ from Gs. † indicates that the episodes are truncated.

3. The manuscript also includes material from Jesus and his family's flight to Egypt.

4. James is presented as author instead of Thomas, and it also includes material from Jesus and his family's flight to Egypt.

5. Cf. the previous note.

6. Sequence of episodes can differ from Gs. See also appendix 7. † indicates that the episodes are truncated.

7. The manuscripts also include material from Jesus and his family's flight to Egypt. The contents vary somewhat and additional episodes occasionally occur, for example 011.

8. The text is integrated into a *Life of Mary* story.

9. See Lm/Lt variants above, and pp. 181–82 above.

APPENDIX 6

Survey of IGT Evidence by Century

Century	Greek Variant	Version	Manuscript	External Evidence
2nd	*Origin*			Justin *Dial.* 88 *Ep. Apos.* 4 Irenaeus *Haer.* 1.20.1–2 *Gos. Truth* I 19, 17–32
3rd		Lat. Syr.		*Acts. Thom.* 79
4th	Gs			*Gos. Bart.* 2:11 *Hist. Jos. Carp.* 17 Epiphanius *Pan.* 51.20.2–3 John Chrysostom *Hom. Jo.* 17 (*Decretum Gelasianum*)
5th			Lv SyrG	Ivory book cover, Milan
6th		Arm. Geo. Eth.	SyrW	Antoninus Placentinus *Itin.* 5;13 *Decretum Gelasianum* Timothy of Const. *PG* 86:21/22C
7th				*Qur'an* 3:46, 49 Anastasius Sinaita *Hodegos* 17

Century	Greek Variant	Version	Manuscript	External Evidence
8th		Arab. Ir.		Later evidence not included
9th	Ga			
10th		Slav.	Geo. (A 95)	
11th	Gd		H Lm Lt	
12th				
13th			T SyrB *Arm. Gos. Inf.*	
14th			S, V, W *Arab.Gos. Inf.* Slav. (various mss.)	
15th	Gb		A, B, C, L, M, O, P, R	
16th			D	
17th			Syr P Eth. (*Mir. of Jes.*) Ir (G 50)	

APPENDIX 7

SURVEY OF EARLY CHRISTIAN
INFANCY STORIES

The *Infancy Gospel of Thomas* belongs among ancient sources that in various ways deal with Jesus' parentage, birth, and childhood. Here follows a survey of the most important sources that contain material in addition to or other than that found in IGT (cf. also appendix 5).[1] The sources are listed chronologically (according to probable time of origin).

Paul's letter to the Galatians (Gal)

Time and language: early 50's, Greek
Contents: Jesus sent as God's Son in "the fullness of time . . . born of a woman, born under the law" (Gal 4:4).

The Gospel of Matthew (Matt)

Time and language: ca. 70–85, Greek
Contents: genealogy and birth of Jesus; visit of the wise men; escape to Egypt; massacre of the infants; return from Egypt (Matt 1–2).

The Gospel of Luke (Luke)

Time and language: ca. 70–85, Greek
Contents: births of John the Baptist and Jesus foretold; Mary's visit to Elizabeth and hymn; birth of John; Zechariah's prophecy; birth of Jesus; shepherds/angels; Jesus presented in temple; return to Nazareth; Jesus at twelve in the temple (Luke 1:5—2:52).

1. For detailed surveys, see Schneemelcher, *New Testament Apocrypha: Gospels and Related Writings*; Elliott, *Apocryphal New Testament*; Elliott, *Synopsis*.

The Gospel of John (John)

Time and language: ca. 80–95, Greek
Contents: the "Word became flesh and lived among us," with "the glory as of a father's only son," the "only begotten God who is in the bosom of the Father" (John 1:14–18).

Infancy Gospel of Thomas (IGT)

Time and language: mid-second century, Greek
Contents: the life, teaching, and miracles of Jesus from age five to twelve.

Infancy Gospel of James/Protevangelium of James (*Prot. Jas.*)

Time and language: mid/late-second century, Greek
Contents: situation of the childless couple Joachim and Anna, and God's promises to them (1:1—5:1); birth of daughter Mary, and life as a child in the temple (5:2—8:3); engagement between Mary and Joseph, Mary's visit to Elizabeth (9–12); Mary's pregnancy, Joseph's anguish, their public acquittal of adultery (13–16); Jesus' birth in cave (17:1—19:2); proof of Mary's continued virginity (19:3—20:3); visit of the Magi (21); Herod's rage and killing of Zecheriah (22–24); postscript (25).

Hippolytus, Refutation of All Heresies (*Haer.*)

Time and language: early third century, Greek
Contents: retelling of Gnostic story about the angel Baruch's visit to the twelve year old shepherd boy Jesus (5.26.29–30).

Pistis Sophia (*Pistis Sophia*)

Time and language: third century, Coptic
Contents: story about how Jesus before his birth sowed in Elizabeth and Mary divine power as a preparation for his own and the Baptist's birth (7–8) and how the union of the child Jesus and the Spirit came about (61).

APPENDIX 7

History of Joseph the Carpenter (*Hist. Jos. Carp.*)

Time and language: fourth–fifth century, Coptic (also Arabic)
Contents: (Joseph's story is told by Jesus); Joseph's old age and piety
(1–2); young Mary in temple becomes nurse in Joseph's house (3–4);
God's election of Joseph, Jesus' conception, annunciation, and birth
(5–7); flight and return from Egypt (8–9); wholesomeness of Joseph,
family life, illness, and prayer (10–13); day of death, deathbed prayer
(14–16); conversation with Jesus, account of Jesus' childhood (17);
grief of family (18–20); Jesus' postpones his death and prays (21–22);
Joseph's death (23–24); neighbors' farewell, Jesus' prayer for Joseph
and those honoring him (25–26); burial, Jesus' memory of flight to
Egypt (27); his lament of death, and grief (28–29); unavoidability of
death, disciples' praise of Jesus (30–32).

Gospel of the Birth of Mary
(*Gos. Bir. Mary, De Nativitate Mariae*)

Time and language: ca. fifth–sixth century, Latin
Contents: lives of Joachim and Anna, their visions about a daughter,
they meet, birth of Mary (1–5); Mary's childhood in the temple, encounters with angels, virginity (6–7); God's election of Joseph, his
engagement with Mary (8); Gabriel's annunciation, uniqueness of
Jesus' conception (9); deliberations and vision of Joseph, marriage of
Joseph and Mary, birth of Jesus (10).

Armenian Gospel of the Infancy (*Arm. Gos. Inf.*)

Time and language: sixth century, Armenian
Contents: reworked variants of parts of *Prot. Jas.* and IGT, with some
additional material.

Ta'amra 'Iyasus (The Miracles of Jesus)

Time and language: sixth century, Ethiopic
Contents: large collection of stories about Jesus, with chapter 8 having
stories about Jesus' childhood.

Gospel fragment (*Pap. Cairensis* 10735)

Time and language: sixth–seventh century, Greek
Contents: annuciation and flight to Egypt.

Gospel of Pseudo-Matthew (*Ps.-Mt.*)

Time and language: ca. seventh century, Latin
Contents: combination and reworking of *Prot. Jas.* and IGT with some
additional episodes inserted. *Prot. Jas.* (1–17); dragons, lions, and
leopards obey and worship Jesus (18–19); palm bowing down with
fruit for Mary at Jesus' bidding (20–21); Jesus' miraculous shortening
of the travel to Egypt (22); temple idols in Egypt fall with face to the
floor worshipping Jesus (23–24); death of Herod (25); IGT (26–34);
lions play with and worship Jesus in their den (35–36); IGT (cont.,
37–39); Jesus makes Joseph raise a rich man from the dead (40); IGT
(cont., 41); Jesus' family and their respect toward him (42).

Serapion, Life of John (*Life of John*)

Time and language: uncertain (seventh–eighth century, purportedly
late fourth), Arabic (Garshuni)
Contents: legend about how the child Jesus while still in Egypt sees and
cares for the orphaned bapist John who is on his way in the desert
back to Nazareth.

Arabic Gospel of the Infancy (*Arab. Gos. Inf.*)

Time and language: eighth century, Arabic
Contents: birth of Jesus; miracles in Egypt (Mary plays a central part);
parts of IGT; some additional episodes.

Leabhar Breac (*Leabhar Breac*)

Time and language: ninth century, Irish
Contents: census in Bethlehem; birth of Jesus; Joseph's and Mary's reaction and experiences; the Magi (Druids); slaying of the Infants; flight
to Egypt; death of Herod; murder of Zecheriah; history of Romans in
Palestine until Pilate.

Liber Flavus Fergusiorum (*Liber Flavus*)

Time and language: ninth century, Irish

Contents: birth and upbringing of Mary; relationship to Joseph; annunciation; Mary's visit to Elizabeth; Joseph's reactions; finding a midwife; midwife's story.

Midwife's Story (*Arundel 404, Liber de Infantia Salvatoris*)

Time and language: before tenth century, Latin

Contents: silence of the world at Jesus' birth (72); birth (73); midwife's awe, child's divine origin (74).

Bibliography

I. Primary Sources

Antoninus Placentinus. *Itinerarium*. In "Antonini Placentini Itinerarium (Recensio Prima Et Altera)." In *Itinera Hierosolymitana Saeculi IIII–VIII*, edited by Paulus Geyer, 157–218. Prague: Tempsky/Freytag, 1898.

Apuleius. *Metamorphoses*. In *Apuleius: Metamorphoses*. Edited and translated by J. Arthur Hanson. 2 vols. LCL. Cambridge: Harvard University Press, 1989.

Aristophanes. *Lysistrata*. In *Aristophanes: Birds, Lysistrata, Women at the Thesmophoria*. Edited and translated by Jeffrey Henderson. LCL. Cambridge: Harvard University Press, 2000.

———. *Wasps*. In *Aristophanes: Clouds, Wasps, Peace*. Edited and translated by Jeffrey Henderson. LCL. Cambridge: Harvard University Press, 1998.

Athenaeus. *Deipnosophistae*. In *Athenaeus: The Deipnosophists*. Translated by Charles Burton Gulick. LCL. London: Heinemann, 1961.

Augustine. *Confessions*. In *St. Augustine's Confessions*. Translated by William Watts. LCL. London: Heinemann, 1946.

Cicero. *On the Nature of the Gods*. In *Cicero: De natura deorum, Academica*. Translated by H. Rackham. LCL. London: Heinemann, 1951.

Dio Chrysostom. *Orations*. In *Dio Chrysostom*. Translated by J. W. Cohoon. LCL. Cambridge: Harvard University Press, 1961.

Epictetus. *Dissertations*. In *Epictetus: The Discourses as Reported by Arrian, The Manual, and Fragments*. Translated by W. A. Oldfather. LCL. London: Heinemann, 1961.

Epiphanius. *Refutation of All Heresies*. In *The Panarion of Epiphanius of Salamis*, translated by Frank Williams. Vol. 2: *Books II and III (Sects 47–80, De Fide)*. NHMS 36. Leiden: Brill, 1994.

Horace. *Satires*. In *Horace: Satires, Epistles, and Ars Poetica*. Translated by H. Rushton Fairclough. LCL. Cambridge: Harvard University Press, 1999.

Irenaeus. *Against Heresies*. In *St. Irenaeus of Lyons: Against the Heresies*. Translated by Dominic J. Unger. Revisions by John J. Dillon. ACW 55. New York: Paulist, 1992.

John Chrysostom. *Homilies on John*. In *Saint John Chrysostom: Commentary on Saint John the Apostle and Evangelist: Homilies 1–47*. Translated by Sister Thomas Aquinas Goggin. FC 33. Washington, DC: Catholic University of America Press, 1969.

———. *On Vainglory*. In M. L. W. Laistner, *Christianity and Pagan Culture in the Later Roman Empire, Together with an English Translation of John Chrysostom's Address on Vainglory and the Right Way for Parents to Bring up Their Children*. Ithaca, NY: Cornell University Press, 1951.

Bibliography

Julian the Apostate. *Orations*. In *The Works of the Emperor Julian*. Translated by Wilmer Cave Wright. LCL. London: Heinemann, 1969.

Justin Martyr. *Dialogue with Trypho*. In *Iustini Martyris: Dialogus cum Tryphone*. Edited by Miroslav Marcovich. PTS 47. Berlin: de Gruyter, 1997.

Lactantius. *Divine Institutes*. Translated with an introduction and notes by Anthony Bowen and Peter Garnsey. Liverpool: Liverpool University Press, 2003.

———. *Divine Institutes*. In *Lactantius: Opera Omnia*. Edited by Samuel Brandt and Georg Laubmann. CSEL 19. Prague: Tempsky, 1890.

Maximus of Tyre. *The Philosophical Orations*. In *Maximi Tyrii: Philosophumena*. Edited by H. Hobein. Leipzig: Teubner, 1910.

———. *The Philosophical Orations*. Translated, with an Introduction and Notes, by M. B. Trapp. Oxford: Clarendon, 1997.

Minucius Felix. *Octavius*. In *Tertullian: Apology, De Spectaculis, Minucius Felix*. Translated by Gerald H. Rendall. LCL. London: Heinemann, 1931.

Origen. *Against Celsus*. In *Contra Celsum*. Translated by Henry Chadwick. Oxford: Clarendon, 1953.

———. *Against Celsus*. In *Origenes: Contra Celsum, Libri VIII*. Edited by M. Marcovich. VCSup 54. Leiden: Brill, 2001.

Ovid. *Metamorphoses*. In *Ovid: Metamorphoses*. Translated by Frank Justus Miller. LCL. London: Heinemann, 1966.

Petronius. *Satyrica*. In *Petronius*. Translated by Michael Heseltine. LCL. London: Heinemann, 1922.

Philostratus. *Life of Apollonius*. In *Philostratus: The Life of Apollonius of Tyana, Books V–VIII*. Edited and Translated by Christopher P. Jones. LCL. Cambridge: Harvard University Press, 2005.

Plato. *Republic*. In *Plato, The Republic*. Vol. 1. Translated by Paul Shorey. LCL. London: Heinemann, 1963.

Pliny the Younger. *Letters*. In *Pliny: Letters and Panegyricus*. Vol. 1. Translated by Betty Radice. LCL. London: Heinemann, 1969.

Quintilian. *The Orator's Education*. In *Quintilian: The Orator's Education, Books 1–2*. Edited ant Translated by Donald A. Russell. LCL. Cambridge: Harvard University Press, 2001.

The Qur'an: A New Translation by M. A. S. Abdel Haleem. Oxford World's Classics. Oxford: Oxford University Press, 2004.

Tacitus. *Dialogus de oratoribus*. In *Tacitus: Agricola, Germania, Dialogus*. LCL. Translated by W. Peterson. Revised by M. Winterbottom. London: Heinemann, 1970.

Tertullian. *Against theValentinians*. In *Tertullien: Contre les Valentiniens*. Vol. 1. Edited and Translated by Jean-Claude Fredouille. SC. Paris: Cerf, 1980.

Tibullus. In *Catullus, Tibullus and Pervigilium Veneris*. Translated by J. P. Postgate. LCL. London: Heinemann, 1968.

II. Secondary Works

Aasgaard, Reidar. "Children in Antiquity and Early Christianity: Research History and Central Issues." *Familia (UPSA, Spain)* 33 (2006) 23–46.

———. "From Boy to Man in Antiquity: Jesus in the Apocryphal Infancy Gospel of Thomas." *THYMOS: Journal of Boyhood Studies* 3 (2009) 3–20.

Bibliography

————. "Liberating Childhood: Reflections on a Child Perspective Reading of the Early Christian Sources." Paper presented at the Society of Biblical Literature Annual Meeting, Washington, DC, November 11, 2006.

————. "Like a Child: Paul's Rhetorical Uses of Childhood." In *The Child in the Bible*, edited by Marcia J. Bunge, 249–77. Grand Rapids: Eerdmans, 2008.

————. *"My Beloved Brothers and Sisters!" Christian Siblingship in Paul.* JSNTSup 265. ECC 2. London: T. & T. Clark 2004.

————. "Paul as a Child: Children and Childhood in the Letters of the Apostle." *JBL* 126 (2007) 129–59.

————. "Uncovering Children's Culture in Late Antiquity: The Testimony of the *Infancy Gospel of Thomas.*" In *Children in Early Christianity*, edited by Cornelia B. Horn, 25 pp. WUNT. Tübingen: Mohr Siebeck, 2009 (forthcoming).

Aland, Barbara. "The Significance of the Chester Beatty Papyri in Early Church History." In *The Earliest Gospels: The Origins and Transmission of the Earliest Christian Gospels—the Contribution of the Chester Beatty Gospel Codex P45*, edited by Charles Horton, 108–21. London: T. & T. Clark, 2004.

Aland, Kurt. "Noch Einmal: Das Rotas/Sator-Rebus." In *Text and Testimony: Essays on New Testament and Apocryphal Literature in Honour of A. F. J. Klijn*, edited by T. Baarda et al., 9–23. Kampen: Kok, 1988.

Amberger-Lahrmann, Mechthild. *Anatomie und Physiognomie in der Hellenistischen Plastik, Dargestellt am Pergamonaltar.* Abhandlungen der Geistes- und Sozialwissenschaftliche Klasse 10. Stuttgart: Steiner, 1996.

Anderson, Graham. *Fairytale in the Ancient World.* London: Routledge, 2000.

————. *Greek and Roman Folklore: A Handbook.* Greenwood Folklore Handbooks. Westport, CT: Greenwood, 2006.

Ankarloo, Bengt, and Stuart Clark, editors. *Witchcraft and Magic in Europe: Ancient Greece and Rome.* Witchcraft and Magic in Europe 2. Philadelphia: University of Pennsylvania Press, 1999.

Applebaum, Shimon. "Animal Husbandry." In *The Roman World*, edited by John Wacher, 2:504–26. London: Routledge & Kegan Paul, 1987.

Ariès, Philippe. *L'enfant et la Vie Familiale sous L'ancien Régime.* Paris: Plon, 1960.

Arras, Victor, and Lucas van Rompay. "Les Manuscrits Éthiopiens des 'Miracles de Jesus.'" *Analecta Bollandiana* 93 (1975) 133–46.

Attridge, Harold W., and George W. MacRae. "The Gospel of Truth (I,3 and XII,2)." In *The Nag Hammadi Library in English*, edited by James M. Robinson, 38–51. San Francisco: HarperSanFrancisco, 1990.

Ault, Bradley A., and Lisa C. Nevett, editors. *Ancient Greek Houses and Households: Chronological, Regional, and Social Diversity.* Philadelphia: University of Pennsylvania Press, 2005.

Baars, W., and J. Helderman. "Neue Materialien Zum Text Und Zur Interpretation Des Kindheitsevangelium Des Pseudo-Thomas (Fortsetzung)." *OrChr* 78 (1994) 1–32.

————. "Neue Materialien zum Text und zur Interpretation des Kindheitsevangelium des Pseudo-Thomas (Teil 1)." *OrChr* 77 (1993) 191–226.

Bagatti, Belarmino. "Nota sul Vangelo di Tommaso Israelita." *Euntes Docete* 29 (1976) 482–89.

Bakke, O. M. *When Children Became People: The Birth of Childhood in Early Christianity.* Minneapolis: Fortress, 2005.

Bibliography

Balla, Peter. *The Child-Parent Relationship in the New Testament and Its Environment.* WUNT 155. Tübingen: Mohr/Siebeck, 2003.

Banaji, Jairus. *Agrarian Change in Late Antiquity: Gold, Labour, and Aristocratic Dominance.* Oxford: Oxford University Press, 2001.

Bandt, Cordula. *Der Traktat "Vom Mysterium der Buchstaben." Kristischer Text mit Einführung, Übersetzung und Anmerkungen.* TU 162. Berlin: de Gruyter, 2007.

Barclay, John M. G. "The Family as the Bearer of Religion in Judaism and Early Christianity." In *Constructing Early Christian Families: Family as Social Reality and Metaphor,* edited by Halvor Moxnes, 66–80. London: Routledge, 1997.

Barker, Graeme, and John Lloyd, editors. *Roman Landscapes: Archaeological Survey in the Mediterranean Region.* Archaeological Monographs of the British School at Rome 2. London: British School at Rome, 1991.

Barton, Stephen. "Can We Identify the Gospel Audiences?" In *The Gospels for All Christians: Rethinking the Gospel Audiences,* edited by Richard Bauckham, 173–94. Grand Rapids: Eerdmans, 1998.

Bauckham, Richard. "For Whom Were Gospels Written?" In *The Gospels for All Christians: Rethinking the Gospel Audiences,* edited by Richard Bauckham, 9–48. Grand Rapids: Eerdmans, 1998.

—————. "Imaginative Literature." In *The Early Christian World,* edited by Philip F. Esler, 2:791–812. London: Routledge, 2000.

Bauer, Johannes Baptist. "Die Entstehung Apokrypher Evangelien." *Bibel und Liturgie* 38 (1964) 268–71.

Bauer, Walter. *Das Leben Jesu im Zeitalter der neutestamentlichen Apokryphen.* Tübingen: Mohr/Siebeck, 1909.

Ben-Amos, Dan. "Folktale." In *Folklore: Critical Concepts in Literary and Cultural Studies,* Volume III: *The Genres of Folklore,* edited by Alan Dundes, 255–67. London: Routledge, 2005.

Benton, Michael. "Readers, Texts, Contexts: Reader-Response Criticism." In *Understanding Children's Literature,* edited by Peter Hunt, 86–102. London: Routledge, 1999.

Benton, Michael, and Geoff Fox. "What Happens When We Read Stories?" In *Children's Literature: Critical Concepts in Literary and Cultural Studies,* edited by Peter Hunt, 2:125–46. London: Routledge, 2006.

Bertelli, Carlo. "The Production and Distribution of Books in Late Antiquity." In *The Sixth Century: Production, Distribution and Demand,* edited by Richard Hodges and William Bowden, 41–60. TRW 3. Leiden: Brill, 1998.

Bilde, Per, Troels Engberg-Pedersen, Lise Hannestad, and Jan Zahle. "Introduction." In *Conventional Values of the Hellenistic Greeks,* edited by Per Bilde, Troels Engberg-Pedersen, Lise Hannestad, and Jan Zahle, 13–27. SHC 8. Århus: Aarhus University Press, 1997.

Bonnington, Malcolm. "Trees, Shrubs and Plants as Sources of Raw Materials." In *Farm Equipment of the Roman World,* by K. D. White, 233–39. Cambridge: Cambridge University Press, 1975.

Borgen, Peder, Kåre Fuglseth, and Roald Skarsten. *The Philo Index: A Complete Word Index to the Writings of Philo of Alexandria.* Grand Rapids: Eerdmans, 2000.

Bottigheimer, Ruth B. "An Important System of Its Own: Defining Children's Literature." In *Children's Literature: Critical Concepts in Literary and Cultural Studies,* edited by Peter Hunt, 1:114–29. London: Routledge, 2006.

Bibliography

Bovon, Francois. "Évangiles Canoniques et Évangiles apocryphes: La Naissance et l'Enfance de Jésus." *Bulletin des facultés catholiques de Lyon* 104 (1980) 19–29.

Bowden, William, and Luke Lavan. "The Late Antique Countryside: An Introduction." In *Recent Research on the Late Antique Countryside*, edited by William Bowden, Luke Lavan, and Carlos Machado, xvii–xxvi. LAA 2. Leiden: Brill, 2004.

Bowden, William, Luke Lavan, and Carlos Machado, editors. *Recent Research on the Late Antique Countryside*. LAA 2. Leiden: Brill, 2004.

Bowden, William, Adam Gutteridge, and Carlos Machado, editors. *Social and Political Life in Late Antiquity*. LAA 3.1. Leiden: Brill, 2006.

Bowes, Kim. "'Christianisation' and the Rural Home." *JECS* 15 (2007) 143–70.

———. *Private Worship, Public Values, and Religious Change in Late Antiquity*. Cambridge: Cambridge University Press, 2008.

Bowie, Ewen. "The Readership of Greek Novels in the Ancient World." In *The Search for the Ancient Novel*, edited by James Tatum, 435–59. Baltimore: Johns Hopkins University Press, 1994.

Bradley, Keith R. "The Roman Child in Sickness and in Health." In *The Roman Family in the Empire: Rome, Italy, and Beyond*, edited by Michele George, 67–92. Oxford: Oxford University Press, 2005.

Brandes, Wolfram, and John Haldon. "Towns, Tax and Transformation: State, Cities and Their Hinterlands in the East Roman Period, C. 500–800." In *Towns and Their Territories between Late Antiquity and the Early Middle Ages*, edited by Gian Pietro Brogiolo, Nancy Gauthier, and Neil Christie, 141–72. TRW 9. Leiden: Brill, 2000.

Braund, Susanna, and Glenn W. Most, editors. *Ancient Anger: Perspectives from Homer to Galen*. YCS 32. Cambridge: Cambridge University Press, 2004.

Bremmer, Jan N. "Performing Myths: Women's Homes and Men's Leschai." In *Myth and Symbol II: Symbolic Phenomena in Ancient Greek Culture*, edited by Synnøve des Bouvrie, 123–40. Bergen, Norway: Norwegian Instituteat Athens, 2004.

Bremmer, Jan N., and Herman Roodenburg, editors. *A Cultural History of Humour: From Antiquity to the Present Day*. Cambridge: Polity, 1997.

Brenk, Beat. "Monasteries as Rural Settlements: Patron-Dependence or Self-Sufficiency?" In *Recent Research on the Late Antique Countryside*, edited by William Bowden, Luke Lavan, and Carlos Machado, 447–76. LAA 2. Leiden: Brill, 2004.

Brogiolo, G. P., N. Gauthier, and Neil Christie, editors. *Towns and Their Territories between Late Antiquity and the Early Middle Ages*. TRW 9. Leiden: Brill, 2000.

Brunt, P. A. "Labour." In *The Roman World*, edited by John Wacher, 2:701–16. London: Routledge & Kegan Paul, 1987.

Brödner, Erika. *Wohnen in der Antike*. Darmstadt: Wissenschaftliche, 1989.

Bunge, Marcia J., editor. *The Child in Christian Thought*. Grand Rapids: Eerdmans, 2001.

———. editor. *The Child in the Bible*. Grand Rapids: Eerdmans, 2008.

Burridge, Richard A. *What Are the Gospels? A Comparison with Graeco-Roman Biography*. 2nd ed. Grand Rapids: Eerdmans, 2004.

Burrus, Virginia, editor. *Late Ancient Christianity*. A People's History of Christianity 2. Minneapolis: Fortress, 2005.

Buxton, Richard, *Imaginary Greece: The Contexts of Mythology*. Cambridge: Cambridge University Press, 1994.

Byrskog, Samuel. *Story as History—History as Story: The Gospel Tradition in the Context of Ancient Oral History*. WUNT 123. Tübingen: Mohr/Siebeck, 2000.

Bibliography

Cameron, Ron, editor. *The Other Gospels: Non-Canonical Gospel Texts*. Philadelphia: Westminster, 1982.

Carney, James. *The Poems of Blathmac, Son of Cu Brettan: Together with the Irish Gospel of Thomas and a Poem on the Virgin Mary*. Dublin: Educational Co. of Ireland, 1964.

———. "Two Old Irish Poems." *Eriu* 18 (1958) 1–43.

Cartlidge, David R., and J. Keith Elliott. *Art and the Christian Apocrypha*. London: Routledge, 2001.

Caseau, Béatrice. "The Fate of Rural Temples in Late Antiquity and the Christianisation of the Countryside." In *Recent Research on the Late Antique Countryside*, edited by William Bowden, Luke Lavan, and Carlos Machado, 105–44. LAA 2. Leiden: Brill, 2004.

Chambers, Aidan. "The Reader in the Book." In *Children's Literature: Critical Concepts in Literary and Cultural Studies*, edited by Peter Hunt, 1:354–74. London: Routledge, 2006.

Charles, J. Daryl. "Vice and Virtue Lists." In *Dictionary of New Testament Background*, edited by Craig A. Evans and Stanley E. Porter, 1252–57. Downers Grove, IL: InterVarsity, 2000.

Chartrand-Burke, Tony. "Authorship and Identity in the Infancy Gospel of Thomas." *TJT* 14 (1998) 27–43.

———. "Completing the Gospel: The Infancy Gospel of Thomas as a Supplement to the Gospel of Luke." In *The Reception and Interpretation of the Bible in Late Antiquity: Proceedings of the Montreal Colloquium in Honour of Charles Kannengeiser, 11–13 October 2006*, edited L. Di Tommaso and L. Turcescu, 102–19. Bible in Ancient Christianity 6. Leiden: Brill, 2008.

———. "Strange New Sayings: The Sayings of Jesus in the Infancy Gospel of Thomas in Light of New Manuscript Evidence." Paper presented at the Society of Biblical Literature Annual Meeting, Nashville, November 2000.

———. "The Greek Manuscript Tradition of the Infancy Gospel of Thomas." *Apocrypha* 14 (2003) 129–51.

———. "The Infancy Gospel of Thomas." In *The Non-Canonical Gospels*, edited by Paul Foster, 126–38. London: T. & T. Clark, 2008.

———. "The Infancy Gospel of Thomas: The Text, Its Origins, and Its Transmission." Ph.D. dissertation, University of Toronto, 2001. http://www.collectionscanada.gc .ca/obj/s4/f2/dsk3/ftp05/NQ63782.pdf.

Chavarría, Alexandra, and Tamara Lewit. "Archaeological Research on the Late Antique Countryside: A Bibliograchic Essay." In *Recent Research on the Late Antique Countryside*, edited by William Bowden, Luke Lavan, and Carlos Machado, 3–51. LAA 2. Leiden: Brill, 2004.

Christie, Neil, *From Constantine to Charlemagne: An Archaeology of Italy, AD 300–800*. Aldershot, UK: Ashgate, 2006.

———. "Landscapes of Change in Late Antiquity and the Early Middle Ages: Themes, Directions and Problems." In *Landscapes of Change: Rural Evolutions in Late Antiquity and the Early Middle Ages*, edited by Neil Christie, 1–37. Aldershot, UK: Ashgate, 2004.

———. editor. *Landscapes of Change: Rural Evolutions in Late Antiquity and the Early Middle Ages*. Aldershot, UK: Ashgate, 2004.

Bibliography

Clarke, John R. *Art in the Lives of Ordinary Romans: Visual Representation and Non-Elite Viewers in Italy, 100 B.C.—A.D. 315*. Berkeley: University of California Press, 2003.

Clines, David J. A. "Paul, the Invisible Man." In *New Testament Masculinities*, edited by Stephen D. Moore and Janice Capel Anderson, 181–92. Semeia Studies 45. Atlanta: Society of Biblical Literature, 2003.

Collins, Raymond F. *First Corinthians*. SacPag 7. Collegeville, MN: Liturgical, 1999.

Conrady, Ludwig. "Das Thomasevangelium: Ein wissenschaftlicher kritischer Versuch." *TSK* 76 (1903) 377–459.

———. *Die Quelle der Kanonischen Kindheitsgeschichte Jesu: Ein Wissenschaftlicher Versuch*. Göttingen: Vandenhoeck & Ruprecht, 1900.

Conway, Colleen M. "'Behold the Man!' Masculine Christology and the Fourth Gospel." In *New Testament Masculinities*, edited by Stephen D. Moore and Janice Capel Anderson, 163–80. Semeia Studies 45. Atlanta: Society of Biblical Literature, 2003.

Cowper, B. Harris. *Apocryphal Gospels and Other Documents Relating to the History of Christ*. London: Norgate, 1881.

Cribiore, Raffaella. *Gymnastics of the Mind: Greek Education in Hellenistic and Roman Egypt*. Princeton: Princeton University Press, 2001.

———. *Writing, Teachers, and Students in Graeco-Roman Egypt*. American Studies in Papyrology 36. Atlanta: Scholars, 1996.

Croom, A. T. *Roman Clothing and Fashion*. Charleston, SC: Tempus, 2000.

Cullmann, Oscar. "Infancy Gospels." In *New Testament Apocrypha*, edited by Wilhelm Schneemelcher, 1:414–69. Translated by R. McL. Wilson. Louisville: Westminster John Knox, 1991.

Currie, Sarah. "Childhood and Christianity from Paul to the Council of Chalcedon." Ph.D. dissertation, University of Cambridge, 1993.

Delatte, Armand. "Évangile de l'Enfance de Jacques: Manuscrit No. 355 de la Bibliothèque Nationale." In *Anecdota Atheniensia, Textes Grecs Inédits Relatifs á L'histoire des Religions*, 264–71. Paris: Champion, 1927.

Dixon, Suzanne. "The Sentimental Ideal of the Roman Family." In *Marriage, Divorce, and Children in Ancient Rome*, edited by Beryl Rawson, 99–113. Oxford: Clarendon, 1991.

Dornseiff, Franz. *Das Alphabet in Mystik und Magie*. Stoicheia 7. Berlin: Teubner, 1922.

Drinkwater, J. F. "Urbanization in Italy and the Western Empire." In *The Roman World*, edited by John Wacher, 1:345–87. London: Routledge & Kegan Paul, 1987.

Dunn, Archibald. "Countryside and Change in the Macedonian Countryside from Gallienus to Justinian." In *Recent Research on the Late Antique Countryside*, edited by William Bowden, Luke Lavan, and Carlos Machado, 534–86. LAA 2. Leiden: Brill, 2004.

Dunn, James D. G. "Jesus in Oral Memory: The Initial Stages of the Jesus Tradition." In *Jesus: A Colloquium in the Holy Land*, edited by Doris Donnelly, 84–145. London: Continuum, 2001.

Dyson, Stephen L. *The Roman Countryside*. Duckworth Debates in Archaeology. London: Duckworth, 2003.

Ehrman, Bart D. *Lost Christianities: The Battles for Scripture and the Faiths We Never Knew*. Oxford: Oxford University Press, 2003.

Elliott, J. Keith, *A Synopsis of the Apocryphal Nativity and Infancy Narratives*. NTTS 34. Leiden: Brill Academic, 2006.

Bibliography

————. editor. *The Apocryphal Jesus: Legends of the Early Church*. Oxford: Oxford University Press, 1996.

————. editor. *The Apocryphal New Testament: A Collection of Apocryphal Christian Literature in an English Translation*. Oxford: Clarendon, 1993.

Ellis, Linda, and Frank L. Kidner, editors. *Travel, Communication and Geography in Late Antiquity: Sacred and Profane*. Aldershot, UK: Ashgate, 2004.

Enslin, Morton S. "Along Highways and Byways." *HTR* 44 (1951) 67–92.

Epp, Eldon Jay. "Issues in New Testament Textual Criticism: Moving from the Nineteenth Century to the Twenty-First Century." In *Rethinking New Testament Textual Criticism*, edited by David Alan Black, 17–76. Grand Rapids: Baker Academic, 2002.

————. "The Oxyrhynchus New Testament Papyri: 'Not without Honor Except in Their Hometown.'" *JBL* 123 (2003) 5–55.

Esbroeck, Michel van. Review of *Das Kirchenslavische Evangelium Des Thomas*, by Aurelio De Santos Otero, *Analecta Bollandiana* 87 (1969) 261–63.

Esler, Philip F., editor. *The Early Christian World*. 2 vols. London: Routledge, 2000.

Evans, Craig A. "Luke's Use of the Elijah/Elisha Narratives and the Ethics of Election." *JBL* 106 (1987) 75–83.

————. *Noncanonical Writings and New Testament Interpretation*. Peabody, MA: Hendrickson, 1992.

Eyben, Emiel. "Fathers and Sons." In *Marriage, Divorce, and Children in Ancient Rome*, edited by Beryl Rawson, 114–43. Oxford: Clarendon, 1991.

Fabricius, Johann Albert. *Codex Apocryphus Novi Testamenti*. 2 vols. Hamburg: Schiller, 1703.

Fideler, David R. *Jesus Christ, Sun of God: Ancient Cosmology and Early Christian Symbolism*. Weaton, IL: Theosophical Publishing House, 1993.

————. editor. *The Pythagorean Sourcebook and Library: An Anthology of Ancient Writings which Relate to Pythagoras and Pythagorean Philosophy*. Grand Rapids: Phanes, 1987.

Fitzgerald, John T., editor. *Greco-Roman Perspectives on Friendship*. SBLRBS 34. Atlanta: Scholars, 1997.

Fox, Sherry C., "Health in Hellenistic and Roman Times: The Case Studies in Paphos, Cyprus and Corinth, Greece." In *Health in Antiquity*, edited by Helen King, 59–82. London: Routledge, 2005.

Frend, W. H. C., *The Donatist Church: A Movement of Protest in Roman North Africa*. Oxford: Clarendon, 1971.

————. *The Rise of Christianity*. Philadelphia: Fortress, 1984.

————. *Town and Country in the Early Christian Centuries*. London: Variorum Reprints, 1980.

Fuchs, Albert, and Franz Weissengruber. *Konkordanz zum Thomasevangelium, Version A und B*. SNTU B4. Linz: Fuchs, 1978.

Gamble, Harry Y. *Books and Readers in the Early Church: A History of Early Christian Texts*. New Haven: Yale University Press, 1995.

Garitte, G. "Le Fragment Géorgien De L'évangile De Thomas." *Revue d'histoire ecclesiastique* 51 (1956) 511–20.

George, Michele. "Repopulating the Roman House." In *The Roman Family in Italy: Status, Sentiment, Space*, edited by Beryl Rawson and Paul Weaver, 299–319. Oxford: Clarendon, 1997.

Bibliography

Gero, Stephen. "Apocryphal Gospels: A Survey of Textual and Literary Problems." In *Aufstieg Und Niedergang Der Römischen Welt*, edited by Wolfgang Haase, II.25.2:3969–96. Berlin: de Gruyter, 1988.

———. "The Infancy Gospel of Thomas: A Study of the Textual and Literary Problems." *NovT* 13 (1971) 46–80.

Gibbs, Laura. *Aesop's Fables*. Oxford World's Classics. Oxford: Oxford University Press, 2002.

Gibson, Elsa. *The "Christians for Christians" Inscriptions of Phrygia: Greek Texts, Translation and Commentary*. HTS 32. Missoula, MT: Scholars, 1978.

Gijsel, Jan, and Rita Beyers, editors. *Libri de Nativitate Mariae: Pseudo-Matthaei Evangelium. Textus et Commentarius*. CCSA 9. Turnhout: Brepols, 1997.

Gilhus, Ingvild. *Laughing Gods, Weeping Virgins: Laughter in the History of Religion*. London: Routledge, 1997.

Gleason, Maud W. *Making Men: Sophists and Self-Presentation in Ancient Rome*. Princeton: Princeton University Press, 1995.

Grubbs, Judith Evans. "Parent-Child Conflict in the Roman Family: The Evidence of the Code of Justinian." In *The Roman Family in the Empire: Rome, Italy, and Beyond*, edited by Michele George, 93–128. Oxford: Oxford University Press, 2005.

Guijarro, Santiago. "Domestic Space, Family Relationships and the Social Location of the Q People." *JSNT* 27 (2004) 69–81.

———. "The Family in First-Century Galilee." In *Constructing Early Christian Families: Family as Social Reality and Metaphor*, edited by Halvor Moxnes, 42–65. London: Routledge, 1997.

Guroian, Vigen, "The Ecclesial Family: John Chrysostom on Parenthood and Children." In *The Child in Christian Thought*, edited by Marcia J. Bunge, 61–77. Grand Rapids: Eerdmans, 2001.

Halsall, Guy, editor. *Humour, History, and Politics in Late Antiquity and the Early Middle Ages*. Cambridge: Cambridge University Press, 2002.

Hanson, K. C. "The Galilean Fishing Economy and the Jesus Tradition." *Biblical Theology Bulletin* 27 (1997) 99–111.

Harlow, Mary, and Ray Laurence. *Growing Up and Growing Old in Ancient Rome: A Life Course Approach*. London: Routledge, 2002.

Harrill, J. Albert. *Slaves in the New Testament: Literary, Social, and Moral Dimensions*. Minneapolis: Fortress, 2006.

Harrington, Daniel J. *The Gospel of Matthew*. SacPag 1. Collegeville, MN: Liturgical, 1991.

Harris, William V. *Ancient Literacy*. Cambridge: Harvard University Press, 1989.

Hearon, Holly E. *The Mary Magdalene Tradition: Witness and Counter-Witness in Early Christian Communities*. Collegeville, MN: Liturgical, 2004.

Hennecke, Edgar, editor. *Handbuch zu den neutestamentlichen Apokryphen*. Tübingen: Mohr/Siebeck, 1904.

———, editor. *Neutestamentliche Apokryphen*. Tübingen: Mohr/Siebeck, 1904.

Herbert, Máire, and Martin McNamara. "A Versified Narrative of the Childhood Deeds of the Lord Jesus." In *Apocrypha Hiberniae I. Evangelia Infantiae*, edited by Martin McNamara et al., 441–83. CCSA 13. Turnhout: Brepols, 2001.

Herren, Michael W., and Shirley Ann Brown. *Christ in Celtic Christianity: Britain and Ireland from the Fifth to the Tenth Century*. Studies in Celtic History 20. Woodbridge, UK: Boydell, 2002.

Bibliography

Hervieux, Jaques, *The New Testament Apocrypha*. New York: Hawthorn, 1960.

Hock, Ronald F. *The Infancy Gospels of James and Thomas*. Scholar's Bible 2. Santa Rosa, CA: Polebridge, 1995.

Hock, Ronald F., J. Bradley Chance, and Judith Perkins, editors. *Ancient Fiction and Early Christian Narrative*, SBLSymS 6. Atlanta: Scholars, 1998.

Hofmann, Rudolph, *Das Leben Jesu nach den Apokryphen im Zusammenhang aus den Quellen erzählt und wissenschaftlich untersucht*. Leipzig: Voigt, 1851.

Honko, Lauri, "Folkloristic Theories of Genre." In *Folklore: Critical Concepts in Literary and Cultural Studies*, edited by Alan Dundes, 4–25. London: Routledge, 2005.

Horn, Cornelia B., "Children's Play as Social Ritual." In *Late Ancient Christianity*, edited by Virginia Burrus, 95–116. A People's History of Christianity 2. Minneapolis: Fortress, 2005.

———. "'Fathers and Mothers Shall Rise up against Their Children and Kill Them': Martyrdom and Children in the Early Church." Paper presented at the Society of Biblical Literature Annual Meeting, Toronto, November, 2002.

Hunt, Peter. "Childist Criticism: The Subculture of the Child, the Book and the Critic." In *Children's Literature: Critical Concepts in Literary and Cultural Studies*, edited by Peter Hunt, 2:263–79. London: Routledge, 2006.

———, editor. *Children's Literature: Critical Concepts in Literary and Cultural Studies*. 4 vols. London: Routledge, 2006.

Hurtado, Larry W. "Beyond the Interlude? Developments and Directions in New Testament Textual Criticism." In *Studies in the Early Text of the Gospels and Acts*, edited by D. G. K. Taylor, 26–48. Birmingham: University of Birmingham Press, 1999.

———. *Lord Jesus Christ: Devotion to Jesus in Earliest Christianity*. Grand Rapids: Eerdmans, 2003.

Hägg, Tomas. "A Professor and His Slave: Conventions and Values in the *Life of Aesop*." In *Conventional Values of the Hellenistic Greeks*, edited by Per Bilde, Troels Engberg-Pedersen, Lise Hannestad, and Jan Zahle, 177–203. SHC 8. Århus: Aarhus University Press, 1997.

———. "Evangelierna som biografier." *Meddelanden från Collegium Patristicum Lundense* 20 (2005) 44–56.

———. *Parthenope: Selected Studies in Ancient Greek Fiction (1969–2004)*. Copenhagen: Museum Tusculanum Press, 2004.

———. *The Novel in Antiquity*. Oxford: Blackwell, 1983.

Haase, Felix. *Literarkritische Untersuchungen zur orientalisch-apokryphen Evangelienliteratur*. Leipzig: Hinrichs, 1913.

Janowitz, Naomi. *Magic in the Roman World: Pagans, Jews and Christians*. Religion in the First Christian Centuries. London: Routledge, 2001.

Jensen, Robin Margaret. *Face to Face: Portraits of the Divine in Early Christianity*. Minneapolis: Fortress, 2005.

———. *Understanding Early Christian Art*. London: Routledge, 2000.

Jónsson, Jakob. *Humour and Irony in the New Testament, Illuminated by Parallels in Talmud and Midrash*. BZRGG 28. Leiden: Brill, 1985.

Kannaday, Wayne C. *Apologetic Discourse and the Scribal Tradition: Evidence of the Influence of Apologetic Interests on the Text of the Canonical Gospels*. Text-Critical Studies 5. Atlanta: Society of Biblical Literature, 2004.

Kartzow, Marianne Bjelland. "Female Gossipers and Their Reputation in the Pastoral Epistles." *Neot* 39 (2005) 255–72.

Bibliography

Kelber, Werner H. *The Oral and the Written Gospel: The Hermeneutics of Speaking and Writing in the Synoptic Tradition, Mark, Paul, and Q.* Bloomington: Indiana University Press, 1997.

Kelly, Joseph F. *The Origins of Christmas.* Collegeville, MN: Liturgical, 2004.

Kent, John. "The Monetary System." In *The Roman World*, edited by John Wacher, 2:568–85. London: Routledge & Kegan Paul, 1987.

King, Karen L. *What Is Gnosticism?* Cambridge, MA: Belknap, 2003.

Klauck, Hans-Josef. *Apocryphal Gospels: An Introduction.* Translated by Brian McNeil. London: T. & T. Clark, 2003.

Knight, Jeremy K. *The End of Antiquity: Archaeology, Society and Religion AD 235–700.* Stroud, UK: Tempus, 1999.

Kuefler, Mathew. *The Manly Eunuch: Masculinity, Gender Ambiguity, and Christian Ideology in Late Antiquity.* Chicago Series on Sexuality, History, and Society. Chicago: University of Chicago Press, 2001.

Labib, Pahor. *Coptic Gnostic Papyri in the Coptic Museum at Old Cairo.* Cairo: Government Press, 1956.

Laes, Christian. "Child Beating in Roman Antiquity: Some Reconsiderations." In *Hoping for Continuity: Childhood, Education and Death in Antiquity and the Middle Ages*, edited by Katariina Mustakallio, Juusi Hanska, and Ville Vuolanto, 75–89. Acta Instituti Romani Finlandiae 33. Rome: Institutum Romanum Finlandiae, 2005.

————. "Children and Fables, Children in Fables in Hellenistic and Roman Antiquity." *Latomus* 65 (2006) 898–914.

————. *Kinderen Bij de Romeinen: Zes Eeuwen Dagelijks Leven.* Leuven: Davidsfonds, 2006.

Laistner, M. L. W. *Christianity and Pagan Culture in the Later Roman Empire, Together with an English Translation of John Chrysostom's Address on Vainglory and the Right Way for Parents to Bring up Their Children.* Ithaca, NY: Cornell University Press, 1951.

Larson, Jennifer. "Paul's Masculinity." *JBL* 123 (2004) 85–97.

Laurence, Ray. "Health and the Life Course at Herculaneum." In *Health in Antiquity*, edited by Helen King, 83–96. London: Routledge, 2005.

Lefort, Jacques, Cecile Morrisson, and Jean-Pierre Sodini, editors. *Les Villages dans l'Empire Byzantin: IVe–XVe Siècle.* Réalités Byzantine 11. Paris: Lethielleux, 2005.

Leyerle, Blake. "Appealing to Children." *JECS* 5 (1997) 243–70.

Liddell, Henry George, and Robert Scott, editors. *A Greek-English Lexicon (with a Revised Supplement).* Oxford: Clarendon, 1996.

Lloyd, John. "Forms of Rural Settlement in the Early Roman Empire." In *Roman Landscapes: Archaeological Survey in the Mediterranean Region*, edited by Graeme Barker and John Lloyd, 233–40. Archaeological Monographs of the British School at Rome 2. London: British School at Rome, 1991.

Long, A. A., and D. N. Sedley. *The Hellenistic Philosophers.* 2 vols. Cambridge: Cambridge University Press, 1987.

Lowe, Malcolm. "*Ioudaioi* of the Apocrypha: A Fresh Approach to the Gospels of James, Pseudo-Thomas, Peter and Nicodemus." *NovT* 23 (1981) 56–90.

Luz, Ulrich. *Matthew 8–20: A Commentary.* Translated by James E. Crouch. Hermeneia. Minneapolis: Fortress, 2001.

————. *The Theology of the Gospel of Matthew.* Translated by J. Bradford Robinson. Cambridge: Cambridge University Press, 1995.

Bibliography

Mackay, E. Anne, editor. *Signs of Orality: The Oral Tradition and Its Influence in the Greek and Roman World*. Mnemosyne 188. Leiden: Brill, 1999.

Malina, Bruce J. *The New Testament World: Insights from Cultural Anthropology*. 3rd ed. Louisville: Westminster John Knox, 2001.

Malina, Bruce J., and Jerome H. Neyrey. *Portraits of Paul: An Archaeology of Ancient Personality*. Louisville: Westminster John Knox, 1996.

Manning, W. H. "Industrial Growth." In *The Roman World*, edited by John Wacher, 2:586–610. London: Routledge & Kegan Paul, 1987.

Mathiesen, Thomas J. *Apollo's Lyre: Greek Music and Music Theory in Antiquity and the Middle Ages*. Publications of the Center for the History of Music Theory 2. Lincoln: University of Nebraska Press, 1999.

McNeil, Brian. "Jesus and the Alphabet." *JTS* 27 (1976) 126–28.

Meeks, Wayne A. *The First Urban Christians: The Social World of the Apostle Paul*. New Haven: Yale University Press, 1983. 2nd ed., 2003.

Metzger, Bruce M. *A Textual Commentary on the Greek New Testament*. 2nd ed. Stuttgart: Deutsche Bibelgesellschaft, 1994.

———. *The Bible in Translation: Ancient and English Versions*. Grand Rapids: Baker Academic, 2001.

———. *The Early Versions of the New Testament: Their Origin, Transmission, and Limitations*. Oxford: Clarendon, 1977.

Meyer, Arnold. "Erzählung des Thomas." In *Neutestamentlichen Apokryphen*, edited by Edgar Hennecke, 63–73. Tübingen: Mohr/Siebeck, 1904.

Miller, Robert J., editor. *The Complete Gospels: Annotated Scholars Version*. San Francisco: HarperSanFrancisco, 1994.

Mirecki, Paul Allan. "The Infancy Gospel of Thomas." In *A Teacher of the True Faith: Essays in Honor of John P. Phillipps*, edited by W. R. Brookman and Ernest R. Freeman, 191–201. Minneapolis: Bupak, 1983.

Mirecki, Paul Allan, and Marvin Meyer, editors. *Magic and Ritual in the Ancient World*. Religions in the Graeco-Roman World 141. Leiden: Brill, 2002.

Mitchell, Margaret M. "Why Family Matters for Early Christian Literature." In *Early Christian Families in Context: An Interdisciplinary Dialogue*, edited by David L. Balch and Carolyn Osiek, 345–58. Grand Rapids: Eerdmans, 2003.

Moffatt, James. "Gospels (Uncanonical)." In *Dictionary of the Apostolic Church*, edited by James Hastings, 485–88. Edinburgh: T. & T. Clark, 1915–1918.

Moore, Stephen D., and Janice Capel Anderson, editors. *New Testament Masculinities*. Semeia Studies 45. Atlanta: Society of Biblical Literature, 2003.

Moreschini, Claudio, and Enrico Norelli. *Early Christian Greek and Latin Literature: A Literary History*. Vol. 1. Peabody, MA: Hendrickson, 2005.

Morey, Charles Rufus. *Early Christian Art: An Outline of the Evolution of Style and Iconography in Sculpture and Painting from Antiquity to the Eighth Century*. Princeton: Princeton University Press, 1953.

Morgan, Teresa. *Literate Education in the Hellenistic and Roman Worlds*. Cambridge Classical Studies. Cambridge: Cambridge University Press, 1998.

Morley, Neville. *Metropolis and Hinterland: The City of Rome and the Italian Economy 200 B.C.–A.D. 200*. Cambridge: Cambridge University Press, 1996.

Mournet, Terence C. *Oral Tradition and Literary Dependency: Variability and Stability in the Synoptic Tradition and Q*. WUNT 195. Tübingen: Mohr/Siebeck, 2005.

Bibliography

Moxnes, Halvor. "Conventional Values in the Hellenistic World: Masculinity." In *Conventional Values of the Hellenistic Greeks*, edited by Per Bilde, Troels Engberg-Pedersen, Lise Hannestad, and Jan Zahle, 263–84. SHC 8. Århus: Aarhus University Press, 1997.

Moxnes, Halvor, Jostein Børtnes, and Dag Øistein Endsjø, editors. *Naturlig sex? Seksualitet og kjønn i den kristne antikken*. Oslo: Gyldendal Akademisk, 2002.

Nathan, Geoffrey S. *The Family in Late Antiquity: The Rise of Christianity and the Endurance of Tradition*. London: Routledge, 2000.

Neils, Jenifer, and John H. Oakley. *Coming of Age in Ancient Greece: Images of Childhood from the Classical Past*. New Haven: Yale University Press, 2003.

Neusner, Jacob. "Zacchaeus/Zakkai." *HTR* 57 (1964) 57–59.

Neyrey, Jerome H. *Paul, in Other Words: A Cultural Reading of His Letters*. Louisville: Westminster John Knox, 1990.

Nicolas, Michel. *Études sur les Évangiles Apocryphes*. Paris: Michel Lévy Frères, 1866.

Nielsen, Hanne Sigismund. "Roman Children at Mealtimes." In *Meals in a Social Context: Aspects of the Communal Meal in the Hellenistic and Roman World*, edited by Inge Nielsen and Hanne Sigismund Nielsen, 56–66. Aarhus Studies in Mediterranean Antiquity 1. Århus: Aarhus University Press, 1998.

Nodelman, Perry. "Pleasure and Genre: Speculations on the Characteristics of Children's Fiction." In *Children's Literature: Critical Concepts in Literary and Cultural Studies*, edited by Peter Hunt, 2:384–95. London: Routledge, 2006.

Orme, Nicholas. *Medieval Children*. New Haven: Yale University Press, 2003.

Osiek, Carolyn, and Margaret Y. MacDonald, with Janet H. Tulloch. *A Woman's Place: House Churches in Earliest Christianity*. Minneapolis: Fortress, 2006.

Parker, A. J., "Trade within the Empire and Beyond the Frontiers." In *The Roman World*, edited by John Wacher, 2:635–57. London: Routledge & Kegan Paul, 1987.

Parkin, Tim G. *Demography and Roman Society*. Ancient Society and History. Baltimore: Johns Hopkins University Press, 1992.

———. *Old Age in the Roman World: A Cultural and Social History*. Ancient Society and History. Baltimore: Johns Hopkins University Press, 2003.

Patrich, Joseph. "Monastic Landscapes." In *Recent Research on the Late Antique Countryside*, edited by William Bowden, Luke Lavan, and Carlos Machado, 413–45. LAA 2. Leiden: Brill, 2004.

Peeters, Paul. "Introduction." In *Évangiles Apocryphes*, edited by Charles Michel and Paul Peeters, 2:i–lix. Textes et documents pour l'étude historique du christianisme, 18. Paris: Picar, 1914.

Percival, John. "The Villa in Italy and the Provinces." In *The Roman World*, edited by John Wacher, 2:527–47. London: Routledge & Kegan Paul, 1987.

Pervo, Richard I. "A Nihilist Fabula: Introducing *The Life of Aesop*." In *Ancient Fiction and Early Christian Narrative*, edited by Ronald F. Hock, J. Bradley Chance, and Judith Perkins, 77–120. SBLSymS 6. Atlanta: Scholars, 1998.

Philippart, Guy. "Fragments Palimpsestes Latins du Vindobonensis 563 (Ve Siècle?) Évangile selon S. Matthieu, Évangile de L'enfance selon Thomas, Évangile de Nicodème." *Analecta Bollandiana* 90 (1972) 391–411.

Pilch, John J., and Bruce J. Malina, editors. *Biblical Social Values and Their Meaning: A Handbook*. Peabody, MA: Hendrickson, 1993.

Price, Simon. *Religions of the Ancient Greeks*, Key Themes in Ancient History. New York: Cambridge University Press, 1999.

Bibliography

Ransom, Caroline L., *Couches and Beds of the Greeks, Etruscans and Romans*. Studies in Ancient Furniture. Chicago: University of Chicago Press, 1905.

Rawson, Beryl. *Children and Childhood in Roman Italy*. Oxford: Oxford University Press, 2003.

————. "Death, Burial, and Commemoration of Children in Roman Italy." In *Early Christian Families in Context: An Interdisciplinary Approach*, edited by David L. Balch and Carolyn Osiek, 277–97. Religion, Marriage and Family. Grand Rapids: Eerdmans, 2003.

————. "Family Life among the Lower Classes at Rome in the First Two Centuries of the Empire." *CP* 61 (1966) 71–83.

Rebell, Walter. *Neutestamentliche Apokryphen und apostolische Väter*. Munich: Kaiser, 1992.

Rees, Sian. "Agriculture and Horticulture." In *The Roman World*, edited by John Wacher, 2:481–503. London: Routledge & Kegan Paul, 1987.

Resch, Alfred. *Aussercanonische Parallelltexte zu den Evangelien*. TUGAL 10.1–4. Leipzig: Hinrichs, 1893–1897.

Rhoads, David. "Performance Criticism: An Emerging Methodology in Second Testament Studies—Part I." *BTB* 36 (2006) 118–33.

————. "Performance Criticism: An Emerging Methodology in Second Testament Studies—Part II." *BTB* 36 (2006) 164–84.

Richardson, Peter. *Building Jewish in the Roman East*. Journal for the Study of Judaism Supplements 92. Waco, TX: Baylor University Press, 2004.

Richter, G. M. A. *The Furniture of the Greeks, Etruscans and Romans*. London: Phaidon, 1966.

Robinson, James M. "Nag Hammadi: The First Fifty Years." In *The Fifth Gospel: The Gospel of Thomas Comes of Age*, edited by Stephen J. Patterson, James M. Robinson, and Hans-Gebhard Bethge, 77–110. Harrisburg, PA: Trinity, 1998.

Rompay, Lucas van. "De Ethiopische Versie van het Kindsheidsevangelie Volgens Thomas de Israëliet." In *Enfant dans les Civilisations Orientales*, edited by J. Théodoriedès, P. Naster, and J. Riesl, 119–32. Acta Orientalia Belgica 2. Leuven: Peeters, 1980.

Rosén, Thomas. *The Slavonic Translation of the Apocryphal Infancy Gospel of Thomas*. Acta Universitatis Upsaliensis 39. Uppsala: Almqvist & Wiksell, 1997.

Saïd, Suzanne. "The City in the Greek Novel." In *The Search for the Ancient Novel*, edited by James Tatum, 216–36. Baltimore: Johns Hopkins University Press, 1994.

Saller, Richard P. *Patriarchy, Property, and Death in the Roman Family*. Cambridge Studies in Population, Economy and Society in Past Time 25. Cambridge: Cambridge University Press, 1994.

Saller, Richard P., and Brent D. Shaw. "Tombstones and Roman Family Relations in the Principate: Civilians, Soldiers and Slaves." *JRS* 74 (1984) 124–56.

Sandnes, Karl Olav. *The Challenge of Homer: School, Pagan Poets and Early Christianity*. LNTS 400. London: T. & T. Clark, 2009.

Santos Otero, Aurelio de. *Das Kirchenslavische Evangelium Des Thomas*. PTS 6. Berlin: de Gruyter, 1967.

Sarris, Peter. "Rehabilitating the Great Estate: Aristocratic Property and Economic Growth in the Late Antique East." In *Recent Research on the Late Antique Countryside*, edited by William Bowden, Luke Lavan, and Carlos Machado, 55–71. LAA 2. Leiden: Brill, 2004.

Bibliography

Schindler, Alfred. *Apokryphen zum Alten Und Neuen Testament*. Zürich: Manesse, 1988.

Schmahl, Günther. "Lk 2,41–52 und die Kindheitserzählung des Thomas 19,1–5." *Bibel und Leben* 15 (1974) 249–58.

Schneemelcher, Wilhelm, editor. *New Testament Apocrypha: Gospels and Related Writings*. Rev. ed. Vol. 1. Louisville: Westminster John Knox, 1991.

———. editor. *New Testament Apocrypha: Writings Related to the Apostles; Apocalypses and Related Subjects*. Rev. ed. Vol. 2. Louisville: Westminster John Knox, 1991.

Schneider, Gerhard. *Evangelia Infantiae Apocrypha: Apocryphe Kindheitsevangelien*. FC 18. Freiburg: Herder, 1995.

Shahar, Shulamith. *Childhood in the Middle Ages*. London: Routledge, 1990.

Shapiro, Helen A. "Fathers and Sons, Men and Boys." In *Coming of Age in Ancient Greece: Images of Childhood from the Classical Past*, edited by Jenifer Neils and John H. Oakley, 85–111. New Haven: Yale University Press, 2003.

Shiner, Whitney. "Creating Plot in Episodic Narratives: The *Life of Aesop* and the Gospel of Mark." In *Ancient Fiction and Early Christian Narrative*, edited by Ronald F. Hock, J. Bradley Chance, and Judith Perkins, 155–76. SBLSymS 6. Atlanta: Scholars, 1998.

———. *Proclaiming the Gospel: First-Century Performance of Mark*. Harrisburg, PA: Trinity, 2003.

Snyder, Graydon F. *Ante Pacem: Archaeological Evidence of Church Life before Constantine*. Rev. ed. Macon, GA: Mercer University Press, 2003.

Stark, Rodney. *The Rise of Christianity: A Sociologist Reconsiders History*. Princeton: Princeton University Press, 1996.

Stephens, Susan A. "Who Read Ancient Novels?" In *The Search for the Ancient Novel*, edited by James Tatum, 405–18. Baltimore: Johns Hopkins University Press, 1994.

Stephens, Susan A., and John J. Winkler, editors. *Ancient Greek Novels: The Fragments. Introduction, Text, Translation, and Commentary*. Princeton: Princeton University Press, 1995.

Stewart, Columba. "Monasticism." In *The Early Christian World*, edited by Philip F. Esler, 1:344–66. 2 vols. London: Routledge, 2000.

Stortz, Martha Ellen. "'Where or When Was Your Servant Innocent?': Augustine on Childhood." In *The Child in Christian Thought*, edited by Marcia J. Bunge, 78–102. Religion, Marriage and Family. Grand Rapids: Eerdmans, 2001.

Stroumsa, Guy G. "Christ's Laughter: Docetic Origins Reconsidered." *JECS* 12 (2004) 267–88.

Stählin, Otto. *Altchristliche griechische Literatur*. Munich: Beck, 1924.

Tabbernee, William. *Montanist Inscriptions and Testimonia: Epigraphic Sources Illustrating the History of Montanism*. Patristic Monograph Series 16. Macon, GA: Mercer University Press, 1997.

Tabbert, Reinbert, and Kristin Wardetzky. "On the Success of Children's Books and Fairy Tales: A Comparative View of Impact Theory and Reception Research." In *Children's Literature: Critical Concepts in Literary and Cultural Studies*, edited by Peter Hunt, 2:21–37. 4 vols. London: Routledge, 2006.

Tatum, James, editor. *The Search for the Ancient Novel*. Baltimore: Johns Hopkins University Press, 1994.

Thatcher, Tom. *The Riddles of Jesus in John: A Study in Tradition and Folklore*. SBLMS 53. Atlanta: Society of Biblical Literature, 2000.

Bibliography

Thilo, Johann C. *Codex apocryphus Novi Testamenti: E libris editis et manuscriptis, maxime gallicanis, germanicis et italicis collectus, recensitus notisque et prolegomenis illustratus, opera et studio Ioannis Caroli Thilo.* Leipzig: Vogel, 1832.

Thomas, Christine M. "Stories without Texts and without Authors: The Problem of Fluidity in Ancient Novelistic Texts and Early Christian Literature." In *Ancient Fiction and Early Christian Narrative*, edited by Ronald F. Hock, J. Bradley Chance, and Judith Perkins, 274–91. SBLSymS 6. Atlanta: Scholars, 1998.

———. *The Acts of Peter, Gospel Literature, and the Ancient Novel: Rewriting the Past.* Oxford: Oxford University Press, 2003.

Thundy, Zacharias P. *Buddha and Christ: Nativity Stories and Indian Traditions.* SHR 60. Leiden: Brill, 1993.

———. "Intertextuality, Buddhism and the Infancy Gospels." In *Religious Writings and Religious Systems: Systemic Analysis of Holy Books in Christianity, Islam, Buddhism, Greco-Roman Religions, Ancient Israel, and Judaism*, edited by Jacob Neusner et al., 17–73. Brown Studies in Religion. Atlanta: Scholars, 1989.

Tischendorf, Constantinus de. *Evangelia apocrypha, adhibitis plurimis codicibus graecis et latinis maximam partem nunc primum consultis atque ineditorum copia insignibus.* Leipzig: Mendelssohn, 1876. 2nd reprint.

Toynbee, J. M. C. *Animals in Roman Life and Art.* London: Thames and Hudson, 1973.

Treu, Kurt. "Der antike Roman und sein Publikum." in Heinrich Kuch, editor, *Der antike Roman: Untersuchungen zur literarischen Kommunikation und Gattungsgeschichte*, 178–97. Veröffentlichungen des Zentralinstituts für Alter Geschichte und Archäologie der Akademie der Wissenschaften der DDR 19. Berlin: Akademie-Verlag, 1989.

Trevett, Christine. *Montanism: Gender, Authority and the New Prophecy.* New York: Cambridge University Press, 1996.

Trombley, Frank R. "Epigraphic Data on Village Culture and Social Institutions: An Interregional Comparison (Syria, Phoenice Libanensis and Arabia)." In *Recent Research on the Late Antique Countryside*, edited by William Bowden, Luke Lavan, and Carlos Machado, 73–101. LAA 2. Leiden: Brill, 2004.

Tropper, Amram. "Children and Childhood in Light of the Demographics of the Jewish Family in Late Antiquity." *Journal for the Study of the Judaism* 37 (2006) 299–343.

Uther, Hans-Jörg. *The Types of International Folktales: A Classification and Bibliography, Based on the System of Antti Aarne and Stith Thompson.* FF Communications 284. Helsinki: Academia Scientiarum Fennica, 2004.

———. *The Types of International Folktales: A Classification and Bibliography, Based on the System of Antti Aarne and Stith Thompson.* FF Communications 285. Helsinki: Academia Scientiarum Fennica, 2004.

Uzzi, Jeannine Diddle. *Children in the Visual Arts of Ancient Rome.* Cambridge: Cambridge University Press, 2005.

Van Aarde, Andries G. "Die Griekse manusckrip van die Kindheidsevangelie van Tomas in Kodeks Sinaïtikus (Gr 453) vertaal in Afrikaans." *Hervormde Teologiese Studies* 61 (2005) 491–516.

———. "Die Kindheidsevangelie van Tomas as 'n Heroïese Mite van die God-kind Jesus in die Konteks van die Ebionitiese vroeë Christendom." D.Lit. thesis, Universiteit van Pretoria, 2005.

Bibliography

————. "Die Kindheidsevangelie van Tomas—Historiese Allegorie of Mite in die Vorm van 'n Biografiese Diskursiewe Evangelie?" *Hervormde Teologiese Studies* 61 (2005) 461–89.

————. "Ebionite Tendencies in the Jesus Tradition: The Infancy Gospel of Thomas Interpreted from the Perspective of Ethnic Identity." *Neot* 40 (2006) 353–82.

————. "The Infancy Gospel of Thomas: Allegory or Myth—Gnostic or Ebionite?" *Verbum et Ecclesia* 26 (2005) 826–50.

Van Voorst, Robert E. *Jesus Outside the New Testament*. Grand Rapids: Eerdmans, 2000.

Variot, Jean. *Les Évangiles Apocryphes: Histoire Littéraire, Forme Primitive, Transformations*. Paris: Berche & Tralin, 1878.

Vielhauer, Philipp. *Geschichte der Urchristlichen Literatur: Einleitung in das Neue Testament, die Apokryphen und die Apostolischen Väter*. De Gruyter Lehrbuch. Berlin: de Gruyter, 1975.

Vitz, Evelyn Birge, Nancy Freeman Regalado, and Marilyn Lawrence, editors. *Performing Medieval Narrative*. Cambridge: Brewer, 2005.

Voicu, Sever J. "Histoire de L'enfance de Jésus." In *Écrits apocryphes chrétiens*, edited by Francois Bovon and Pierre Geoltrain, 191–204. Paris: Gallimard, 1997.

————. "Notes sur l'histoire du texte de l'histoire de l'enfance de Jésus." *Apocrypha* 2 (1991) 119–32.

————. "Verso il Testo Primitivo dei *Paidika tou Kyriou Iesou* 'Racconti dell' Infanzia dell Signore Gesu.'" *Apocrypha* 9 (1998) 7–95.

Vööbus, Arthur. *The Didascalia Apostolorum in Syriac*. Vol. 1: *Chapters 1–X*. CSCO 402. 2 vols. in 4. Louvain: Secrétariat du CorpusSCO, 1979.

Voorwinde, Stephen. *Jesus' Emotions in the Fourth Gospel: Human or Divine?* LNTS 284. London: T. & T. Clark, 2005.

Vroom, Joanita. "Late Antique Pottery, Settlement and Trade in the East Mediterranean: A Preliminary Comparison of Ceramics from Limyra (Lycia) and Boeotia." In *Recent Research on the Late Antique Countryside*, edited by William Bowden, Luke Lavan, and Carlos Machado, 281–331. LAA 2. Leiden: Brill, 2004.

White, K. D. *Agricultural Implements of the Roman World*. Cambridge: Cambridge University Press, 1967.

————. *Farm Equipment of the Roman World*. Cambridge: Cambridge University Press, 1975.

Wiedemann, Thomas. *Adults and Children in the Roman Empire*. London: Routledge, 1989.

Wilkins, John, David Harvey, and Mike Dobson, editors. *Food in Antiquity*. Exeter: University of Exeter Press, 1995.

Williams, Craig A. *Roman Homosexuality: Ideologies of Masculinity in Classical Antiquity*. Ideologies of Desire. Oxford: Oxford University Press, 1999.

Wilson, Stephen G. *Related Strangers: Jews and Christians 70–170 C.E.* Minneapolis: Fortress, 1995.

Winter, Bruce W. *Seek the Welfare of the City: Christians as Benefactors and Citizens*. First-Century Christians in the Greco-Roman World. Grand Rapids: Eerdmans, 1994.

Wire, Antoinette Clark. *Holy Lives, Holy Deaths: A Close Hearing of Early Jewish Storytellers*. Studies in Biblical Literature 1. Atlanta: Society of Biblical Literature, 2002.

Bibliography

Witakowski, Witold. "The Miracles of Jesus: An Ethiopian Apocryphal Gospel." *Apocrypha* 6 (1995) 279–98.

Young, Frances, Lewis Ayres, Andrew Louth, and Augustine Casiday, editors. *The Cambridge History of Early Christian Literature*. Cambridge: Cambridge University Press, 2004.

Zipes, Jack. *Breaking the Magic Spell: Radical Theories of Folk and Fairy Tales*. Revised and Expanded Edition. Lexington: University Press of Kentucky, 2002.

Index of Biblical Writings

SEPTUAGINT (OLD TESTAMENT)

116, 117, 124, 130–32, 134, 135, 157–60, 160

Genesis

1–3	128, 129–30, 134, 135
1–2	128, 163
3	128
3:15	131

Numbers

11:32	124
23:7	159

Joshua

8:34	122

1–2 Kings

129, 130, 134, 135

1 Kings

5:12	159

Nehemiah

13:2	122

Esther

50

2 Maccabees

134

9:24	124

4 Maccabees

117, 134

5:4	126

Psalms

32:9	130, 134
48:3	155
81:3	131, 134
108:17	122, 134

Proverbs

3:33	122, 134
9:18	134, 155
23:33	159
30:4	130, 134

Sirach

3:9	122, 134
13:26	134, 159
27:17	74
43:25	134

Tobit

50

Wisdom

5:2	124
7:1	155

Hosea

9:8	159

Joel

1:15	124

Daniel

7:1	159

NEW TESTAMENT

123, 125–27, 130–32,
132–36, 152–57, 160,
164

Matthew

54, 131, 133, 134, 153,
254

1–2	254
7:29	121
9:6	124–25
9:18	125
9:23–26	125
11:16–17	201
11:25–27	42, 147
13:55	131
18:20	122, 141
21:18–19	128, 130, 135
26:56	131

Mark

36, 52, 114, 115, 125,
133, 153, 164, 172–73

1:22	121
2:11	124–25
2:24	130
4:1–34	154
4:3–8	129, 135
5:21–43	41
6:3	131, 176
11:12–21	128
14:50	131

Luke

51, 124, 131, 134, 135,
153

1–4	132
1–2	111, 123
1:5—2:40	129, 130
1:42	116
1:44	143
2:19	117
2:41–52	115–18, 135, 254
2:48	241
2:52	154
3:2	127
4:16–22	129, 130
4:24–27	129, 130
5:17–26	153
5:17	126
11	126, 132
11:14–28	117
11:27	116
11:37–54	116
11:53	116
16:7	124
17:21	122, 141
19:1–10	126
20:17	124

John

120–21, 123, 124, 133,
134, 135, 153–56, 157,
172, 204, 255

1:1–3	128
1:14–18	255
2:11	178
3:3	121
3:10	120
6:22–65	154
7:27–28	120
7:34–36	120
7:46	121
7:53—8:11	30
8:57	120
8:58	120
9:39	121, 147
11:43	125
17:5	121
17:24	121
18:13	127
18:24	127

Acts

	113, 124–25, 132, 133, 153
3:12	124
4:6	127
5:1–11	153
5:34	126
13:6–12	153
20:9–12	76, 131
28:3–6	131

Paul

| | 122, 133, 134, 157 |

Romans

| 12:14 | 18, 122, 133 |

1 Corinthians

7:21	122
12–13	120, 133
13:1	61, 118–20, 133

Galatians

| 4:4 | 254 |

Ephesians

| 1:3–14 | 156 |

Philippians

| 2:6–11 | 156 |
| 4:8 | 117 |

Colossians

| 1:15–20 | 156 |

1 Timothy

1:7	126
3:2–5	198
3:11	197
4:7	197, 200
5:13	197

2 Timothy

| 1:5 | 198 |
| 4:19 | 127 |

Titus

| 2:3 | 197 |
| 3:13 | 126 |

Hebrews

| 8:1 | 159 |

1 Peter

| 2:9 | 117 |

2 Peter

| 1:3, 5 | 117 |
| 2:11 | 122 |

3 John

| 7 | 141 |

Revelation

	36, 52, 123, 124, 125, 133, 134, 171
3:14	121, 133
17:6	133
19:17	125, 133
21:6	122, 133, 152
22:13	122, 152

INDEX OF *INFANCY GOSPEL OF THOMAS*

INFANCY GOSPEL OF THOMAS

(selection, cf. *Gs*)

1	14, 39, 40
2–3	38, 40–41, 124
2	128, 130, 177, 179–80, 208
3	124, 126–27, 128, 208
4–5	38, 41, 120, 124
4	17–19, 28, 122, 138, 208
5	138–39, 147–48
6–8	38, 39, 41–42, 48, 77–78, 120–21, 130, 158, 179
6	19–22, 23, 27–28, 73–74, 118–20, 122, 124, 126, 140–46, 174–75
7	39, 48, 75–76, 79, 122, 124–25, 207
8	41–42, 121, 146–47, 154–55
9	29, 38, 42, 56, 62, 125, 131, 152, 162
10–12	38, 42–43, 100
10	59, 208, 211
11	78–79, 129, 131, 179
12	70–71, 78, 131, 211
13–14	39, 43–44, 130, 179
13	38, 158
14	38, 77–78, 81, 82–83, 129, 158
15–16	44
15	22–23, 38, 131, 132, 177
16	14
17	14, 44–45, 115–118, 158–59

Greek variants

Ga	2, 7, 9, 15, 16–23, 28, 30, 35, 38, 40, 44, 47, 48, 49, 56, 63, 65, 79, 107, 118, 142, 145, 147, 157, 162, 173, 183, 184, 186, 205, 208, 225, 228, 230, 231–32, 239, 241–42, 243–44, 245, 248, 253
Gb	2, 7, 9, 10, 15, 16, 18, 24, 30, 35, 38, 40, 48, 49, 56, 57, 58, 62, 63, 64, 65, 107, 110, 147, 173, 184, 205, 206, 208, 243, 248, 253
Gd	2, 5, 8, 9, 15–16, 16–23, 28, 35, 38, 40, 47, 56, 57, 63, 65, 79, 107, 110, 118, 126, 140, 142, 145, 147, 153, 157, 162, 173, 206, 208, 222, 225, 228, 230, 241–42, 243–44, 245, 248, 253
Gs	2, 6, 8, 9, 14, 15, 16–23, 28, 29, 34, 37–38, 40, 41, 43, 44, 45, 47, 48, 49, 53, 72, 99, 114, 132, 133, 137, 138, 139, 140, 141, 142, 145, 147, 150, 153, 157, 162, 164, 169, 173, 181, 182, 183, 184, 205, 206, 214, 215, 219–30, 233–41, 243–44, 248, 252

Latin versions

2, 3, 6, 9, 14, 29, 33, 34,
40, 62, 118, 181–82, 184,
186, 249 (see also *Ps.-Mt.*)

Lm   29, 35, 107, 182, 186, 249,
251, 253

Lt   3, 182, 184, 249, 251, 253

Lv   3, 29, 181, 182, 186, 249,
252

Syriac versions

Syr   2, 4, 8, 9, 14, 29, 34, 40,
43, 118, 140, 151, 182–83,
184, 186, 230, 249, 252,
253

Other versions

Arab   2, 6, 250, 253 (see also
Arab. Gos. Inf.)

Arm   2, 250, 253 (see also *Arm.
Gos. Inf.*)

Eth   2, 4, 6, 8, 118, 140, 183,
186, 252, 253

Geo   2, 4, 5, 40, 118, 183, 252,
253

Ir   2, 5, 29, 33, 182, 184, 250,
253

Slav   2, 4, 6, 9, 23, 151, 183–84,
231, 242, 250, 253

INDEX OF ANCIENT AUTHORS AND WRITINGS

Old Testament Pseudepigrapha

Jos. Asen., 50
Jub., 90

Apostolic fathers

1 Clem., 74, 188
Herm. Vis., 159
Ignatius Pol., 74

Nag Hammadi books

Ap. Jas., 129
Dial. Sav., 120
Gos. Mary, 120, 134, 203
Gos. Thom., 3, 5, 6, 51, 134, 151, 174
2   120
3   122
9   129
38   120
40   124
92   120
94   120

Gos. Truth, 175, 176, 252

New Testament Apocrypha and Pseudepigrapha

Acts Andr., 203
Acts John, 153
Acts Paul, 50, 127, 153
Acts Pet., 50, 153
Acts Thom., 153, 177, 252
Arab. Gos. Inf., 183, 184, 185, 186, 245, 250, 253, 257

Arm. Gos. Inf., 29, 183, 185, 250, 253, 256
Arundel 404, 258
Assum. Vir., 186
Didasc. apost., 81
Ep. Apos., 174, 175, 176, 252
Gos. Bart., 177, 203, 252
Gos. Heb., 120, 134
Gos. Nic., 127, 186
Gos. Bir. Mary, 256
Ps.-Mt., 2, 31, 182, 185, 186, 212, 245, 249, 250, 257
Hist. Jos. Carp., 177, 252, 256
Infancy Gospel of James, see Prot. Jas.
Infancy Gospel of Thomas, see index of Infancy Gospel of Thomas
Leabhar Breac, 257
Life of Mary, 182, 185, 251
Liber Flavus, 258
Pap. Cairensis, 35, 107, 257
Pap. Eg., 129
Pilate's Letter to Tiberius, 186
Pistis Sophia, 255
Prot. Jas., 1, 51, 160, 161, 169, 171, 181, 182, 183, 186, 187, 203, 204, 255, 256, 257
1–17   257
9:1   131
13:1   131
15:1   127
21   173

Ta'amra 'Iyasus, 183, 185, 186, 256

Patristic writings

Ambrose
Exp. Luc., 203

Anastasius Sinaita
Hodegos, 179, 252

Antoninus Placentinus
Itin., 179, 252

Arnobius of Sicca, 197

Athanasius
Life of Antony, 50

Augustine
Conf., 96, 201
Civ., 95

Decretum Gelasianum, 179, 182, 252

Epiphanius
Pan., 177, 178, 252

Hippolytus
Haer., 255

Irenaeus
Haer., 151, 174–75, 176, 178, 180, 182, 212, 252

John Chrysostom
Hom. Jo., 178, 252
Inan. glor., 96, 98, 142, 178, 180, 186, 193, 194, 195, 212

25	98
34	201, 202
36–53	195
37–38	195, 198
38	196
38–39	197
39	96, 195, 200
39–40	169
39–43	194
39–46	201
41	143, 203
52	194, 195

Justin Martyr
Dial., 174, 175, 176, 252

Lactantius
Inst., 194, 197

Minucius Felix
Oct., 200

Origen
Cels., 194, 207
Hom. Luc., 203

Serapion
Life of John, 257

Tatian
Diatessaron, 133

Tertullian
Val., 194, 196, 200

Timothy of Constantinople
Recept. haer., 179, 252

Greek and Latin authors/ writings (non-Christian)

Aeschylus, 131

Aetius, 138

Alexander Romance, 8

Apollonius Rhodius, 131

Apuleius
Metam., 170, 195, 196, 200

Aristophanes
Lys., 194
Vesp., 197, 200

Athenaeus
Deipn., 144–45

Cato
Agr., 190

Catullus
  Poems, 58

Cicero
  Nat. d., 95, 196, 200

Dio Chrysostom
  Or., 170, 195, 196

Diogenes Laertius, 62

Epictetus
  Diatr., 200

Euripides, 131

Hellenistic novels, 40, 166, 168,
  170, 171, 181, 190, 199, 205,
  211

Hermeneumata Ps.-Dositheana, 60

Herodotus, 155

Hippocrates, 98

Homer
  Il., 81, 201
  Od., 201

Horace
  Sat., 200

Josephus
  Ant., 74, 124
  J.W., 74

Julian the Apostate
  Or., 195, 201

Libanius, 98

Life of Aesop, 36, 48, 49, 52, 171,
  181, 199, 202, 207

Lucian
  Philops., 200
  Vit. auct., 48

Maximus of Tyre
  Or., 195

Ovid
  Epistulae ex Ponto, 194
  Metam., 170, 200

Persius
  Sat., 194

Petronius
  Satyrica, 170, 200

Philo, 159
  Moses, 49

Philostratus the Athenian
  Vit. Apoll., 48, 199

Philostratus the Elder
  Imag., 194

Plato, 116, 155
  Gorg., 200
  Hipp. maj., 200
  Leg., 194
  Resp., 194, 200, 201
  Symp., 170
  Theaet., 200

Pliny the Elder
  Nat., 190

Pliny the Younger, 95
  Ep., 170, 188–89

Plutarch 95, 116, 131
  Sept. sap. Conv., 170
  Mor., 195
  Thes., 195

Pythagorean school, 163

Quintilian
  Inst., 96–97, 144, 193, 199, 200,
  201, 202, 207, 212

Sophocles, 131

Strabo
  Geogr., 200

Suetonius, 49
  Emperor Biographies, 98

Tacitus
  Dial., 197

Tibullus
  Elegies, 194, 195, 200

Varro
  Rust., 190

Virgil
  Aen., 201

Xenophon, 131

Other
Qur'an, 179–80, 252